Grimms' Fairy Tales

Jacob (1785–1863) and Wilhelm Grimm (1786–1859). German literary scholars, philologists and editors of the famous collection of folktales.

Born in Hanau they both studied at Marburg, and from 1808 to 1829 mainly worked in Kassel as state-appointed librarians, with Jacob also assisting in diplomatic missions between 1813 and 1815 and again in 1848. Both brothers had been professors at Göttingen University for several years when in 1837 they were among the seven leading academics dismissed from their posts by the new King of Hanover for their liberal political views. In 1840 they were invited by Frederick William IV of Prussia to settle in Berlin as members of the Academy of Sciences, and here they stayed until their deaths. Jacob is regarded as one of Germany's greatest scholars and is the rightful founder of the scientific study of the German language and medieval German literature. His most monumental achievements were the *Deutsche Grammatik* and the initiation of the great *Deutsches Wörterbuch* (the many volumes of which were finally completed by scholars in 1961), which is the equivalent of the *Oxford English Dictionary*.

The joint ambition of the brothers was to bring together the entire oral tradition of Germany, and in trying to do so they took as their basis not information from written documents but information from the peasants whom they interviewed. Many of the stories collected here, such as 'Cinderella' or 'Rumplestiltskin', have their equivalents in other languages and cultures, but the Grimm brothers' selection remains the most extensive. Between them they were responsible for pioneering work on medieval texts, legends and mythology and other contributions to the study of ancient German culture. The publication of *Kinder- und Hausmärchen* (*Children's and Household Tales*, 1812) remains to this day the most famous collection of folktales in the world.

PENGUIN BOOKS

Published by the Penguin Group
Penguin Books Ltd, 80 Strand, London WC2R ORL, England
Penguin Putnam Inc., 375 Hudson Street, New York, New York 10014, USA
Penguin Books Australia Ltd, Ringwood, Victoria, Australia
Penguin Books Canada Ltd, 10 Alcorn Avenue, Toronto, Ontario, Canada M4V 3B2
Penguin Books India (P) Ltd, 11 Community Centre, Panchsheel Park,
New Delhi – 110 017, India
Penguin Books (NZ) Ltd, Cnr Rosedale and Airborne Roads, Albany, Auckland,
New Zealand
Penguin Books (South Africa) (Pty) Ltd, 24 Sturdee Avenue, Rosebank 2196, South Africa

Penguin Books Ltd, Registered Offices: 80 Strand, London WC2R ORL, England

www.penguin.com

First published 1823
Published in Penguin Popular Classics 1996
1

Printed in the UK by CPI Bookmarque, Croydon, CR0 4TD

ISBN 978-0-14062-432-8

CONTENTS

CONTENTS

LIST OF ILLUSTRATIONS

—

The Brothers Grimm and
their Fairy Tales

THE brothers Grimm, who gave us the fairy tales generally known by their name, were grave scholarly men who spent most of their lives in research.

Jacob was born in 1785 and Wilhelm a year later. Their father, a lawyer, died when they were children, but their mother was bent on seeing her sons follow in his footsteps, and this they did with financial aid from an aunt. They were born at Hanau in Hesse, and went to the University at Cassel, where they both qualified successfully in law. There was no money to help them to a position, and they had their mother to keep, so they took what work offered. Jacob became assistant to a famous specialist in Roman law, Professor Savigny, who showed him what research meant and implanted in his mind such a love of it that he became one of the great men of his time – not, however, on matters of law, but in philology, the study of language. Both brothers were captivated by it and their interest was so wide and deep that Professor William P. Ker described it as being for them, not only the study of words but of History, of Germany and the Middle Ages, of the Humanities and the Human Race.

Soon Jacob and Wilhelm obtained positions which left them time for private work, and they started on a treatise on the German language. They evolved a theory which is known universally as Grimms' Law. In all their work they were pioneers, starting from scratch, with no other men's work to help them, not even a dictionary; no guides to roots or the derivation of words, absolutely nothing. Jacob was rather the greater scholar, Wilhelm the greater writer; but their collaboration was such that it is almost impossible to separate their contributions. For ten years they worked on the *German Grammar*; then tackled the mythology of their people in the same dogged fashion, determined to establish something comparable to the Norse and Slav myths which were already well known. It was this task which gave the world these fairy tales, which they collected as part of the evidence needed for the greater work.

The tales had been handed down by word of mouth from mother to child, over no one knew how many generations, with never a printed page to fix the shapes of the stories. A family who had lived for centuries, as say woodcutters or charcoal burners, in thick forests might, thus, tell them quite differently from another family who had lived always under the open sky on valley farms.

Jacob and Wilhelm had listened to the tales often in childhood, but now they looked at them with different, critical eyes, expecting them to throw light on the history, beliefs and ways of life of the succession of German peasants who had given the stories their final form. They valued the tales for their folklore material, so it was essential that as many versions as possible should be obtained of each story and that each should be taken down with absolute accuracy as it was told in the peasants' huts. 'We have added nothing of our own', they said when the tales were published, 'embellished no incident or feature. Each is given substantially as we received it, though skill was needed to distinguish one version from another.' They found one or two reliable people and sent them out, to go into the kitchens where old women told them tales. Sometimes they had to hear the same story over and over again before they got hold of the full flavour of dialect and detail. Then the Brothers worked with all their native thoroughness over the reports, taking a phrase here, a word there, as token of forgotten myths and legends. To them the elves, fairies, giants, kobolds and brownies were part of that forgotten past; the bowl of milk on the hearth at night, set there by the wife to please the brownies, was, in the philologists' eyes, a direct link with the living sacrifices on the ancient altars of the gods. They observed that a giant could, apparently, be as old as the hills, though a dwarf was already grown up in his third year, and a greybeard at seven: that the reason for 'changelings' was that fairies snatched healthy human babies, substituting one of their own, to improve their puny physique; that knotholes in wood were the doors through which elves and fairies entered human habitations along with the sunbeams.

In character, the Grimms possessed the thoroughness and solemnity typical of the Teutons, had little humour but a certain strain of romance which caused Jacob to admit that even as he grew old the mere word 'mysterious' never failed to thrill him. In youth at least, he had also a very real feeling for sweet country things. They dedicated their *Grammar* to Savigny, and Jacob wrote that the true poet '*is like a man who is happy anywhere, in endless measure, if he is allowed to look at leaves and grass, to see the sun rise and set. The false poet travels abroad in strange countries and hopes to be uplifted by the mountains of Switzerland, the sky and sea of Italy. He comes to them and is dissatisfied. He is not as happy as the man who stays at home and sees the apple trees flower in spring, and hears the small birds singing among the branches.*'

The first volume of the *Kindermärchen* was published in 1812, the second in 1815, the year of Waterloo. It is strange to think of these brothers stubbornly pursuing their researches into Teutonic folklore, right through the troubled years of Napoleonic wars, which so directly affected their own native soil – Napoleon had incorporated both Hesse and Cassel in the new Kingdom of Westphalia. Perhaps it is stranger still that the tales should have reached England in translation so soon – only eight years afterwards.

Fairy-tales in this country had been almost frowned out of existence at that time. They were classed as injurious nonsense, liable to upset children; and an era of moral tales and interesting facts in capsule form had set in. Probably the very seriousness with which the brothers Grimm had collected the tales helped to make them more acceptable here, and so opened once again the gateway of fairyland to children.

Sir Walter Scott had worked in much the same way when he scoured the Borders in search of the ballads which he collected and preserved in his *Border Minstrelsy*. He understood what the Brothers Grimm had been after, and recommended the English edition of their tales to every home.

As soon as the Theory of Teutonic Mythology was completed – and it took thirteen years – the brothers embarked on the gigantic task of producing a German Dictionary, but both died before it could be completed. Towards the end of his life Jacob used sometimes to hold up his hands, fingers outspread, and say sadly: 'I have a book ready to run out at the tip of each of my ten fingers – but I am not free.'

In his early thirties Jacob had held a post at the University of Göttingen, and was one of the seven Professors who signed a protest against interference with their academic liberties by the King of Hanover (who was that doubtful character, Ernest, Duke of Cumberland). Jacob was dismissed from the University and banished from the kingdom. It seemed like disaster, for how could he work without access to a scholars' library? He went back to Cassel and plodded along there as best he could and after three years there, was offered a post at Berlin University by the King of Prussia, where he was able to resume his work.

Another famous philologist, Vigfusson, left a vivid description of Jacob Grimm at the age of seventy-four, living in a flat in the Linkstrasse in Berlin. He was not very tall, but carried himself bolt upright, with his big head bent a little, as though in thought. He was clean-shaven, with an unsmiling face that showed little change of expression. His hair was thick, straight and silvery. Reading and writing had worn his eyes, but he had no spectacles; he seemed adept, nevertheless, at picking out just the book he wanted, and even at opening it at the very line he needed. He was neat in his dress and did not smoke. The room he worked in was fresh and airy. Its walls were lined with books, and the only furniture was a strong table in the middle of the floor and a bench or couch with no back or head-rest. Great folio volumes lay about, and some leant against the table-legs. Jacob showed no signs of pride or vanity, had no desire to talk about himself, but only of other men's work.

There is a story that Hans Andersen (a very different character, working always with heart as well as imagination, too sensitive, too tender for happiness) once set out delightedly from Copenhagen to call upon these (as he thought) brother artists. He found their flat and inquired for them. He was asked which Mr Grimm he would see. 'Th-the one who writes the fairy-tales,' he stammered, beginning at once to wish he had never come. He was taken to Wilhelm. They bowed. 'Long' Andersen looked down from his awkward height at the grave, self-possessed Grimm.

Wilhelm repeated the name and shook his head. He had never heard of Hans Christian Andersen.

Andersen tried to explain. He wrote fairy-tales. His work and that of the brothers had just been included in one volume in translation ...

Still Wilhelm shook his head. No, there were no two ways about it; he knew nothing of Andersen or his tales. Perhaps

Jacob could help? No? But Andersen, wounded, weeping, was already backing away.

The text here used is that of Edgar Taylor who made the first translation of these tales; and George Cruikshank's illustrations are also taken from the first English edition, published in two volumes in 1823-26.

E. G.

GRIMMS'
FAIRY TALES

—

G Cruikshank fec

HANS IN LUCK

HANS had served his master seven years, and at last said to him, 'Master, my time is up, I should like to go home and see my mother; so give me my wages.' And the master said, 'You have been a faithful and good servant, so your pay shall be handsome.' Then he gave him a piece of silver that was as big as his head.

Hans took out his pocket-handkerchief, put the piece of silver into it, threw it over his shoulder, and jogged off homewards. As he went lazily on, dragging one foot after another, a man came in sight, trotting along gaily on a capital horse. 'Ah!' said Hans aloud, 'what a fine thing it is to ride on horseback! there he sits as if he was at home in his chair; he trips against no stones, spares his shoes, and yet gets on he hardly knows how.' The horseman heard this, and said, 'Well, Hans, why do you go on foot then?' 'Ah!' said he, 'I have this load to carry; to be sure it is silver, but it is so heavy that I can't hold up my head, and it hurts my shoulder sadly.' 'What do you say to changing?' said the horseman; 'I will give you my horse, and you shall give me the silver.' 'With all my heart,' said Hans: 'but I tell you one thing, – you'll have a weary task to drag it along.' The horseman got off, took the silver, helped Hans up, gave him the bridle into his hand, and said, 'When you want to go very fast, you must smack your lips loud, and cry "Jip."'

Hans was delighted as he sat on the horse, and rode merrily on. After a time he thought he should like to go a little faster, so he smacked his lips, and cried 'Jip'. Away went the horse full gallop; and before Hans knew what he was about, he was thrown off, and lay in a ditch by the road side; and his horse would have run off, if a shepherd who was coming by, driving a cow, had not stopt it. Hans soon came to himself, and got upon his legs again. He was sadly vexed, and said to the shepherd, 'This riding is no joke when a man gets on a beast like this, that stumbles and flings him off as if he would break his neck. However, I'm off now once for all: I like your cow a great deal better; one can walk along at one's leisure behind her, and have milk, butter, and cheese, every day into the bargain. What would I give to have such a cow!' 'Well,' said the shepherd, 'if you are so fond of her, I will change my cow for your horse.' 'Done!' said Hans merrily. The shepherd jumped upon the horse, and away he rode.

Hans drove off his cow quietly, and thought his bargain a very lucky one. 'If I have only a piece of bread (and I certainly shall be able to get that), I can, whenever I like, eat my butter and cheese with it; and when I am thirsty I can milk my cow and drink the milk: what can I wish for more?' When he came to an inn, he halted, ate up all his bread, and gave away his last penny for a glass of beer: then he drove his cow towards his mother's village; and the heat grew greater as noon came on, till at last he found himself on a wide heath that would take him more than an hour to cross, and he began to be so hot and parched that his tongue clave to the roof of his mouth. 'I can find a cure for this,' thought he, 'now will I milk my cow and quench my thirst;' so he tied her to the stump of a tree, and held his leathern cap to milk into; but not a drop was to be had.

While he was trying his luck and managing the matter very clumsily, the uneasy beast gave him a kick on the head that knocked him down, and there he lay a long while senseless. Luckily a butcher soon came by driving a pig in a wheel-barrow. 'What is the matter with you?' said the butcher as he helped him up. Hans told him what had happened, and the butcher gave him a flask, saying, 'There, drink and refresh yourself; your cow will give you no milk, she is an old beast good for nothing but the slaughter-house.' 'Alas, alas! said Hans, 'who would have thought it? If I kill her, what will she be good for? I hate cow-beef, it is not tender enough for me. If it were a pig now, one could do something with it, it would at any rate make some sausages.' 'Well,' said the butcher, 'to please you, I'll change, and give you the pig for the cow.' 'Heaven reward you for your kindness!' said Hans as he gave the butcher the cow, and took the pig off the wheel-barrow, and drove it off, holding it by the string that was tied to its leg.

So on he jogged, and all seemed now to go right with him; he had met with some misfortunes, to be sure; but he was now well repaid for all. The next person he met was a countryman carrying a fine white goose under his arm. The countryman stopped to ask what was o'clock; and Hans told him all his luck, and how he had made so many good bargains. The countryman said he was going to take the goose to a christening; 'Feel,' said he, 'how heavy it is, and yet it is only eight weeks old. Whoever roasts and eats it may cut plenty of fat off it, it has lived so well!' 'You're right,' said Hans as he weighed it in his hand; 'but my pig is no trifle.' Meantime the countryman began to look grave, and shook his head. 'Hark ye,' said he, 'my good friend; your pig may get you into a scrape; in the village I just come from, the squire has had a pig stolen out of his stye. I was dreadfully afraid, when I saw you, that you had got the squire's pig; it will be a bad job if they catch you; the least they'll do, will be to throw you into the horsepond.'

Poor Hans was sadly frightened. 'Good man,' cried he, 'pray get me out of this scrape; you know this country better than I, take my pig and give me the goose.' 'I ought to have something into the bargain,' said the countryman;

'however, I will not bear hard upon you, as you are in trouble.' Then he took the string in his hand, and drove off the pig by a side path; while Hans went on the way homewards free from care. 'After all,' thought he, 'I have the best of the bargain: first there will be a capital roast; then the fat will find me in goose grease for six months; and then there are all the beautiful white feathers; I will put them into my pillow, and then I am sure I shall sleep soundly without rocking. How happy my mother will be!'

As he came to the last village, he saw a scissor-grinder, with his wheel, working away, and singing

> O'er hill and o'er dale so happy I roam,
> Work light and live well, all the world is my home;
> Who so blythe, so merry as I?

Hans stood looking for a while, and at last said, 'You must be well off, master grinder, you seem so happy at your work.' 'Yes,' said the other, 'mine is a golden trade; a good grinder never puts his hand in his pocket without finding money in it:— but where did you get that beautiful goose?' 'I did not buy it, but changed a pig for it.' 'And where did you get the pig?' 'I gave a cow for it.' 'And the cow?' 'I gave a horse for it.' 'And the horse?' 'I gave a piece of silver as big as my head for that.' 'And the silver?' 'Oh! I worked hard for that seven long years.' 'You have thriven well in the world hitherto,' said the grinder; 'now if you could find money in your pocket whenever you put your hand into it, your fortune would be made.' 'Very true: but how is that to be managed?' 'You must turn grinder like me,' said the other; 'you only want a grindstone; the rest will come of itself. Here is one that is a little the worse for wear: I would not ask more than the value of your goose for it; — will you buy?' 'How can you ask such a question?' replied Hans; 'I should be the happiest man in the world, if I could have money whenever I put my hand in my pocket;

what could I want more? there's the goose!' 'Now,' said the grinder, as he gave him a common rough stone that lay by his side, 'this is a most capital stone; do but manage it cleverly, and you can make an old nail cut with it.'

Hans took the stone and went off with a light heart: his eyes sparkled for joy, and he said to himself, 'I must have been born in a lucky hour; every thing that I want or wish for comes to me of itself.'

Meantime he began to be tired, for he had been travelling ever since day-break; he was hungry too, for he had given away his last penny in his joy at getting the cow. At last he could go no farther, and the stone tired him terribly; he dragged himself to the side of a pond, that he might drink some water, and rest a while; so he laid the stone carefully by his side on the bank: but as he stooped down to drink, he forgot it, pushed it a little, and down it went plump into the pond. For a while he watched it sinking in the deep clear water, then sprang up for joy, and again fell upon his knees, and thanked heaven with tears in his eyes for its kindness in taking away his only plague, the ugly heavy stone. 'How happy am I!' cried he: 'no mortal was ever so lucky as I am.' Then up he got with a light and merry heart and walked on free from all his troubles, till he reached his mother's house.

THE TRAVELLING MUSICIANS

An honest farmer had once an ass, that had been a faithful servant to him a great many years, but was now growing old and every day more and more unfit for work. His master therefore was tired of keeping him and began to think of putting an end to him; but the ass, who saw that some mischief was in the wind, took himself slyly off, and began his journey towards the great city, 'for there,' thought he, 'I may turn musician.'

After he had travelled a little way, he spied a dog lying by the road-side and panting as if he were very tired. 'What makes you pant so, my friend?' said the ass. 'Alas!' said the dog, 'my master was going to knock me on the head, because I am old and weak, and can no longer make myself useful to him in hunting; so I ran away: but what can I do to earn my livelihood?' 'Hark ye!' said the ass, 'I am going to the great city to turn musician: suppose you go with me, and try what you can do in the same way?' The dog said he was willing, and they jogged on together.

They had not gone far before they saw a cat sitting in the middle of the road and making a most rueful face. 'Pray, my good lady,' said the ass, 'what's the matter with you? you look quite out of spirits!' 'Ah me!' said the cat, 'how can one be in good spirits when one's life is in danger? Because I am beginning to grow old, and had rather lie at my ease by the fire than run about the house after the mice, my mistress laid hold of me, and was going to drown me; and though I have been lucky enough to get away from her, I do not know what I am to live upon.' 'O!' said the ass, 'by all means go with us to the great city; you are a good night singer, and may make your fortune as a musician.' The cat was pleased with the thought, and joined the party.

Soon afterwards, as they were passing by a farmyard, they saw a cock perched upon a gate, and screaming out with all his might and main. 'Bravo!' said the ass; 'upon my word you make a famous noise; pray what is all this about?' 'Why,' said the cock, 'I was just now saying that we should have fine weather for our washing-day, and yet my mistress and the cook don't thank me for my pains, but threaten to cut off my head tomorrow, and make broth of me for the guests that are coming on Sunday!' 'Heaven forbid!' said the ass; 'come with us, Master Chanticleer; it

THE TRAVELLING MUSICIANS 25

will be better, at any rate, than staying here to have your head cut off! Besides, who knows? If we take care to sing in tune, we may get up some kind of a concert: so come along with us.' 'With all my heart,' said the cock: so they all four went on jollily together.

They could not, however, reach the great city the first day; so when night came on, they went into a wood to sleep. The ass and the dog laid themselves down under a great tree, and the cat climbed up into the branches; while the cock, thinking that the higher he sat the safer he should be, flew up to the very top of the tree, and then, according to his custom, before he went to sleep, looked out on all sides of him to see that every thing was well. In doing this, he saw afar off something bright and shining; and calling to his companions said, 'There must be a house no great way off, for I see a light.' 'If that be the case,' said the ass, 'we had better change our quarters, for our lodging is not the best in the world!' 'Besides,' added the dog, 'I should not be the worse for a bone or two, or a bit of meat.' So they walked off together towards the spot where Chanticleer had seen the light; and as they drew near, it became larger and brighter, till they at last came close to a house in which a gang of robbers lived.

The ass, being the tallest of the company, marched up to the window and peeped in. 'Well, Donkey,' said Chanticleer, 'what do you see?' 'What do I see?' replied the ass, 'why I see a table spread with all kinds of good things, and robbers sitting round it making merry.' 'That would be a noble lodging for us,' said the cock. 'Yes,' said the ass, 'if we could only get in:' so they consulted together how they should contrive to get the robbers out; and at last they hit upon a plan. The ass placed himself upright on his hind-legs, with his fore-feet resting against the window; the dog got upon his back; the cat scrambled up to the dog's shoulders, and the cock flew up and sat upon the cat's head.

When all was ready, a signal was given, and they began their music. The ass brayed, the dog barked, the cat mewed, and the cock screamed; and then they all broke through the window at once, and came tumbling into the room, amongst the broken glass, with a most hideous clatter! The robbers, who had been not a little frightened by the opening concert, had now no doubt that some frightful hobgoblin had broken in upon them, and scampered away as fast as they could.

The coast once clear, our travellers soon sat down, and dispatched what the robbers had left, with as much eagerness as if they had not expected to eat again for a month. As soon as they had satisfied themselves, they put out the lights, and each once more sought out a resting-place to his own liking. The donkey laid himself down upon a heap of straw in the yard; the dog stretched himself upon a mat behind the door; the cat rolled herself up on the hearth before the warm ashes; and the cock perched upon a beam on top of the house; and, as they were all rather tired with their journey, they soon fell asleep.

But about midnight, when the robbers saw from afar that the lights were out and that all seemed quiet, they began to think that they had been in too great a hurry to run away; and one of them, who was bolder than the rest, went to see what was going on. Finding every thing still, he marched into the kitchen, and groped about till he found a match in order to light a candle; and then, espying the glittering fiery eyes of the cat, he mistook them for live coals, and held the match to them to light it. But the cat, not understanding this joke, sprung at his face, and spit, and scratched at him. This frightened him dreadfully, and away he ran to the back door; but there the dog jumped up and bit him in the leg; and as he was crossing over the yard the ass kicked him; and the cock, who had been awakened by the noise, crowed with all his might. At this the robber ran back as fast as he could to his comrades, and told the captain 'how a horrid witch had got into the house, and had spit at him and scratched his face with her long bony fingers; how a man with a knife in his hand had hidden himself behind the door, and stabbed him in the leg; how a black monster stood in the yard and struck him with a club, and how the devil sat upon the top of the house and cried out, 'Throw the rascal up here!' After this the robbers never dared to go back to the house: but the musicians were so pleased with their quarters, that they took up their abode there; and there they are, I dare say, at this very day.

THE GOLDEN BIRD

A CERTAIN king had a beautiful garden, and in the garden stood a tree which bore golden apples. These apples were always counted, and about the time when they began to grow ripe it was found that every night one of them was gone. The king became very angry at this, and ordered the gardener to keep watch all night under the tree. The gardener set his eldest son to watch; but about twelve o'clock he fell asleep, and in the morning another of the apples was missing. Then the second son was ordered to watch; and at midnight he too fell asleep, and in the morning another apple was gone. Then the third son offered to keep watch; but the gardener at first would not let him, for fear some harm should come to him: however, at last he consented, and the young man laid himself under the tree to watch. As the clock struck twelve he heard a rustling noise in the air, and a bird came flying that was of pure gold; and as it was snapping at one of the apples with its beak, the gardener's son jumped up and shot an arrow at it. But the arrow did the bird no harm; only it dropped a golden feather from its tail, and then flew away. The golden feather was brought to the king in the morning, and all the council was called together. Every one agreed that it was worth more than all the wealth of the kingdom: but the king said, 'One feather is of no use to me, I must have the whole bird.'

Then the gardener's eldest son set out and thought to find the golden bird very easily; and when he had gone but a little way, he came to a wood, and by the side of the wood he saw a fox sitting; so he took his bow and made ready to shoot at it. Then the fox said, 'Do not shoot me, for I will give you good counsel; I know what your business is, and that you want to find the golden bird. You will reach a village in the evening; and when you get there, you will see two inns opposite to each other, one of which is very pleasant and beautiful to look at: go not in there, but rest for the night in the other, though it may appear to you to be very poor and mean.' But the son thought to himself, 'What can such a beast as this know about the matter?' So he shot his arrow at the fox; but he missed it, and it set up its tail above its back and ran into the wood. Then he went his way, and in the evening came to the village where the two inns were; and in one of these were people singing, and dancing, and feasting; but the other looked very dirty, and poor. 'I should be very silly,' said he, 'if I went to that shabby house, and left this charming place;' so he went into the smart house, and ate and drank at his ease, and forgot the bird, and his country too.

Time passed on; and as the eldest son did not come back, and no tidings were heard of him, the second son set out, and the same thing happened to him. He met the fox, who gave him the same good advice: but when he came to the two inns, his eldest brother was standing at the window where the merrymaking was, and called to him to come in; and he could not withstand the temptation, but went in, and forgot the golden bird and his country in the same manner.

Time passed on again, and the youngest son too wished to set out into the wide world to seek for the golden bird; but his father would not listen to it for a long while, for he was very fond of his son, and was afraid that some ill luck might happen to him also, and prevent his coming back. However, at last it was agreed he should go, for he would not rest at home; and as he came to the wood, he met the

fox, and heard the same good counsel. But he was thankful to the fox, and did not attempt his life as his brothers had done; so the fox said, 'Sit upon my tail, and you will travel faster.' So he sat down, and the fox began to run, and away they went over stock and stone so quick that their hair whistled in the wind.

When they came to the village, the son followed the fox's counsel, and without looking about him went to the shabby inn and rested there all night at his ease. In the morning came the fox again and met him as he was beginning his journey, and said, 'Go straight forward, till you come to a castle, before which lie a whole troop of soldiers fast asleep and snoring: take no notice of them, but go into the castle and pass on and on till you come to a room, where the golden bird sits in a wooden cage; close by it stands a beautiful golden cage; but do not try to take the bird out of the shabby cage and put it into the handsome one, otherwise you will repent it.' Then the fox stretched out his tail again, and the young man sat himself down, and away they went over stock and stone till their hair whistled in the wind.

Before the castle gate all was as the fox had said: so the son went in and found the chamber where the golden bird hung in a wooden cage, and below stood the golden cage, and the three golden apples that had been lost were lying close by it. Then thought he to himself, 'It will be a very droll thing to bring away such a fine bird in this shabby cage;' so he opened the door and took hold of it and put it into the golden cage. But the bird set up such a loud scream that all the soldiers awoke, and they took him prisoner and carried him before the king. The next morning the court sat to judge him; and when all was heard, it sentenced him to die, unless he should bring the king the golden horse which could run as swiftly as the wind; and if he did this, he was to have the golden bird given him for his own.

So he set out once more on his journey, sighing, and in great despair, when on a sudden his good friend the fox met him, and said, 'You see now what has happened on account of your not listening to my counsel. I will still, however, tell you how to find the golden horse, if you will do as I bid you. You must go straight on till you come to the castle where the horse stands in his stall: by his side will lie the groom fast asleep and snoring: take away the horse quietly, but be sure to put the old leathern saddle upon him, and not the golden one that is close by it.' Then the son sat down on the

fox's tail, and away they went over stock and stone till
their hair whistled in the wind.

All went right, and the groom lay snoring with his hand
upon the golden saddle. But when the son looked at the
horse, he thought it a great pity to put the leathern saddle
upon it. 'I will give him the good one,' said he; 'I am sure
he deserves it.' As he took up the golden saddle the groom
awoke and cried out so loud, that all the guards ran in and
took him prisoner, and in the morning he was again brought
before the court to be judged, and was sentenced to die.
But it was agreed, that, if he could bring thither the beautiful princess, he should live, and have the bird and the horse
given him for his own.

Then he went his way again very sorrowful; but the old
fox came and said, 'Why did not you listen to me? If you
had, you would have carried away both the bird and the
horse; yet will I once more give you counsel. Go straight on,
and in the evening you will arrive at a castle. At twelve
o'clock at night the princess goes to the bathing-house: go
up to her and give her a kiss, and she will let you lead her
away; but take care you do not suffer her to go and take
leave of her father and mother.' Then the fox stretched out
his tail, and so away they went over stock and stone till
their hair whistled again.

As they came to the castle, all was as the fox had said,
and at twelve o'clock the young man met the princess going
to the bath and gave her the kiss, and she agreed to run
away with him, but begged with many tears that he would
let her take leave of her father. At first he refused, but she
wept still more and more, and fell at his feet, till at last he
consented; but the moment she came to her father's house
the guards awoke and he was taken prisoner again.

Then he was brought before the king, and the king said,
'You shall never have my daughter unless in eight days you
dig away the hill that stops the view from my window.'

Now this hill was so big that the whole world could not take it away: and when he had worked for seven days, and had done very little, the fox came and said, 'Lie down and go to sleep; I will work for you.' And in the morning he awoke and the hill was gone; so he went merrily to the king, and told him that now that it was removed he must give him the princess.

Then the king was obliged to keep his word, and away went the young man and the princess; and the fox came and said to him, 'We will have all three, the princess, the horse, and the bird.' 'Ah!' said the young man, 'that would be a great thing, but how can you contrive it?'

'If you will only listen,' said the fox, 'it can soon be done. When you come to the king, and he asks for the beautiful princess, you must say, "Here she is!" Then he will be very joyful; and you will mount the golden horse that they are to give you, and put out your hand to take leave of them; but shake hands with the princess last. Then lift her quickly on to the horse behind you; clap your spurs to his side, and gallop away as fast as you can.'

All went right: then the fox said, 'When you come to the castle where the bird is, I will stay with the princess at the door, and you will ride in and speak to the king; and when he sees that it is the right horse, he will bring out the bird; but you must sit still, and say that you want to look at it, to see whether it is the true golden bird; and when you get it into your hand, ride away.'

This, too, happened as the fox said; they carried off the bird, the princess mounted again, and they rode on to a great wood. Then the fox came, and said, 'Pray kill me, and cut off my head and my feet.' But the young man refused to do it: so the fox said, 'I will at any rate give you good counsel: beware of two things; ransom no one from the gallows, and sit down by the side of no river.' Then away he went. 'Well,' thought the young man, 'it is no hard matter to keep that advice.'

He rode on with the princess, till at last he came to the village where he had left his two brothers. And there he heard a great noise and uproar; and when he asked what was the matter, the people said, 'Two men are going to be hanged.' As he came nearer, he saw that the two men were his brothers, who had turned robbers; so he said, 'Cannot they in any way be saved?' But the people said 'No,' unless he would bestow all his money upon the rascals and buy their liberty. Then he did not stay to think about the matter, but paid what was asked, and his brothers were given up, and went on with him towards their home.

And as they came to the wood where the fox first met them, it was so cool and pleasant that the two brothers said, 'Let us sit down by the side of the river, and rest a while, to eat and drink.' So he said, 'Yes,' and forgot the fox's counsel, and sat down on the side of the river; and while he suspected nothing, they came behind, and threw him down the bank, and took the princess, the horse, and the bird, and went home to the king their master, and said, 'All this have we won by our labour.' Then there was great rejoicing made; but the horse would not eat, the bird would not sing, and the princess wept.

The youngest son fell to the bottom of the river's bed: luckily it was nearly dry, but his bones were almost broken, and the bank was so steep that he could find no way to get out. Then the old fox came once more, and scolded him for not following his advice; otherwise no evil would have befallen him: 'Yet,' said he, 'I cannot leave you here, so lay hold of my tail and hold fast.' Then he pulled him out of the river, and said to him, as he got upon the bank, 'Your brothers have set watch to kill you, if they find you in the kingdom.' So he dressed himself as a poor man, and came secretly to the king's court, and was scarcely within the doors when the horse began to eat, and the bird to sing, and the princess left off weeping. Then he went to the king, and told him all his brothers' roguery; and they were seized and punished, and he had the princess given to him again; and after the king's death he was heir to his kingdom.

A long while after, he went to walk one day in the wood, and the old fox met him, and besought him with tears in his eyes to kill him, and cut off his head and feet. And at last he did so, and in a moment the fox was changed into a man, and turned out to be the brother of the princess, who had been lost a great many many years.

THE FISHERMAN AND HIS WIFE

THERE was once a fisherman who lived with his wife in a ditch, close by the sea-side. The fisherman used to go out all day a-fishing; and one day, as he sat on the shore with his rod, looking at the shining water and watching his line, all on a sudden his float was dragged away deep under the sea: and in drawing it up he pulled a great fish out of the water. The fish said to him, 'Pray let me live: I am not a real fish; I am an enchanted prince, put me in the water again, and let me go.' 'Oh!' said the man, 'you need not make so many words about the matter; I wish to have nothing to do with a fish that can talk; so swim away as soon as you please.' Then he put him back into the water, and the fish darted straight down to the bottom, and left a long streak of blood behind him.

When the fisherman went home to his wife in the ditch, he told her how he had caught a great fish, and how it had told him it was an enchanted prince, and that on hearing it speak he had let it go again. 'Did yóu not ask it for any

thing?' said the wife. 'No,' said the man, 'what should I
ask for?' 'Ah!' said the wife, 'we live very wretchedly here
in this nasty stinking ditch; do go back, and tell the fish we
want a little cottage.'

The fisherman did not much like the business: however,
he went to the sea, and when he came there the water
looked all yellow and green. And he stood at the water's
edge, and said,

> 'O man of the sea!
> Come listen to me,
> For Alice my wife,
> The plague of my life,
> Has sent me to beg a boon of thee!'

Then the fish came swimming to him, and said, 'Well,
what does she want?' 'Ah!' answered the fisherman, 'my
wife says that when I had caught you, I ought to have
asked you for something before I let you go again; she does
not like living any longer in the ditch, and wants a little
cottage.' 'Go home, then,' said the fish, 'she is in the cottage
already.' So the man went home, and saw his wife standing
at the door of a cottage. 'Come in, come in,' said she; 'is not
this much better than the ditch?' And there was a parlour,
and a bed-chamber, and a kitchen; and behind the cottage
there was a little garden with all sorts of flowers and fruits,
and a court-yard full of ducks and chickens. 'Ah!' said the
fisherman, 'how happily we shall live!' 'We will try to do
so at least,' said his wife.

Every thing went right for a week or two, and then
Dame Alice said, 'Husband, there is not room enough in
this cottage, the court-yard and garden are a great deal too
small; I should like to have a large stone castle to live in;
so go to the fish again, and tell him to give us a castle.'
'Wife,' said the fisherman, 'I don't like to go to him again,
for perhaps he will be angry; we ought to be content with

the cottage.' 'Nonsense!' said the wife; 'he will do it very willingly; go along, and try.'

The fisherman went; but his heart was very heavy: and when he came to the sea, it looked blue and gloomy, though it was quite calm, and he went close to it, and said,

> 'O man of the sea!
> Come listen to me,
> For Alice my wife,
> The plague of my life,
> Hath sent me to beg a boon of thee!'

'Well, what does she want now?' said the fish. 'Ah!' said the man very sorrowfully, 'my wife wants to live in a stone castle.' 'Go home then,' said the fish, 'she is standing at the door of it already.' So away went the fisherman, and found his wife standing before a great castle. 'See,' said she, 'is not this grand?' With that they went into the castle together, and found a great many servants there, and the rooms all richly furnished and full of golden chairs and tables; and behind the castle was a garden, and a wood half a mile long, full of sheep, and goats, and hares, and deer; and in the court-yard were stables and cow-houses. 'Well,' said the man, 'now will we live contented and happy in this beautiful castle for the rest of our lives.' 'Perhaps we may,' said the wife; 'but let us consider and sleep upon it before we make up our minds:' so they went to bed.

The next morning, when Dame Alice awoke, it was broad day-light, and she jogged the fisherman with her elbow, and said, 'Get up, husband, and bestir yourself, for we must be king of all the land.' 'Wife, wife,' said the man, 'why should we wish to be king? I will not be king.' 'Then I will,' said Alice. 'But, wife,' answered the fisherman, 'how can you be king? the fish cannot make you a king.' 'Husband,' said she, 'say no more about it, but go and try;

I will be king!' So the man went away, quite sorrowful to think that his wife should want to be king. The sea looked a dark grey colour, and was covered with foam as he cried out,

> 'O man of the sea!
> Come listen to me,
> For Alice my wife,
> The plague of my life,
> Hath sent me to beg a boon of thee!'

'Well, what would she have now?' said the fish. 'Alas!' said the man, 'my wife wants to be king.' 'Go home,' said the fish; 'she is king already.'

Then the fisherman went home; and as he came close to the palace, he saw a troop of soldiers, and heard the sound of drums and trumpets; and when he entered in, he saw his wife sitting on a high throne of gold and diamonds, with a golden crown upon her head; and on each side of her stood six beautiful maidens, each a head taller than the other. 'Well, wife,' said the fisherman, 'are you king?' 'Yes,' said she, 'I am king.' And when he had looked at her for a long time, he said, 'Ah, wife! what a fine thing it is to be king! now we shall never have any thing more to wish for.' 'I don't know how that may be,' said she; 'never is a long time. I am king, 'tis true, but I begin to be tired of it, and I think I should like to be emperor.' 'Alas, wife! why should you wish to be emperor?' said the fisherman. 'Husband,' said she; 'go to the fish; I say I will be emperor.' 'Ah, wife!' replied the fisherman, 'the fish cannot make an emperor, and I should not like to ask for such a thing.' 'I am king,' said Alice, 'and you are my slave, so go directly!' So the fisherman was obliged to go; and he muttered as he went along, 'This will come to no good, it is too much to ask, the fish will be tired at last, and then we shall repent of what we have done.' He soon arrived at the sea, and the water was quite black and muddy, and a mighty whirlwind blew over it; but he went to the shore, and said,

'O man of the sea!
Come listen to me,
For Alice my wife,
The plague of my life,
Hath sent me to beg a boon of thee!'

'What would she have now!' said the fish. 'Ah!' said the fisherman, 'she wants to be emperor.' 'Go home,' said the fish; 'she is emperor already.'

So he went home again; and as he came near he saw his wife sitting on a very lofty throne made of solid gold, with a great crown on her head full two yards high, and on each side of her stood her guards and attendants in a row, each one smaller than the other, from the tallest giant down to a little dwarf no bigger than my finger. And before her stood princes, and dukes, and earls: and the fisherman went up to her and said, 'Wife, are you emperor?' 'Yes,' said she, 'I am emperor.' 'Ah!' said the man as he gazed upon her, 'what a fine thing it is to be emperor!' 'Husband,' said she, 'why should we stay at being emperor; I will be pope next.' 'O wife, wife!' said he, 'how can you be pope? there is but one pope at a time in Christendom.' 'Husband,' said she, 'I will be pope this very day.' 'But,' replied the husband, 'the fish cannot make you pope.' 'What nonsense!' said she, 'if he can make an emperor, he can make a pope, go and try him.' So the fisherman went. But when he came to the shore the wind was raging, and the sea was tossed up and down like boiling water, and the ships were in the greatest distress and danced upon the waves most fearfully; in the middle of the sky there was a little blue, but towards the south it was all red as if a dreadful storm was rising. At this the fisherman was terribly frightened, and trembled, so that his knees knocked together: but he went to the shore and said,

'O man of the sea!
Come listen to me,
For Alice my wife,
The plague of my life,
Hath sent me to beg a boon of thee!'

'What does she want now?' said the fish. 'Ah!' said the fisherman, 'my wife wants to be pope.' 'Go home,' said the fish, 'she is pope already.'

Then the fisherman went home, and found his wife sitting on a throne that was two miles high; and she had three great crowns on her head, and around stood all the pomp and power of the Church; and on each side were two rows of burning lights, of all sizes, the greatest as large as the highest and biggest tower in the world, and the least no larger than a small rushlight. 'Wife,' said the fisherman as he looked at all this grandeur, 'Are you pope?' 'Yes,' said she, 'I am pope.' 'Well, wife,' replied he, 'it is a grand thing to be pope; and now you must be content, for you can be nothing greater.' 'I will consider of that,' said the wife. Then they went to bed: but Dame Alice could not sleep all night for thinking what she should be next. At last morning came, and the sun rose. 'Ha!' thought she as she looked at it through the window, 'cannot I prevent the sun rising?' At this she was very angry, and she wakened her husband, and said, 'Husband, go to the fish and tell him I want to be lord of the sun and moon.' The fisherman was half asleep, but the thought frightened him so much, that he started and fell out of bed. 'Alas, wife!' said he, 'cannot you be content to be pope?' 'No,'' said she, 'I am very uneasy, and cannot bear to see the sun and moon rise without my leave. Go to the fish directly.'

Then the man went trembling for fear; and as he was going down to the shore a dreadful storm arose, so that the trees and the rocks shook; and the heavens became black, and the lightning played, and the thunder rolled; and you

might have seen in the sea great black waves like mountains with a white crown of foam upon them; and the
fisherman said,

> 'O man of the sea!
> Come listen to me,
> For Alice my wife,
> The plague of my life,
> Hath sent me to beg a boon of thee!'

'What does she want now?' said the fish. 'Ah!' said he,
'she wants to be lord of the sun and moon.' 'Go home,'
said the fish, 'to your ditch again!' And there they live to
this very day.

THE TOM-TIT AND THE BEAR

ONE summer day, as the wolf and the bear were walking
together in a wood, they heard a bird singing most delightfully. 'Brother,' said the bear, 'what can that bird be that
is singing so sweetly?' 'O!' said the wolf, 'that is his majesty the king of the birds, we must take care to show him all
possible respect.' (Now I should tell you that this bird was
after all no other than the tom-tit.) 'If that is the case,'
said the bear, 'I should like to see the royal palace; so pray
come along and show it to me.' 'Gently, my friend,' said
the wolf, 'we cannot see it just yet, we must wait till the
queen comes home.'

Soon afterwards the queen came with food in her beak,
and she and the king began to feed their young ones. 'Now
for it!' said the bear; and was about to follow them, to see
what was to be seen. 'Stop a little, master Bruin,' said the
wolf, 'we must wait now till their majesties are gone again.'
So they marked the hole where they had seen the nest, and
went away. But the bear, being very eager to see the royal

palace, soon came back again, and peeping into the nest, saw five or six young birds lying at the bottom of it. 'What nonsense!' said Bruin, 'this is not a royal palace: I never saw such a filthy place in my life; and you are no royal children, you little base-born brats!' As soon as the young tom-tits heard this they were very angry, and screamed out, 'We are not base-born, you stupid bear! our father and mother are honest good sort of people: and depend upon it you shall suffer for your insolence!' At this the wolf and the bear grew frightened, and ran away to their dens. But the young tom-tits kept crying and screaming; and when their father and mother came home and offered them food, they all said, 'We will not touch a bit; no, not the leg of a fly, though we should die of hunger, till that rascal Bruin has been punished for calling us base-born brats.' 'Make yourselves easy, my darlings,' said the old king, 'you may be sure he shall meet with his deserts.'

So he went out and stood before the bear's den, and cried out with a loud voice, 'Bruin the bear! thou hast shamefully insulted our lawful children: we therefore hereby declare bloody and cruel war against thee and thine, which shall never cease until thou hast been punished as thou so richly deservest.' Now when the bear heard this, he called together the ox, the ass, the stag, and all the beasts of the earth, in order to consult about the means of his defence. And the tom-tit also enlisted on his side all the birds of the air, both great and small, and a very large army of hornets, gnats, bees, and flies, and other insects.

As the time approached when the war was to begin, the tom-tit sent out spies to see who was the commander-in-chief of the enemy's forces; and the gnat, who was by far the cleverest spy of them all, flew backwards and forwards in the wood where the enemy's troops were, and at last hid himself under a leaf on a tree, close by which the orders of the day were given out. And the bear, who was standing so near the tree that the gnat could hear all he said, called to the fox and said, 'Reynard, you are the cleverest of all the beasts; therefore you shall be our general and lead us to battle: but we must first agree upon some signal, by which we may know what you want us to do.' 'Behold,' said the fox, 'I have a fine, long, bushy tail, which is very like a plume of red feathers, and gives me a very warlike air: now remember, when you see me raise up my tail, you may be sure that the battle is won, and you have then nothing to do but to rush down upon the enemy with all your force. On the other hand, if I drop my tail, the day is lost, and you must run away as fast as you can.' Now when the gnat had heard all this, she flew back to the tom-tit and told him every thing that had passed.

At length the day came when the battle was to be fought; and as soon as it was light, behold! the army of beasts came rushing forward with such a fearful sound that the earth shook. And his majesty the tom-tit, with his troops, came flying along in warlike array, flapping and fluttering, and beating the air, so that it was quite frightful to hear; and both armies set themselves in order of battle upon the field. Now the tom-tit gave orders to a troop of hornets that at the first onset they should march straight towards Captain Reynard, and fixing themselves about his tail, should sting him with all their might and main. The hornets did as they were told: and when Reynard felt the first sting, he started aside and shook one of his legs, but still held up his tail with wonderful bravery; at the second sting he was forced to drop his tail for a moment; but when the third hornet had fixed itself, he could bear it no longer, but clapped his tail between his legs and scampered away as fast as he could. As soon as the beasts saw this, they thought of course all was lost, and scoured across the country in the greatest dismay, leaving the birds masters of the field.

And now the king and queen flew back in triumph to
their children, and said, 'Now, children, eat, drink, and be
merry, for the victory is ours!' But the young birds said,
'No: not till Bruin has humbly begged our pardon for calling us base-born.' So the king flew back to the bear's den,
and cried out, 'Thou villain bear! come forthwith to my
abode, and humbly beseech my children to forgive thee the
insult thou hast offered them; for, if thou wilt not do this,
every bone in thy wretched body shall be broken to pieces.'
So the bear was forced to crawl out of his den very sulkily,
and do what the king bade him: and after that the young
birds sat down together, and ate and drank and made
merry till midnight.

THE TWELVE DANCING PRINCESSES

THERE was a king who had twelve beautiful daughters.
They slept in twelve beds all in one room; and when they
went to bed, the doors were shut and locked up; but every
morning their shoes were found to be quite worn through,
as if they had been danced in all night; and yet nobody
could find out how it happened, or where they had been.

Then the king made it known to all the land, that if any
person could discover the secret, and find out where it was
that the princesses danced in the night, he should have the
one he liked best for his wife, and should be king after his
death; but whoever tried and did not succeed, after three
days and nights, should be put to death.

A king's son soon came. He was well entertained, and in
the evening was taken to the chamber next to the one
where the princesses lay in their twelve beds. There he was
to sit and watch where they went to dance; and, in order
that nothing might pass without his hearing it, the door

of his chamber was left open. But the king's son soon fell asleep; and when he awoke in the morning he found that the princesses had all been dancing, for the soles of their shoes were full of holes. The same thing happened the second and third night: so the king ordered his head to be cut off. After him came several others; but they had all the same luck, and all lost their lives in the same manner.

Now it chanced that an old soldier, who had been wounded in battle and could fight no longer, passed through the country where this king reigned: and as he was travelling through a wood, he met an old woman, who asked him where he was going. 'I hardly know where I am going, or what I had better do,' said the soldier; 'but I think I should like very well to find out where it is that the princesses dance, and then in time I might be a king.' 'Well,' said the old dame, 'that is no very hard task: only take care not to drink any of the wine which one of the princesses will bring to you in the evening; and as soon as she leaves you pretend to be fast asleep.'

Then she gave him a cloak, and said, 'As soon as you put that on you will become invisible, and you will then be able to follow the princesses wherever they go.' When the soldier heard all this good counsel, he determined to try his luck: so he went to the king, and said he was willing to undertake the task.

He was as well received as the others had been, and the king ordered fine royal robes to be given him; and when the evening came he was led to the outer chamber. Just as he was going to lie down, the eldest of the princesses brought him a cup of wine; but the soldier threw it all away secretly, taking care not to drink a drop. Then he laid himself down on his bed, and in a little while began to snore very loud as if he was fast asleep. When the twelve princesses heard this they laughed heartily; and the eldest said, 'This fellow too might have done a wiser thing than lose his life in this way!' Then they rose up and opened their drawers and boxes, and took out all their fine clothes, and dressed themselves at the glass, and skipped about as if they were eager to begin dancing. But the youngest said, 'I don't know how it is, while you are so happy I feel very uneasy; I am sure some mischance will befall us.' 'You simpleton,' said the eldest, 'you are always afraid; have you forgotten how many kings' sons have already watched us in vain? And as for this soldier, even if I had not given him his sleeping draught, he would have slept soundly enough.'

When they were all ready, they went and looked at the soldier; but he snored on, and did not stir hand or foot: so they thought they were quite safe; and the eldest went up to her own bed and clapped her hands, and the bed sunk into the floor and a trap-door flew open. The soldier saw them going down through the trap-door one after another, the eldest leading the way; and thinking he had no time to lose, he jumped up, put on the cloak which the old woman had given him, and followed them; but in the middle of the stairs he trod on the gown of the youngest princess, and she cried out to her sisters, 'All is not right; some one took hold of my gown.' 'You silly creature!' said the eldest, 'it is nothing but a nail in the wall.' Then down they all went, and at the bottom they found themselves in a most delightful grove of trees; and the leaves were all of silver, and glittered and sparkled beautifully. The soldier wished to take away some token of the place; so he broke off a little branch, and there came a loud noise from the tree. Then the youngest daughter said again, 'I am sure all is not right – did not you hear that noise? That never happened before.' But the eldest said, 'It is only our princes, who are shouting for joy at our approach.'

Then they came to another grove of trees, where all the leaves were of gold; and afterwards to a third, where the leaves were all glittering diamonds. And the soldier broke a branch from each; and every time there was a loud noise, which made the youngest sister tremble with fear; but the eldest still said, It was only the princes, who were crying for joy. So they went on till they came to a great lake; and at the side of the lake there lay twelve little boats with twelve handsome princes in them, who seemed to be waiting there for the princesses.

One of the princesses went into each boat, and the soldier stepped into the same boat with the youngest. As they were rowing over the lake, the prince who was in the boat with the youngest princess and the soldier said, 'I do not know why it is, but though I am rowing with all my might we do not get on so fast as usual, and I am quite tired: the boat seems very heavy to-day.' 'It is only the heat of the weather,' said the princess; 'I feel it very warm too.'

On the other side of the lake stood a fine illuminated castle, from which came the merry music of horns and trumpets. There they all landed, and went into the castle, and each prince danced with his princess; and the soldier, who was all the time invisible, danced with them too; and when any of the princesses had a cup of wine set by her, he drank it all up, so that when she put the cup to her mouth it was empty. At this, too, the youngest sister was terribly frightened, but the eldest always silenced her. They danced on till three o'clock in the morning, and then all their shoes were worn out, so that they were obliged to leave off. The princes rowed them back again over the lake; (but this time the soldier placed himself in the boat with the eldest princess;) and on the opposite shore they took leave of each other, the princesses promising to come again the next night.

When they came to the stairs, the soldier ran on before the princesses, and laid himself down; and as the twelve sisters slowly came up very much tired, they heard him snoring in his bed; so they said, 'Now all is quite safe;' then they undressed themselves, put away their fine clothes, pulled off their shoes, and went to bed. In the morning the soldier said nothing about what had happened, but determined to see more of this strange adventure, and went again the second and third night; and every thing happened just as before; the princesses danced each time till their shoes were worn to pieces, and then returned home. However, on the third night the soldier carried away one of the golden cups as a token of where he had been.

As soon as the time came when he was to declare the secret, he was taken before the king with the three branches and the golden cup; and the twelve princesses stood listening behind the door to hear what he would say. And when the king asked him, 'Where do my twelve daughters dance at night?' he answered, 'With twelve princes in a castle under ground.' And then he told the king all that had happened, and showed him the three branches and the golden cup which he had brought with him. Then the king called for the princesses, and asked them whether what the soldier said was true: and when they saw that they were discovered, and that it was of no use to deny what had happened, they confessed it all. And the king asked the soldier which of them he would choose for his wife; and he answered, 'I am not very young, so I will have the eldest.'— And they were married that very day, and the soldier was chosen to be the king's heir.

ROSE-BUD

ONCE upon a time there lived a king and queen who had no children; and this they lamented very much. But one day as the queen was walking by the side of the river, a little fish lifted its head out of the water, and said, 'Your wish

shall be fulfilled, and you shall soon have a daughter.'
What the little fish had foretold soon came to pass; and the
queen had a little girl that was so very beautiful that the
king could not cease looking on it for joy, and determined
to hold a great feast. So he invited not only his relations,
friends, and neighbours, but also all the fairies, that they
might be kind and good to his little daughter. Now there
were thirteen fairies in his kingdom, and he had only
twelve golden dishes for them to eat out of, so that he was
obliged to leave one of the fairies without an invitation.
The rest came, and after the feast was over they gave all
their best gifts to the little princess: one gave her virtue,
another beauty, another riches, and so on till she had all
that was excellent in the world. When eleven had done
blessing her, the thirteenth, who had not been invited, and
was very angry on that account, came in, and determined
to take her revenge. So she cried out, 'The king's daughter
shall in her fifteenth year be wounded by a spindle, and fall
down dead.' Then the twelfth, who had not yet given her
gift, came forward and said that the bad wish must be fulfilled, but that she could soften it, and that the king's
daughter should not die, but fall asleep for a hundred
years.

But the king hoped to save his dear child from the
threatened evil, and ordered that all the spindles in the
kingdom should be bought up and destroyed. All the
fairies' gifts were in the mean time fulfilled; for the princess
was so beautiful, and well-behaved, and amiable, and wise,
that every one who knew her loved her. Now it happened
that on the very day she was fifteen years old the king and
queen were not at home, and she was left alone in the
palace. So she roved about by herself, and looked at all the
rooms and chambers, till at last she came to an old tower,
to which there was a narrow staircase ending with a little
door. In the door there was a golden key, and when she

turned it the door sprang open, and there sat an old lady
spinning away very busily. 'Why, how now, good mother,'
said the princess, 'what are you doing there?' 'Spinning,'
said the old lady, and nodded her head. 'How prettily that
little thing turns round!' said the princess, and took the
spindle and began to spin. But scarcely had she touched it,
before the prophecy was fulfilled, and she fell down lifeless
on the ground.

However, she was not dead, but had only fallen into a
deep sleep; and the king and the queen, who just then came
home, and all their court, fell asleep too; and the horses
slept in the stables, and the dogs in the court, the pigeons
on the house-top and the flies on the walls. Even the fire on
the hearth left off blazing, and went to sleep; and the meat
that was roasting stood still; and the cook, who was at that
moment pulling the kitchen-boy by the hair to give him a
box on the ear for something he had done amiss, let him go,
and both fell asleep; and so every thing stood still, and
slept soundly.

A large hedge of thorns soon grew round the palace, and
every year it became higher and thicker, till at last the
whole palace was surrounded and hid, so that not even the
roof or the chimneys could be seen. But there went a report
through all the land of the beautiful sleeping Rose-Bud (for
so was the king's daughter called); so that from time to
time several kings' sons came, and tried to break through
the thicket into the palace. This they could never do; for
the thorns and bushes laid hold of them as it were with
hands, and there they stuck fast and died miserably.

After many many years there came a king's son into that
land, and an old man told him the story of the thicket of
thorns, and how a beautiful palace stood behind it, in
which was a wondrous princess, called Rose-Bud, asleep
with all her court. He told, too, how he had heard from his
grandfather that many many princes had come, and had

tried to break through the thicket, but had stuck fast and died. Then the young prince said, 'All this shall not frighten me, I will go and see Rose-Bud.' The old man tried to dissuade him, but he persisted in going.

Now that very day were the hundred years completed; and as the prince came to the thicket, he saw nothing but beautiful flowering shrubs, through which he passed with ease, and they closed after him as firm as ever. Then he came at last to the palace, and there in the court lay the dogs asleep, and the horses in the stables, and on the roof sat the pigeons fast asleep with their heads under their wings; and when he came into the palace, the flies slept on the walls, and the cook in the kitchen was still holding up her hand as if she would beat the boy, and the maid sat with a black fowl in her hand ready to be plucked.

Then he went on still farther, and all was so still that he could hear every breath he drew; till at last he came to the old tower and opened the door of the little room in which Rose-Bud was, and there she lay fast asleep, and looked so beautiful that he could not take his eyes off, and he stooped down and gave her a kiss. But the moment he kissed her she opened her eyes and awoke, and smiled upon him. Then they went out together, and presently the king and queen also awoke, and all the court, and they gazed on each other with great wonder. And the horses got up and shook themselves, and the dogs jumped about and barked; the pigeons took their heads from under their wings, and looked about and flew into the fields; the flies on the walls buzzed away; the fire in the kitchen blazed up and cooked the dinner, and the roast meat turned round again; the cook gave the boy the box on his ear so that he cried out, and the maid went on plucking the fowl. And then was the wedding of the prince and Rose-Bud celebrated, and they lived happily together all their lives long.

TOM THUMB

THERE was once a poor woodman sitting by the fire in his cottage, and his wife sat by his side spinning. 'How lonely it is,' said he, 'for you and me to sit here by ourselves without any children to play about and amuse us, while other people seem so happy and merry with their children!' 'What you say is very true,' said the wife, sighing and turning round her wheel, 'how happy should I be if I had but one child! and if it were ever so small, nay, if it were no bigger than my thumb, I should be very happy, and love it dearly.' Now it came to pass that this good woman's wish was fulfilled just as she desired; for, some time afterwards, she had a little boy who was quite healthy and strong, but not much bigger than my thumb. So they said, 'Well, we cannot say we have not got what we wished for, and, little as he is, we all love him dearly;' and they called him Tom Thumb.

They gave him plenty of food, yet he never grew bigger, but remained just the same size as when he was born; still his eyes were sharp and sparkling, and he soon showed himself to be a clever little fellow, who always knew well what he was about. One day, as the woodman was getting ready to go into the wood to cut fuel, he said, 'I wish I had some one to bring the cart after me, for I want to make haste.' 'O father!' cried Tom, 'I will take care of that; the cart shall be in the wood by the time you want it.' Then the woodman laughed, and said, 'How can that be? you cannot reach up to the horse's bridle.' 'Never mind that, father,' said Tom: 'if my mother will only harness the horse, I will get into his ear and tell him which way to go.' 'Well,' said the father, 'we will try for once.'

When the time came, the mother harnessed the horse to the cart, and put Tom into his ear; and as he sat there, the

little man told the beast how to go, crying out, 'Go on,' and
'Stop,' as he wanted; so the horse went on just as if the
woodman had driven it himself into the wood. It happened
that, as the horse was going a little too fast, and Tom was
calling out 'Gently! gently!' two strangers came up. 'What
an odd thing that is!' said one, 'there is a cart going along,
and I hear a carter talking to the horse, but can see no one.'
'That is strange,' said the other; 'let us follow the cart and
see where it goes.' So they went on into the wood, till at
last they came to the place where the woodman was. Then
Tom Thumb, seeing his father, cried out, 'See, father, here
I am, with the cart, all right and safe; now take me down.'
So his father took hold of the horse with one hand, and
with the other took his son out of the ear; then he put him
down upon a straw, where he sat as merry as you please.
The two strangers were all this time looking on, and did not
know what to say for wonder. At last one took the other
aside and said, 'That little urchin will make our fortune if
we can get him and carry him about from town to town as a
show: we must buy him.' So they went to the woodman and
asked him what he would take for the little man: 'He will
be better off,' said they, 'with us than with you.' 'I won't
sell him at all,' said the father, 'my own flesh and blood is
dearer to me than all the silver and gold in the world.' But
Tom, hearing of the bargain they wanted to make, crept up
his father's coat to his shoulder, and whispered in his ear,
'Take the money, father, and let them have me, I'll soon
come back to you.'

So the woodman at last agreed to sell Tom to the strangers for a large piece of gold. 'Where do you like to sit?'
said one of them. 'Oh! put me on the rim of your hat, that
will be a nice gallery for me; I can walk about there, and
see the country as we go along.' So they did as he wished;
and when Tom had taken leave of his father, they took him
away with them. They journeyed on till it began to be

dusky, and then the little man said, 'Let me get down, I'm tired.' So the man took off his hat and set him down on a clod of earth in a ploughed field by the side of the road. But Tom ran about amongst the furrows, and at last slipt into an old mouse-hole. 'Good night, masters,' said he, 'I'm off! mind and look sharp after me the next time.' They ran directly to the place, and poked the ends of their sticks into the mouse-hole, but all in vain; Tom only crawled farther and farther in, and at last it became quite dark, so that they were obliged to go their way without their prize, as sulky as you please.

When Tom found they were gone, he came out of his hiding-place. 'What dangerous walking it is,' said he, 'in this ploughed field! If I were to fall from one of these great clods, I should certainly break my neck.' At last, by good luck, he found a large empty snail-shell. 'This is lucky,' said he, 'I can sleep here very well,' and in he crept. Just as he was falling asleep he heard two men passing, and one said to the other, 'How shall we manage to steal that rich parson's silver and gold?' 'I'll tell you,' cried Tom. 'What noise was that?' said the thief, frightened, 'I am sure I heard some one speak.' They stood still listening, and Tom said, 'Take me with you, and I'll soon show you how to get the parson's money.' 'But where are you?' said they. 'Look about on the ground,' answered he, 'and listen where the sound comes from.' At last the thieves found him out, and lifted him up in their hands. 'You little urchin!' said they, 'what can you do for us?' 'Why I can get between the iron window-bars of the parson's house, and throw you out whatever you want.' 'That's a good thought,' said the thieves, 'come along, we shall see what you can do.'

When they came to the parson's house, Tom slipt through the window-bars into the room, and then called out as loud as he could bawl, 'Will you have all that is here?'

At this the thieves were frightened, and said, 'Softly, softly! Speak low, that you may not awaken any body.' But Tom pretended not to understand them, and bawled out again, 'How much will you have? Shall I throw it all out?' Now the cook lay in the next room, and hearing a noise she raised herself in her bed and listened. Meantime the thieves were frightened, and ran off to a little distance; but at last they plucked up courage, and said, 'The little urchin is only trying to make fools of us.' So they came back and whispered softly to him, saying, 'Now let us have no more of your jokes, but throw out some of the money.' Then Tom called out as loud as he could, 'Very well: hold your hands, here it comes.' The cook heard this quite plain, so she sprang out of bed and ran to open the door. The thieves ran off as if a wolf was at their tails; and the maid, having groped about and found nothing, went away for a light. By the time she returned, Tom had slipt off into the barn; and when the cook had looked about and searched every hole and corner, and found nobody, she went to bed, thinking she must have been dreaming with her eyes open. The little man crawled about in the hay-loft, and at last found a glorious place to finish his night's rest in; so he laid himself down, meaning to sleep till day-light, and then find his way home to his father and mother. But, alas! how cruelly was he disappointed! what crosses and sorrows happen in this world! The cook got up early before day-break to feed the cows: she went straight to the hay-loft, and carried away a large bundle of hay with the little man in the middle of it fast asleep. He still, however, slept on, and did not awake till he found himself in the mouth of the cow, who had taken him up with a mouthful of hay: 'Good lack-a-day!' said he, 'how did I manage to tumble into the mill?' But he soon found out where he really was, and was obliged to have all his wits about him in order that he might not get between the cow's teeth, and so be crushed to death. At last down he went into her stomach. 'It is rather dark here,' said he; 'they forgot to build windows in this room to let the sun in: a candle would be no bad thing.'

Though he made the best of his bad luck, he did not like his quarters at all; and the worst of it was, that more and more hay was always coming down, and the space in which he was became smaller and smaller. At last he cried out as loud as he could, 'Don't bring me any more hay! Don't bring me any more hay!' The maid happened to be just then milking the cow, and hearing some one speak and seeing nobody, and yet being quite sure it was the same voice that she had heard in the night, she was so frightened that she fell off her stool and overset the milk-pail. She ran off as fast as she could to her master the parson, and said, 'Sir, sir, the cow is talking!' But the parson said, 'Woman, thou art surely mad!' However, he went with her into the cow-house to see what was the matter. Scarcely had they set their foot on the threshold, when Tom called out, 'Don't bring me any more hay!' Then the parson himself was frightened; and thinking the cow was surely bewitched, ordered that she should be killed directly. So the cow was killed, and the stomach, in which Tom lay, was thrown out upon a dunghill.

Tom soon set himself to work to get out, which was not a very easy task; but at last, just as he had made room to get his head out, a new misfortune befell him: a hungry wolf sprang out, and swallowed the whole stomach with Tom in it at a single gulp, and ran away. Tom, however, was not disheartened; and, thinking the wolf would not dislike having some chat with him as he was going along, he called out, 'My good friend, I can show you a famous treat.' 'Where's that?' said the wolf. 'In such and such a house,' said Tom, describing his father's house, 'you can crawl through the drain into the kitchen, and there you will find cakes, ham, beef, and every thing your heart can desire.' The wolf did

not want to be asked twice; so that very night he went to
the house and crawled through the drain into the kitchen,
and ate and drank there to his heart's content. As soon as
he was satisfied, he wanted to get away, but he had eaten so
much that he could not get out the same way that he came
in. This was just what Tom had reckoned upon; and he
now began to set up a great shout, making all the noise he
could. 'Will you be quiet?' said the wolf: 'you'll awaken
every body in the house.' 'What's that to me?' said the
little man: 'you have had your frolic, now I've a mind to
be merry myself;' and he began again singing and shouting
as loud as he could.

The woodman and his wife, being awakened by the noise,
peeped through a crack in the door; but when they saw
that the wolf was there, you may well suppose that they
were terribly frightened; and the woodman ran for his axe,
and gave his wife a scythe. — 'Now do you stay behind,'
said the woodman; 'and when I have knocked him on the
head, do you rip up his belly for him with the scythe.' Tom
heard all this, and said, 'Father, father! I am here, the wolf
has swallowed me:' and his father said, 'Heaven be
praised! we have found our dear child again;' and he told
his wife not to use the scythe, for fear she should hurt him.
Then he aimed a great blow, and struck the wolf on the
head, and killed him on the spot; and when he was dead
they cut open his body and set Tommy free. 'Ah!' said the
father, 'what fears we have had for you!' 'Yes, father,'
answered he, 'I have travelled all over the world, since we
parted, in one way or other; and now I am very glad to get
fresh air again.' 'Why, where have you been?' said his
father. 'I have been in a mouse-hole, in a snail-shell, down
a cow's throat, and in the wolf's belly; and yet here I am
again safe and sound.' 'Well,' said they 'we will not sell you
again for all the riches in the world.' So they hugged and
kissed their dear little son, and gave him plenty to eat and

drink, and fetched new clothes for him, for his old ones were quite spoiled on his journey.

THE GRATEFUL BEASTS

A CERTAIN man, who had lost almost all his money, resolved to set off with the little that was left him, and travel into the wide world. Then the first place he came to was a village, where the young people were running about crying and shouting. 'What is the matter?' asked he. 'See here,' answered they, 'we have got a mouse that we make dance to please us. Do look at him: what a droll sight it is! how he jumps about!' But the man pitied the poor little thing, and said, 'Let the mouse go, and I will give you money.' So he gave them some, and took the mouse and let him run; and he soon jumped into a hole that was close by, and was out of their reach.

Then he travelled on and came to another village, and there the children had got an ass that they made stand on its hind legs and tumble, at which they laughed and shouted, and gave the poor beast no rest. So the good man gave them also some money to let the poor ass alone.

At the next village he came to, the young people had got a bear that had been taught to dance, and they were plaguing the poor thing sadly. Then he gave them too some money to let the beast go, and the bear was very glad to get on his four feet, and seemed quite happy.

But the man had now given away all the money he had in the world, and had not a shilling in his pocket. Then said he to himself, 'The king has heaps of gold in his treasury that he never uses; I cannot die of hunger, I hope I shall be forgiven if I borrow a little, and when I get rich again I will repay it all.'

Then he managed to get into the treasury, and took a very little money; but as he came out the king's guards saw him; so they said he was a thief, and took him to the Judge, and he was sentenced to be thrown into the water in a box. The lid of the box was full of holes to let in air, and a jug of water and a loaf of bread were given him.

Whilst he was swimming along in the water very sorrowfully, he heard something nibbling and biting at the lock; and all of a sudden it fell off, the lid flew open, and there stood his old friend the little mouse, who had done him this service. And then came the ass and the bear, and pulled the box ashore; and all helped him because he had been kind to them.

But now they did not know what to do next, and began to consult together; when on a sudden a wave threw on the shore a beautiful white stone that looked like an egg. Then the bear said, 'That's a lucky thing: this is the wonderful stone, and whoever has it may have every thing else that he wishes.' So the man went and picked up the stone, and wished for a palace and a garden, and a stud of horses; and his wish was fulfilled as soon as he had made it. And there he lived in his castle and garden, with fine stables and horses; and all was so grand and beautiful, that he never could wonder and gaze at it enough.

After some time, some merchants passed by that way. 'See,' said they, 'what a princely palace! The last time we were here, it was nothing but a desert waste.' They were very curious to know how all this had happened; so they went in and asked the master of the palace how it had been so quickly raised. 'I have done nothing myself,' answered he, 'it is the wonderful stone that did all.' – 'What a strange stone that must be!' said they: then he invited them in and showed it to them. They asked him whether he would sell it, and offered him all their goods for it; and the goods seemed so fine and costly, that he quite forgot that the stone would bring him in a moment a thousand better and richer things, and he agreed to make the bargain.

Scarcely was the stone, however, out of his hands before all his riches were gone, and he found himself sitting in his box in the water, with his jug of water and loaf of bread by his side. The grateful beasts, the mouse, the ass, and the bear, came directly to help him; but the mouse found she could not nibble off the lock this time, for it was a great deal stronger than before. Then the bear said, 'We must find the wonderful stone again, or all our endeavours will be fruitless.'

The merchants, meantime, had taken up their abode in the palace; so away went the three friends, and when they came near, the bear said, 'Mouse, go in and look through the key-hole and see where the stone is kept: you are small, nobody will see you.' The mouse did as she was told, but soon came back and said, 'Bad news! I have looked in, and the stone hangs under the looking-glass by a red silk string, and on each side of it sits a great cat with fiery eyes to watch it.'

Then the others took council together and said, 'Go back again, and wait till the master of the palace is in bed asleep, then nip his nose and pull his hair.' Away went the mouse, and did as they directed her; and the master jumped up very angry, and rubbed his nose, and cried, 'Those rascally cats are good for nothing at all, they let the mice eat my very nose and pull the hair off my head.' Then he hunted them out of the room; and so the mouse had the best of the game.

Next night as soon as the master was asleep, the mouse crept in again, and nibbled at the red silken string to which the stone hung, till down it dropped, and she rolled it along to the door; but when it got there, the poor little mouse was quite tired; so she said to the ass, 'Put in your foot, and lift it over the threshold.' This was soon done: and they took up the stone, and set off for the water side. Then the ass said, 'How shall we reach the box?' But the bear answered, 'That is easily managed; I can swim very well, and do you, donkey, put your fore feet over my shoulders; – mind and hold fast, and take the stone in your mouth: as for you, mouse, you can sit in my ear.'

It was all settled thus, and away they swam. After a time, the bear began to brag and boast: 'We are brave fellows, are not we, ass?' said he; 'what do you think?' But the ass held his tongue, and said not a word. 'Why don't you answer me?' said the bear, 'you must be an ill-mannered brute not to speak when you're spoken to.' When the ass heard this, he could hold no longer; so he opened his mouth, and dropped the wonderful stone. 'I could not speak,' said he; 'did not you know I had the stone in my mouth? now 'tis lost, and that's your fault.' 'Do but hold your tongue and be quiet,' said the bear; 'and let us think what's to be done.'

Then a council was held: and at last they called together all the frogs, their wives and families, relations and friends, and said: 'A great enemy is coming to eat you all up; but never mind, bring us up plenty of stones, and we'll build a strong wall to guard you.' The frogs hearing this were dreadfully frightened, and set to work, bringing up all the stones they could find. At last came a large fat frog pulling along the wonderful stone by the silken string: and when the bear saw it, he jumped for joy, and said, 'Now we have found what we wanted.' So he released the old frog from his load, and told him to tell his friends they might go about their business as soon as they pleased.

Then the three friends swam off again for the box; and the lid flew open, and they found that they were but just in time, for the bread was all eaten, and the jug almost empty. But as soon as the good man had the stone in his hand, he wished himself safe and sound in his palace again; and in a

moment there he was, with his garden and his stables and
his horses; and his three faithful friends dwelt with him,
and they all spent their time happily and merrily as long
as they lived.

JORINDA AND JORINDEL

THERE was once an old castle that stood in the middle of a
large thick wood, and in the castle lived an old fairy. All
the day long she flew about in the form of an owl, or crept
about the country like a cat; but at night she always became an old woman again. When any youth came within a
hundred paces of her castle, he became quite fixed, and
could not move a step till she came and set him free: but
when any pretty maiden came within that distance, she
was changed into a bird; and the fairy put her into a cage
and hung her up in a chamber in the castle. There were
seven hundred of these cages hanging in the castle, and all
with beautiful birds in them.

Now there was once a maiden whose name was Jorinda:
she was prettier than all the pretty girls that ever were
seen; and a shepherd whose name was Jorindel was very
fond of her, and they were soon to be married. One day
they went to walk in the wood, that they might be alone:
and Jorindel said, 'We must take care that we don't go too
near to the castle.' It was a beautiful evening; the last rays
of the setting sun shone bright through the long stems of
the trees, upon the green underwood beneath, and the
turtledoves sang plaintively from the tall birches.

Jorinda sat down to gaze upon the sun; Jorindel sat by
her side; and both felt sad, they knew not why; but it
seemed as if they were to be parted from one another for
ever. They had wandered a long way; and when they

looked to see which way they should go home, they found
themselves at a loss to know what path to take.

The sun was setting fast, and already half of his circle
had disappeared behind the hill: Jorindel on a sudden
looked behind him, and as he saw through the bushes that
they had, without knowing it, sat down close under the old
walls of the castle, he shrank for fear, turned pale, and
trembled. Jorinda was singing,

> The ring-dove sang from the willow spray,
>> Well-a-day! well-a-day!
> He mourn'd for the fate
> Of his lovely mate,
>> Well-a-day!

The song ceased suddenly. Jorindel turned to see the
reason, and beheld his Jorinda changed into a nightingale;
so that her song ended with a mournful *jug, jug*. An owl
with fiery eyes flew three times round them, and three
times screamed Tu whu! Tu whu! Tu whu! Jorindel could
not move: he stood fixed as a stone, and could neither weep,
nor speak, nor stir hand or foot. And now the sun went
quite down; the gloomy night came; the owl flew into a
bush; and a moment after the old fairy came, forth pale and
meagre, with staring eyes, and a nose and chin that almost
met one another.

She mumbled something to herself, seized the nightingale, and went away with it in her hand. Poor Jorindel saw
the nightingale was gone, – but what could he do? he could
not move from the spot where he stood. At last the fairy
came back, and sung with a hoarse voice,

> Till the prisoner's fast,
> And her doom is cast,
>> There stay! Oh, stay!
> When the charm is around her,
> And the spell has bound her,
>> Hie away! away!

On a sudden Jorindel found himself free. Then he fell on his knees before the fairy, and prayed her to give him back his dear Jorinda: but she said he should never see her again, and went her way.

He prayed, he wept, he sorrowed, but all in vain. 'Alas!' he said, 'what will become of me?'

He could not return to his own home, so he went to a strange village, and employed himself in keeping sheep. Many a time did he walk round and round as near to the hated castle as he dared go. At last he dreamt one night that he found a beautiful purple flower, and in the middle of it lay a costly pearl; and he dreamt that he plucked the flower, and went with it in his hand into the castle, and that every thing he touched with it was disenchanted, and that there he found his dear Jorinda again.

In the morning when he awoke, he began to search over hill and dale for this pretty flower; and eight long days he sought for it in vain: but on the ninth day early in the morning he found the beautiful purple flower; and in the middle of it was a large dew drop as big as a costly pearl.

Then he plucked the flower, and set out and travelled day and night till he came again to the castle. He walked nearer than a hundred paces to it, and yet he did not become fixed as before, but found that he could go close up to the door.

Jorindel was very glad to see this: he touched the door with the flower, and it sprang open, so that he went in through the court, and listened when he heard so many birds singing. At last he came to the chamber where the fairy sat, with the seven hundred birds singing in the seven hundred cages. And when she saw Jorindel she was very angry, and screamed with rage; but she could not come within two yards of him; for the flower he held in his hand protected him. He looked around at the birds, but alas! there were many many nightingales, and how then should

he find his Jorinda? While he was thinking what to do, he observed that the fairy had taken down one of the cages, and was making her escape through the door. He ran or flew to her, touched the cage with the flower, – and his Jorinda stood before him. She threw her arms round his neck and looked as beautiful as ever, as beautiful as when they walked together in the wood.

Then he touched all the other birds with the flower, so that they resumed their old forms; and took his dear Jorinda home, where they lived happily together many years.

THE WONDERFUL MUSICIAN

THERE was once a capital musician who played delightfully on the fiddle, and he went rambling in a forest in a merry mood. Then he said to himself, 'Time goes rather heavily on, I must find a companion.' So he took up his fiddle, and fiddled away till the wood resounded with his music.

Presently up came a wolf. 'Dear me! there's a wolf coming to see me,' said the musician. But the wolf came up to him, and said, 'How very prettily you play! I wish you would teach me.' 'That is easily done,' said the musician, 'if you will only do what I bid you.' 'Yes,' replied the wolf, 'I shall be a very apt scholar.' So they went on a little way together, and came at last to an old oak tree that was hollow within, and had a large crack in the middle of the trunk. 'Look there,' said the musician, 'if you wish to learn to fiddle, put your fore feet into that crack.' The wolf did as he was bid: but the musician picked up a large stone and wedged both his forefeet fast into the crack, so as to make him a prisoner. 'Now be so good as to wait there till I come back,' said he, and jogged on.

After a while, he said again to himself, 'Time goes very heavily, I must find another companion.' So he took his fiddle, and fiddled away again in the wood. Presently up came a fox that was wandering close by. 'Ah! there is a fox,' said he. The fox came up and said, 'You delightful musician, how prettily you play! I must and will learn to play as you do.' 'That you may soon do,' said the musician, 'if you do as I tell you.' 'That I will,' said the fox. So they travelled on together till they came to a narrow footpath with high bushes on each side. Then the musician bent a stout hazel stem down to the ground from one side of the path, and set his foot on the top, and held it fast; and bent another from the other side, and said to the fox, 'Now, pretty fox, if you want to fiddle, give me hold of your left paw.' So the fox gave him his paw; and he tied it fast to the top of one of the hazel stems. 'Now give me your right,' said he; and the fox did as he was told: then the musician tied that paw to the other hazel; and took off his foot, and away up flew the bushes, and the fox too, and hung sprawling and swinging in the air. 'Now be so kind as to stay there till I come back,' said the musician, and jogged on.

But he soon said to himself, 'Time begins to hang heavy, I must find a companion.' So he took up his fiddle and fiddled away divinely. Then up came a hare running along. 'Ah! there is a hare,' said the musician. And the hare said to him, 'You fine fiddler, how beautifully you play! will you teach me?' 'Yes,' said the musician, 'I will soon do that, if you will follow my orders.' 'Yes,' said the hare, 'I shall make a good scholar.' Then they went on together very well for a long while, till they came to an open space in the wood. The musician tied a string round the hare's neck, and fastened the other end to the tree. 'Now,' said he, 'pretty hare, quick, jump about, run round the tree twenty times.' So the silly hare did as she was bid: and when she had run twenty times round the tree, she had twisted the string twenty times round the trunk, and was fast prisoner; and she might pull and pull away as long as she pleased, and only pulled the string faster about her neck. 'Now wait there till I come back,' said the musician.

But the wolf had pulled and bitten and scratched at the stone a long while, till at last he had got his feet out and was at liberty. Then he said in a great passion, 'I will run after that rascally musician and tear him in pieces.' As the fox saw him run by, he said, 'Ah, brother wolf, pray let me down, the musician has played tricks with me.' So the wolf set to work at the bottom of the hazel stem, and bit it in two; and away went both together to find the musician:

and as they came to the hare, she cried out too for help. So
they went and set her free, and all followed the enemy
together.

Meantime the musician had been fiddling away, and
found another companion; for a poor woodcutter had been
pleased with the music, and could not help following him
with his axe under his arm. The musician was pleased to get
a man for his companion, and behaved very civilly to him,
and played him no tricks, but stopped and played his pret-

tiest tunes till his heart overflowed for joy. While the wood-
cutter was standing listening, he saw the wolf, the fox, and
the hare coming, and knew by their faces that they were in
a great rage, and coming to do some mischief. So he stood
before the musician with his great axe, as much as to say,
No one shall hurt him as long as I have this axe. And when
the beasts saw this, they were so frightened that they ran
back into the wood. Then the musician played the wood-
cutter one of his best tunes for his pains, and went on with
his journey.

THE QUEEN BEE

Two king's sons once upon a time went out into the world
to seek their fortunes; but they soon fell into a wasteful
foolish way of living, so that they could not return home
again. Then their young brother, who was a little insignifi-
cant dwarf, went out to seek for his brothers: but when he
had found them they only laughed at him, to think that he,
who was so young and simple, should try to travel through
the world, when they, who were so much wiser, had been
unable to get on. However, they all set out on their journey
together, and came at last to an ant-hill. The two elder
brothers would have pulled it down, in order to see how the
poor ants in their fright would run about and carry off their
eggs. But the little dwarf said, 'Let the poor things enjoy
themselves, I will not suffer you to trouble them.'

So on they went, and came to a lake where many many
ducks were swimming about. The two brothers wanted to
catch two, and roast them. But the dwarf said, 'Let the
poor things enjoy themselves, you shall not kill them.'
Next they came to a bees' nest in a hollow tree, and there
was so much honey that it ran down the trunk; and the two
brothers wanted to light a fire under the tree and kill the

bees, so as to get their honey. But the dwarf held them back, and said, 'Let the pretty insects enjoy themselves, I cannot let you burn them.'

At length the three brothers came to a castle: and as they passed by the stables they saw fine horses standing there, but all were of marble, and no man was to be seen. Then they went through all the rooms, till they came to a door on which were three locks: but in the middle of the door there was a wicket, so that they could look into the next room. There they saw a little grey old man sitting at a table; and they called to him once or twice, but he did not hear: however, they called a third time, and then he rose and came out to them.

He said nothing, but took hold of them and led them to a beautiful table covered with all sorts of good things: and when they had eaten and drunk, he showed each of them to a bedchamber.

The next morning he came to the eldest and took him to a marble table, where were three tablets, containing an account of the means by which the castle might be disenchanted. The first tablet said – 'In the wood, under the moss, lie the thousand pearls belonging to the king's daughter; they must all be found: and if one be missing by set of sun, he who seeks them will be turned into marble.'

The eldest brother set out, and sought for the pearls the whole day; but the evening came, and he had not found the first hundred: so he was turned into stone as the tablet had foretold.

The next day the second brother undertook the task; but he succeeded no better than the first; for he could only find the second hundred of the pearls; and therefore he too was turned into stone.

At last came the little dwarf's turn: and he looked in the moss; but it was so hard to find the pearls, and the job was so tiresome! – so he sat down upon a stone and cried. And as he sat there, the king of the ants (whose life he had saved) came to help him, with five thousand ants; and it was not long before they had found all the pearls and lay them in a heap.

The second tablet said – 'The key of the princess's bed-chamber must be fished up out of the lake.' And as the dwarf came to the brink of it, he saw the two ducks whose lives he had saved swimming about; and they dived down and soon brought up the key from the bottom.

The third task was the hardest. It was to choose out the youngest and the best of the king's three daughters. Now they were all beautiful, and all exactly alike: but he was told that the eldest had eaten a piece of sugar, the next some sweet syrup, and the youngest a spoonful of honey; so he was to guess which it was that had eaten the honey.

Then came the queen of the bees, who had been saved by the little dwarf from the fire, and she tried the lips of all three; but at last she sat upon the lips of the one that had eaten the honey; and so the dwarf knew which was the youngest. Thus the spell was broken, and all who had been turned into stones awoke, and took their proper forms. And the dwarf married the youngest and the best of the prin-cesses, and was king after her father's death; but his two brothers married the other two sisters.

THE DOG AND THE SPARROW

A SHEPHERD'S dog had a master who took no care of him, but often let him suffer the greatest hunger. At last he could bear it no longer; so he took to his heels, and off he ran in a very sad and sorrowful mood. On the road he met a sparrow, that said to him, 'Why are you so sad, my friend?' 'Because,' said the dog, 'I am very very hungry, and have nothing to eat.' 'If that be all,' answered the sparrow, 'come with me into the next town, and I will soon find you plenty of food.' So on they went together into the town: and as they passed by a butcher's shop, the sparrow said to the dog, 'Stand there a little while, till I peck you down a piece of meat.' So the sparrow perched upon the shelf: and having first looked carefully about her to see if any one was watching her, she pecked and scratched at a steak that lay upon the edge of the shelf, till at last down it fell. Then the dog snapped it up, and scrambled away with it into a corner, where he soon ate it all up. 'Well,' said the sparrow, 'you shall have some more if you will; so come with me to the next shop, and I will peck you down another steak.' When the dog had eaten this too, the sparrow said to him, 'Well, my good friend, have you had enough now?' 'I have had plenty of meat,' answered he, 'but I should like to have a piece of bread to eat after it.' 'Come with me then,' said the sparrow, 'and you shall soon have that too.' So she took him to a baker's shop, and pecked at two rolls that lay in the window, till they fell down: and as the dog still wished for more, she took him to another shop and pecked down some more for him. When that was eaten, the sparrow asked him whether he had had enough now. 'Yes,' said he; 'and now let us take a walk a little way out of the town.' So they both went out upon the high road: but as the weather was warm, they had not gone far before the dog said, 'I am very much tired, – I should like to take a nap.' 'Very well,' answered the sparrow, 'do so, and in the meantime I will perch upon that bush.' So the dog stretched himself out on the road, and fell fast asleep. Whilst he slept, there came by a carter with a cart drawn by three horses, and loaded with two casks of wine. The sparrow, seeing that the carter did not turn out of the way, but would go on in the track in which the dog lay, so as to drive over him, called out, 'Stop! stop! Mr Carter, or it shall be the worse for you.' But the carter, grumbling to himself, 'You make it the worse for me, indeed! what can you do!' cracked his whip, and drove his cart over the poor dog, so that the wheels crushed him to death. 'There,' cried the sparrow, 'thou cruel villain, thou hast killed my friend the dog. Now mind what I say. This deed of thine shall cost thee all thou art worth.' 'Do your worst, and welcome,' said the brute, 'what harm can you do me?' and passed on. But the sparrow crept under the tilt of the cart, and pecked at the bung of one of the casks till she loosened it; and then all the wine ran out, without the carter seeing it. At last he looked round, and saw that the cart was dripping, and the cask quite empty. 'What an unlucky wretch I am!' cried he. 'Not wretch enough yet!' said the sparrow, as she alighted upon the head of one of the horses, and pecked at him till he reared up and kicked. When the carter saw this, he drew out his hatchet and aimed a blow at the sparrow, meaning to kill her; but she flew away, and the blow fell upon the poor horse's head with such force, that he fell down dead. 'Unlucky wretch that I am!' cried he. 'Not wretch enough yet!' said the sparrow. And as the carter went on with the other two horses, she again crept under the tilt of the cart, and pecked out the bung of the second cask, so that all the wine ran out. When the carter saw this, he again cried out, 'Miserable wretch that I am!' But the sparrow answered, 'Not wretch enough yet!' and perched on the head of the second horse, and pecked at him too. The carter ran up and struck at her again with his hatchet; but away she flew, and the blow fell upon the second horse and killed him on the spot. 'Unlucky wretch that I am!' said he. 'Not wretch enough yet!' said the sparrow; and perching upon the third horse, she began to peck him too. The carrier was mad with fury; and without looking about him, or caring what he was about, struck again at the sparrow; but killed his third horse as he had done the other two. 'Alas! miserable wretch that I am!' cried he. 'Not wretch enough yet!' answered the sparrow as she flew away; 'now will I plague and punish thee at thy own house.' The carter was forced at last to leave his cart behind him, and to go home overflowing with rage and vexation. 'Alas!' said he to his wife, 'what ill luck has befallen me! – my wine is all spilt, and my horses all three dead.' 'Alas! husband,' replied she, 'and a wicked bird has come into the house, and has brought with her all the birds in the world, I am sure, and they have fallen upon our corn in the loft, and are eating it up at such a rate!' Away ran the husband up stairs, and saw thousands of birds sitting upon the floor eating up his corn, with the sparrow in the midst of them. 'Unlucky wretch that I am!' cried the carter; for he saw that the corn was almost all gone. 'Not wretch enough yet!' said the sparrow; 'thy cruelty shall cost thee thy life yet!' and away she flew.

The carter seeing that he had thus lost all that he had, went down into his kitchen; and was still not sorry for what he had done, but sat himself angrily and sulkily in the chimney corner. But the sparrow sat on the outside of the window, and cried 'Carter! thy cruelty shall cost thee thy life!' With that he jumped up in a rage, seized his hatchet, and threw it at the sparrow; but it missed her, and only broke the window. The sparrow now hopped in, perched upon the window-seat, and cried, 'Carter! it shall cost thee thy life!' Then he became mad and blind with rage, and struck the window seat with such force that he cleft it in two: and as the sparrow flew from place to place, the carter and his wife were so furious, that they broke all their furniture, glasses, chairs, benches, the table, and at last the walls, without touching the bird at all. In the end, however, they caught her: and the wife said, 'Shall I kill her at once?' 'No,' cried he, 'that is letting her off too easily: she shall die a much more cruel death; I will eat her.' But the sparrow began to flutter about, and stretched out her neck and cried, 'Carter! it shall cost thee thy life yet!' With that he could wait no longer: so he gave his wife the hatchet, and cried, 'Wife, strike at the bird and kill her in my hand.' And the wife struck; but she missed her aim, and hit her husband on the head so that he fell down dead, and the sparrow flew quietly home to her nest.

FREDERICK AND CATHERINE

THERE was once a man called Frederick: he had a wife whose name was Catherine, and they had not long been married. One day Frederick said, 'Kate! I am going to work in the fields; when I come back I shall be hungry, so let me have something nice cooked, and a good draught of ale.' 'Very well,' said she, 'it shall all be ready.' When dinner-time drew nigh, Catherine took a nice steak, which was all the meat she had, and put it on the fire to fry. The steak soon began to look brown, and to crackle in the pan; and Catherine stood by with a fork and turned it: then she said to herself, 'The steak is almost ready, I may as well go to the cellar for the ale.' So she left the pan on the fire, and took a large jug and went into the cellar and tapped the ale cask. The beer ran into the jug, and Catherine stood looking on. At last it popped into her head, 'The dog is not shut up – he may be running away with the steak; that's well thought of.' So up she ran from the cellar; and sure enough the rascally cur had got the steak in his mouth, and was making off with it.

Away ran Catherine, and away ran the dog across the field! but he ran faster than she, and stuck close to the steak. 'It's all gone, and "what can't be cured must be endured,"' said Catherine. So she turned round; and as she had run a good way and was tired, she walked home leisurely to cool herself.

Now all this time the ale was running too, for Catherine had not turned the cock; and when the jug was full the liquor ran upon the floor till the cask was empty. When she got to the cellar stairs she saw what had happened. 'My stars!' said she, 'what shall I do to keep Frederick from seeing all this slopping about?' So she thought a while; and at last remembered that there was a sack of fine meal bought at the last fair, and that if she sprinkled this over the floor it would suck up the ale nicely. 'What a lucky thing,' said she, 'that we kept that meal! we have now a good use for it.' So away she went for it: but she managed to set it down just upon the great jug full of beer, and upset it; and thus all the ale that had been saved was set swimming on the floor also. 'Ah! well,' said she, 'when one goes, another may as well follow.' Then she strewed the meal all about the cellar, and was quite pleased with her cleverness, and said, 'How very neat and clean it looks!'

At noon Frederick came home. 'Now, wife,' cried he, 'what have you for dinner?' 'O Frederick!' answered she, 'I was cooking you a steak; but while I went down to draw the ale, the dog ran away with it; and while I ran after him, the ale all ran out; and when I went to dry up the ale with the sack of meal that we got at the fair, I upset the jug: but the cellar is now quite dry, and looks so clean!' 'Kate, Kate,' said he, 'how could you do all this? Why did you leave the steak to fry, and the ale to run, and then spoil all the meal?' 'Why, Frederick,' said she, 'I did not know I was doing wrong, you should have told me before.'

The husband thought to himself, If my wife manages matters thus, I must look sharp myself. Now he had a good deal of gold in the house: so he said to Catherine, 'What pretty yellow buttons these are! I shall put them into a box and bury them in the garden; but take care that you never go near or meddle with them.' 'No, Frederick,' said she, 'that I never will.' As soon as he was gone, there came by some pedlars with earthenware plates and dishes, and they asked her whether she would buy. 'Oh dear me, I should like to buy very much, but I have no money: if you had any use for yellow buttons, I might deal with you.' 'Yellow buttons!' said they: 'let us have a look at them.' 'Go into the garden and dig where I tell you, and you will find the yellow buttons: I dare not go myself.' So the rogues went: and when they found what these yellow buttons were, they took them all away, and left her plenty of plates and dishes. Then she set them all about the house for a show: and when Frederick came back, he cried out, 'Kate, what have you been doing?' 'See,' said she, 'I have bought all these with your yellow buttons: but I did not touch them myself; the pedlars went themselves and dug them up.' 'Wife, wife,' said Frederick, 'what a pretty piece of work you have made! those yellow buttons were all my money: How came you to do such a thing?' 'Why,' answered she, 'I did not know there was any harm in it; you should have told me.'

Catherine stood musing for a while, and at last said to her husband, 'Hark ye, Frederick, we will soon get the gold back: let us run after the thieves.' 'Well, we will try,' answered he; 'but take some butter and cheese with you, that we may have something to eat by the way.' 'Very well,' said she; and they set out: and as Frederick walked the fastest, he left his wife some way behind. 'It does not matter,' thought she: 'when we turn back, I shall be so much nearer home than he.'

Presently she came to the top of a hill; down the side of which there was a road so narrow that the cart-wheels always chafed the trees on each side as they passed. 'Ah, see now,' said she, 'how they have bruised and wounded those poor trees; they will never get well.' So she took pity on them, and made use of the butter to grease them all, so that the wheels might not hurt them so much. While she was doing this kind office, one of her cheeses fell out of the basket, and rolled down the hill. Catherine looked, but could not see where it was gone; so she said, 'Well, I suppose the other will go the same way and find you; he has younger legs than I have.' Then she rolled the other cheese after it; and away it went, nobody knows where, down the hill. But she said she supposed they knew the road, and would follow her, and she could not stay there all day waiting for them.

At last she overtook Frederick, who desired her to give him something to eat. Then she gave him the dry bread. 'Where are the butter and cheese?' said he. 'Oh!' answered she, 'I used the butter to grease those poor trees that the wheels chafed so: and one of the cheeses ran away, so I sent the other after it to find it, and I suppose they are both on the road together somewhere.' 'What a goose you are to do such silly things!' said the husband. 'How can you say so?' said she; 'I am sure you never told me not.'

They ate the dry bread together; and Frederick said, 'Kate, I hope you locked the door safe when you came away.' 'No,' answered she, 'you did not tell me.' 'Then go home, and do it now before we go any farther,' said Frederick, 'and bring with you something to eat.'

Catherine did as he told her, and thought to herself by the way, 'Frederick wants something to eat; but I don't think he is very fond of butter and cheese: I'll bring him a bag of fine nuts, and the vinegar, for I have often seen him take some.'

When she reached home, she bolted the back door, but the front door she took off the hinges, and said, 'Frederick told me to lock the door, but surely it can no where be so safe as if I take it with me.' So she took her time by the way: and when she overtook her husband she cried out,

'There, Frederick, there is the door itself, now you may watch it as carefully as you please.' 'Alas! alas!' said he, 'what a clever wife I have! I sent you to make the house fast, and you take the door away, so that every body may go in and out as they please: — however, as you have brought the door, you shall carry it about with you for your pains.' 'Very well,' answered she, 'I'll carry the door; but I'll not carry the nuts and vinegar bottle also, — that would be too much of a load; so, if you please, I'll fasten them to the door.'

Frederick of course made no objection to that plan, and they set off into the wood to look for the thieves; but they could not find them: and when it grew dark, they climbed up into a tree to spend the night there. Scarcely were they up, than who should come by but the very rogues they were looking for. They were in truth great rascals, and belonged to that class of people who find things before they are lost: they were tired; so they sat down and made a fire under the very tree where Frederick and Catherine were. Frederick slipped down on the other side, and picked up some stones. Then he climbed up again, and tried to hit the thieves on the head with them: but they only said, 'It must be near morning, for the wind shakes the fir-apples down.'

Catherine, who had the door on her shoulder, began to be very tired; but she thought it was the nuts upon it that were so heavy: so she said softly, 'Frederick, I must let the nuts go.' 'No,' answered he, 'not now, they will discover us.' 'I can't help that, they must go.' 'Well then, make haste and throw them down, if you will.' Then away rattled the nuts down among the boughs; and one of the thieves cried, 'Bless me, it is hailing.'

A little while after, Catherine thought the door was still very heavy: so she whispered to Frederick, 'I must throw the vinegar down.' 'Pray don't,' answered he, 'it will discover us.' 'I can't help that,' said she, 'go it must.' So she poured all the vinegar down; and the thieves said, 'What a heavy dew there is!'

At last it popped into Catherine's head that it was the door itself that was so heavy all the time: so she whispered Frederick, 'I must throw the door down soon.' But he begged and prayed her not to do so, for he was sure it would betray them. 'Here goes, however,' said she: and down went the door with such a clatter upon the thieves, that they cried out 'Murder!' and not knowing what was coming, ran away as fast as they could, and left all the gold. So when Frederick and Catherine came down, there they found all their money safe and sound.

THE THREE CHILDREN OF FORTUNE

ONCE upon a time a father sent for his three sons, and gave to the eldest a cock, to the second a scythe, and to the third a cat. 'I am now old,' said he, 'my end is approaching, and I would fain provide for you before I die. Money I have none, and what I now give you seems of but little worth; yet it rests with yourselves alone to turn my gifts to good account. Only seek out for a land where what you have is as yet unknown, and your fortune is made.'

After the death of the father, the eldest set out with his cock: but wherever he went, in every town he saw from afar off a cock sitting upon the church steeple, and turning round with the wind. In the villages he always heard plenty of them crowing, and his bird was therefore nothing new; so there did not seem much chance of his making his fortune. At length it happened that he came to an island where the people who lived there had never heard of a cock, and knew not even how to reckon the time. They knew, indeed, if it were morning or evening; but at night, if they lay awake, they had no means of knowing how time went. 'Behold,' said he to them, 'what a noble animal this is! how like a knight he is! he carries a bright red crest upon his head, and spurs upon his heels; he crows three times every night, at stated hours, and at the third time the sun is about to rise. But this is not all; sometimes he screams in broad day-light, and then you must take warning, for the weather is surely about to change.' This pleased the natives mightily; they kept awake one whole night, and heard, to their great joy, how gloriously the cock called the hour, at two, four, and six o'clock. Then they asked him whether the bird was to be sold, and how much he would sell it for. 'About as much gold as an ass can carry,' said he. 'A very fair price for such an animal,' cried they with one voice; and agreed to give him what he asked.

When he returned home with his wealth, his brothers wondered greatly; and the second said, 'I will now set forth likewise, and see if I can turn my scythe to as good an account.' There did not seem, however, much likelihood of this; for go where he would, he was met by peasants who had as good a scythe on their shoulders as he had. But at last, as good luck would have it, he came to an island where the people had never heard of a scythe: there, as soon as the corn was ripe, they went into the fields and pulled it up; but this was very hard work, and a great deal of it was lost. The man then set to work with his scythe; and mowed down their whole crop so quickly, that the people stood staring open-mouthed with wonder. They were willing to give him what he asked for such a marvellous thing: but he only took a horse laden with as much gold as it could carry.

Now the third brother had a great longing to go and see what he could make of his cat. So he set out: and at first it happened to him as it had to the others, so long as he kept upon the main land, he met with no success; there were plenty of cats every where, indeed too many, so that the young ones were for the most part, as soon as they came into the world, drowned in the water. At last he passed over to an island, where, as it chanced most luckily for him, nobody had ever seen a cat; and they were overrun with mice to such a degree, that the little wretches danced upon the tables and chairs, whether the master of the house were at home or not. The people complained loudly of this grievance; the king himself knew not how to rid himself of them in his palace; in every corner mice were squeaking, and they gnawed everything that their teeth could lay hold of. Here was a fine field for Puss – she soon began her chase, and had cleared two rooms in the twinkling of an eye; when the people besought their king to buy the wonderful animal, for the good of the public, at any price. The king willingly gave what was asked, – a mule laden with gold and jewels; and thus the third brother returned home with a richer prize than either of the others.

Meantime the cat feasted away upon the mice in the royal palace, and devoured so many that they were no longer in any great numbers. At length, quite spent and tired with her work, she became extremely thirsty; so she stood still, drew up her head, and cried, 'Miau, Miau!' The king gathered together all his subjects when they heard this strange cry, and many ran shrieking in a great fright out of the palace. But the king held a great council below as to what was best to be done; and it was at length fixed to send a herald to the cat, to warn her to leave the castle forth-with, or that force would be used to remove her. 'For,' said the counsellors, 'we would far more willingly put up with the mice (since we are used to that evil), than get rid of them at the risk of our lives.' A page accordingly went, and asked the cat 'whether she were willing to quit the castle?' But Puss, whose thirst became every moment more and

more pressing, answered nothing but 'Miau! Miau!' which
the page interpreted to mean 'No! No!' and therefore carried this answer to the king. 'Well,' said the counsellors,
'then we must try what force will do.' So the guns were
planted, and the palace was fired upon from all sides. When
the fire reached the room where the cat was, she sprang out
of the window and ran away; but the besiegers did not see
her, and went on firing until the whole palace was burnt to
the ground.

KING GRISLY-BEARD

A GREAT king had a daughter who was very beautiful, but
so proud and haughty and conceited, that none of the
princes who came to ask her in marriage were good enough
for her, and she only made sport of them.

Once upon a time the king held a great feast, and invited
all her suitors; and they sat in a row according to their
rank, kings and princes and dukes and earls. Then the princess came in and passed by them all, but she had something
spiteful to say to every one. The first was too fat: 'He's as
round as a tub,' said she. The next was too tall: 'What a
maypole!' said she. The next was too short: 'What a
dumpling!' said she. The fourth was too pale, and she
called him 'Wallface.' The fifth was too red, so she called
him 'Cockscomb.' The sixth was not straight enough, so
she said he was like a green stick that had been laid to dry
over a baker's oven. And thus she had some joke to crack
upon every one: but she laughed more than all at a good
king who was there. 'Look at him,' said she, 'his beard is
like an old mop, he shall be called Grisly-beard.' So the king
got the nickname of Grisly-beard.

But the old king was very angry when he saw how his
daughter behaved, and how she ill-treated all his guests;

and he vowed that, willing or unwilling, she should marry the first beggar that came to the door.

Two days after there came by a travelling musician, who began to sing under the window, and beg alms: and when the king heard him, he said, 'Let him come in.' So they brought in a dirty-looking fellow; and when he had sung before the king and the princess, he begged a boon. Then the king said, 'You have sung so well, that I will give you my daughter for your wife.' The princess begged and prayed; but the king said, 'I have sworn to give you to the first beggar, and I will keep my word.' So words and tears were of no avail; the parson was sent for, and she was married to the musician. When this was over, the king said, 'Now get ready to go; you must not stay here; you must travel on with your husband.'

Then the beggar departed, and took her with him; and they soon came to a great wood. 'Pray,' said she, 'whose is this wood?' 'It belongs to king Grisly-beard,' answered he; 'hadst thou taken him, all had been thine.' 'Ah! unlucky wretch that I am!' sighed she, 'would that I had married king Grisly-beard!' Next they came to some fine meadows. 'Whose are these beautiful green meadows?' said she. 'They belong to king Grisly-beard; hadst thou taken him, they had all been thine.' 'Ah! unlucky wretch that I am!' said she, 'would that I had married king Grisly-beard!'

Then they came to a great city. 'Whose is this noble city?' said she. 'It belongs to king Grisly-beard; hadst thou taken him, it had all been thine.' 'Ah! miserable wretch that I am!' sighed she, 'why did I not marry king Grisly-beard?' 'That is no business of mine,' said the musician; 'why should you wish for another husband? am not I good enough for you?'

At last they came to a small cottage. 'What a paltry place!' said she; 'to whom does that little dirty hole belong?' The musician answered, 'That is your and my house, where we are to live.' 'Where are your servants?' cried she. 'What do we want with servants?' said he, 'you must do for yourself whatever is to be done. Now make the fire, and put on water and cook my supper, for I am very tired.' But the princess knew nothing of making fires and cooking, and the beggar was forced to help her. When they had eaten a very scanty meal they went to bed; but the musician called her up very early in the morning to clean the house. Thus they lived for two days: and when they had eaten up all there was in the cottage, the man said, 'Wife, we can't go on thus, spending money and earning nothing. You must learn to weave baskets.' Then he went out and cut willows and brought them home, and she began to weave: but it made her fingers very sore. 'I see this work won't do,' said he, 'try and spin; perhaps you will do that better.' So she sat down and tried to spin; but the threads cut her tender fingers till the blood ran. 'See now,' said the musician, 'you are good for nothing, you can do no work; — what a bargain I have got! However, I'll try and set up a trade in pots and pans, and you shall stand in the market and sell them.' 'Alas!' sighed she, 'when I stand in the market and any of my father's court pass by and see me there, how they will laugh at me!'

But the beggar did not care for that; and said she must work, if she did not wish to die of hunger. At first the trade went well; for many people, seeing such a beautiful woman, went to buy her wares, and paid their money without thinking of taking away the goods. They lived on this as long as it lasted, and then her husband bought a fresh lot of ware, and she sat herself down with it in a corner of the market; but a drunken soldier soon came by, and rode his horse against her stall and broke all her goods into a thousand pieces. Then she began to weep, and knew not what to do. 'Ah! what will become of me!' said she; 'what will my husband say?' So she ran home and told him all.

'Who would have thought you would have been so silly,' said he, 'as to put an earthenware stall in the corner of the market, where every body passes? – But let us have no more crying; I see you are not fit for this sort of work: so I have been to the king's palace, and asked if they did not want a kitchen-maid, and they have promised to take you, and there you will have plenty to eat.'

Thus the princess became a kitchen-maid, and helped the cook to do all the dirtiest work: she was allowed to carry home some of the meat that was left, and on this she and her husband lived.

She had not been there long, before she heard that the king's eldest son was passing by, going to be married; and she went to one of the windows and looked out. Every thing was ready, and all the pomp and splendour of the court was there. Then she thought with an aching heart on her own sad fate, and bitterly grieved for the pride and folly which had brought her so low. And the servants gave her some of the rich meats, which she put into her basket to take home.

All on a sudden, as she was going out, in came the king's son in golden clothes: and when he saw a beautiful woman at the door, he took her by the hand, and said she should be his partner in the dance: but she trembled for fear, for she saw that it was king Grisly-beard, who was making sport of her. However, he kept fast hold and led her in; and the cover of the basket came off, so that the meats in it fell all about. Then every body laughed and jeered at her; and she was so abashed that she wished herself a thousand feet deep in the earth. She sprang to the door to run away; but on the steps king Grisly-beard overtook and brought her back, and said, 'Fear me not! I am the musician who has lived with you in the hut: I brought you there because I loved you. I am also the soldier who overset your stall. I have done all this only to cure you of pride, and to punish you

for the ill-treatment you bestowed on me. Now all is over;
you have learnt wisdom, your faults are gone, and it is
time to celebrate our marriage feast!'

Then the chamberlains came and brought her the most
beautiful robes: and her father and his whole court were
there already, and congratulated her on her marriage. Joy
was in every face. The feast was grand, and all were merry;
and I wish you and I had been of the party.

THE ADVENTURES OF
CHANTICLEER AND PARTLET

1. *How they went to the Mountains to eat Nuts*

'THE nuts are quite ripe now,' said Chanticleer to his wife
Partlet, 'suppose we go together to the mountains, and eat
as many as we can, before the squirrel takes them all away.'
'With all my heart,' said Partlet, 'let us go and make a
holiday of it together.' So they went to the mountains; and
as it was a lovely day they stayed there till the evening.
Now, whether it was that they had eaten so many nuts that
they could not walk, or whether they were lazy and would
not, I do not know: however, they took it into their heads
that it did not become them to go home on foot. So Chanticleer began to build a little carriage of nut-shells: and when
it was finished, Partlet jumped into it and sat down, and
bid Chanticleer harness himself to it and draw her home.
'That's a good joke!' said Chanticleer; 'no, that will never
do; I had rather by half walk home; I'll sit on the box and
be coachman, if you like, but I'll not draw.' While this was
passing, a duck came quacking up, and cried out, 'You
thieving vagabonds, what business have you in my
grounds; I'll give it you well for your insolence!' and upon

that she fell upon Chanticleer most lustily. But Chanticleer was no coward, and returned the duck's blows with his sharp spurs so fiercely, that she soon began to cry out for mercy; which was only granted her upon condition that she would draw the carriage home for them. This she agreed to do; and Chanticleer got upon the box, and drove, crying, 'Now, duck, get on as fast as you can.' And away they went at a pretty good pace.

After they had travelled along a little way, they met a needle and a pin walking together along the road: and the needle cried out, 'Stop! stop!' and said it was so dark that they could hardly find their way, and such dirty walking they could not get on at all: he told them that he and his friend, the pin, had been at a public house a few miles off, and had sat drinking till they had forgotten how late it was; he begged therefore that the travellers would be so kind as to give them a lift in their carriage. Chanticleer, observing that they were but thin fellows, and not likely to take up much room, told them they might ride, but made them promise not to dirty the wheels of the carriage in getting in, nor to tread on Partlet's toes.

Late at night they arrived at an inn; and as it was bad travelling in the dark, and the duck seemed much tired, and waddled about a good deal from one side to the other, they made up their minds to fix their quarters there: but the landlord at first was unwilling, and said his house was full, thinking they might not be very respectable company: however, they spoke civilly to him, and gave him the egg which Partlet had laid by the way, and said they would give him the duck, who was in the habit of laying one every day: so at last he let them come in, and they bespoke a handsome supper, and spent the evening very jollily.

Early in the morning, before it was quite light, and when no body was stirring in the inn, Chanticleer awakened his wife, and, fetching the egg, they pecked a hole in it, ate it

up, and threw the shells into the fire-place: they then went
to the pin and needle, who were fast asleep, and, seizing
them by their heads, stuck one into the landlord's easy
chair, and the other into his handkerchief; and having done
this, they crept away as softly as possible. However, the
duck, who slept in the open air in the yard, heard them
coming, and jumping into the brook which ran close by the
inn, soon swam out of their reach.

An hour or two afterwards the landlord got up, and took
his handkerchief to wipe his face, but the pin ran into him
and pricked him: then he walked into the kitchen to light
his pipe at the fire, but when he stirred it up the egg-shells
flew into his eyes, and almost blinded him. 'Bless me!' said
he, 'all the world seems to have a design against my head
this morning:' and so saying, he threw himself sulkily into
his easy chair; but, oh dear! the needle ran into him; and
this time the pain was not in his head. He now flew into a
very great passion, and, suspecting the company who had
come in the night before, he went to look after them, but
they were all off; so he swore that he never again would
take in such a troop of vagabonds, who ate a great deal,
paid no reckoning, and gave him nothing for his trouble but
their apish tricks.

2. *How Chanticleer and Partlet went to visit Mr Korbes*

Another day, Chanticleer and Partlet wished to ride out
together; so Chanticleer built a handsome carriage with
four red wheels, and harnessed six mice to it; and then he
and Partlet got into the carriage, and away they drove.
Soon afterwards a cat met them, and said, 'Where are you
going?' And Chanticleer replied,

> 'All on our way
> A visit to pay
> To Mr Korbes, the fox, to-day.'

Then the cat said, 'Take me with you.' Chanticleer said, 'With all my heart: get up behind, and be sure you do not fall off.'

> 'Take care of this handsome coach of mine,
> Nor dirty my pretty red wheels so fine!
>   Now, mice, be ready,
>   And, wheels, run steady!
> For we are going a visit to pay
> To Mr Korbes, the fox, to-day.'

Soon after came up a mill-stone, an egg, a duck, and a pin; and Chanticleer gave them all leave to get into the carriage and go with them.

When they arrived at Mr Korbes's house, he was not at home; so the mice drew the carriage into the coach-house, Chanticleer and Partlet flew upon a beam, the cat sat down in the fire-place, the duck got into the washing cistern, the pin stuck himself into the bed pillow, the mill-stone laid himself over the house door, and the egg rolled herself up in the towel.

When Mr Korbes came home, he went to the fire-place to make a fire; but the cat threw all the ashes in his eyes: so he ran to the kitchen to wash himself; but there the duck splashed all the water in his face; and when he tried to wipe himself, the egg broke to pieces in the towel all over his face and eyes. Then he was very angry, and went without his supper to bed; but when he laid his head on the pillow, the pin ran into his cheek: at this he became quite furious, and, jumping up, would have run out of the house; but when he came to the door, the mill-stone fell down on his head, and killed him on the spot.

3. *How Partlet died and was buried, and how Chanticleer died of grief*

Another day Chanticleer and Partlet agreed to go again to the mountains to eat nuts; and it was settled that all the nuts which they found should be shared equally between them. Now Partlet found a very large nut; but she said nothing about it to Chanticleer, and kept it all to herself: however, it was so big that she could not swallow it, and it stuck in her throat. Then she was in a great fright, and cried out to Chanticleer, 'Pray run as fast as you can, and fetch me some water, or I shall be choked.' Chanticleer ran as fast as he could to the river, and said, 'River, give me some water, for Partlet lies on the mountain, and will be choked by a great nut.' The river said, 'Run first to the bride, and ask her for a silken cord to draw up the water.' Chanticleer ran to the bride, and said, 'Bride, you must give me a silken cord, for then the river will give me water, and the water I will carry to Partlet, who lies on the mountain, and will be choked by a great nut.' But the bride said, 'Run first, and bring me my garland that is hanging on a willow in the garden.' Then Chanticleer ran to the garden, and took the garland from the bough where it hung, and brought it to the bride; and then the bride gave him the silken cord, and he took the silken cord to the river, and the river gave him water, and he carried the water to Partlet; but in the mean time she was choked by the great nut, and lay quite dead, and never moved any more.

Then Chanticleer was very sorry, and cried bitterly; and all the beasts came and wept with him over poor Partlet. And six mice built a little hearse to carry her to her grave; and when it was ready they harnessed themselves before it, and Chanticleer drove them. On the way they met the fox. 'Where are you going, Chanticleer?' said he. 'To bury my Partlet,' said the other, 'May I go with you?' said the fox. 'Yes; but you must get up behind, or my horses will not be able to draw you.' Then the fox got up behind; and presently the wolf, the bear, the goat, and all the beasts of the wood, came and climbed upon the hearse.

So on they went till they came to a rapid stream. 'How

shall we get over?' said Chanticleer. Then said a straw, 'I
will lay myself across, and you may pass over upon me.'
But as the mice were going over, the straw slipped away
and fell into the water, and the six mice all fell in and were
drowned. What was to be done? Then a large log of wood
came and said, 'I am big enough; I will lay myself across
the stream, and you shall pass over upon me.' So he laid
himself down; but they managed so clumsily, that the log
of wood fell in and was carried away by the stream. Then
a stone, who saw what had happened, came up and kindly
offered to help poor Chanticleer by laying himself across
the stream; and this time he got safely to the other side
with the hearse, and managed to get Partlet out of it; but
the fox and the other mourners, who were sitting behind,
were too heavy, and fell back into the water and were all
carried away by the stream, and drowned.

Thus Chanticleer was left alone with his dead Partlet;
and having dug a grave for her, he laid her in it, and made a
little hillock over her. Then he sat down by the grave, and
wept and mourned, till at last he died too: and so all were
dead.

SNOW-DROP

IT was in the middle of winter, when the broad flakes of
snow were falling around, that a certain queen sat working
at a window, the frame of which was made of fine black
ebony; and as she was looking out upon the snow, she
pricked her finger, and three drops of blood fell upon it.
Then she gazed thoughtfully upon the red drops which
sprinkled the white snow, and said, 'Would that my little
daughter may be as white as that snow, as red as the blood,
and as black as the ebony window-frame!' And so the little
girl grew up: her skin was as white as snow, her cheeks as

rosy as the blood, and her hair as black as ebony; and she was called Snow-drop.

But this queen died; and the king soon married another wife, who was very beautiful, but so proud that she could not bear to think that any one could surpass her. She had a magical looking-glass, to which she used to go and gaze upon herself in it, and say,

'Tell me, glass, tell me true!
Of all the ladies in the land,
Who is the fairest? tell me who?'

And the glass answered,

'Thou, queen, art fairest in the land.'

But Snow-drop grew more and more beautiful; and when she was seven years old, she was as bright as the day, and fairer than the queen herself. Then the glass one day answered the queen, when she went to consult it as usual,

'Thou, queen, may'st fair and beauteous be,
But Snow-drop is lovelier far than thee!'

When she heard this, she turned pale with rage and envy; and called to one of her servants and said, 'Take Snow-drop away into the wide wood, that I may never see her more.' Then the servant led her away; but his heart melted when she begged him to spare her life, and he said, 'I will not hurt thee, thou pretty child.' So he left her by herself; and though he thought it most likely that the wild beasts would tear her in pieces, he felt as if a great weight were taken off his heart when he had made up his mind not to kill her, but leave her to her fate.

Then poor Snow-drop wandered along through the wood in great fear; and the wild beasts roared about her, but none did her any harm. In the evening she came to a little cottage, and went in there to rest herself, for her little feet would carry her no farther. Every thing was spruce and neat in the cottage: on the table was spread a white cloth, and there were seven little plates with seven little loaves, and seven little glasses with wine in them; and knives and forks laid in order; and by the wall stood seven little beds. Then, as she was very hungry, she picked a little piece off each loaf, and drank a very little wine out of each glass; and after that she thought she would lie down and rest. So she tried all the little beds; and one was too long, and another was too short, till at last the seventh suited her; and there she laid herself down, and went to sleep.

Presently in came the masters of the cottage, who were seven little dwarfs that lived among the mountains, and dug and searched for gold. They lighted up their seven lamps, and saw directly that all was not right. The first said, 'Who has been sitting on my stool?' The second, 'Who has been eating off my plate?' The third, 'Who has been picking my bread?' The fourth, 'Who has been meddling with my spoon?' The fifth, 'Who has been handling my fork?' The sixth, 'Who has been cutting with my knife?' The seventh, 'Who has been drinking my wine?' Then the first looked round and said, 'Who has been lying on my bed?' And the rest came running to him, and every one cried out that somebody had been upon his bed. But the seventh saw Snow-drop, and called all his brethren to come and see her; and they cried out with wonder and astonishment, and brought their lamps to look at her, and said, 'Good heavens! what a lovely child she is!' And they were delighted to see her, and took care not to wake her; and the seventh dwarf slept an hour with each of the other dwarfs in turn, till the night was gone.

In the morning, Snow-drop told them all her story; and they pitied her, and said if she would keep all things in order, and cook and wash, and knit and spin for them, she might stay where she was, and they would take good care of her. Then they went out all day long to their work, seek-

ing for gold and silver in the mountains; and Snow-drop remained at home: and they warned her, and said, 'The
queen will soon find out where you are, so take care and let
no one in.'

But the queen, now that she thought Snow-drop was
dead, believed that she was certainly the handsomest lady
in the land; and she went to her glass and said,

> 'Tell me, glass, tell me true!
>   Of all the ladies in the land,
> Who is fairest? tell me who?'

And the glass answered,

> 'Thou, queen, art the fairest in all this land;
> But over the hills, in the greenwood shade,
> Where the seven dwarfs their dwelling have made,
> There Snow-drop is hiding her head, and she
> Is lovelier far, O queen! than thee.'

Then the queen was very much alarmed; for she knew
that the glass always spoke the truth, and was sure that
the servant had betrayed her. And she could not bear to
think that any one lived who was more beautiful than she
was; so she disguised herself as an old pedlar, and went her
way over the hills to the place where the dwarfs dwelt.
Then she knocked at the door, and cried 'Fine wares to
sell!' Snow-drop looked out at the window, and said,
'Good-day, good-woman; what have you to sell?' 'Good
wares, fine wares,' said she; 'laces and bobbins of all
colours.' 'I will let the old lady in; she seems to be a very
good sort of body,' thought Snow-drop; so she ran down,
and unbolted the door. 'Bless me!' said the old woman, 'how
badly your stays are laced! Let me lace them up with one
of my nice new laces.' Snow-drop did not dream of any
mischief; so she stood up before the old woman; but she set
to work so nimbly, and pulled the lace so tight, that Snow-
drop lost her breath, and fell down as if she were dead.

'There's an end of all thy beauty,' said the spiteful queen, and went away home.

In the evening the seven dwarfs returned; and I need not say how grieved they were to see their faithful Snow-drop stretched upon the ground motionless, as if she were quite dead. However, they lifted her up, and when they found what was the matter, they cut the lace; and in a little time she began to breathe, and soon came to life again. Then they said, 'The old woman was the queen herself; take care another time, and let no one in when we are away.'

When the queen got home, she went straight to her glass, and spoke to it as usual; but to her great surprise it still said,

> 'Thou, queen, art the fairest in all this land;
> But over the hills, in the greenwood shade,
> Where the seven dwarfs their dwelling have made,
> There Snow-drop is hiding her head; and she
> Is lovelier far, O queen! than thee.'

Then the blood ran cold in her heart with spite and malice to see that Snow-drop still lived; and she dressed herself up again in a disguise, but very different from the one she wore before, and took with her a poisoned comb. When she reached the dwarfs' cottage, she knocked at the door, and cried 'Fine wares to sell!' But Snow-drop said, 'I dare not let any one in.' Then the queen said, 'Only look at my beautiful combs;' and gave her the poisoned one. And it looked so pretty that she took it up and put it into her hair to try it; but the moment it touched her head the poison was so powerful that she fell down senseless. 'There you may lie,' said the queen, and went her way. But by good luck the dwarfs returned very early that evening; and when they saw Snow-drop lying on the ground, they thought what had happened, and soon found the poisoned comb. And when they took it away, she recovered, and told

them all that had passed; and they warned her once more
not to open the door to any one.

Meantime the queen went home to her glass, and
trembled with rage when she received exactly the same
answer as before; and she said, 'Snow-drop shall die, if it
costs me my life.' So she went secretly into a chamber, and
prepared a poisoned apple: the outside looked very rosy
and tempting, but whoever tasted it was sure to die. Then
she dressed herself up as a peasant's wife, and travelled
over the hills to the dwarfs' cottage, and knocked at the
door; but Snow-drop put her head out of the window and
said, 'I dare not let any one in, for the dwarfs have told me
not.' 'Do as you please,' said the old woman, 'but at any
rate take this pretty apple; I will make you a present of it.'
'No,' said Snow-drop, 'I dare not take it.' 'You silly girl!'
answered the other, 'what are you afraid of? do you think
it is poisoned? Come! do you eat one part, and I will eat
the other.' Now the apple was so prepared that one side
was good, though the other side was poisoned. Then Snow-
drop was very much tempted to taste, for the apple looked
exceedingly nice; and when she saw the old woman eat, she
could refrain no longer. But she had scarcely put the piece
into her mouth, when she fell down dead upon the ground.
'This time nothing will save thee,' said the queen; and she
went home to her glass, and at last it said

'Thou, queen, art the fairest of all the fair.'

And then her envious heart was glad, and as happy as such
a heart could be.

When evening came, and the dwarfs returned home, they
found Snow-drop lying on the ground: no breath passed
her lips, and they were afraid that she was quite dead.
They lifted her up, and combed her hair, and washed her
face with wine and water; but all was in vain, for the little
girl seemed quite dead. So they laid her down upon a bier,

and all seven watched and bewailed her three whole days; and then they proposed to bury her: but her cheeks were still rosy, and her face looked just as it did while she was alive; so they said, 'We will never bury her in the cold ground.' And they made a coffin of glass, so that they might still look at her, and wrote her name upon it, in golden letters, and that she was a king's daughter. And the coffin was placed upon the hill, and one of the dwarfs always sat by it and watched. And the birds of the air came too, and bemoaned Snow-drop: first of all came an owl, and then a raven, but at last came a dove.

And thus Snow-drop lay for a long long time, and still only looked as though she were asleep; for she was even now as white as snow, and as red as blood, and as black as ebony. At last a prince came and called at the dwarfs' house; and he saw Snow-drop, and read what was written in golden letters. Then he offered the dwarfs' money, and earnestly prayed them to let him take her away; but they said, 'We will not part with her for all the gold in the world.' At last however they had pity on him, and gave him the coffin: but the moment he lifted it up to carry it home with him, the piece of apple fell from between her lips, and Snow-drop awoke, and said, 'Where am I?' And the prince answered, 'Thou art safe with me.' Then he told her all that had happened, and said, 'I love you better than all the world: come with me to my father's palace, and you shall be my wife.' And Snow-drop consented, and went home with the prince; and every thing was prepared with great pomp and splendour for their wedding.

To the feast was invited, among the rest, Snow-drop's old enemy the queen; and as she was dressing herself in fine rich clothes, she looked in the glass, and said,

> 'Tell me, glass, tell me true!
> Of all the ladies in the land,
> Who is fairest? tell me who?'

And the glass answered,

> 'Thou, lady, art loveliest *here*, I ween;
> But lovelier far is the new-made queen.'

When she heard this, she started with rage; but her envy and curiosity were so great, that she could not help setting out to see the bride. And when she arrived, and saw that it was no other than Snow-drop, who, as she thought, had been dead a long while, she choked with passion, and fell ill and died; but Snow-drop and the prince lived and reigned happily over that land many many years.

THE ELVES AND THE SHOEMAKER

THERE was once a shoemaker who worked very hard and was very honest; but still he could not earn enough to live upon, and at last all he had in the world was gone, except just leather enough to make one pair of shoes. Then he cut them all ready to make up the next day, meaning to get up early in the morning to work. His conscience was clear and his heart light amidst all his troubles; so he went peaceably to bed, left all his cares to heaven, and fell asleep. In the morning, after he had said his prayers, he set himself down to his work, when, to his great wonder, there stood the shoes, all ready made, upon the table. The good man knew not what to say or think of this strange event. He looked at the workmanship; there was not one false stitch in the whole job; and all was so neat and true, that it was a complete masterpiece.

That same day a customer came in, and the shoes pleased him so well that he willingly paid a price higher than usual for them; and the poor shoemaker with the money bought leather enough to make two pairs more. In

the evening he cut out the work, and went to bed early
that he might get up and begin betimes next day: but he
was saved all the trouble, for when he got up in the morning the work was finished ready to his hand. Presently in
came buyers, who paid him handsomely for his goods, so
that he bought leather enough for four pairs more. He cut
out the work again over night, and found it finished in the
morning as before; and so it went on for some time: what
was got ready in the evening was always done by day-
break, and the good man soon became thriving and pros-
perous again.

One evening about Christmas time, as he and his wife
were sitting over the fire chatting together, he said to her,
'I should like to sit up and watch to-night, that we may see
who it is that comes and does my work for me.' The wife
liked the thought; so they left a light burning, and hid
themselves in the corner of the room behind a curtain that
was hung up there, and watched what should happen.

As soon as it was midnight, there came two little naked
dwarfs; and they sat themselves upon the shoemaker's
bench, took up all the work that was cut out, and began to
ply with their little fingers, stitching and rapping and tapping away at such a rate, that the shoemaker was all amaze-
ment, and could not take his eyes off for a moment. And on
they went till the job was quite finished, and the shoes stood
ready for use upon the table. This was long before day-
break; and then they bustled away as quick as lightning.

The next day the wife said to the shoemaker, 'These
little wights have made us rich, and we ought to be thankful to them, and do them a good office in return. I am quite
vexed to see them run about as they do; they have nothing
upon their backs to keep off the cold. I'll tell you what, I
will make each of them a shirt, and a coat and waistcoat,
and a pair of pantaloons into the bargain; do you make
each of them a little pair of shoes.'

The thought pleased the good shoemaker very much; and one evening, when all the things were ready, they laid them on the table instead of the work that they used to cut out, and then went and hid themselves to watch what the little elves would do. About midnight they came in, and were going to sit down to their work as usual; but when they saw the clothes lying for them, they laughed and were greatly delighted. Then they dressed themselves in the twinkling of an eye, and danced and capered and sprang about as merry as could be, till at last they danced out at the door over the green; and the shoemaker saw them no more: but every thing went well with him from that time forward, as long as he lived.

THE TURNIP

THERE were two brothers who were both soldiers; the one was rich and the other poor. The poor man thought he would try to better himself; so, pulling off his red coat, he became a gardener, and dug his ground well, and sowed turnips.

When the seed came up, there was one plant bigger than all the rest; and it kept getting larger and larger, and seemed as if it would never cease growing; so that it might have been called the prince of turnips for there never was such a one seen before, and never will again. At last it was so big that it filled a cart, and two oxen could hardly draw it; and the gardener knew not what in the world to do with it, nor whether it would be a blessing or a curse to him. One day he said to himself, 'What shall I do with it? if I sell it, it will bring no more than another; and for eating, the little turnips are better than this; the best thing perhaps is to carry it and give it to the king as a mark of respect.'

Then he yoked his oxen, and drew the turnip to the Court, and gave it to the king. 'What a wonderful thing!' said the king; 'I have seen many strange things, but such a monster as this I never saw. Where did you get the seed? or is it only your good luck? If so, you are a true child of fortune.' 'Ah, no!' answered the gardener, 'I am no child of fortune; I am a poor soldier, who never could get enough to live upon; so I laid aside my red coat, and set to work, tilling the ground. I have a brother, who is rich, and your majesty knows him well, and all the world knows him; but because I am poor, every body forgets me.'

The king then took pity on him, and said, 'You shall be poor no longer. I will give you so much that you shall be even richer than your brother.' Then he gave him gold and lands and flocks, and made him so rich that his brother's fortune could not at all be compared with his.

When the brother heard of all this, and how a turnip had made the gardener so rich, he envied him sorely, and bethought himself how he could contrive to get the same good fortune for himself. However, he determined to manage more cleverly than his brother, and got together a rich present of gold and fine horses for the king; and thought he must have a much larger gift in return: for if his brother had received so much for only a turnip, what must his present be worth?

The king took the gift very graciously, and said he knew not what to give in return more valuable and wonderful than the great turnip; so the soldier was forced to put it into a cart, and drag it home with him. When he reached home, he knew not upon whom to vent his rage and spite; and at length wicked thoughts came into his head, and he resolved to kill his brother.

So he hired some villains to murder him; and having shown them where to lie in ambush, he went to his brother, and said, 'Dear brother, I have found a hidden treasure; let us go and dig it up, and share it between us.' The other had no suspicions of his roguery: so they went out together, and as they were travelling along, the murderers rushed out upon him, bound him, and were going to hang him on a tree. But whilst they were getting all ready, they heard the trampling of a horse at a distance, which so frightened them that they pushed their prisoner neck and shoulders together into a sack, and swung him up by a cord to the tree, where they left him dangling, and ran away. Meantime he worked and worked away, till he made a hole large enough to put out his head.

When the horseman came up, he proved to be a student, a merry fellow, who was journeying along on his nag, and singing as he went. As soon as the man in the sack saw him

passing under the tree, he cried out, 'Good morning! good
morning to thee, my friend!' The student looked about
every where; and seeing no one, and not knowing where
the voice came from, cried out, 'Who calls me?'

Then the man in the tree answered, 'Lift up thine eyes,
for behold here I sit in the sack of wisdom; here have I, in
a short time, learned great and wondrous things. Compared to this seat, all the learning of the schools is as empty

air. A little longer, and I shall know all that man can know, and shall come forth wiser than the wisest of mankind. Here I discern the signs and motions of the heavens and the stars; the laws that control the winds; the number of the sands on the sea-shore; the healing of the sick; the virtues of all simples, of birds, and of precious stones. Wert thou but once here, my friend, thou wouldst feel and own the power of knowledge.'

The student listened to all this and wondered much; at last he said, 'Blessed be the day and hour when I found you; cannot you contrive to let me into the sack for a little while?' Then the other answered, as if very unwillingly, 'A little space I may allow thee to sit here, if thou wilt reward me well and entreat me kindly; but thou must tarry yet an hour below, till I have learnt some little matters that are yet unknown to me.'

So the student sat himself down and waited a while; but the time hung heavy upon him, and he begged earnestly that he might ascend forthwith, for his thirst of knowledge was great. Then the other pretended to give way, and said, 'Thou must let the sack of wisdom descend, by untying yonder cord, and then thou shalt enter.' So the student let him down, opened the sack, and set him free. 'Now then,' cried he, 'let me ascend quickly.' As he began to put himself into the sack heels first, 'Wait a while,' said the gardener, 'that is not the way.' Then he pushed him in head first, tied up the sack, and soon swung up the searcher after wisdom dangling in the air. 'How is it with thee, friend?' said he, 'dost thou not feel that wisdom comes unto thee? Rest there in peace, till thou art a wiser man than thou wert.'

So saying, he trotted off on the student's nag, and left the poor fellow to gather wisdom till somebody should come and let him down.

OLD SULTAN

A SHEPHERD had a faithful dog, called Sultan, who was grown very old, and had lost all his teeth. And one day when the shepherd and his wife were standing together before the house, the shepherd said, 'I will shoot old Sultan to-morrow morning, for he is of no use now.' But his wife said, 'Pray let the poor faithful creature live; he has served us well a great many years, and we ought to give him a livelihood for the rest of his days.' 'But what can we do with him?' said the shepherd, 'he has not a tooth in his head, and the thieves don't care for him at all; to be sure he has served us, but then he did it to earn his livelihood; to-morrow shall be his last day, depend upon it.'

Poor Sultan, who was lying close by them, heard all that the shepherd and his wife said to one another, and was very much frightened to think to-morrow would be his last day; so in the evening he went to his good friend the wolf, who lived in the wood, and told him all his sorrows, and how his master meant to kill him in the morning. 'Make yourself easy,' said the wolf, 'I will give you some good advice. Your master, you know, goes out every morning very early with his wife into the field; and they take their little child with them, and lay it down behind the hedge in the shade while they are at work. Now do you lie down close by the child, and pretend to be watching it, and I will come out of the wood and run away with it: you must run after me as fast as you can, and I will let it drop; then you may carry it back, and they will think you have saved their child, and will be so thankful to you that they will take care of you as long as you live.' The dog liked this plan very well; and accordingly so it was managed. The wolf ran with the child a little way; the shepherd and his wife screamed out; but Sultan soon overtook him, and carried the poor little thing back to his master and mistress. Then the shepherd patted him on the head, and said, 'Old Sultan has saved our child from the wolf, and therefore he shall live and be well taken care of, and have plenty to eat. Wife, go home, and give him a good dinner, and let him have my old cushion to sleep on as long as he lives.' So from this time forward Sultan had all that he could wish for.

Soon afterwards the wolf came and wished him joy, and said, 'Now, my good fellow, you must tell no tales, but turn your head the other way when I want to taste one of the old shepherd's fine fat sheep.' 'No,' said Sultan; 'I will be true to my master.' However, the wolf thought he was in joke, and came one night to get a dainty morsel. But Sultan had told his master what the wolf meant to do; so he laid wait for him behind the barn-door, and when the wolf was busy looking out for a good fat sheep, he had a stout cudgel laid about his back, that combed his locks for him finely.

Then the wolf was very angry, and called Sultan 'an old rogue,' and swore he would have his revenge. So the next morning the wolf sent the boar to challenge Sultan to come into the wood to fight the matter out. Now Sultan had no body he could ask to be his second but the shepherd's old three-legged cat; so he took her with him, and as the poor thing limped along with some trouble, she stuck up her tail straight in the air.

The wolf and the wild boar were first on the ground; and when they espied their enemies coming, and saw the cat's long tail standing straight in the air, they thought she was carrying a sword for Sultan to fight with; and every time she limped, they thought she was picking up a stone to throw at them; so they said they should not like this way of fighting, and the boar lay down behind a bush, and the wolf jumped up into a tree. Sultan and the cat soon came up, and looked about, and wondered that no one was there. The boar, however, had not quite hidden himself, for his ears stuck out of the bush; and when he shook one of them a little, the cat, seeing something move, and thinking it was a mouse, sprang upon it, and bit and scratched it, so that the boar jumped up and grunted, and ran away, roaring out, 'Look up in the tree, there sits the one who is to blame.' So they looked up, and espied the wolf sitting amongst the branches; and they called him a cowardly rascal, and would not suffer him to come down till he was heartily ashamed of himself, and had promised to be good friends again with old Sultan.

THE LADY AND THE LION

A MERCHANT, who had three daughters, was once setting out upon a journey; but before he went he asked each daughter what gift he should bring back for her. The eldest wished for pearls; the second for jewels; but the third said, 'Dear father, bring me a rose.' Now it was no easy task to find a rose, for it was the middle of winter; yet, as she was the fairest daughter, and was very fond of flowers, her father said he would try what he could do. So he kissed all three, and bid them good-bye. And when the time came for his return, he had bought pearls and jewels for the two eldest, but he had sought every where in vain for the rose; and when he went into any garden and inquired for such a thing, the people laughed at him, and asked him whether he thought roses grew in snow. This grieved him very much, for his third daughter was his dearest child; and as he was journeying home, thinking what he should bring her, he came to a fine castle; and around the castle was a garden, in half of which it appeared to be summer time, and in the other half winter. On one side the finest flowers were in full bloom, and on the other every thing looked desolate and

buried in snow. 'A lucky hit!' said he as he called to his servant, and told him to go to a beautiful bed of roses that was
there, and bring him away one of the flowers. This done,
they were riding away well pleased, when a fierce lion
sprang up, and roared out, 'Whoever dares to steal my
roses shall be eaten up alive.' Then the man said, 'I knew
not that the garden belonged to you; can nothing save my
life?' 'No!' said the lion, 'nothing, unless you promise to
give me whatever meets you first on your return home; if
you agree to this, I will give you your life, and the rose too
for your daughter.' But the man was unwilling to do so,
and said, 'It may be my youngest daughter, who loves me
most, and always runs to meet me when I go home.' Then
the servant was greatly frightened, and said, 'It may perhaps be only a cat or a dog.' And at last the man yielded
with a heavy heart, and took the rose; and promised the
lion whatever should meet him first on his return.

And as he came near home, it was his youngest and dearest daughter that met him; she came running and kissed
him, and welcomed him home; and when she saw that he
had brought her the rose, she rejoiced still more. But her
father began to be very melancholy, and to weep, saying,
'Alas! my dearest child! I have bought this flower dear, for
I have promised to give you to a wild lion, and when he has
you, he will tear you in pieces, and eat you.' And he told
her all that had happened; and said she should not go, let
what would happen.

But she comforted him, and said, 'Dear father, what you
have promised must be fulfilled; I will go to the lion, and
soothe him, that he may let me return again safe home.'

The next morning she asked the way she was to go, and
took leave of her father, and went forth with a bold heart
into the wood. But the lion was an enchanted prince, and
by day he and all his court were lions, but in the evening
they took their proper forms again. And when the lady

came to the castle, he welcomed her so courteously that she consented to marry him. The wedding-feast was held, and they lived happily together a long time. The prince was only to be seen as soon as evening came, and then he held his court; but every morning he left his bride, and went away by himself, she knew not whither, till night came again.

After some time he said to her, 'To-morrow there will be a great feast in your father's house, for your eldest sister is to be married; and, if you wish to go to visit her, my lions shall lead you thither.' Then she rejoiced much at the thoughts of seeing her father once more, and set out with the lions; and every one was overjoyed to see her, for they had thought her dead long since. But she told them how happy she was; and stayed till the feast was over, and then went back to the wood.

Her second sister was soon after married; and when she was invited to the wedding, she said to the prince, 'I will not go alone this time; you must go with me.' But he would not, and said that would be a very hazardous thing, for if the least ray of the torch light should fall upon him, his enchantment would become still worse, for he should be changed into a dove, and be obliged to wander about the world for seven long years. However, she gave him no rest, and said she would take care no light should fall upon him. So at last they set out together, and took with them their little child too; and she chose a large hall with thick walls, for him to sit in while the wedding torches were lighted; but unluckily no one observed that there was a crack in the door. Then the wedding was held with great pomp; but as the train came from the church, and passed with the torches before the hall, a very small ray of light fell upon the prince. In a moment he disappeared; and when his wife came in, and sought him, she found only a white dove. Then he said to her, 'Seven years must I fly up and down

over the face of the earth; but every now and then I will let
fall a white feather, that shall show you the way I am
going; follow it, and at last you may overtake and set me
free.'

This said, he flew out at the door, and she followed; and
every now and then a white feather fell, and showed her
the way she was to journey. Thus she went roving on
through the wide world, and looked neither to the right
hand nor to the left, nor took any rest for seven years.
Then she began to rejoice, and thought to herself that the
time was fast coming when all her troubles should cease;
yet repose was still far off: for one day as she was travelling
on, she missed the white feather, and when she lifted up her
eyes she could no where see the dove. 'Now,' thought she to
herself, 'no human aid can be of use to me;' so she went to
the sun, and said, 'Thou shinest every where, on the mountain's top, and the valley's depth: hast thou any where
seen a white dove?' 'No,' said the sun, 'I have not seen it;
but I will give thee a casket – open it when thy hour of need
comes.' So she thanked the sun, and went on her way till
eventide; and when the moon arose, she cried unto it, and
said, 'Thou shinest through all the night, over field and
grove: hast thou no where seen a white dove?' 'No,' said
the moon, 'I cannot help thee; but I will give thee an egg –
break it when need comes.' Then she thanked the moon,
and went on till the night-wind blew; and she raised up her
voice to it, and said, 'Thou blowest through every tree and
under every leaf: hast thou not seen the white dove?' 'No,'
said the night-wind; 'but I will ask three other winds; perhaps they have seen it.' Then the east wind and the west
wind came, and said they too had not seen it; but the south
wind said, 'I have seen the white dove; he has fled to the
Red Sea, and is changed once more into a lion, for the
seven years are passed away; and there he is fighting with a
dragon, and the dragon is an enchanted princess, who seeks

to separate him from you.' Then the night-wind said, 'I will give thee counsel: go to the Red Sea; on the right shore stand many rods; number them, and when thou comest to the eleventh, break it off and smite the dragon with it; so the lion will have the victory, and both of them will appear to you in their human forms. Then instantly set out with thy beloved prince, and journey home over sea and land.'

So our poor wanderer went forth, and found all as the night-wind had said; and she plucked the eleventh rod, and smote the dragon, and immediately the lion became a prince and the dragon a princess again. But she forgot the counsel which the night-wind had given; and the false princess watched her opportunity, and took the prince by the arm, and carried him away.

Thus the unfortunate traveller was again forsaken and forlorn; but she took courage and said, 'As far as the wind blows, and so long as the cock crows, I will journey on till I find him once again.' She went on for a long long way, till at length she came to the castle whither the princess had carried the prince; and there was a feast prepared, and she heard that the wedding was about to be held. 'Heaven aid me now!' said she; and she took the casket that the sun had given her, and found that within it lay a dress as dazzling as the sun itself. So she put it on, and went into the palace; and all the people gazed upon her; and the dress pleased the bride so much that she asked whether it was to be sold: 'Not for gold and silver,' answered she; 'but for flesh and blood.' The princess asked what she meant; and she said, 'Let me speak with the bridegroom this night in his chamber, and I will give thee the dress.' At last the princess agreed; but she told her chamberlain to give the prince a sleeping-draught, that he might not hear or see her. When evening came, and the prince had fallen asleep, she was led into his chamber, and she sat herself down at his

feet and said, 'I have followed thee seven years; I have
been to the sun, the moon, and the night-wind, to seek
thee; and at last I have helped thee to overcome the
dragon. Wilt thou then forget me quite?' But the prince
slept so soundly that her voice only passed over him, and
seemed like the murmuring of the wind among the fir-trees.

Then she was led away, and forced to give up the golden
dress; and when she saw that there was no help for her, she
went out into a meadow and sat herself down and wept.
But as she sat she bethought herself of the egg that the
moon had given her; and when she broke it, there ran out a
hen and twelve chickens of pure gold, that played about,
and then nestled under the old one's wings, so as to form
the most beautiful sight in the world. And she rose up, and
drove them before her till the bride saw them from her
window, and was so pleased that she came forth, and asked
her if she would sell the brood. 'Not for gold or silver; but
for flesh and blood: let me again this evening speak with
the bridegroom in his chamber.'

Then the princess thought to betray her as before, and
agreed to what she asked; but when the prince went to his
chamber, he asked the chamberlain why the wind had mur-
mured so in the night. And the chamberlain told him all;
how he had given him a sleeping-draught, and a poor
maiden had come and spoken to him in his chamber, and
was to come again that night. Then the prince took care to
throw away the sleeping-draught; and when she came and
began again to tell him what woes had befallen her, and
how faithful and true to him she had been, he knew his beloved wife's voice, and sprung up, and said, 'You have
awakened me as from a dream; for the strange princess had
thrown a spell around me, so that I had altogether forgotten you: but heaven hath sent you to me in a lucky
hour.'

And they stole away out of the palace by night secretly

(for they feared the princess), and journeyed home; and there they found their child, now grown comely and fair, and lived happily together to the end of their days.

THE KING OF THE GOLDEN MOUNTAIN

A CERTAIN merchant had two children, a son and daughter, both very young, and scarcely able to run alone. He had two richly laden ships then making a voyage upon the seas, in which he had embarked all his property, in the hope of making great gains, when the news came that they were lost. Thus from being a rich man he became very poor, so that nothing was left him but one small plot of land; and, to relieve his mind a little of his trouble, he often went out to walk there.

One day, as he was roving along, a little rough-looking dwarf stood before him, and asked him why he was so sorrowful, and what it was that he took so deeply to heart. But the merchant replied, 'If you could do me any good, I would tell you.' 'Who knows but I may?' said the little man; 'tell me what is the matter, and perhaps I can be of some service.' Then the merchant told him how all his wealth was gone to the bottom of the sea, and how he had nothing left except that little plot of land. 'Oh! trouble not yourself about that,' said the dwarf; 'only promise to bring me here, twelve years hence, whatever meets you first on your return home, and I will give you as much gold as you please.' The merchant thought this was no great request; that it would most likely be his dog, or something of that sort, but forgot his little child: so he agreed to the bargain, and signed and sealed the engagement to do what was required.

But as he drew near home, his little boy was so pleased to see him, that he crept behind him and laid fast hold of his legs. Then the father started with fear, and saw what it was that he had bound himself to do; but as no gold was come, he consoled himself by thinking that it was only a joke that the dwarf was playing him.

About a month afterwards he went up stairs into an old lumber room to look for some old iron, that he might sell it and raise a little money; and there he saw a large pile of gold lying on the floor. At the sight of this he was greatly delighted, went into trade again, and became a greater merchant than before.

Meantime his son grew up, and as the end of the twelve years drew near, the merchant became very anxious and thoughtful; so that care and sorrow were written upon his face. The son one day asked what was the matter: but his father refused to tell for some time; at last however he said that he had, without knowing it, sold him to a little ugly-looking dwarf for a great quantity of gold; and that the twelve years were coming round when he must perform his agreement. Then the son said, 'Father, give yourself very little trouble about that; depend upon it I shall be too much for the little man.'

When the time came, they went out together to the appointed place; and the son drew a circle on the ground, and set himself and his father in the middle. The little dwarf soon came, and said to the merchant, 'Have you brought me what you promised?' The old man was silent, but his son answered, 'What do you want here?' The dwarf said, 'I come to talk with your father, not with you.' 'You have deceived and betrayed my father,' said the son; 'give him up his bond.' 'No,' replied the other, 'I will not yield up my rights.' Upon this a long dispute arose; and at last it was agreed that the son should be put into an open boat, that lay on the side of a piece of water hard by, and that the father should push him off with his own hand; so that he should be turned adrift. Then he took leave of his father, and set himself in the boat; and as it was pushed off it heaved, and fell on one side into the water: so the merchant thought that his son was lost, and went home very sorrowful.

But the boat went safely on, and did not sink; and the young man sat securely within, till at length it ran ashore upon an unknown land. As he jumped upon the shore, he saw before him a beautiful castle, but empty and desolate within, for it was enchanted. At last, however, he found a white snake in one of the chambers.

Now the white snake was an enchanted princess; and she rejoiced greatly to see him, and said, 'Art thou at last come to be my deliverer? Twelve long years have I waited for thee, for thou alone canst save me. This night twelve men will come: their faces will be black, and they will be hung round with chains. They will ask what thou dost here; but be silent, give no answer, and let them do what they will – beat and torment thee. Suffer all, only speak not a word, and at twelve o'clock they must depart. The second night twelve others will come; and the third night twenty-four, who will even cut off thy head; but at the twelfth hour of that night their power is gone, and I shall be free, and will come and bring thee the water of life, and will wash thee with it, and restore thee to life and health.' And all came to pass as she had said; the merchant's son spoke not a word, and the third night the princess appeared, and fell on his neck and kissed him; joy and gladness burst forth throughout the castle; the wedding was celebrated, and he was king of the Golden Mountain.

They lived together very happily, and the queen had a son. Eight years had passed over their heads when the king thought of his father: and his heart was moved, and he longed to see him once again. But the queen opposed his going, and said, 'I know well that misfortunes will come.' However, he gave her no rest till she consented. At his de-

parture she presented him with a wishing-ring, and said,
'Take this ring, and put it on your finger; whatever you
wish it will bring you: only promise that you will not make
use of it to bring me hence to your father's.' Then he
promised what she asked, and put the ring on his finger,
and wished himself near the town where his father lived.
He found himself at the gates in a moment; but the guards
would not let him enter, because he was so strangely clad.
So he went up to a neighbouring mountain where a shepherd dwelt, and borrowed his old frock, and thus passed un-
observed into the town. When he came to his father's
house, he said he was his son; but the merchant would not
believe him, and said he had had but one son, who he knew
was long since dead; and as he was only dressed like a poor
shepherd, he would not even offer him any thing to eat.
The king however persisted that he was his son, and said,
'Is there no mark by which you would know if I am really
your son?' 'Yes,' observed his mother, 'our son has a mark
like a raspberry under the right arm.' Then he showed them
the mark, and they were satisfied that what he had said
was true. He next told them how he was king of the Golden
Mountain, and was married to a princess, and had a son
seven years old. But the merchant said, 'That can never be
true; he must be a fine king truly who travels about in a
shepherd's frock.' At this the son was very angry; and, for-
getting his promise, turned his ring, and wished for his
queen and son. In an instant they stood before him; but
the queen wept, and said he had broken his word, and misfortune would follow. He did all he could to soothe her, and
she at last appeared to be appeased; but she was not so in
reality, and only meditated how she should take her
revenge.

One day he took her to walk with him out of the town, and
showed her the spot where the boat was turned adrift upon
the wide waters. Then he sat himself down, and said, 'I am

very much tired; sit by me, I will rest my head in your lap, and sleep a while.' As soon as he had fallen asleep, however, she drew the ring from his finger, and crept softly away, and wished herself and her son at home in their kingdom. And when the king awoke, he found himself alone, and saw that the ring was gone from his finger. 'I can never return to my father's house,' said he; 'they would say I am a sorcerer; I will journey forth into the world till I come again to my kingdom.'

So saying, he set out and travelled till he came to a

mountain, where three giants were sharing their inheritance; and as they saw him pass, they cried out and said, 'Little men have sharp wits; he shall divide the inheritance between us.' Now it consisted of a sword that cut off an enemy's head whenever the wearer gave the words 'Heads off!' – a cloak that made the owner invisible, or gave him any form he pleased; and a pair of boots that transported the person who put them on wherever he wished. The king said they must first let him try these wonderful things, that he might know how to set a value upon them. Then they gave him the cloak, and he wished himself a fly, and in a moment he was a fly. 'The cloak is very well,' said he; 'now give me the sword.' 'No,' said they, 'not unless you promise not to say "Heads off!" for if you do, we are all dead men.' So they gave it him on condition that he tried its virtue only on a tree. He next asked for the boots also; and the moment he had all three in his possession he wished himself at the Golden Mountain; and there he was in an instant. So the giants were left behind with no inheritance to divide or quarrel about.

As he came near to the castle he heard the sound of merry music; and the people around told him that his queen was about to celebrate her marriage with another prince. Then he threw his cloak around him, and passed through the castle, and placed himself by the side of his queen, where no one saw him. But when any thing to eat was put upon her plate, he took it away and ate it himself; and when a glass of wine was handed to her, he took and drank it: and thus, though they kept on serving her with meat and drink, her plate continued always empty.

Upon this, fear and remorse came over her, and she went into her chamber and wept; and he followed her there. 'Alas!' said she to herself, 'did not my deliverer come? why then doth enchantment still surround me?'

'Thou traitress!' said he, 'thy deliverer indeed came, and

now is near thee: has he deserved this of thee?' And he went out and dismissed the company, and said the wedding was at an end, for that he was returned to his kingdom: but the princes and nobles and counsellors mocked at him. However, he would enter into no parley with them, but only demanded whether they would depart in peace, or not. Then they turned and tried to seize him; but he drew his sword, and, with a word, the traitors' heads fell before him; and he was once more king of the Golden Mountain.

THE GOLDEN GOOSE

THERE was a man who had three sons. The youngest was called Dummling, and was on all occasions despised and ill-treated by the whole family. It happened that the eldest took it into his head one day to go into the wood to cut fuel; and his mother gave him a delicious pasty and a bottle of wine to take with him, that he might refresh himself at his work. As he went into the wood, a little old man bid him good day, and said, 'Give me a little piece of meat from your plate, and a little wine out of your bottle; I am very hungry and thirsty.' But this clever young man said, 'Give you my meat and wine! No, I thank you; I should not have enough left for myself:' and away he went. He soon began to cut down a tree; but he had not worked long before he missed his stroke, and cut himself, and was obliged to go home to have the wound dressed. Now it was the little old man that caused him this mischief.

Next went out the second son to work; and his mother gave him too a pasty and a bottle of wine. And the same little old man met him also, and asked him for something to eat and drink. But he too thought himself vastly clever, and said, 'Whatever you get, I shall lose; so go your way!'

The little man took care that he should have his reward; and the second stroke that he aimed against a tree, hit him on the leg; so that he too was forced to go home.

Then Dummling said, 'Father, I should like to go and cut wood too.' But his father answered, 'Your brothers have both lamed themselves; you had better stay at home, for you know nothing of the business.' But Dummling was very pressing; and at last his father said, 'Go your way; you will be wiser when you have suffered for your folly.' And his mother gave him only some dry bread, and a bottle of sour beer; but when he went into the wood, he met the little old man, who said, 'Give me some meat and drink, for I am very hungry and thirsty.' Dummling said, 'I have only dry bread and sour beer; if that will suit you, we will sit down and eat it together.' So they sat down; and when the lad pulled out his bread, behold it was turned into a capital pasty, and his sour beer became delightful wine. They ate and drank heartily; and when they had done, the little man said, 'As you have a kind heart, and have been willing to share every thing with me, I will send a blessing upon you. There stands an old tree; cut it down, and you will find something at the root.' Then he took his leave, and went his way.

Dummling set to work, and cut down the tree; and when it fell, he found in a hollow under the roots a goose with feathers of pure gold. He took it up, and went on to an inn, where he proposed to sleep for the night. The landlord had three daughters; and when they saw the goose, they were very curious to examine what this wonderful bird could be, and wished very much to pluck one of the feathers out of its tail. At last the eldest said, 'I must and will have a feather.' So she waited till his back was turned, and then seized the goose by the wing; but to her great surprise there she stuck, for neither hand nor finger could she get away again. Presently in came the second sister, and

thought to have a feather too; but the moment she touched
her sister, there she too hung fast. At last came the third,
and wanted a feather; but the other two cried out, 'Keep
away! for heaven's sake, keep away!' However, she did not
understand what they meant. 'If they are there,' thought
she, 'I may as well be there too.' So she went up to them;
but the moment she touched her sisters she stuck fast, and
hung to the goose as they did. And so they kept company
with the goose all night.

The next morning Dummling carried off the goose under
his arm; and took no notice of the three girls, but went out

with them sticking fast behind; and wherever he travelled, they too were obliged to follow, whether they would or no, as fast as their legs could carry them.

In the middle of a field the parson met them; and when he saw the train, he said, 'Are you not ashamed of yourselves, you bold girls, to run after the young man in that way over the fields? is that proper behaviour?' Then he took the youngest by the hand to lead her away; but the moment he touched her he too hung fast, and followed in the train. Presently up came the clerk; and when he saw his master the parson running after the three girls, he wondered greatly, and said, 'Hollo! hollo! your reverence! whither so fast? there is a christening to-day.' Then he ran up, and took him by the gown, and in a moment he was fast too. As the five were thus trudging along, one behind another, they met two labourers with their mattocks coming from work; and the parson cried out to them to set him free. But scarcely had they touched him, when they too fell into the ranks, and so made seven, all running after Dummling and his goose.

At last they arrived at a city, where reigned a king who had an only daughter. The princess was of so thoughtful and serious a turn of mind that no one could make her laugh; and the king had proclaimed to all the world, that whoever could make her laugh should have her for his wife. When the young man heard this, he went to her with his goose and all its train; and as soon as she saw the seven all hanging together, and running about, treading on each other's heels, she could not help bursting into a long and loud laugh. Then Dummling claimed her for his wife; the wedding was celebrated, and he was heir to the kingdom, and lived long and happily with his wife.

MRS FOX

THERE was once a sly old fox with nine tails, who was very
curious to know whether his wife was true to him: so he
stretched himself out under a bench, and pretended to be as
dead as a mouse.

Then Mrs Fox went up into her own room and locked the
door: but her maid, the cat, sat at the kitchen fire cooking;
and soon after it became known that the old fox was dead,
some one knocked at the door, saying,

> 'Miss Pussy! Miss Pussy! how fare you today?
> Are you sleeping or watching the time away?'

Then the cat went and opened the door, and there stood
a young fox; so she said to him,

> 'No, no, Master Fox, I don't sleep in the day,
> I'm making some capital white wine whey.
> Will your honour be pleased to dinner to stay?'

'No, I thank you,' said the fox; 'but how is poor Mrs
Fox?' Then the cat answered,

> 'She sits all alone in her chamber up stairs,
> And bewails her misfortune with floods of tears:
> She weeps till her beautiful eyes are red;
> For, alas! alas! Mr Fox is dead.'

'Go to her,' said the other, 'and say that there is a young
fox come, who wishes to marry her.'

> Then up went the cat, – trippety trap,
> And knocked at the door, – tippety tap;
> 'Is good Mrs Fox within?' said she.
> 'Alas! my dear, what want you with me?'
> 'There waits a suitor below at the gate.'

Then said Mrs Fox,

> 'How looks he, my dear? is he tall and straight?
> Has he nine good tails? There must be nine,
> Or he never shall be a suitor of mine.'

'Ah!' said the cat, 'he has but one.' 'Then I will never have him,' answered Mrs Fox.

So the cat went down, and sent this suitor about his business. Soon after, some one else knocked at the door; it was another fox that had two tails, but he was not better welcomed than the first. After this came several others, till at last one came that had really nine tails just like the old fox.

When the widow heard this, she jumped up and said,

> 'Now, Pussy, my dear, open windows and doors,
> And bid all our friends at our wedding to meet;
> And as for that nasty old master of ours,
> Throw him out of the window, Puss, into the street.'

But when the wedding feast was all ready, up sprung the old gentleman on a sudden, and taking a club, drove the whole company, together with Mrs Fox, out of doors.

*

After some time, however, the old fox really died; and soon afterwards a wolf came to pay his respects, and knocked at the door.

> *Wolf.* 'Good day, Mrs Cat, with your whiskers so trim;
> How comes it you're sitting alone so prim?
> What's that you are cooking so nicely, I pray?'
> *Cat.* 'O, that's bread and milk for my dinner to-day.
> Will your worship be pleased to stay and dine,
> Or shall I fetch you a glass of wine?'

'No, I thank you: Mrs Fox is not at home, I suppose?'

> *Cat.* 'She sits all alone,
> Her griefs to bemoan;
> For, alas! alas! Mr Fox is gone.'

Wolf. 'Ah! dear Mrs Puss! that's a loss indeed:
    D'ye think she'd take *me* for a husband instead?'
Cat. 'Indeed, Mr Wolf, I don't know but she may
    If you'll sit down a moment, I'll step up and see.'
So she gave him a chair, and shaking her ears,
She very obligingly tripped it up stairs.
She knocked at the door with the rings on her toes,
And said, 'Mrs Fox, you're within, I suppose?'
'O yes,' said the widow, 'pray come in, my dear,
And tell me whose voice in the kitchen I hear.'
'It's a wolf,' said the cat,' 'with a nice smooth skin,
Who was passing this way, and just stepped in
To see (as old Mr Fox is dead)
If you like to take him for a husband instead.'

'But,' said Mrs Fox, 'has he red feet and a sharp snout?'
'No,' said the cat. 'Then he won't do for me.' Soon after
the wolf was sent about his business, there came a dog, then
a goat, and after that a bear, a lion, and all the beasts, one
after another. But they all wanted something that old Mr
Fox had, and the cat was ordered to send them all away.
At last came a young fox, and Mrs Fox said, 'Has he four
red feet and a sharp snout?' 'Yes,' said the cat.

'Then, Puss, make the parlour look clean and neat,
And throw the old gentleman into the street;
A stupid old rascal! I'm glad that he's dead,
Now I've got such a charming young fox instead.'
So the wedding was held, and the merry bells rung,
And the friends and relations they danced and they sung,
And feasted and drank, I can't tell how long.

HANSEL AND GRETTEL

Hansel one day took his sister Grettel by the hand, and
said, 'Since our poor mother died we have had no happy

days; for our new mother beats us all day long, and when we go near her, she pushes us away. We have nothing but hard crusts to eat; and the little dog that lies by the fire is better off than we; for he sometimes has a nice piece of meat thrown to him. Heaven have mercy upon us! O if our poor mother knew how we are used! Come, we will go and travel over the wide world.' They went the whole day walking over the fields, till in the evening they came to a great wood; and then they were so tired and hungry that they sat down in a hollow tree and went to sleep.

In the morning when they awoke, the sun had risen high above the trees, and shone warm upon the hollow tree. Then Hansel said, 'Sister, I am very thirsty; if I could find a brook, I would go and drink, and fetch you some water too. Listen, I think I hear the sound of one.' Then Hansel rose up and took Grettel by the hand and went in search of the brook. But their cruel step-mother was a fairy, and had followed them into the wood to work them mischief: and when they had found a brook that ran sparkling over the pebbles, Hansel wanted to drink; but Grettel thought she heard the brook, as it babbled along, say, 'Whoever drinks here will be turned into a tiger.' Then she cried out, 'Ah, brother! do not drink, or you will be turned into a wild beast and tear me to pieces.' Then Hansel yielded, although he was parched with thirst. 'I will wait,' said he, 'for the next brook.' But when they came to the next, Grettel listened again, and thought she heard, 'Whoever drinks here will become a wolf.' Then she cried out, 'Brother, brother, do not drink, or you will become a wolf and eat me.' So he did not drink, but said, 'I will wait for the next brook; there I must drink, say what you will, I am so thirsty.'

As they came to the third brook, Grettel listened, and heard, 'Whoever drinks here will become a fawn.' 'Ah, brother!' said she, 'do not drink, or you will be turned into a fawn and run away from me.' But Hansel had already stooped down upon his knees, and the moment he put his lips into the water he was turned into a fawn.

Grettel wept bitterly over the poor creature, and the tears too rolled down his eyes as he laid himself beside her. Then she said, 'Rest in peace, dear fawn, I will never never leave thee.' So she took off her golden necklace and put it round his neck, and plucked some rushes and plaited them into a soft string to fasten to it; and led the poor little thing by her side farther into the wood.

After they had travelled a long way, they came at last to a little cottage; and Grettel, having looked in and seen that it was quite empty, thought to herself, 'We can stay and live here.' Then she went and gathered leaves and moss to make a soft bed for the fawn: and every morning she went out and plucked nuts, roots, and berries for herself, and sweet shrubs and tender grass for her companion; and it ate out of her hand, and was pleased, and played and frisked about her. In the evening, when Grettel was tired, and had said her prayers, she laid her head upon the fawn for her pillow, and slept: and if poor Hansel could but have his right form again, they thought they should lead a very happy life.

They lived thus a long while in the wood by themselves, till it chanced that the king of that country came to hold a great hunt there. And when the fawn heard all around the echoing of the horns, and the baying of the dogs, and the merry shouts of the huntsmen, he wished very much to go and see what was going on. 'Ah sister! sister!' said he, 'let me go out into the wood, I can stay no longer.' And he begged so long, that she at last agreed to let him go. 'But,' said she, 'be sure to come to me in the evening: I shall shut up the door to keep out those wild huntsmen; and if you tap at it, and say, "Sister, let me in," I shall know you; but if you don't speak, I shall keep the door fast.' Then away sprang the fawn, and frisked and bounded along in the open air. The king and his huntsmen saw the beautiful creature, and followed but could not overtake him; for when they thought they were sure of their prize, he sprung over the bushes and was out of sight in a moment.

As it grew dark he came running home to the hut, and tapped, and said 'Sister, sister, let me in.' Then she opened the little door, and in he jumped and slept soundly all night on his soft bed.

Next morning the hunt began again; and when he heard the huntsmen's horns, he said, 'Sister, open the door for me, I must go again.' Then she let him out, and said, 'Come back in the evening, and remember what you are to say.' When the king and the huntsmen saw the fawn with the golden collar again, they gave him chase; but he was too quick for them. The chase lasted the whole day; but at last the huntsmen nearly surrounded him, and one of them wounded him in the foot, so that he became sadly lame and could hardly crawl home. The man who had wounded him followed close behind, and hid himself, and heard the little fawn say, 'Sister, sister, let me in:' upon which the door opened and soon shut again. The huntsman marked all well, and went to the king and told him what he had seen and heard; then the king said, 'To-morrow we will have another chase.'

Grettel was very much frightened when she saw that her dear little fawn was wounded; but she washed the blood away and put some healing herbs on it, and said, 'Now go to bed, dear fawn, and you will soon be well again.' The wound was so small, that in the morning there was nothing to be seen of it; and when the horn blew, the little creature said, 'I can't stay here, I must go and look on; I will take care that none of them shall catch me.' But Grettel said, 'I am sure they will kill you this time, I will not let you go.' 'I shall die of vexation,' answered he, 'if you keep me here; when I hear the horns, I feel as if I could fly.' Then Grettel

was forced to let him go; so she opened the door with a
heavy heart, and he bounded out gaily into the wood.

When the king saw him, he said to his huntsman, 'Now
chase him all day long till you catch him; but let none of
you do him any harm.' The sun set, however, without their
being able to overtake him, and the king called away the
huntsmen, and said to the one who had watched, 'Now
come and show me the little hut.' So they went to the door
and tapped, and said, 'Sister, sister, let me in.' Then the
door opened and the king went in, and there stood a
maiden more lovely than any he had ever seen. Grettel was
frightened to see that it was not her fawn, but a king with a
golden crown, that was come into her hut: however, he
spoke kindly to her, and took her hand, and said, 'Will you
come with me to my castle and be my wife?' 'Yes,' said the
maiden; 'but my fawn must go with me, I cannot part with
that.' 'Well,' said the king, 'he shall come and live with you
all your life, and want for nothing.' Just at that moment in
sprung the little fawn; and his sister tied the string to his
neck, and they left the hut in the wood together.

Then the king took Grettel to his palace, and celebrated
the marriage in great state. And she told the king all her
story; and he sent for the fairy and punished her: and the
fawn was changed into Hansel again, and he and his sister
loved one another, and lived happily together all their days.

THE GIANT WITH THE THREE
GOLDEN HAIRS

THERE was once a poor man who had an only son born to
him. The child was born under a lucky star; and those who
told his fortune said that in his fourteenth year he would
marry the king's daughter. It so happened that the king of

that land soon after the child's birth passed through the village in disguise, and asked whether there was any news. 'Yes,' said the people, 'a child has just been born, that they say is to be a lucky one, and when he is fourteen years old, he is fated to marry the king's daughter.' This did not please the king; so he went to the poor child's parents and asked them whether they would sell him their son? 'No,' said they; but the stranger begged very hard and offered a great deal of money, and they had scarcely bread to eat, so at last they consented, thinking to themselves, he is a luck's child, he can come to no harm.

The king took the child, put it into a box, and rode away; but when he came to a deep stream, he threw it into the current, and said to himself, 'That young gentleman will never be my daughter's husband.' The box however floated down the stream; some kind spirit watched over it so that no water reached the child, and at last about two miles from the king's capital it stopt at the dam of a mill. The miller soon saw it, and took a long pole, and drew it towards the shore, and finding it heavy, thought there was gold inside; but when he opened it, he found a pretty little boy, that smiled upon him merrily. Now the miller and his wife had no children, and therefore rejoiced to see their prize, saying, 'Heaven has sent it to us;' so they treated it very kindly, and brought it up with such care that every one admired and loved it.

About thirteen years passed over their heads, when the king came by accident to the mill, and asked the miller if that was his son. 'No,' said he, 'I found him when a babe in a box in the mill-dam.' 'How long ago?' asked the king. 'Some thirteen years,' replied the miller. 'He is a fine fellow,' said the king, 'can you spare him to carry a letter to the queen? it will please me very much, and I will give him two pieces of gold for his trouble.' 'As your majesty pleases,' answered the miller.

Now the king had soon guessed that this was the child whom he had tried to drown; and he wrote a letter by him to the queen, saying, 'As soon as the bearer of this arrives let him be killed and immediately buried, so that all may be over before I return.'

The young man set out with this letter, but missed his way, and came in the evening to a dark wood. Through the gloom he perceived a light at a distance, towards which he directed his course, and found that it proceeded from a little cottage. There was no one within except an old woman, who was frightened at seeing him, and said, 'Why do you come hither, and whither are you going?' 'I am going to the queen, to whom I was to have delivered a letter; but I have lost my way, and shall be glad if you will give me a night's rest.' 'You are very unlucky,' said she, 'for this is a robbers' hut, and if the band returns while you are here it may be worse for you.' 'I am so tired, however, replied he, 'that I must take my chance, for I can go no farther;' so he laid the letter on the table, stretched himself out upon a bench, and fell asleep.

When the robbers came home and saw him, they asked the old woman who the strange lad was. 'I have given him shelter for charity,' said she; 'he had a letter to carry to the queen, and lost his way.' The robbers took up the letter, broke it open and read the directions which it contained to murder the bearer. Then their leader tore it, and wrote a fresh one desiring the queen, as soon as the young man arrived, to marry him to the king's daughter. Meantime they let him sleep on till morning broke, and then showed him the right way to the queen's palace; where, as soon as she had read the letter, she had all possible preparations made for the wedding; and as the young man was very beautiful, the princess took him willingly for her husband.

After a while the king returned; and when he saw the prediction fulfilled, and that this child of fortune was, notwithstanding all his cunning, married to his daughter, he inquired eagerly how this had happened, and what were the orders which he had given. 'Dear husband,' said the queen, 'here is your letter, read it for yourself.' The king took it, and seeing that an exchange had been made, asked his son-in-law what he had done with the letter which he had given him to carry. 'I know nothing of it,' answered he; 'it must have been taken away in the night while I slept.' Then the king was very wroth, and said, 'No man shall have my daughter who does not descend into the wonderful cave and bring me three golden hairs from the head of the giant king who reigns there; do this and you shall have my consent.' 'I will soon manage that,' said the youth; – so he took leave of his wife and set out on his journey.

At the first city that he came to, the guard of the gate stopt him, and asked what trade he followed and what he knew. 'I know every thing,' said he. 'If that be so,' replied they, 'you are just the man we want; be so good as to tell us why our fountain in the market-place is dry and will give no water; find out the cause of that, and we will give you two asses loaded with gold.' 'With all my heart,' said he, 'when I come back.'

Then he journeyed on and came to another city, and there the guard also asked him what trade he followed, and what he understood. 'I know every thing,' answered he. 'Then pray do us a piece of service,' said they, 'tell us why a tree which used to bear us golden apples, now does not even produce a leaf.' 'Most willingly,' answered he, 'as I come back.'

At last his way led him to the side of a great lake of water over which he must pass. The ferryman soon began to ask, as the others had done, what was his trade, and what he knew. 'Every thing,' said he. 'Then,' said the other, 'pray inform me why I am bound for ever to ferry over this water, and have never been able to get my liberty; I will reward you handsomely.' 'I will tell you all about it,' said the young man, 'as I come home.'

When he had passed the water, he came to the wonderful cave, which looked terribly black and gloomy. But the wizard king was not at home, and his grandmother sat at the door in her easy chair. 'What do you seek?' said she. 'Three golden hairs from the giant's head,' answered he. 'You run a great risk,' said she, 'when he returns home; yet I will try what I can do for you.' Then she changed him into an ant, and told him to hide himself in the folds of her cloak. 'Very well,' said he: 'but I want also to know why the city fountain is dry, why the tree that bore golden apples is now leafless, and what it is that binds the ferry-man to his post.' 'Those are three puzzling questions,' said the old dame; 'but lie quiet and listen to what the giant says when I pull the golden hairs.'

Presently night set in and the old gentleman returned home. As soon as he entered he began to snuff up the air, and cried, 'All is not right here: I smell man's flesh.' Then he searched all round in vain, and the old dame scolded, and said, 'Why should you turn every thing topsy-turvy? I have just set all in order.' Upon this he laid his head in her lap and soon fell asleep. As soon as he began to snore, she seized one of the golden hairs and pulled it out. 'Mercy!' cried he, starting up, 'what are you about?' 'I had a dream that disturbed me,' said she, 'and in my trouble I seized your hair: I dreamt that the fountain in the market-place of the city was become dry and would give no water; what can be the cause?' 'Ah! if they could find that out, they would be glad,' said the giant: 'under a stone in the fountain sits a toad; when they kill him, it will flow again.'

This said, he fell asleep, and the old lady pulled out another hair. 'What would you be at?' cried he in a rage. 'Don't be angry,' said she, 'I did it in my sleep; I dreamt that in a great kingdom there was a beautiful tree that used to bear golden apples, and now has not even a leaf upon it; what is the reason of that?' 'Aha!' said the giant, 'they would like very well to know that secret: at the root of the tree a mouse is gnawing; if they were to kill him, the tree would bear golden apples again; if not, it will soon die. Now let me sleep in peace; if you wake me again, you shall rue it.'

Then he fell once more asleep; and when she heard him snore she pulled out the third golden hair, and the giant jumped up and threatened her sorely; but she soothed him, and said, 'It was a strange dream: methought I saw a ferryman who was fated to ply backwards and forwards over a lake, and could never be set at liberty; what is the charm that binds him?' 'A silly fool!' said the giant; 'if he were to give the rudder into the hand of any passenger, he would find himself at liberty, and the other would be obliged to take his place. Now let me sleep.'

In the morning the giant arose and went out; and the old woman gave the young man the three golden hairs, reminded him of the answers to his three questions, and sent him on his way.

He soon came to the ferryman, who knew him again, and asked for the answer which he had promised him. 'Ferry me over first,' said he, 'and then I will tell you.' When the boat arrived on the other side, he told him to give the rudder to any of his passengers, and then he might run away as soon as he pleased. The next place he came to was the city where the barren tree stood: 'Kill the mouse,' said he, 'that gnaws the root, and you will have golden apples again.' They gave him a rich present, and he journeyed on to the city where the fountain had dried up, and the guard demanded his answer to their question. So he told them how to cure the mischief, and they thanked him and gave him the two asses laden with gold.

And now at last this child of fortune reached home, and

his wife rejoiced greatly to see him, and to hear how well everything had gone with him. He gave the three golden hairs to the king, who could no longer raise any objection to him, and when he saw all the treasure, cried out in a transport of joy, 'Dear son, where did you find all this gold?' 'By the side of a lake,' said the youth, 'where there is plenty more to be had.' 'Pray, tell me,' said the king, 'that I may go and get some too.' 'As much as you please,' replied the other; 'you will see the ferryman on the lake, let him carry you across, and there you will see gold as plentiful as sand upon the shore.'

Away went the greedy king; and when he came to the lake, he beckoned to the ferryman, who took him into his boat, and as soon as he was there gave the rudder into his hand, and sprung ashore, leaving the old king to ferry away as a reward for his sins.

'And is his majesty plying there to this day?' You may be sure of that, for nobody will trouble himself to take the rudder out of his hands.

THE FROG-PRINCE

ONE fine evening a young princess went into a wood, and sat down by the side of a cool spring of water. She had a golden ball in her hand, which was her favourite plaything, and she amused herself with tossing it into the air and catching it again as it fell. After a time she threw it up so high that when she stretched out her hand to catch it, the ball bounded away and rolled along upon the ground, till at last it fell into the spring. The princess looked into the spring after her ball; but it was very deep, so deep that she could not see the bottom of it. Then she began to lament her loss, and said, 'Alas! if I could only get my ball

again, I would give all my fine clothes and jewels, and
every thing that I have in the world.' Whilst she was speaking a frog put its head out of the water, and said, 'Princess,
why do you weep so bitterly?' 'Alas!' said she, 'what can
you do for me, you nasty frog? My golden ball has fallen
into the spring.' The frog said, 'I want not your pearls and
jewels and fine clothes; but if you will love me and let me
live with you, and eat from your little golden plate, and
sleep upon your little bed, I will bring you your ball again.'
'What nonsense,' thought the princess, 'this silly frog is
talking! He can never get out of the well: however, he may
be able to get my ball for me; and therefore I will promise
him what he asks.' So she said to the frog, 'Well, if you will
bring me my ball, I promise to do all you require.' Then
the frog put his head down, and dived deep under the
water; and after a little while he came up again with the
ball in his mouth, and threw it on the ground. As soon as
the young princess saw her ball, she ran to pick it up, and was
so overjoyed to have it in her hand again, that she never
thought of the frog, but ran home with it as fast as she could.
The frog called after her, 'Stay, princess, and take me with
you as you promised;' but she did not stop to hear a word.

The next day, just as the princess had sat down to dinner, she heard a strange noise, tap-tap, as if somebody was
coming up the marble staircase; and soon afterwards
something knocked gently at the door, and said,

'Open the door, my princess dear,
Open the door to thy true love here!
And mind the words that thou and I said
By the fountain cool in the greenwood shade.'

Then the princess ran to the door and opened it, and there
she saw the frog, whom she had quite forgotten; she was
terribly frightened, and shutting the door as fast as she
could, came back to her seat. The king her father asked her
what had frightened her. 'There is a nasty frog,' said she,

'at the door, who lifted my ball out of the spring this morning: I promised him that he should live with me here, thinking that he could never get out of the spring; but there he is at the door and wants to come in!' While she was speaking the frog knocked again at the door, and said,

'Open the door, my princess dear,
Open the door to thy true love here!
And mind the words that thou and I said
By the fountain cool in the greenwood shade.'

The king said to the young princess, 'As you have made a promise, you must keep it; so go and let him in.' She did so, and the frog hopped into the room, and came up close to the table. 'Pray lift me upon a chair,' said he to the princess, 'and let me sit next to you.' As soon as she had done this, the frog said, 'Put your plate closer to me that I may eat out of it.' This she did, and when he had eaten as much as he could, he said, 'Now I am tired; carry me up stairs and put me into your little bed.' And the princess took him up in her hand and put him upon the pillow of her own little bed, where he slept all night long. As soon as it was light he jumped up, hopped down stairs, and went out of the house. 'Now,' thought the princess, 'he is gone, and I shall be troubled with him no more.'

But she was mistaken; for when night came again, she heard the same tapping at the door, and when she opened it, the frog came in and slept upon her pillow as before till the morning broke: and the third night he did the same; but when the princess awoke on the following morning, she was astonished to see, instead of the frog, a handsome prince gazing on her with the most beautiful eyes that ever were seen, and standing at the head of her bed.

He told her that he had been enchanted by a malicious fairy, who had changed him into the form of a frog, in which he was fated to remain till some princess should take him out of the spring and let him sleep upon her bed for three nights. 'You,' said the prince, 'have broken this cruel charm, and now I have nothing to wish for but that you should go with me into my father's kingdom, where I will marry you, and love you as long as you live.'

The young princess, you may be sure, was not long in giving her consent; and as they spoke a splendid carriage drove up with eight beautiful horses decked with plumes of feathers and golden harness, and behind rode the prince's servant, the faithful Henry, who had bewailed the misfortune of his dear master so long and bitterly that his heart had well nigh burst. Then all set out full of joy for the Prince's kingdom; where they arrived safely, and lived happily a great many years.

THE FOX AND THE HORSE

A FARMER had a horse that had been an excellent faithful servant to him: but he was now grown too old to work; so the farmer would give him nothing more to eat, and said, 'I want you no longer, so take yourself off out of my stable; I shall not take you back again until you are stronger than a lion.' Then he opened the door and turned him adrift.

The poor horse was very melancholy, and wandered up and down in the wood, seeking some little shelter from the cold wind and rain. Presently a fox met him: 'What's the matter, my friend?' said he, 'why do you hang down your head and look so lonely and woe-begone?' 'Ah!' replied the horse, 'justice and avarice never dwell in one house; my master has forgotten all that I have done for him so many years, and because I can no longer work he has turned me adrift, and says unless I become stronger than a lion he will not take me back again; what chance can I have of that? he knows I have none, or he would not talk so.'

However, the fox bid him be of good cheer, and said, 'I will help you; lie down there, stretch yourself out quite stiff, and pretend to be dead.' The horse did as he was told, and the fox went straight to the lion who lived in a cave close by, and said to him, 'A little way off lies a dead horse; come with me and you may make an excellent meal of his carcase.' The lion was greatly pleased, and set off immediately; and when they came to the horse, the fox said, 'You will not be able to eat him comfortably here; I'll tell you what – I will tie you fast to his tail, and then you can draw him to your den, and eat him at your leisure.'

This advice pleased the lion, so he laid himself down quietly for the fox to make him fast to the horse. But the fox managed to tie his legs together and bound all so hard and fast that with all his strength he could not set himself free. When the work was done, the fox clapped the horse on the shoulder, and said, 'Jip! Dobbin! Jip!' Then up he sprang, and moved off, dragging the lion behind him. The beast began to roar and bellow, till all the birds of the wood flew away for fright; but the horse let him sing on, and made his way quietly over the fields to his master's house.

'Here he is, master,' said he, 'I have got the better of him:' and when the farmer saw his old servant, his heart relented, and he said, 'Thou shalt stay in thy stable and be well taken care of.' And so the poor old horse had plenty to eat, and lived – till he died.

RUMPEL-STILTS-KIN

In a certain kingdom once lived a poor miller who had a very beautiful daughter. She was moreover exceedingly shrewd and clever; and the miller was so vain and proud of her, that he one day told the king of the land that his

daughter could spin gold out of straw. Now this king was
very fond of money; and when he heard the miller's boast,
his avarice was excited, and he ordered the girl to be
brought before him. Then he led her to a chamber where
there was a great quantity of straw, gave her a spinning-
wheel, and said, 'All this must be spun into gold before
morning, as you value your life.' It was in vain that the
poor maiden declared that she could do no such thing, the
chamber was locked and she remained alone.

She sat down in one corner of the room and began to lament over her hard fate, when on a sudden the door opened,
and a droll-looking little man hobbled in, and said, 'Good
morrow to you, my good lass, what are you weeping for?'
'Alas!' answered she, 'I must spin this straw into gold, and
I know not how.' 'What will you give me,' said the little
man, 'to do it for you?' 'My necklace,' replied the maiden.
He took her at her word, and sat himself down to the
wheel; round about it went merrily, and presently the work
was done and the gold all spun.

When the king came and saw this, he was greatly astonished and pleased; but his heart grew still more greedy of
gain, and he shut up the poor miller's daughter again with a
fresh task. Then she knew not what to do, and sat down
once more to weep; but the little man presently opened the
door, and said, 'What will you give me to do your task?'
'The ring on my finger,' replied she. So her little friend took
the ring, and began to work at the wheel, till by the
morning all was finished again.

The king was vastly delighted to see all this glittering
treasure; but still he was not satisfied, and took the miller's
daughter into a yet larger room, and said, 'All this must be
spun to-night; and if you succeed, you shall be my queen.'
As soon as she was alone the dwarf came in, and said,
'What will you give me to spin gold for you this third
time?' 'I have nothing left,' said he. 'Then promise me,'

said the little man, 'your first little child when you are
queen.' 'That may never be,' thought the miller's daughter; and as she knew no other way to get her task done, she
promised him what he asked, and he spun once more the
whole heap of gold. The king came in the morning, and
finding all he wanted, married her, and so the miller's
daughter really became queen.

At the birth of her first little child the queen rejoiced
very much, and forgot the little man and her promise: but
one day he came into her chamber and reminded her of it.
Then she grieved sorely at her misfortune, and offered him

all the treasures of the kingdom in exchange; but in vain, till at last her tears softened him, and he said, 'I will give you three days' grace, and if during that time you tell me my name, you shall keep your child.'

Now the queen lay awake all night, thinking of all the odd names that she had ever heard, and dispatched messengers all over the land to inquire after new ones. The next day the little man came, and she began with Timothy, Benjamin, Jeremiah, and all the names she could remember; but to all of them he said, 'That's not my name.'

The second day she began with all the comical names she could hear of, Bandy-legs, Hunch-back, Crook-shanks, and so on, but the little gentleman still said to every one of them, 'That's not my name.'

The third day came back one of the messengers, and said, 'I can hear of no one other name; but yesterday, as I was climbing a high hill among the trees of the forest where the fox and the hare bid each other good night, I saw a little hut, and before the hut burnt a fire, and round about the fire danced a funny little man upon one leg, and sung

'Merrily the feast I'll make,
To-day I'll brew, to-morrow bake;
Merrily I'll dance and sing,
For next day will a stranger bring:
Little does my lady dream
Rumpel-Stilts-Kin is my name!'

When the queen heard this, she jumped for joy, and as soon as her little visitor came, and said, 'Now, lady, what is my name?' 'Is it John?' asked she. 'No!' 'Is it Tom?' 'No!'

'Can your name be Rumpel-stilts-kin?'

'Some witch told you that! Some witch told you that!' cried the little man, and dashed his right foot in a rage so deep into the floor, that he was forced to lay hold of it with both hands to pull it out. Then he made the best of his way

off, while every body laughed at him for having had all his
trouble for nothing.

THE GOOSE-GIRL

An old queen, whose husband had been dead some years,
had a beautiful daughter. When she grew up, she was betrothed to a prince who lived a great way off; and as the
time drew near for her to be married, she got ready to set
off on her journey to his country. Then the queen her
mother packed up a great many costly things; jewels, and
gold, and silver; trinkets, fine dresses, and in short every
thing that became a royal bride; for she loved her child
very dearly: and she gave her a waiting-maid to ride with
her, and gave her into the bridegroom's hands; and each
had a horse for the journey. Now the princess's horse was
called Falada, and could speak.

When the time came for them to set out, the old queen
went into her bed-chamber, and took a little knife, and cut
off a lock of her hair, and gave it to her daughter, and said,
'Take care of it, dear child; for it is a charm that may be of
use to you on the road.' Then they took a sorrowful leave of
each other, and the princess put the lock of her mother's
hair into her bosom, got upon her horse, and set off on her
journey to her bridegroom's kingdom. One day, as they
were riding along by the side of a brook, the princess began
to feel very thirsty, and said to her maid, 'Pray get down
and fetch me some water in my golden cup out of yonder
brook, for I want to drink.' 'Nay,' said the maid, 'if you
are thirsty, get down yourself, and lie down by the water
and drink; I shall not be your waiting-maid any longer.'
Then she was so thirsty that she got down, and knelt over
the little brook, and drank, for she was frightened, and

dared not bring out her golden cup; and then she wept, and said, 'Alas! what will become of me?' And the lock of hair answered her, and said,

> 'Alas! alas! if thy mother knew it,
> Sadly, sadly her heart would rue it.'

But the princess was very humble and meek, so she said nothing to her maid's ill behaviour, but got upon her horse again.

Then all rode farther on their journey, till the day grew so warm, and the sun so scorching, that the bride began to feel very thirsty again; and at last when they came to a river she forgot her maid's rude speech, and said, 'Pray get down and fetch me some water to drink in my golden cup.' But the maid answered her, and even spoke more haughtily than before, 'Drink if you will, but I shall not be your waiting-maid.' Then the princess was so thirsty that she got off her horse, and lay down, and held her head over the running stream, and cried, and said, 'What will become of me?' And the lock of hair answered her again,

> 'Alas! alas! if thy mother knew it,
> Sadly, sadly her heart would rue it.'

And as she leaned down to drink, the lock of hair fell from her bosom, and floated away with the water, without her seeing it, she was so frightened. But her maid saw it, and was very glad, for she knew the charm, and saw that the poor bride would be in her power, now that she had lost the hair. So when the bride had done, and would have got upon Falada again, the maid said, 'I shall ride upon Falada, and you may have my horse instead:' so she was forced to give up her horse, and soon afterwards to take off her royal clothes, and put on her maid's shabby ones.

At last, as they drew near the end of their journey, this treacherous servant threatened to kill her mistress if she ever told any one what had happened. But Falada saw it all, and marked it well. Then the waiting-maid got upon Falada, and the real bride was set upon the other horse, and they went on in this way till at last they came to the royal court. There was great joy at their coming, and the prince flew to meet them, and lifted the maid from her horse, thinking she was the one who was to be his wife; and she was led up stairs to the royal chamber, but the true princess was told to stay in the court below.

But the old king happened to be looking out of the window, and saw her in the yard below; and as she looked very pretty, and too delicate for a waiting-maid, he went into the royal chamber to ask the bride who it was she had brought with her, that was thus left standing in the court below. 'I brought her with me for the sake of her company on the road,' said she; 'pray give the girl some work to do, that she may not be idle.' The old king could not for some time think of any work for her to do; but at last he said, 'I have a lad who takes care of my geese; she may go and help him.' Now the name of this lad, that the real bride was to help in watching the king's geese, was Curdken.

Soon after, the false bride said to the prince, 'Dear husband, pray do me one piece of kindness.' 'That I will,' said the prince. 'Then tell one of your slaughterers to cut off the head of the horse I rode upon, for it was very unruly, and plagued me sadly on the road:' but the truth was, she was very much afraid lest Falada should speak, and tell all she had done to the princess. She carried her point, and the faithful Falada was killed: but when the true princess heard of it, she wept, and begged the man to nail up Falada's head against a large dark gate of the city, through which she had to pass every morning and evening, that there she might still see him sometimes. Then the slaughterer said he would do as she wished; and cut off the head, and nailed it fast under the dark gate.

Early the next morning, as she and Curdken went out through the gate, she said sorrowfully,

'Falada, Falada, there thou art hanging!'

and the head answered,

'Bride, bride, there thou art ganging!
Alas! alas! if thy mother knew it,
Sadly, sadly her heart would rue it.'

Then they went out of the city, and drove the geese on. And when she came to the meadow, she sat down upon a bank there, and let down her waving locks of hair, which were all of pure silver; and when Curdken saw it glitter in the sun, he ran up, and would have pulled some of the locks out; but she cried,

'Blow, breezes, blow!
Let Curdken's hat go!
Blow, breezes, blow!
Let him after it go!
O'er hills, dales, and rocks,
Away be it whirl'd,
Till the silvery locks
Are all comb'd and curl'd!'

Then there came a wind, so strong that it blew off Curdken's hat; and away it flew over the hills, and he after it; till, by the time he came back, she had done combing and curling her hair, and put it up again safe. Then he was very angry and sulky, and would not speak to her at all; but they watched the geese until it grew dark in the evening, and then drove them homewards.

The next morning, as they were going through the dark gate, the poor girl looked up at Falada's head, and cried,

'Falada, Falada, there thou art hanging!'

and it answered,

'Bride, bride, there thou art ganging!
Alas! alas! if thy mother knew it,
Sadly, sadly her heart would rue it.'

Then she drove on the geese, and sat down again in the meadow, and began to comb out her hair as before; and Curdken ran up to her, and wanted to take hold of it; but she cried out quickly,

> 'Blow, breezes, blow!
> Let Curdken's hat go!
> Blow, breezes, blow!
> Let him after it go!
> O'er hills, dales, and rocks,
> Away be it whirl'd,
> Till the silvery locks
> Are all comb'd and curl'd!'

Then the wind came and blew his hat, and off it flew a great way, over the hills and far away, so that he had to run after it; and when he came back, she had done up her hair again, and all was safe. So they watched the geese till it grew dark.

In the evening, after they came home, Curdken went to the old king, and said, 'I cannot have that strange girl to help me to keep the geese any longer.' 'Why?' said the king. 'Because she does nothing but tease me all day long.' Then the king made him tell him all that had passed. And Curdken said, 'When we go in the morning through the dark gate with our flock of geese, she weeps, and talks with the head of a horse that hangs upon the wall, and says,

> "Falada, Falada, there thou art hanging!"

and the head answers,

> "Bride, bride, there thou art ganging!
> Alas! alas! if thy mother knew it,
> Sadly, sadly her heart would rue it."'

And Curdken went on telling the king what had happened upon the meadow where the geese fed; and how his hat was blown away, and he was forced to run after it, and leave his flock. But the old king told him to go out again

as usual the next day; and when morning came, he placed
himself behind the dark gate, and heard how she spoke to
Falada, and how Falada answered; and then he went into
the field, and hid himself in a bush by the meadow's side,
and soon saw with his own eyes how they drove the flock of
geese, and how, after a little time, she let down her hair
that glittered in the sun; and then he heard her say,

> 'Blow, breezes, blow!
> Let Curdken's hat go!
> Blow, breezes, blow!
> Let him after it go!

O'er hills, dales, and rocks,
Away be it whirl'd,
Till the silver locks
Are all comb'd and curl'd!'

And soon came a gale of wind, and carried away Curdken's hat, while the girl went on combing and curling her hair. All this the old king saw: so he went home without being seen; and when the little goose-girl came back in the evening, he called her aside, and asked her why she did so; but she burst into tears, and said, 'That I must not tell you or any man, or I shall lose my life.'

But the old king begged so hard, that she had no peace till she had told him all, word for word: and it was very lucky for her that she did so, for the king ordered royal clothes to be put upon her, and gazed on her with wonder she was so beautiful. Then he called his son, and told him that he had only the false bride, for that she was merely a waiting-maid, while the true one stood by. And the young king rejoiced when he saw her beauty, and heard how meek and patient she had been; and, without saying any thing, ordered a great feast to be got ready for all his court. The bridegroom sat at the top, with the false princess on one side, and the true one on the other; but nobody knew her, for she was quite dazzling to their eyes, and was not at all like the little goose-girl, now that she had her brilliant dress.

When they had eaten and drank, and were very merry, the old king told all the story, as one that he had once heard of, and asked the true waiting-maid what she thought ought to be done to any one who would behave thus. 'Nothing better,' said this false bride, 'than that she should be thrown into a cask stuck round with sharp nails, and that two white horses should be put to it, and should drag it from street to street till she is dead.' 'Thou art she!' said the old king, 'and since thou hast judged thyself, it shall be so done to thee.' And the young king was married to his true wife, and they reigned over the kingdom in peace and happiness all their lives.

———————

FAITHFUL JOHN

An old king fell sick; and when he found his end drawing near, he said, 'Let Faithful John come to me.' Now Faithful John was the servant that he was fondest of, and was so called because he had been true to his master all his life long. Then when he came to the bed-side, the king said, 'My faithful John, I feel that my end draws nigh, and I have now no cares save for my son, who is still young, and stands in need of good counsel. I have no friend to leave him but you; if you do not pledge yourself to teach him all he should know, and to be a father to him, I shall not shut my eyes in peace.' Then John said, 'I will never leave him, but will serve him faithfully, even though it should cost me my life.' And the king said, 'I shall now die in peace: after my death, show him the whole palace; all the rooms and vaults, and all the treasures and stores which lie there: but take care how you show him one room, – I mean the one where hangs the picture of the daughter of the king of the golden roof. If he sees it, he will fall deeply in love with her, and will then be plunged into great dangers on her account: guard him in this peril.' And when Faithful John had once more pledged his word to the old king, he laid his head on his pillow, and died in peace.

Now when the old king had been carried to his grave, Faithful John told the young king what had passed upon his death-bed, and said, 'I will keep my word truly, and be faithful to you as I was always to your father, though it should cost me my life.' And the young king wept, and said, 'Neither will I ever forget your faithfulness.'

The days of mourning passed away, and then Faithful John said to his master, 'It is now time that you should see your heritage; I will show you your father's palace.' Then he led him about every where, up and down, and let him see all the riches and all the costly rooms; only one room, where the picture stood, he did not open. Now the picture was so placed, that the moment the door opened, you could see it; and it was so beautifully done, that one would think it breathed and had life, and that there was nothing more lovely in the whole world. When the young king saw that Faithful John always went by this door, he said, 'Why do you not open that room?' 'There is something inside,' he answered, 'which would frighten you.' But the king said, 'I have seen the whole palace, and I must also know what is in there;' and he went and began to force open the door: but Faithful John held him back, and said, 'I gave my word to your father before his death, that I would take heed how I showed you what stands in that room, lest it should lead you and me into great trouble.' 'The greatest trouble to me,' said the young king, 'will be not to go in and see the room; I shall have no peace by day or by night until I do; so I shall not go hence until you open it.'

Then Faithful John saw that with all he could do or say the young king would have his way; so, with a heavy heart and many foreboding sighs, he sought for the key out of his great bunch; and he opened the door of the room, and entered in first, so as to stand between the king and the picture, hoping he might not see it: but he raised himself upon tiptoes, and looked over John's shoulders; and as soon as he saw the likeness of the lady, so beautiful and shining with gold, he fell down upon the floor senseless. Then Faithful John lifted him up in his arms, and carried him to his bed, and was full of care, and thought to himself, 'This trouble has come upon us; O Heaven! what will come of it?'

At last the king came to himself again; but the first thing that he said was, 'Whose is that beautiful picture?' 'It is the picture of the daughter of the king of the golden roof,' said Faithful John. But the king went on, saying, 'My love towards her is so great, that if all the leaves on the trees were tongues, they could not speak it; I care not to risk my life to win her; you are my faithful friend, you must aid me.'

Then John thought for a long time what was now to be done; and at length said to the king, 'All that she has about her is of gold: the tables, stools, cups, dishes, and all the things in her house are of gold; and she is always seeking new treasures. Now in your stores there is much gold; let it be worked up into every kind of vessel, and into all sorts of birds, wild beasts, and wonderful animals; then we will take it, and try our fortune.' So the king ordered all the goldsmiths to be sought for; and they worked day and night, until at last the most beautiful things were made: and Faithful John had a ship loaded with them, and put on a merchant's dress, and the king did the same, that they might not be known.

When all was ready, they put out to sea, and sailed till they came to the coast of the land where the king of the golden roof reigned. Faithful John told the king to stay in the ship, and wait for him; 'for perhaps,' said he, 'I may be able to bring away the king's daughter with me: therefore take care that every thing be in order; let the golden vessels and ornaments be brought forth, and the whole ship be decked out with them.' And he chose out something of each of the golden things to put into his basket, and got ashore, and went towards the king's palace. And when he came to the castle yard, there stood by the well side a beautiful maiden, who had two golden pails in her hand, drawing water. And as she drew up the water, which was glittering with gold, she turned herself round, and saw the stranger,

and asked him who he was. Then he drew near, and said, 'I
am a merchant,' and opened his basket, and let her look
into it; and she cried out, 'Oh! what beautiful things!' and
set down her pails, and looked at one after the other. Then
she said, 'The king's daughter must see all these; she is so
fond of such things, that she will buy all of you.' So she
took him by the hand, and led him in; for she was one of
the waiting-maids of the daughter of the king.

When the princess saw the wares, she was greatly
pleased, and said, 'They are so beautiful that I will buy
them all.' But Faithful John said, 'I am only the servant of
a rich merchant; what I have here is nothing to what he
has lying in yonder ship: there he has the finest and most
costly things that ever were made in gold.' The princess
wanted to have them all brought ashore; but he said, 'That
would take up many days, there are such a number; and
more rooms would be wanted to place them in than there
are in the greatest house.' But her wish to see them grew
still greater, and at last she said, 'Take me to the ship, I
will go myself, and look at your master's wares.'

Then Faithful John led her joyfully to the ship, and the
king, when he saw her, thought that his heart would leap
out of his breast; and it was with the greatest trouble that
he kept himself still. So she got into the ship, and the king
led her down; but Faithful John stayed behind with the
steersman, and ordered the ship to put off: 'Spread all your
sail,' cried he, 'that she may fly over the waves like a bird
through the air.'

And the king showed the princess the golden wares, each
one singly; the dishes, cups, basins, and the wild and wonderful beasts; so that many hours flew away, and she
looked at every thing with delight, and was not aware that
the ship was sailing away. And after she had looked at the
last, she thanked the merchant, and said she would go
home; but when she came upon the deck, she saw that the

ship was sailing far away from land upon the deep sea, and that it flew along at full sail. 'Alas!' she cried out in her fright, 'I am betrayed; I am carried off, and have fallen into the power of a roving trader; I would sooner have died.' But then the king took her by the hand, and said, 'I am not a merchant, I am a king, and of as noble birth as you. I have taken you away by stealth, but I did so because of the very great love I have for you; for the first time that I saw your face, I fell on the ground in a swoon.' When the daughter of the king of the golden roof heard all, she was comforted, and her heart soon turned towards him, and she was willing to become his wife.

But it so happened, that whilst they were sailing on the deep sea, Faithful John, as he sat on the prow of the ship playing on his flute, saw three ravens flying in the air towards him. Then he left off playing, and listened to what they said to each other, for he understood their tongue. The first said, 'There he goes! he is bearing away the daughter of the king of the golden roof; let him go!' 'Nay,' said the second, 'there he goes, but he has not got her yet.' And the third said, 'There he goes; he surely has her, for she is sitting by his side in the ship.' Then the first began again, and cried out, 'What boots it to him? See you not that when they come to land, a horse of a foxy-red colour will spring towards him; and then he will try to get upon it, and if he does, it will spring away with him into the air, so that he will never see his love again.' 'True! true!' said the second, 'but is there no help?' 'Oh! yes, yes!' said the first; 'if he who sits upon the horse takes the dagger which is stuck in the saddle and strikes him dead, the young king is saved: but who knows that? and who will tell him, that he who thus saves the king's life will turn to stone from the toes of his feet to his knee?' Then the second said, 'True! true! but I know more still; though the horse be dead, the king loses his bride: when they go together into the palace, there lies the bridal dress on the couch, and looks as if it were woven of gold and silver, but it is all brimstone and pitch; and if he puts it on, it will burn him, marrow and bones.' 'Alas! alas! is there no help?' said the third. 'Oh! yes, yes!' said the second, 'if some one draws near and throws it into the fire, the young king will be saved. But what boots that? who knows and will tell him, that, if he does, his body from the knee to the heart will be turned to stone?' 'More! more! I know more,' said the third: 'were the dress burnt, still the king loses his bride. After the wedding, when the dance begins, and the young queen dances on, she will turn pale, and fall as though she were dead; and if some one does not draw near and lift her up, and take from her right breast three drops of blood, she will surely die. But if any one knew this, he would tell him, that if he does do so, his body will turn to stone, from the crown of his head to the tip of his toe.'

Then the ravens flapped their wings, and flew on; but Faithful John, who had understood it all, from that time was sorrowful, and did not tell his master what he had heard; for he saw that if he told him, he must himself lay down his life to save him: at last he said to himself, 'I will be faithful to my word, and save my master, if it costs me my life.'

Now when they came to land, it happened just as the ravens had foretold; for there sprang out a fine foxy-red horse. 'See,' said the king, 'he shall bear me to my palace:' and he tried to mount, but Faithful John leaped before him, and swung himself quickly upon it, drew the dagger, and smote the horse dead. Then the other servants of the king, who were jealous of Faithful John, cried out, 'What a shame to kill the fine beast that was to take the king to his palace!' But the king said, 'Let him alone, it is my Faithful John; who knows but he did it for some good end?'

Then they went on to the castle, and there stood a couch in one room, and a fine dress lay upon it, that shone with gold and silver; and the young king went up to it to take hold of it, but Faithful John cast it in the fire, and burnt it. And the other servants began again to grumble, and said, 'See, now he is burning the wedding dress.' But the king said, 'Who knows what he does it for? let him alone! he is my faithful servant John.'

Then the wedding feast was held, and the dance began, and the bride came in; but Faithful John took good heed, and looked in her face; and on a sudden she turned pale, and fell as though she were dead upon the ground. But he sprung towards her quickly, lifted her up, and took her and laid her upon a couch, and drew three drops of blood from her right breast. And she breathed again, and came to herself. But the young king had seen all, and did not know why Faithful John had done it; so he was angry at his boldness, and said, 'Throw him into prison.'

The next morning Faithful John was led forth, and stood upon the gallows, and said, 'May I speak out before I die?' and when the king answered, 'It shall be granted thee,' he said, 'I am wrongly judged, for I have always been faithful and true:' and then he told what he had heard the ravens say upon the sea, and how he meant to save his master, and had therefore done all these things.

When he had told all, the king called out, 'O my most faithful John! pardon! pardon! take him down!' But Faithful John had fallen down lifeless at the last word he spoke, and lay as a stone: and the king and the queen mourned over him; and the king said, 'Oh, how ill have I rewarded thy truth!' And he ordered the stone figure to be taken up, and placed in his own room near to his bed; and as often as he looked at it he wept, and said, 'O that I could bring thee back to life again, my Faithful John!'

After a time, the queen had two little sons, who grew up,

and were her great joy. One day, when she was at church, the two children stayed with their father; and as they played about, he looked at the stone figure, and sighed, and cried out, 'Oh that I could bring thee back to life, my Faithful John!' Then the stone began to speak, and said, 'O king! thou canst bring me back to life if thou wilt give up for my sake what is dearest to thee.' But the king said, 'All that I have in the world would I give up for thee.' 'Then,' said the stone, 'cut off the heads of thy children, sprinkle their blood over me, and I shall live again.' Then the king was greatly shocked: but he thought how Faithful John had died for his sake, and because of his great truth towards him; and rose up and drew his sword to cut off his children's heads and sprinkle the stone with their blood; but the moment he drew his sword Faithful John was alive again, and stood before his face, and said, 'Your truth is rewarded.' And the children sprang about and played as if nothing had happened.

Then the king was full of joy: and when he saw the queen coming, to try her, he put Faithful John and the two children in a large closet; and when she came in he said to her, 'Have you been at church?' 'Yes,' said she, 'but I could not help thinking of Faithful John, who was so true to us.' 'Dear wife,' said the king, 'we can bring him back to life again, but it will cost us both our little sons, and we must give them up for his sake.' When the queen heard this, she turned pale and was frightened in her heart; but she said, 'Let it be so; we owe him all, for his great faith and truth.' Then he rejoiced because she thought as he had thought, and went in and opened the closet, and brought out the children and Faithful John, and said, 'Heaven be praised! he is ours again, and we have our sons safe too.' So he told her the whole story; and all lived happily together the rest of their lives.

THE BLUE LIGHT

A SOLDIER had served a king his master many years, till at last he was turned off without pay or reward. How he should get his living he did not know: so he set out and journeyed homeward all day in a very downcast mood, until in the evening he came to the edge of a deep wood. The road leading that way, he pushed forward, but had not gone far before he saw a light glimmering through the trees, towards which he bent his weary steps; and soon came to a hut where no one lived but an old witch. The poor fellow begged for a night's lodging and something to eat and drink; but she would listen to nothing: however, he was not easily got rid of; and at last she said, 'I think I will take pity on you this once; but if I do, you must dig over all my garden for me in the morning.' The soldier agreed very willingly to any thing she asked, and he became her guest.

The next day he kept his word and dug the garden very neatly. The job lasted all day; and in the evening, when his mistress would have sent him away, he said, 'I am so tired with my work that I must beg you to let me stay over the night.' The old lady vowed at first she would not do any such thing; but after a great deal of talk he carried his point, agreeing to chop up a whole cart-load of wood for her the next day.

This task too was duly ended; but not till towards night; and then he found himself so tired, that he begged a third night's rest: and this too was given, but only on his pledging his word that he next day would fetch the witch the blue light that burnt at the bottom of the well.

When morning came she led him to the well's mouth, tied him to a long rope, and let him down. At the bottom sure enough he found the blue light as the witch had said, and at once made the signal for her to draw him up again.

But when she had pulled him up so near to the top that she could reach him with her hands, she said, 'Give me the light, I will take care of it,' – meaning to play him a trick, by taking it for herself and letting him fall again to the bottom of the well. But the soldier saw through her wicked thoughts, and said, 'No, I shall not give you the light till I find myself safe and sound out of the well.' At this she became very angry, and dashed him, with the light she had longed for many a year, down to the bottom. And there lay the poor soldier for a while in despair, on the damp mud below, and feared that his end was nigh. But his pipe happened to be in his pocket still half full, and he thought to himself, 'I may as well make an end of smoking you out; it is the last pleasure I shall have in this world.' So he lit at the blue light, and began to smoke.

Up rose a cloud of smoke, and on a sudden a little black dwarf was seen making his way through the midst of it, 'What do you want with me, soldier?' said he. 'I have no business with you,' answered he. But the dwarf said, 'I am bound to serve you in every thing, as lord and master of the blue light.' 'Then first of all be so good as to help me out of this well.' No sooner said than done: the dwarf took him by the hand and drew him up, and the blue light of course with him. 'Now do me another piece of kindness,' said the soldier: 'pray let that old lady take my place in the well.' When the dwarf had done this, and lodged the witch safely at the bottom, they began to ransack her treasures; and the soldier made bold to carry off as much of her gold and silver as he well could. Then the dwarf said, 'If you should chance at any time to want me, you have nothing to do but to light your pipe at the blue light, and I will soon be with you.'

The soldier was not a little pleased at his good luck, and went to the best inn in the first town he came to, and ordered some fine clothes to be made, and a handsome room

to be got ready for him. When all was ready, he called his little man to him, and said, 'The king sent me away penniless, and left me to hunger and want: I have a mind to show him that it is my turn to be master now; so bring me his daughter here this evening, that she may wait upon me, and do what I bid her.' 'That is rather a dangerous task,' said the dwarf. But away he went, took the princess out of her bed, fast asleep as she was, and brought her to the soldier.

Very early in the morning he carried her back: and as soon as she saw her father, she said, 'I had a strange dream last night: I thought I was carried away through the air to a soldier's house, and there I waited upon him as his servant.' Then the king wondered greatly at such a story; but told her to make a hole in her pocket and fill it with peas, so that if it were really as she said, and the whole was not a dream, the peas might fall out in the streets as she passed through, and leave a clue to tell whither she had been taken. She did so; but the dwarf had heard the king's plot; and when evening came, and the soldier said he must bring him the princess again, he strewed peas over several of the streets, so that the few that fell from her pocket were not known from the others; and the people amused themselves all the next day picking up peas, and wondering where so many came from.

When the princess told her father what had happened to her the second time, he said, 'Take one of your shoes with you, and hide it in the room you are taken to.' The dwarf heard this also; and when the soldier told him to bring the king's daughter again, he said, 'I cannot save you this time; it will be an unlucky thing for you if you are found out – as I think you will.' But the soldier would have his own way. 'Then you must take care and make the best of your way out of the city gate very early in the morning,' said the dwarf. The princess kept one shoe on as her father bid her, and hid it in the soldier's room: and when she got back to her father, he ordered it to be sought for all over the town; and at last it was found where she had hid it. The soldier had run away, it is true; but he had been too slow, and was soon caught and thrown into a strong prison, and loaded with chains: – what was worse, in the hurry of his flight, he had left behind him his great treasure the blue

light and all his gold, and had nothing left in his pocket but
one poor ducat.

As he was standing very sorrowful at the prison grating,
he saw one of his comrades, and calling out to him said, 'If
you will bring me a little bundle I left in the inn, I will give
you a ducat.' His comrade thought this very good pay for
such a job: so he went away, and soon came back bringing
the blue light and the gold. Then the prisoner soon lit his
pipe: up rose the smoke, and with it came his old friend the
little dwarf. 'Do not fear, master,' said he: 'keep up your
heart at your trial, and leave everything to take its course;
– only mind to take the blue light with you.' The trial soon
came on; the matter was sifted to the bottom; the prisoner
found guilty, and his doom passed: – he was ordered to be
hung forthwith on the gallows-tree.

But as he was led out, he said he had one favour to beg of
the king. 'What is it?' said his majesty. 'That you will
deign to let me smoke one pipe on the road.' 'Two, if you
like,' said the king. Then he lit his pipe at the blue light,
and the black dwarf was before him in a moment. 'Be so
good as to kill, slay, or put to flight all these people,' said
the soldier: 'and as for the king, you may cut him into
three pieces.' Then the dwarf began to lay about him, and
soon got rid of the crowd around: but the king begged hard
for mercy; and, to save his life, agreed to let the soldier
have the princess for his wife, and to leave the kingdom to
him when he died.

ASHPUTTEL

THE wife of a rich man fell sick: and when she felt that her
end drew nigh, she called her only daughter to her bed-
side, and said, 'Always be a good girl, and I will look

down from heaven and watch over you.' Soon afterwards she shut her eyes and died, and was buried in the garden; and the little girl went every day to her grave and wept, and was always good and kind to all about her. And the snow spread a beautiful white covering over the grave; but by the time the sun had melted it away again, her father had married another wife. This new wife had two daughters of her own, that she brought home with her: they were fair in face, but foul at heart, and it was now a sorry time for the poor little girl. 'What does the good-for-nothing thing want in the parlour?' said they; 'they who would eat bread should first earn it; away with the kitchen maid!' Then they took away her fine clothes, and gave her an old grey frock to put on, and laughed at her and turned her into the kitchen.

There she was forced to do hard work; to rise early before day-light, to bring the water, to make the fire, to cook and to wash. Besides that, the sisters plagued her in all sorts of ways and laughed at her. In the evening when she was tired she had no bed to lie down on, but was made to lie by the hearth among the ashes; and then, as she was of course always dusty and dirty, they called her Ashputtel.

It happened once that the father was going to the fair, and asked his wife's daughters what he should bring them. 'Fine clothes,' said the first: 'Pearls and diamonds,' cried the second. 'Now, child,' said he to his own daughter, 'what will you have?' 'The first sprig, dear father, that rubs against your hat on your way home,' said she. Then he bought for the two first the fine clothes and pearls and diamonds they had asked for: and on his way home as he rode through a green copse, a sprig of hazel brushed against him, and almost pushed off his hat: so he broke it off and brought it away; and when he got home he gave it to his daughter. Then she took it and went to her mother's grave and planted it there, and cried so much that it was watered

with her tears; and there it grew and became a fine tree.
Three times every day she went to it and wept; and soon a
little bird came and built its nest upon the tree, and talked
with her, and watched over her, and brought her whatever
she wished for.

Now it happened that the king of the land held a feast
which was to last three days, and out of those who came to
it his son was to choose a bride for himself: and Ashputtel's
two sisters were asked to come. So they called her up, and
said, 'Now, comb our hair, brush our shoes, and tie our
sashes for us, for we are going to dance at the king's feast.'
Then she did as she was told, but when all was done she
could not help crying, for she thought to herself, she should
have liked to go to the dance too; and at last she begged
her mother very hard to let her go. 'You! Ashputtel?'said
she; 'you who have nothing to wear, no clothes at all, and
who cannot even dance – you want to go to the ball?' And
when she kept on begging, – to get rid of her, she said at
last, 'I will throw this basin-full of peas into the ash heap,
and if you have picked them all out in two hours' time you
shall go to the feast too.' Then she threw the peas into the
ashes: but the little maiden ran out at the back door into
the garden, and cried out –

> 'Hither, hither, through the sky,
> Turtle-doves and linnets, fly!
> Blackbird, thrush, and chaffinch gay,
> Hither, hither, haste away!
> One and all, come help me quick,
> Haste ye, haste ye, – pick, pick, pick!'

Then first came two white doves flying in at the kitchen
window; and next came two turtle-doves; and after them
all the little birds under heaven came chirping and fluttering in, and flew down into the ashes: and the little doves
stooped their heads down and set to work, pick, pick, pick;
and then the others began to pick, pick, pick; and picked

out all the good grain and put it in a dish, and left the
ashes. At the end of one hour the work was done, and all
flew out again at the windows. Then she brought the dish to
her mother, overjoyed at the thought that now she should
go to the wedding. But she said, 'No, no! you slut, you
have no clothes and cannot dance, you shall not go.' And
when Ashputtel begged very hard to go, she said, 'If you
can in one hour's time pick two of those dishes of peas out
of the ashes, you shall go too.' And thus she thought she
should at last get rid of her. So she shook two dishes of peas
into the ashes; but the little maiden went out into the garden at the back of the house, and cried out as before –

> 'Hither, hither, through the sky,
> Turtle-doves and linnets, fly!
> Blackbird, thrush, and chaffinch gay,
> Hither, hither, haste away!
> One and all, come help me quick,
> Haste ye, haste ye, – pick, pick pick!'

Then first came two white doves in at the kitchen window; and next came the turtle-doves; and after them all
the little birds under heaven came chirping and hopping
about, and flew down about the ashes: and the little doves
put their heads down and set to work, pick, pick, pick; and
then the others began pick, pick, pick; and they put all the
good grain into the dishes, and left all the ashes. Before
half an hour's time all was done, and out they flew again.
And then Ashputtel took the dishes to her mother, rejoicing
to think that she should now go to the ball. But her
mother said, 'It is all of no use, you cannot go; you have no
clothes, and cannot dance, and you would only put us to
shame:' and off she went with her two daughters to the
feast.

Now when all were gone, and nobody left at home, Ashputtel went sorrowfully and sat down under the hazel-tree,
and cried out –

'Shake, shake, hazel-tree,
Gold and silver over me!'

Then her friend the bird flew out of the tree and brought a gold and silver dress for her, and slippers of spangled silk: and she put them on, and followed her sisters to the feast. But they did not know her, and thought it must be some strange princess, she looked so fine and beautiful in her rich clothes: and they never once thought of Ashputtel, but took for granted that she was safe at home in the dirt.

The king's son soon came up to her, and took her by the hand and danced with her and no one else: and he never left her hand; but when any one else came to ask her to dance, he said, 'This lady is dancing with me.' Thus they danced till a late hour of the night; and then she wanted to go home: and the king's son said, 'I shall go and take care of you to your home;' for he wanted to see where the beautiful maid lived. But she slipped away from him unawares, and ran off towards home, and the prince followed her; but she jumped up into the pigeon-house and shut the door. Then he waited till her father came home, and told him that the unknown maiden who had been at the feast had hid herself in the pigeon-house. But when they had broken open the door they found no one within; and as they came back into the house, Ashputtel lay, as she always did, in her dirty frock by the ashes, and her dim little lamp burnt in the chimney: for she had run as quickly as she could through the pigeon-house and on to the hazel-tree, and had there taken off her beautiful clothes, and laid them beneath the tree, that the bird might carry them away, and had seated herself amid the ashes again in her little grey frock.

The next day when the feast was again held, and her father, mother, and sisters were gone, Ashputtel went to the hazel-tree, and said –

'Shake, shake, hazel-tree,
Gold and silver over me!'

And the bird came and brought a still finer dress than the one she had worn the day before. And when she came in it to the ball, every one wondered at her beauty: but the king's son, who was waiting for her, took her by the hand, and danced with her; and when any one asked her to dance, he said as before, 'This lady is dancing with me.' When night came she wanted to go home; and the king's son followed her as before, that he might see into what house she went: but she sprung away from him all at once into the garden behind her father's house. In this garden stood a fine large pear-tree full of ripe fruit; and Ashputtel not knowing where to hide herself jumped up into it without being seen. Then the king's son could not find out where she was gone, but waited till her father came home, and said to him, 'The unknown lady who danced with me has slipt away, and I think she must have sprung into the pear-tree.' The father thought to himself, 'Can it be Ashputtel?' So he ordered an axe to be brought; and they cut down the tree, but found no one upon it. And when they came back into the kitchen, there lay Ashputtel in the ashes as usual; for she had slipped down on the other side of the tree, and carried her beautiful clothes back to the bird at the hazel-tree, and then put on her little grey frock.

The third day, when her father and mother and sisters were gone, she went again into the garden, and said –

'Shake, shake, hazel-tree,
Gold and silver over me!'

Then her kind friend the bird brought a dress still finer than the former one, and slippers which were all of gold: so that when she came to the feast no one knew what to say for wonder at her beauty: and the king's son danced with her alone; and when any one else asked her to dance, he

said, 'This lady is my partner.' Now when night came she
wanted to go home; and the king's son would go with her,
and said to himself, 'I will not lose her this time;' but however she managed to slip away from him, though in such a
hurry that she dropped her left golden slipper upon the
stairs.

So the prince took the shoe, and went the next day to the
king his father, and said, 'I will take for my wife the lady
that this golden slipper fits.' Then both the sisters were
overjoyed to hear this; for they had beautiful feet, and had
no doubt that they could wear the golden slipper. The
eldest went first into the room where the slipper was and
wanted to try it on, and the mother stood by. But her great
toe could not go into it, and the shoe was altogether much
too small for her. Then the mother gave her a knife, and
said, 'Never mind, cut it off; when you are queen you will
not care about toes, you will not want to go on foot.' So the
silly girl cut her great toe off, and squeezed the shoe on, and
went to the king's son. Then he took her for his bride, and
set her beside him on his horse and rode away with her.

But on their way home they had to pass by the hazel-tree
that Ashputtel had planted, and there sat a little dove on
the branch singing –

> 'Back again! back again! look to the shoe!
> The shoe is too small, and not made for you!
> Prince! prince! look again for thy bride,
> For she's not the true one that sits by thy side.'

Then the prince got down and looked at her foot, and
saw by the blood that streamed from it what a trick she
had played him. So he turned his horse round and brought
the false bride back to her home, and said, 'This is not the
right bride; let the other sister try and put on the slipper.'
Then she went into the room and got her foot into the shoe,
all but the heel, which was too large. But her mother
squeezed it in till the blood came, and took her to the king's

son; and he set her as his bride by his side on his horse, and
rode away with her.

But when they came to the hazel-tree the little dove sat
there still, and sang –

> 'Back again! back again! look to the shoe!
> The shoe is too small, and not made for you!
> Prince! prince! look again for thy bride,
> For she's not the true one that sits by thy side.'

Then he looked down and saw that the blood streamed so
from the shoe that her white stockings were quite red. So
he turned his horse and brought her back again also. 'This
is not the true bride,' said he to the father; 'have you no
other daughters?' 'No,' said he; 'there is only a little dirty
Ashputtel here, the child of my first wife; I am sure she
cannot be the bride.' However, the prince told him to send
her. But the mother said 'No, no, she is much too dirty, she
will not dare to show herself:' however, the prince would
have her come. And she first washed her face and hands,
and then went in and curtsied to him, and he reached her
the golden slipper. Then she took her clumsy shoe off her
left foot, and put on the golden slipper; and it fitted her as
if it had been made for her. And when he drew near and
looked at her face he knew her, and said, 'This is the right
bride.' But the mother and both the sisters were frightened
and turned pale with anger as he took Ashputtel on his
horse, and rode away with her. And when they came to the
hazel-tree, the white dove sang –

> 'Home! home! look at the shoe!
> Princess! the shoe was made for you!
> Prince! prince! take home thy bride,
> For she is the true one that sits by thy side!'

And when the dove had done its song, it came flying and
perched upon her right shoulder, and so went home with
her.

THE YOUNG GIANT AND THE TAILOR

A HUSBANDMAN had once a son, who was born no bigger than my thumb, and for many years did not grow a hair's breadth taller. One day as the father was going to plough in the field, the little fellow said, 'Father, let me go too.' 'No,' said his father; 'stay where you are, you can do no good out of doors, and if you go perhaps I may lose you.' Then little Thumbling fell a-crying: and his father, to quiet him, at last said he might go. So he put him in his pocket, and when he was in the field pulled him out and set him upon a newly made furrow, that he might look about. While he was sitting there, a great giant came striding over the hill. 'Do you see that tall steeple-man?' said the father: 'he will run away with you.' (Now he only said this to frighten the little boy if he should be naughty.) But the giant had long legs, and with two or three strides he really came close to the furrow, and picked up little Thumbling to look at him; and taking a liking to the little chap went off with him. The father stood by all the time, but could not say a word for fright; for he thought his child was really lost, and that he should never see him again.

But the giant took care of him at his house in the woods, and laid him in his bosom and fed him with the same food that he lived on himself. So Thumbling, instead of being a little dwarf, became like the giant — tall and stout and strong: so that at the end of two years when the old giant took him into the wood to try him, and said, 'Pull up that birch-tree for yourself to walk with;' the lad was so strong that he tore it up by the root. The giant thought he should make him a still stronger man than this: so after taking care of him two years more, he took him into the wood to try his strength again. This time he took hold of one of the thickest oaks, and pulled it up as if it were mere sport

to him. Then the old giant said, 'Well done, my man, you will do now.' So he carried him back to the field where he first found him.

His father happened to be just then ploughing as the young giant went up to him, saying, 'Look here, father, see who I am; – don't you see I am your son?' But the husbandman was frightened, and cried out, 'No, no, you are not my son; begone about your business.' 'Indeed, I am your son; let me plough a little, I can plough as well as you.' 'No, go your ways,' said the father, but as he was afraid of the tall man, he at last let go the plough and sat down on the ground beside it. Then the youth laid hold of the ploughshare, and though he only pushed with one hand, he drove it deep into the earth. The ploughman cried out, 'If you must plough, pray do not push so hard; you are doing more harm than good;' but he took off the horses, and said, 'Father, go home and tell my mother to get ready a good dinner; I'll go round the field meanwhile.' So he went on driving the plough without any horses, till he had done two mornings' work by himself; then he harrowed it, and when all was over, took up plough, harrow, horses and all, and carried them home like a bundle of straw.

When he reached the house he sat himself down on the bench, saying, 'Now, mother, is dinner ready?' 'Yes,' said she, for she dared not deny him; so she brought two large dishes full, enough to have lasted herself and her husband eight days; however, he soon ate it all up, and said that was but a taste. 'I see very well, father, that I shan't get enough to eat at your house; so if you will give me an iron walking-stick, so strong that I cannot break it against my knees, I will go away again.' The husbandman very gladly put his two horses to the cart and drove them to the forge, and brought back a bar of iron as long and as thick as his two horses could draw; but the lad laid it against his knee; and snap! it went like a broken beanstalk. 'I see, father,' said he, 'you can get no stick that will do for me, so I'll go and try my luck by myself.'

Then away he went, and turned blacksmith, and travelled till he came to a village where lived a miserly smith, who earned a good deal of money, but kept all he got to himself, and gave nothing away to any body. The first thing he did was to step into the smithy, and ask if the smith did not want a journeyman. 'Aye,' said the cunning fellow, (as he looked at him and thought what a stout chap he was, and how lustily he would work and earn his bread,) 'what wages do you ask?' 'I want no pay,' said he; 'but every fortnight when the other workmen are paid, you shall let me give you two strokes over the shoulders to amuse myself.' The old smith thought to himself he could bear this very well, and reckoned on saving a great deal of money; so the bargain was soon struck.

The next morning the new workman was about to begin to work; but at the first stroke that he hit, when his master brought him the iron red hot, he shivered it in pieces, and the anvil sunk so deep into the earth, that he could not get it out again. This made the old fellow very angry; 'Halloo!' cried he, 'I can't have you for a workman, you are too clumsy; we must put an end to our bargain.' 'Very well,' said the other, 'but you must pay for what I have done, so let me give you only one little stroke, and then the bargain is all over.' So saying, he gave him a thump that tossed him over a load of hay that stood near. Then he took the thickest bar of iron on the forge for a walking-stick, and went on his way.

When he had journeyed some way, he came to a farmhouse, and asked the farmer if he wanted a foreman. The farmer said, 'Yes,' and the same wages were agreed for as before with the blacksmith. The next morning the workmen were all to go into the wood; but the giant was found to be fast asleep in his bed when the rest were all up and ready to start. 'Come, get up,' said one of them to him, 'it is high time to be stirring; you must go with us.' 'Go your way,' muttered he sulkily, 'I shall have done my work and get home long before you.' So he lay in bed two hours longer, and at last got up and cooked and ate his breakfast, and then at his leisure harnessed his horses to go to the wood. Just before the wood was a hollow, through which all must pass; so he drove the cart on first, and built up behind him such a mound of faggots and briars that no horse could pass. This done, he drove on, and as he was going into the wood met the others coming out on their road home; 'Drive away,' said he, 'I shall be home before you still.' However, he only went a very little way into the wood and tore up one of the largest timber trees, put it into his cart, and turned about homewards. When he came to the pile of faggots, he found all the others standing there, not being able to pass by. 'So,' said he, 'you see if you had stayed with me, you would have been home just as soon, and might have slept an hour or two longer.' Then he took his tree on one shoulder, and his cart on the other, and pushed through as easily as though he were laden with feathers, and when he reached the yard showed the tree to the farmer, and asked if it was not a famous walking-stick. 'Wife,' said the farmer, 'this man is worth something; if he sleeps longer, still he works better than the rest.'

Time rolled on, and he had served the farmer his whole year; so when his fellow-labourers were paid, he said he also had a right to take his wages. But great dread came upon the farmer, at the thought of the blows he was to have, so he begged him to give up the old bargain, and take his whole farm and stock instead. 'Not I,' said he, 'I will be no farmer; I am foreman, and so I mean to keep, and be paid as we agreed.' Finding he could do nothing with him, the farmer only begged one fortnight's respite, and called together all his friends, to ask their advice in the matter. They bethought themselves for a long time, and at last agreed that the shortest way was to kill this troublesome foreman. The next thing was to settle how it was to be done; and it was agreed that he should be ordered to carry into the yard some great mill-stones, and to put them on the edge of a well; that then he should be sent down to clean it out, and when he was at the bottom, the mill-stones should be pushed down upon his head. Every thing went right, and when the foreman was safe in the well, the stones were rolled in. As they struck the bottom, the water splashed to the very top. Of course they thought his head must be crashed to pieces; but he only cried out, 'Drive away the chickens from the well; they are pecking about in the sand above me, and throwing it into my eyes, so that I cannot see.' When his job was done, up he sprung from the well, saying, 'Look here! see what a fine neck-cloth I have!' as he pointed to one of the mill-stones, that had fallen over his head, and hung about his neck.

The farmer was again overcome with fear, and begged another fortnight to think of it. So his friends were called together again, and at last gave this advice; that the fore-man should be sent and made to grind corn by night at the haunted mill, whence no man had ever yet come out in the morning alive. That very evening he was told to carry eight bushels of corn to the mill, and grind them in the night. Away he went to the loft, put two bushels in his right pocket, two in his left, and four in a long sack slung over his shoulders, and then set off to the mill. The miller told him he might grind there in the day time, but not by night, for the mill was bewitched, and whoever went in at night had been dead in the morning: 'Never mind, miller, I shall come out safe,' said he; 'only make haste and get out of the way, and look out for me in the morning.'

So he went into the mill and put the corn into the hop-per, and about twelve o'clock sat himself down on the bench in the miller's room. After a little time the door all at once opened of itself, and in came a large table. On the table stood wine and meat, and many good things besides: all seemed placed there by themselves; at any rate there was no one to be seen. The chairs next moved themselves round it, but still neither guests nor servants came; till all at once he saw fingers handling the knives and forks and putting food on the plates, but still nothing else was to be seen. Now our friend felt somewhat hungry as he looked at the dishes, so he sat himself down at the table and ate whatever he liked best; and when he had had enough, and the plates were empty, on a sudden he heard something blow out the lights. When it was pitch dark he felt a tremendous blow upon his head; 'If I get such another box on the ear,' said he, 'I shall just give it back again;' and this he really did, when the next blow came. Thus the game went on all night; and he never let fear get the better of him, but kept dealing his blows round, till at day-break all was still. 'Well, miller,' said he in the morning, 'I have had some little slaps on the face, but I've given as good, I'll warrant you; and meantime I have eaten as much as I liked.' The miller was glad to find the charm was broken, and would have given him a great deal of money; 'I want no money, I have quite enough,' said he, as he took the meal on his back, and went home to his master to claim his wages.

But the farmer was in a rage, knowing there was no help for him, and paced the room up and down till the drops of sweat ran down his forehead. Then he opened the window for a little fresh air, and before he was aware, his foreman gave him the first blow, and kicked him out of the window over the hills and far away, and next sent his wife after him; and there, for aught I know, they may be flying in the air still: but the young giant took up his iron walking-stick and walked off.

Perhaps this was the same giant that the Bold little Tailor met, when he set out on his travels, as I will tell you next.

*

It was a fine summer morning when this little man bound his girdle round his body, and looked about his house to see if there was any thing good to take with him on his journey into the wide world. He could only find an old cheese; but that was better than nothing; so he took it up; and, as he was going out, the old hen met him at the door, and he packed her too into his wallet with the cheese. Then off he set, and when he had climbed a high hill, he found the giant sitting on the top. 'Good day, comrade,' said he; 'there you sit at your ease, and look the wide world over: I have a mind to go and try my luck in that same world; what do you say to going with me?' Then the giant looked at him, and said, 'You are a poor trumpery little knave.' 'That may be,' said the tailor; 'but we shall see who is the best man of the two.' The giant, finding the little man so bold, began to be a little more respectful, and said they would soon try who was master. So he took a large stone in his hand and squeezed it till water dropped from it; 'Do that,' said he, 'if you have a mind to be thought a strong man.' 'Is that all?' said the tailor; 'I will soon do as much;' so he put his hand in his wallet, pulled out the cheese (which was quite new), and squeezed it till the whey ran out. 'What do you say now, Mr Giant? my squeeze was a better one than yours.' Then the giant, not seeing that it was only a cheese, did not know what to say for himself, though he could hardly believe his eyes; at last he took up a stone, and threw it up so high that it went almost out of sight; 'Now then, little pygmy, do that if you can.' 'Very good,' said the other; 'your throw was not a bad one, but after all your stone fell to the ground; I will throw something that shall not fall at all.' 'That you can't do,' said the giant: but the tailor took his old hen out of the wallet, and threw her up in the air, and she, pleased enough to be set free, flew away out of sight. 'Now, comrade,' said he, 'what do you say to that?' 'I say you are a clever hand,' said the giant, 'but we will now try how you can work.'

Then he led him into the wood, where a fine oak tree lay felled. 'Now let us drag it out of the wood together.' 'Very

well; do you take the thick end, and I will carry all the top
and branches, which are much the largest and heaviest.' So
the giant took the trunk and laid it on his shoulder; but the
cunning little rogue, instead of carrying any thing, sat himself at his ease among the branches, and let the giant carry
stem, branches, and tailor into the bargain. All the way
they went he made merry, and whistled and sang his song
as if carrying the tree were mere sport; while the giant after
he had borne it a good way could carry it no longer, and
said, 'I must let it fall.' Then the tailor sprung down and
held the tree as if he were carrying it, saying, 'What a

shame that such a big lout as you cannot carry a tree like
this!' Then on they went together till they came to a tall
cherry tree; and the giant took hold of the top stem, and
bent it down to pluck the ripest fruit, and when he had
done, gave it over to his friend that he too might eat; but
the little man was so weak that he could not hold the tree
down, and up he went with it swinging in the air. 'Halloo!'
said the giant, 'what now? can't you hold that twig?' 'To
be sure I could,' said the other; 'but don't you see there's a
huntsman, who is going to shoot into the bush where we
stood? so I took a jump over the tree to be out of his way;
do you do the same.' The giant tried to follow, but the tree
was far too high to jump over, and he only stuck fast in
the branches, for the tailor to laugh at him. 'Well! you are
a fine fellow after all,' said the giant; 'so come home and
sleep with me and a friend of mine in the mountains to-
night.'

The tailor had no business upon his hands, so he did as he
was bid, and the giant gave him a good supper, and a bed
to sleep upon; but the tailor was too cunning to lie down
upon it, and crept slily into a corner, and slept there
soundly. When midnight came, the giant came softly in
with his iron walking-stick, and gave such a stroke upon
the bed where he thought his guest was lying, that he said
to himself, 'It's all up now with that grasshopper; I shall
have no more of his tricks.' In the morning the giants went
off into the woods, and quite forgot him, till all on a sudden
they met him trudging along, whistling a merry tune; and
so frightened were they at the sight, that they both ran
away as fast as they could.

Then on went the little tailor following his spuddy nose,
till at last he reached the king's court, and began to brag
very loud of his mighty deeds, saying he was come to serve
the king. To try him, they told him that the two giants
who lived in a part of the kingdom a long way off, were be-

come the dread of the whole land; for they had begun to
rob, plunder and ravage all about them, and that if he was
so great a man as he said, he should have a hundred soldiers
and should set out to fight these giants, and if he beat them
he should have half the kingdom. 'With all my heart!'
said he; 'but as for your hundred soldiers, I believe I shall
do as well without them.' However, they set off together
till they came to a wood: 'Wait here, my friends,' said he to
the soldiers, 'I will soon give a good account of these
giants:' and on he went casting his sharp little eye here,
there, and every where around him. After a while he spied
them both lying under a tree, and snoring away till the
very boughs whistled with the breeze. 'The game's won,
for a penny,' said the little man, as he filled his wallet with
stones, and climbed the tree under which they lay.

As soon as he was safely up, he threw one stone after
another at the nearest giant, till at last he woke up in a
rage, and shook his companion, crying out, 'What did you
strike me for?' 'Nonsense! you are dreaming,' said the
other, 'I did not strike you.' Then both lay down to sleep
again, and the tailor threw stones at the second giant, till
he sprung up and cried, 'What are you about? you struck
me.' 'I did not,' said the other; and on they wrangled for a
while, till as both were tired they made up the matter, and
fell asleep again. But then the tailor began his game once
more, and flung the largest stone he had in his wallet with
all his force and hit the first giant on the nose. 'That is too
bad,' cried he, as if he was mad, 'I will not bear it.' So he
struck the other a mighty blow; he of course was not
pleased at this, and gave him just such another box on the
ear; and at last a bloody battle began; up flew the trees by
the roots, the rocks and stones went bang at one another's
heads, and in the end both lay dead upon the spot. 'It is a
good thing,' said the tailor, 'that they let my tree stand, or
I must have made a fine jump.' Then down he ran, and

took his sword and gave each of them a very fine wound or two on the breast and set off to look for the soldiers. 'There lie the giants,' said he; 'I have killed them, but it has been no small job, for they even tore trees up in their struggle.' 'Have you any wounds?' asked they. 'That is a likely matter, truly,' said he; 'they have not touched a hair of my head.' But the soldiers would not believe him till they rode into the wood and found the giants weltering in their blood, and the trees lying around torn up by the roots.

The king, after he had got rid of his enemies, was not much pleased at the thoughts of giving up half his king-dom to a tailor; so he said, 'You have not yet done; in the palace court lies a bear with whom you must pass the night, and if when I rise in the morning I find you still liv-ing, you shall then have your reward.' Now he thought he had got rid of him, for the bear had never yet let any one go away alive who had come within reach of his claws. 'Very well,' said the tailor, 'I am willing.'

So when evening came our little tailor was led out and shut up in the court with the bear, who rose at once to give him a friendly welcome with his paw. 'Softly, softly, my friend,' said he; 'I know a way to please you;' then at his ease and as if he cared nothing about the matter, he pulled out of his pocket some fine walnuts, cracked them, and ate the kernels. When the bear saw this, he took a great fancy to having some nuts too; so the tailor felt in his pocket and gave him a handful, not of walnuts, but nice round pebbles. The bear snapt them up, but could not crack one of them, do what he would. 'What a clumsy thick head thou art!' thought the beast to itself; 'thou canst not crack a nut to-day.' Then said he to the tailor, 'Friend, pray crack me the nuts.' 'Why, what a lout you are,' said the tailor, 'to have such a jaw as that, and not be able to crack a little nut! Well! engage to be friends with me and I'll help you.' So he took the stones, and slily changed them for nuts, put them in his mouth, and crack! they went. 'I must try for myself, however,' said the bear; 'now I see how you do it, I am sure I can do it myself.' Then the tailor gave him the cobble stones again, and the bear lay down and worked away as hard as he could, and bit and bit with all his force till he broke all his teeth, and lay down quite tired.

But the tailor began to think this would not last long, and that the bear might find him out and break the bargain; so he pulled a fiddle out from under his coat and played him a tune. As soon as the bear heard it, he could

not help jumping up and beginning to dance; and when he had jigged away for a while, the thing pleased him so much that he said, 'Hark ye, friend! is the fiddle hard to play upon?' 'No! not at all!' said the other; 'look ye, I lay my left hand here, and then I take the bow with my right hand thus, and scrape it over the strings there, and away it goes merrily, hop, sa, sa! fal, lal, la!' 'Will you teach me to fiddle,' said the bear, 'so that I may have music whenever I want to dance?' 'With all my heart; but let me look at your claws, they are so very long that I must first clip your nails a little bit.' Then the bear lifted up his paws one after another, and the tailor screwed them down tight, and said, 'Now wait till I come with my scissors.' So he left the bear to growl as loud as he liked, and laid himself down on a heap of straw in the corner and slept soundly. In the morning when the king came, he found the tailor sitting merrily eating his breakfast, and could no longer help keeping his word; and thus the little man became a great one.

THE CROWS AND THE SOLDIER

A WORTHY soldier had saved a good deal of money out of his pay; for he worked hard, and did not spend all he earned in eating and drinking, as many others do. Now he had two comrades who were great rogues, and wanted to rob him of his money, but behaved outwardly towards him in a friendly way. 'Comrade,' said they to him one day, 'why should we stay here shut up in this town like prisoners, when you at any rate have earned enough to live upon for the rest of your days in peace and plenty at home by your own fireside?' They talked so often to him in this manner, that he at last said he would go and try his luck with them; but they all the time thought of nothing but how they should manage to steal his money from him.

When they had gone a little way, the two rogues said, 'We must go by the right hand road, for that will take us quickest into another country where we shall be safe.' Now they knew all the while that what they were saying was untrue; and as soon as the soldier said, 'No, that will take us straight back into the town we came from; we must keep on the left hand;' they picked a quarrel with him, and said, 'What do you give yourself airs for? you know nothing about it;' and then they fell upon him and knocked him down, and beat him over the head till he was blind. Then they took all the money out of his pockets and dragged him to a gallows tree that stood hard by, bound him fast down at the foot of it, and went back into the town with the money; but the poor blind man did not know where he was; and he felt all around him, and finding that he was bound to a large beam of wood, thought it was a cross, and said, 'After all, they have done kindly in leaving me under a cross; now Heaven will guard me;' so he raised himself up and began to pray.

When night came on, he heard something fluttering over his head. It turned out to be three crows, who flew round and round, and at last perched upon the tree. By and by they began to talk together, and he heard one of them say, 'Sister, what is the best news with you to-day?' 'Oh, if men knew what we know!' said the other; 'the princess is ill, and the king has vowed to marry her to any one who will cure her; but this none can do, for she will not be well until yonder flower is burnt to ashes and swallowed by her.' 'Oh, indeed,' said the other crow, 'if men did but know what we know! to-night will fall from heaven a dew of such healing power, that even the blind man who washes his eyes with it will see again;' and the third spoke, and said, 'Oh, if men knew what we know! the flower is wanted but for one, the dew is wanted but for few; but there is a great dearth of water in the town; all the wells are dried up; and no one knows that they must take away the large square stone out of the market-place, and dig underneath it, and that then the finest water 'will spring up.'

When the three crows had done talking, he heard them fluttering round again, and at last away they flew. Greatly wondering at what he had heard, and overjoyed at the thoughts of getting his sight, he tried with all his strength to break loose from his bonds; at last he found himself free, and plucked some of the grass that grew beneath him and washed his eyes with the dew that had fallen upon it. At once his eye-sight came to him again, and he saw by the light of the moon and the stars that he was beneath the gallows-tree, and not the cross, as he had thought. Then he gathered together in a bottle as much of the dew as he could to take away with him, and looked around till he saw the flower that grew close by; and when he had burned it he gathered up the ashes, and set out on his way towards the king's court.

When he reached the palace, he told the king he was come to cure the princess; and when she had taken of the ashes and been made well, he claimed her for his wife, as the reward that was to be given; but the king looking upon him and seeing that his clothes were so shabby, would not keep his word, and thought to get rid of him by saying, 'Whoever wants to have the princess for his wife, must find enough water for the use of the town, where there is this summer a great dearth.' Then the soldier went out and told the people to take up the square stone in the market-place and dig for water underneath; and when they had done so there came up a fine spring, that gave enough water for the whole town. So the king could no longer get off giving him his daughter, and they were married and lived happily together.

Some time after, as he was walking one day through a field, he met his two wicked comrades who had treated him so basely. Though they did not know him, he knew them at once, and went up to them and said, 'Look upon me, I am your old comrade whom you beat and robbed and left blind; Heaven has defeated your wicked wishes, and turned all the mischief which you brought upon me into good luck.' When they heard this they fell at his feet and begged for pardon, and he had a kind and good heart, so he forgave them, and took them to his palace and gave them food and clothes. And he told them all that had happened to him, and how he had reached these honours. After they had heard the whole story they said to themselves, 'Why should not we go and sit some night under the gallows? we may hear something that will bring us good luck too.'

Next night they stole away; and, when they had sat under the tree a little while, they heard a fluttering noise over their heads; and the three crows came and perched upon it. 'Sisters,' said one of them, 'some one must have overheard us, for all the world is talking of the wonderful things that have happened: the princess is well; the flower has been plucked and burnt; a blind man's sight has been given him again, and they have dug a fresh well that gives water to the whole town: let us look about, perhaps we may find some one near; if we do he shall rue the day.' Then they began to flutter about, and soon found out the two men below, and flew at them in a rage, beating and pecking them in the face with their wings and beaks till they were quite blind, and lay nearly dead upon the ground under the gallows. The next day passed over and they did not return to the palace; and their old comrade began to wonder where they had been, and went out the following morning in search of them, and at last found them where they lay, dreadfully repaid for all their folly and baseness.

PEE-WIT

A POOR countryman whose name was Pee-wit lived with
his wife in a very quiet way in the parish where he was
born. One day, as he was ploughing with his two oxen in
the field, he heard all on a sudden some one calling out his
name. Turning round, he saw nothing but a bird that kept
crying Pee-wit! Pee-wit! Now this poor bird is called a Pee-
wit, and like the cuckoo always keeps crying out its own
name. But the countryman thought it was mocking him, so
he took up a huge stone and threw at it; the bird flew off
safe and sound, but the stone fell upon the head of one of
the oxen, and killed him on the spot. 'What is to be done
with the odd one?' thought Pee-wit to himself as he looked
at the ox that was left; so without more ado he killed him
too, skinned them both, and set out for the neighbouring
town, to sell the hides to the tanner for as much as he could
get. He soon found out where the tanner lived, and knocked
at the door. Before, however, the door was opened, he saw
through the window that the mistress of the house was
hiding in an old chest a friend of hers, whom she seemed to
wish no one should see. By and by the door was opened,
'What do you want?' said the woman. Then he told her
that he wanted to sell his hides; and it came out that the
tanner was not at home, and that no one there ever made
bargains but himself. The countryman said he would sell
cheap, and did not mind giving his hides for the old chest
in the corner; meaning the one he had seen the good
woman's friend get into. Of course the wife would not agree
to this; and they went on talking the matter over so long,
that at last in came the tanner and asked what it was all
about. Pee-wit told him the whole story, and asked him
whether he would give the old chest for the hides. 'To be
sure I will,' said he; and scolded his wife for saying nay to

such a bargain, which she ought to have been glad to make
if the countryman was willing. Then up he took the chest
on his shoulders, and all the good woman could say mat-
tered nothing; away it went into the countryman's cart,
and off he drove. But when they had gone some way, the
young man within began to make himself heard, and to beg
and pray to be let out. Pee-wit, however, was not to be
bought over; till at last after a long parley a thousand
dollars were bid and taken; the money was paid, and at
that price the poor fellow was set free, and went about his
business.

Then Pee-wit went home very happy, and built a new
house and seemed so rich that his neighbours wondered,
and said, 'Pee-wit must have been where the golden snow
falls.' So they took him before the next justice of the peace,
to give an account of himself, and show that he came
honestly by his wealth; and then he told them that he had
sold his hides for one thousand dollars. When they heard
it they all killed their oxen and would sell the hides to the
same tanner; but the justice said, 'My maid shall have the
first chance;' so off she went, and when she came to the
tanner, he laughed at them all, and said he had given their
neighbour nothing but an old chest.

At this they were all very angry, and laid their heads together to work him some mischief, which they thought they
could do while he was digging in his garden. All this, however, came to the ears of the countryman, who was plagued
with a sad scold for his wife; and he thought to himself, 'If
any one is to come into trouble, I don't see why it should
not be my wife, rather than me;' so he said to her that he
wished she would humour him in a whim he had taken into
his head, and would put on his clothes, and dig the garden
in his stead. The wife did what was asked, and next morning began digging; but soon came some of the neighbours,
and, thinking it was Pee-wit, threw a stone at her, (harder

perhaps than they meant,) and killed her at once. Poor
Pee-wit was rather sorry at this, but still thought that he
had had a lucky escape for himself, and that perhaps he
might after all turn the death of his wife to some account:
so he dressed her in her own clothes, put a basket with fine
fruit (which was now scarce, it being winter) into her hand,
and set her by the road side on a broad bench.

After a while came by a fine coach with six horses, servants, and outriders, and within sat a noble lord who lived
not far off. When his lordship saw the beautiful fruit, he
sent one of the servants to the woman to ask what was the
price of her goods. The man went and asked ·'What is the
price of this fruit?' No answer. He asked again. No answer:
and when this had happened three times, he became angry;
and, thinking she was asleep, gave her a blow, and down
she fell backwards into the pond that was behind the seat.
Then up ran Pee-wit, and cried and sorrowed because they
had drowned his poor wife, and threatened to have the lord
and his servants tried for what they had done. His lordship begged him to be easy, and offered to give him the
coach and horses, servants and all; so the countryman after
a long time let himself be appeased a little, took what they
gave, got into the coach and set off towards his own home
again.

As he came near, the neighbours wondered much at the
beautiful coach and horses, and still more when they
stopped, and Pee-wit got out at his own door. Then he told
them the whole story, which only vexed them still more;
so they took him and fastened him up in a tub and were
going to throw him into the lake that was hard by. Whilst
they were rolling the tub on before them towards the
water, they passed by an alehouse and stopped to refresh
themselves a little before they put an end to Pee-wit;
meantime they tied the tub to a tree and there left it while
they were enjoying themselves within doors.

Pee-wit no sooner found himself alone than he began to turn over in his mind how he could get free. He listened, and soon heard Ba, ba! from a flock of sheep and lambs that were coming by. Then he lifted up his voice, and shouted out, 'I will not be burgomaster, I say; I will not be made burgomaster.' The shepherd hearing this went up, and said, 'What is all this noise about?' 'Oh!' said Pee-wit, 'my neighbours will make me burgomaster against my will; and when I told them I would not agree, they put me into the cask and are going to throw me into the lake.' 'I should like very well to be burgomaster if I were you,' said the shepherd. 'Open the cask then,' said the other, 'and let me out, and get in yourself, and they will make you burgomaster instead of me.' No sooner said than done, the shepherd was in, Pee-wit was out; and as there was nobody to take care of the shepherd's flock, he drove it off merrily towards his own house.

When the neighbours came out of the alehouse, they rolled the cask on, and the shepherd began to cry out, 'I *will* be burgomaster now; I *will* be burgomaster now.' 'I dare say you will, but you shall take a swim first,' said a neighbour, as he gave the cask the last push over into the lake. This done, away they went home merrily, leaving the shepherd to get out as well as he could.

But as they came in at one side of the village, who should they meet coming in the other way but Pee-wit driving a fine flock of sheep and lambs before him. 'How came you here?' cried all with one voice. 'Oh! the lake is enchanted,' said he; 'when you threw me in, I sunk deep and deep into the water, till at last I came to the bottom; there I knocked out the bottom of the cask and found myself in a beautiful meadow with fine flocks grazing upon it, so I chose a few for myself, and here I am.' 'Cannot we have some too?' said they. 'Why not? there are hundreds and thousands left; you have nothing to do but jump in and fetch them out.'

So all agreed they would dive for sheep; the justice first, then the clerk, then the constables, and then the rest of the parish, one after the other. When they came to the side of the lake, the blue sky was covered with little white clouds like flocks of sheep, and all were reflected in the clear water: so they called out, 'There they are, there they are already;' and fearing lest the justice should get every thing, they jumped in all at once; and Pee-wit jogged home, and made himself happy with what he had got, leaving them to find their flocks by themselves as well as they could.

———

HANS AND HIS WIFE GRETTEL

I. *Showing who Grettel was*

THERE was once a little maid named Grettel: she wore
shoes with red heels, and when she went abroad she turned
out her toes, and was very merry, and thought to herself,
'What a pretty girl I am!' And when she came home, to put
herself in good spirits, she would tipple down a drop or two
of wine; and as wine gives a relish for eating, she would
take a taste of every thing when she was cooking, saying,
'A cook ought to know whether a thing tastes well.' It happened one day that her master said, 'Grettel, this evening I
have a friend coming to sup with me; get two fine fowls
ready.' 'Very well, sir,' said Grettel. Then she killed the
fowls, plucked, and trussed them, put them on the spit, and
when evening came put them to the fire to roast. The fowls
turned round and round, and soon began to look nice and
brown, but the guest did not come. Then Grettel cried out,
'Master, if the guest does not come I must take up the
fowls, but it will be a shame and a pity if they are not eaten
while they are hot and good.' 'Well,' said her master, 'I'll
run and tell him to come.' As soon as he had turned his
back, Grettel stopped the spit, and laid it with the fowls
upon it on one side, and thought to herself, 'Standing by
the fire makes one very tired and thirsty; who knows how
long they will be? meanwhile I will just step into the cellar
and take a drop.' So off she ran, put down her pitcher, and
said 'Your health, Grettel,' and took a good draught. 'This
wine is a good friend,' said she to herself, 'it breaks one's
heart to leave it.' Then up she trotted, put the fowls down
to the fire, spread some butter over them, and turned the
spit merrily round again.

The fowls soon smelt so good, that she thought to herself,
'They are very good, but they may want something still; I

had better taste them and see.' So she licked her fingers, and and said, 'Oh! how good! what a shame and a pity that they are not eaten!' Away she ran to the window to see if her master and his friend were coming; but nobody was in sight: so she turned to the fowls again, and thought it would be better for her to eat a wing than that it should be burnt. So she cut one wing off, and ate it, and it tasted very well; and as the other was quite done enough, she thought it had better be cut off too, or else her master would see one was wanting. When the two wings were gone, she went again to look out for her master, but could not see him. 'Ah!' thought she to herself, 'who knows whether they will come at all? very likely they have turned into some tavern: O Grettel! Grettel! make yourself happy, take another draught, and eat the rest of the fowl; it looks so oddly as it is; when you have eaten all, you will be easy: why should such good things be wasted?' So she ran once more to the cellar, took another drink, and ate up the rest of the fowl with the greatest glee.

Still her master did not come, and she cast a lingering eye upon the other fowl, and said, 'Where the other went, this had better go too; they belong to each other; they who have a right to one must have a right to the other; but if I were to take another draught first, it would not hurt me.' So she tippled down another drop of wine, and sent the second fowl to look after the first. While she was making an end of this famous meal, her master came home and called out, 'Now quick, Grettel, my friend is just as hand!' 'Yes, master, I will dish up this minute,' said she. In the mean time he looked to see if the cloth was laid, and took up the carving-knife to sharpen it. Whilst this was going on, the guest came and knocked softly and gently at the house door; then Grettel ran to see who was there, and when she saw him she put her finger upon her lips, and said, 'Hush! hush! run away as fast as you can, for if my master catches

you, it will be worse for you; he owes you a grudge, and
asked you to supper only that he might cut off your ears;
only listen how he is sharpening his knife.' The guest listened, and when he heard the knife, he made as much haste
as he could down the steps and ran off. Grettel was not idle
in the mean time, but ran screaming, 'Master, master!
what a fine guest you have asked to supper!' 'Why, Grettel, what's the matter?' 'Oh!' said she, 'he has taken both
the fowls that I was going to bring up, and has run away
with them.' 'That is a rascally trick to play,' said the master, sorry to lose the fine chickens; 'at least he might have
left me one, that I might have had something to eat; call
out to him to stay.' But the guest would not hear; so he ran
after him with his knife in his hand, crying out, 'Only one,
only one, I want only one;' meaning that the guest should
leave him one of the fowls, and not take both: but he
thought that his host meant nothing less than that he
would cut off at least one of his ears; so he ran away to save
them both, as if he had hot coals under his feet.

II. *Hans in love*

Hans's mother says to him, 'Whither so fast?' 'To see
Grettel,' says Hans. 'Behave well.' 'Very well: Good-bye,
mother!' Hans comes to Grettel; 'Good day, Grettel!'
'Good day, Hans! do you bring me any thing good?'
'Nothing at all: have you any thing for me?' Grettel gives
Hans a needle. Hans says, 'Good-bye, Grettel!' 'Good-bye,
Hans!' Hans takes the needle, sticks it in a truss of hay, and
takes both off home. 'Good evening, mother!' 'Good evening, Hans! where have you been?' 'To see Grettel.' 'What
did you take her?' 'Nothing at all.' 'What did she give
you?' 'She gave me a needle.' 'Where is it, Hans?' 'Stuck
in the truss.' 'How silly you are! you should have stuck

it in your sleeve.' 'Let me alone! I'll do better next time.'

'Where now, Hans?' 'To see Grettel, mother.' 'Behave yourself well.' 'Very well: Good-bye, mother!' Hans comes to Grettel; 'Good day, Grettel!' 'Good day, Hans! what have you brought me?' 'Nothing at all: have you any thing for me?' Grettel gives Hans a knife. 'Good-bye, Grettel!' 'Good-bye, Hans!' Hans takes the knife. sticks it in his sleeve, and goes home. 'Good evening, mother!' 'Good evening, Hans! where have you been?' 'To see Grettel.' 'What did you carry her?' 'Nothing at all.' 'What has she given you?' 'A knife.' 'Where is the knife, Hans?' 'Stuck in my sleeve, mother.' 'You silly goose! you should have put it in your pocket.' 'Let me alone! I'll do better next time.'

'Where now, Hans?' 'To see Grettel.' 'Behave yourself well.' 'Very well: Good-bye, mother!' Hans comes to Grettel; 'Good day, Grettel!' 'Good day, Hans! have you any thing good?' 'No: have you any thing for me?' Grettel gives Hans a kid. 'Good-bye, Grettel!' 'Good-bye, Hans!' Hans takes the kid, ties it up with a cord, stuffs it into his pocket, and chokes it to death. 'Good evening, mother!' 'Good evening, Hans! where have you been?' 'To see Grettel, mother!' 'What did you take her?' 'Nothing at all.' 'What did she give you?' 'She gave me a kid,' 'Where is the kid, Hans?' 'Safe in my pocket.' 'You silly goose! you should have led it with a string.' 'Never mind, mother, I'll do better next time.'

'Where now, Hans?' 'To Grettel's, mother.' 'Behave well.' 'Quite well, mother; Good-bye!' Hans comes to Grettel; 'Good day, Grettel!' 'Good day, Hans! what have you brought me?' 'Nothing at all: have you any thing for me?' Grettel gives Hans a piece of bacon; Hans ties the bacon to a string and drags it behind him; the dog comes after and eats it all up as he walks home. 'Good evening,

mother!' 'Good evening, Hans! where have you been?'
'To Grettel's.' 'What did you take her?' 'Nothing at all.'
'What did she give you?' 'A piece of bacon.' 'Where is the
bacon, Hans?' 'Tied to the string, and dragged home, but
somehow or other all gone.' 'What a silly trick, Hans! you
should have brought it on your head.' 'Never mind,
mother, I'll do better another time.'

'Where now, Hans?' 'Going to Grettel.' 'Take care of
yourself.' 'Very well, mother: Good-bye.' Hans comes to
Grettel; – 'Good day, Grettel!' 'Good day, Hans! what
have you brought me?' 'Nothing: have you any thing for
me?' Grettel gives Hans a calf. Hans sets it upon his head,
and it kicks him in the face. 'Good evening, mother!'
'Good evening, Hans! where have you been?' 'To see
Grettel.' 'What did you take her?' 'Nothing.' 'What did
she give you?' 'She gave me a calf.' 'Where is the calf,
Hans?' 'I put it on my head, and it scratched my face.'
'You silly goose! you should have led it home and put it in
the stall.' 'Very well; I'll do better another time.'

'Where now, Hans?' 'To see Grettel.' 'Mind and behave
well.' 'Good-bye, mother!' Hans comes to Grettel; 'Good
day, Grettel!' 'Good day, Hans! what have you brought?'
'Nothing at all: have you any thing for me?' 'I'll go home
with you.' Hans ties a string round her neck, leads her
along, and ties her up in the stall. 'Good evening, mother!'
'Good evening, Hans! where have you been?' 'At Grettel's.' 'What has she given you?' 'She has come herself.'
'Where have you put her?' 'Fast in the stall with plenty of
hay.' 'How silly you are! you should have taken good care
of her, and brought her home.' Then Hans went back to
the stall; but Grettel was in a great rage, and had got loose
and run away: yet, after all, she was Hans's bride.

III. *Hans married*

Hans and Grettel lived in the village together, but Grettel did as she pleased, and was so lazy that she never would work; and when her husband gave her any yarn to spin she did it in a slovenly way; and when it was spun she did not wind it on the reel, but left it to lie all tangled about. Hans sometimes scolded, but she was always before-hand with her tongue, and said, 'Why, how should I wind it when I have no reel? go into the wood and make one.' 'If that's all,' said he, 'I will go into the wood and cut reel-sticks.' Then Grettel was frightened lest when he had cut the sticks he should make a reel, and thus she would be forced to wind the yarn and spin again. So she pondered a while, till at last a bright thought came into her head, and she ran slyly after her husband into the wood. As soon as he had got into a tree and began to bend down a bough to cut it, she crept into the bush below, where he could not see her, and sung:

> 'Bend not the bough;
> He who bends it shall die!
> Reel not the reel;
> He who reels it shall die!'

Hans listened a while, laid down his axe, and thought to himself, 'What can that be?' 'What indeed can it be?' said he at last; 'it is only a singing in your ears, Hans! pluck up your heart, man!' So he raised up his axe again, and took hold of the bough, but once more the voice sung:

> 'Bend not the bough;
> He who bends it shall die!
> Reel not the reel;
> He who reels it shall die!'

Once more he stopped his hand; fear came over him, and he began pondering what it could mean. After a while, however, he plucked up his courage again, and took up his axe and began for the third time to cut the wood; again the third time began the song –

> 'Bend not the bough;
> He who bends it shall die!
> Reel not the reel;
> He who reels it shall die!'

At this he could hold no longer, down he dropped from the tree and set off homewards as fast as he could. Away too ran Grettel by a shorter cut, so as to reach home first, and when he opened the door met him quite innocently, as if nothing had happened, and said, 'Well! have you brought a good piece of wood for the reel?' 'No,' said he, 'I see plainly that no luck comes of that reel;' and then he told her all that had happened, and left her for that time in peace.

But soon afterwards Hans began again to reproach her with the untidiness of her house. 'Wife,' said he; 'is it not a sin and a shame that the spun yarn should lie all about in that way?' 'It may be so,' said she; 'but you know very well that we have no reel; if it must be done, lie down there and hold up your hands and legs, and so I'll make a reel of you, and wind off the yarn into skeins.' 'Very well,' said Hans (who did not much like the job, but saw no help for it if his wife was to be set to work); so he did as she said, and when all was wound, 'The yarn is all in skeins,' said he; 'now take care and get up early and heat the water and boil it well, so that it may be ready for sale.' Grettel disliked this part of the work very much, but said to him, 'Very well, I'll be sure to do it very early to-morrow morning.' But all the time she was thinking to herself what plan she should take for getting off such work for the future.

Betimes in the morning she got up, made the fire and put on the boiler; but instead of the yarn she laid a large ball of

tow in it and let it boil. Then she went up to her husband,
who was still in bed, and said to him, 'I must go out, pray
look meantime to the yarn in the boiler over the fire; but do
it soon and take good care, for if the cock crows and you
are not looking to it, they say it will turn to tow.' Hans
soon after got up that he might run no risk, and went (but
not perhaps as quickly as he might have done) into the
kitchen, and when he lifted up the boiler lid and looked in,
to his great terror nothing was there but a ball of tow.
Then off he slunk as dumb as a mouse, for he thought to
himself that he was to blame for his laziness; and left Grettel to get on with her yarn and her spinning as fast as she
pleased and no faster.

One day, however, he said to her, 'Wife, I must go a
little way this morning; do you go into the field and cut the
corn.' 'Yes, to be sure, dear Hans!' said she; so when he
was gone she cooked herself a fine mess and took it with her
into the field. When she came into the field, she sat down
for a while and said to herself, 'What shall I do? shall I
sleep first or eat first? Heigho! I'll first eat a bit.' Then she
ate her dinner heartily, and when she had had enough she
said again to herself, 'What shall I do? shall I reap first or
sleep first? Heigho! I'll first sleep a bit.' So she laid herself
down among the corn and went fast asleep. By and by
Hans came home, but no Grettel was to be seen, and he
said to himself, 'What a clever wife I have! she works so
hard that she does not even come home to her dinner!'
Evening came and still she did not come; then Hans set off
to see how much of the corn was reaped, but there it all
stood untouched, and Grettel lay fast asleep in the middle.
So he ran home and got a string of little bells and tied them
quietly round her waist, and went back and set himself
down on his stool and locked the house door.

At last Grettel woke when it was quite dark, and as she
rose up the bells jingled around her every step she took. At

this she was greatly frightened, and puzzled to tell whether she was really Grettel or not. 'Is it I, or is it not?' said she as she stood doubting what she ought to think. At last, after she had pondered a while, she thought to herself, 'I will go home and ask if it is I or not; Hans will know.' So she ran to the house door, and when she found it locked she knocked at the window and cried out, 'Hans! is Grettel within?' 'She is where she ought to be, to be sure,' said Hans; 'Oh dear then!' said she frightened, 'this is not I.' Then away she went and knocked at the neighbours' doors; but when they heard her bells rattling no one would let her in, and so at last off she ran back to the field again.

CHERRY, OR THE FROG-BRIDE

THERE was once a king who had three sons. Not far from his kingdom lived an old woman who had an only daughter called Cherry. The king sent his sons out to see the world, that they might learn the ways of foreign lands, and get wisdom and skill in ruling the kingdom that they were one day to have for their own. But the old woman lived at peace at home with her daughter, who was called Cherry, because she liked cherries better than any other kind of food, and would eat scarcely any thing else. Now her poor old mother had no garden, and no money to buy cherries every day for her daughter; and at last there was no other plan left but to go to a neighbouring nunnery-garden and beg the finest she could get of the nuns; for she dared not let her daughter go out by herself, as she was very pretty, and she feared some mischance might befall her. Cherry's taste was, however, very well known; and as it happened that the abbess was as fond of cherries as she was, it was soon found out where all the best fruit went; and the holy mother was not a little angry at missing some of her stock and finding whither it had gone.

The princes while wandering on came one day to the town where Cherry and her mother lived; and as they passed along the street saw the fair maiden standing at the window, combing her long and beautiful locks of hair. Then each of the three fell deeply in love with her, and began to say how much he longed to have her for his wife! Scarcely had the wish been spoken, when all drew their swords, and a dreadful battle began; the fight lasted long, and their rage grew hotter and hotter, when at last the abbess hearing the uproar came to the gate. Finding that her neighbour was the cause, her old spite against her broke forth at once, and in her rage she wished Cherry turned into an ugly frog, and sitting in the water under the bridge at the world's end. No sooner said than done; and poor Cherry became a frog, and vanished out of their sight. The princes had now nothing to fight for; so sheathing their swords again, they shook hands as brothers, and went on towards their father's home.

The old king meanwhile found that he grew weak and ill fitted for the business of reigning: so he thought of giving up his kingdom; but to whom should it be? This was a point that his fatherly heart could not settle; for he loved all his sons alike. 'My dear children,' said he, 'I grow old and weak, and should like to give up my kingdom; but I cannot make up my mind which of you to choose for my heir, for I love you all three; and besides, I should wish to give my people the cleverest and best of you for their king. However, I will give you three trials, and the one who wins the prize shall have the kingdom. The first is to seek me out one hundred ells of cloth, so fine that I can draw it through my golden ring.' The sons said they would do their best, and set out on the search.

The two eldest brothers took with them many followers,

and coaches and horses of all sorts, to bring home all the
beautiful cloths which they should find; but the youngest
went alone by himself. They soon came to where the roads
branched off into several ways; two ran through smiling
meadows, with smooth paths and shady groves, but the
third looked dreary and dirty, and went over barren wastes.
The two eldest chose the pleasant ways; and the youngest
took his leave and whistled along over the dreary road.
Whenever fine linen was to be seen, the two elder brothers
bought it, and bought so much that their coaches and
horses bent under their burthen. The youngest, on the
other hand, journeyed on many a weary day, and found
not a place where he could buy even one piece of cloth that
was at all fine and good. His heart sunk beneath him, and
every mile he grew more and more heavy and sorrowful.
At last he came to a bridge over a stream, and there he sat
himself down to rest and sigh over his bad luck, when an
ugly-looking frog popped its head out of the water, and
asked, with a voice that had not at all a harsh sound to
his ears, what was the matter. The prince said in a pet,
'Silly frog! thou canst not help me.' 'Who told you so?'
said the frog; 'tell me what ails you.' After a while the
prince opened the whole story, and told why his father had
sent him out. 'I will help you,' said the frog; so it jumped
back into the stream and soon came back dragging a small
piece of linen not bigger than one's hand, and by no means
the cleanest in the world in its look. However, there it was,
and the prince was told to take it away with him. He had
no great liking for such a dirty rag; but still there was
something in the frog's speech that pleased him much, and
he thought to himself, 'It can do no harm, it is better than
nothing;' so he picked it up, put it in his pocket, and
thanked the frog, who dived down again, panting and quite
tired, as it seemed, with its work. The farther he went the
heavier he found to his great joy the pocket grow, and so he

turned himself homewards, trusting greatly in his good luck.

He reached home nearly about the same time that his brothers came up, with their horses and coaches all heavily laden. Then the old king was very glad to see his children again, and pulled the ring off his finger to try who had done the best; but in all the stock which the two eldest had brought there was not one piece a tenth part of which would go through the ring. At this they were greatly abashed; for they had made a laugh of their brother, who came home, as they thought, empty-handed. But how great was their anger, when they saw him pull from his pocket a piece that for softness, beauty, and whiteness, was a thousand times better than any thing that was ever before seen! It was so fine that it passed with ease through the ring; indeed, two such pieces would readily have gone in together. The father embraced the lucky youth, told his servants to throw the coarse linen into the sea, and said to his children, 'Now you must set about the second task which I am to set you; – bring me home a little dog, so small that it will lie in a nut-shell.'

His sons were not a little frightened at such a task; but they all longed for the crown, and made up their minds to go and try their hands, and so after a few days they set out once more on their travels. At the cross-ways they parted as before, and the youngest chose his old dreary rugged road with all the bright hopes that his former good luck gave him. Scarcely had he sat himself down again at the bridge foot, when his old friend the frog jumped out, set itself beside him, and as before opened its big wide mouth, and croaked out, 'What is the matter?' The prince had this time no doubt of the frog's power, and therefore told what he wanted. 'It shall be done for you,' said the frog; and springing into the stream it soon brought up a hazel-nut, laid it at his feet, and told him to take it home to his father, and crack it gently, and then see what would happen. The prince went his way very well pleased, and the frog, tired with its task, jumped back into the water.

His brothers had reached home first, and brought with them a great many very pretty little dogs. The old king, willing to help them all he could, sent for a large walnut-shell and tried it with every one of the little dogs; but one stuck fast with the hind-foot out, and another with the head, and a third with the forefoot, and a fourth with its tail, – in short, some one way and some another; but none was at all likely to sit easily in this new kind of kennel. When all had been tried, the youngest made his father a dutiful bow, and gave him the hazel-nut, begging him to crack it very carefully: the moment this was done out ran a beautiful little white dog upon the king's hand, wagged its tail, fondled his new master, and soon turned about and barked at the other little beasts in the most graceful manner, to the delight of the whole court. The joy of every one was great; the old king again embraced his lucky son, told his people to drown all the other dogs in the sea, and said to his children, 'Dear sons! your weightiest tasks are now over; listen to my last wish; whoever brings home the fairest lady shall be at once the heir to my crown.'

The prize was so tempting and the chance so fair for all, that none made any doubts about setting to work, each in his own way, to try and be the winner. The youngest was not in such good spirits as he was the last time; he thought to himself, 'The old frog has been able to do a great deal for me; but all its power must be nothing to me now, for where should it find me a fair maiden, still less a fairer maiden than was ever seen at my father's court? The swamps where it lives have no living things in them, but toads, snakes, and such vermin.' Meantime he went on, and sighed as he sat down again with a heavy heart by the bridge. 'Ah frog!' said he, 'this time thou canst do me no

G. Cruikshank —

good.' 'Never mind,' croaked the frog; 'only tell me what
is the matter now.' Then the prince told his old friend what
trouble had now come upon him. 'Go thy ways home,' said
the frog; 'the fair maiden will follow hard after; but take
care and do not laugh at whatever may happen!' This said,
it sprang as before into the water and was soon out of sight.
The prince still sighed on, for he trusted very little this
time to the frog's word; but he had not set many steps towards home before he heard a noise behind him, and looking round saw six large water rats dragging along a large
pumpkin like a coach, full trot. On the box sat an old fat

toad as coachman, and behind stood two little frogs as
footmen, and two fine mice with stately whiskers ran before as outriders; within sat his old friend the frog, rather
misshapen and unseemly to be sure, but still with somewhat of a graceful air as it bowed to him in passing. Much
too deeply wrapt in thought as to his chance of finding the
fair lady whom he was seeking, to take any heed of the
strange scene before him, the prince scarcely looked at it,
and had still less mind to laugh. The coach passed on a little
way, and soon turned a corner that hid it from his sight;
but how astonished was he, on turning the corner himself,
to find a handsome coach and six black horses standing
there, with a coachman in gay livery, and within, the most
beautiful lady he had ever seen, whom he soon knew to be
the fair Cherry, for whom his heart had so long ago panted!
As he came up, the servants opened the coach door, and he
was allowed to seat himself by the beautiful lady.

They soon came to his father's city, where his brothers
also came, with trains of fair ladies; but as soon as Cherry
was seen, all the court gave her with one voice the crown of
beauty. The delighted father embraced his son, and
named him the heir to his crown, and ordered all the other
ladies to be thrown like the little dogs into the sea and
drowned. Then the prince married Cherry, and lived long
and happily with her, and indeed lives with her still – if he
be not dead.

MOTHER HOLLE

A WIDOW had two daughters; one of them was very pretty
and thrifty, but the other was ugly and idle.

Odd as you may think it, she loved the ugly and idle one
much the best, and the other was made to do all the work,
and was in short quite the drudge of the whole house.

Every day she had to sit on a bench by a well on the side of the high-road before the house, and spin so much that her fingers were quite sore, and at length the blood would come. Now it happened that once when her fingers had bled and the spindle was all bloody, she dipt it into the well, and meant to wash it, but unluckily it fell from her hand and dropt in. Then she ran crying to her mother, and told her what had happened; but she scolded her sharply, and said, 'If you have been so silly as to let the spindle fall in, you must get it out again as well as you can.' So the poor little girl went back to the well, and knew not how to begin, but in her sorrow threw herself into the water, and sank down to the bottom senseless. In a short time she seemed to awake as from a trance, and came to herself again; and when she opened her eyes and looked around, she saw she was in a beautiful meadow, where the sun shone brightly, the birds sang sweetly on the boughs, and thousands of flowers sprang beneath her feet.

Then she rose up, and walked along this delightful meadow, and came to a pretty cottage by the side of a wood; and when she went in she saw an oven full of new bread baking, and the bread said, 'Pull me out! pull me out! or I shall be burnt, for I am quite done enough.' So she stepped up quickly and took it all out. Then she went on farther, and came to a tree that was full of fine rosy-cheeked apples, and it said to her, 'Shake me! shake me! we are all quite ripe!' So she shook the tree, and the apples fell down like a shower, until there were no more upon the tree. Then she went on again, and at length came to a small cottage where an old woman was sitting at the door: the little girl would have run away, but the old woman called out after her, 'Don't be frightened, my dear child! stay with me, I should like to have you for my little maid, and if you do all the work in the house neatly you shall fare well; but take care to make my bed nicely, and shake it

every morning out at the door, so that the feathers may
fly, for then the good people below say it snows. – I am
Mother Holle.'

As the old woman spoke so kindly to her, the girl was
willing to do as she said; so she went into her employ, and
took care to do every thing to please her, and always shook
the bed well, so that she led a very quiet life with her, and
every day had good meat both boiled and roast to eat for
her dinner.

But when she had been some time with the old lady, she
became sorrowful, and although she was much better off
here than at home, still she had a longing towards it, and at
length said to her mistress, 'I used to grieve at my troubles
at home, but if they were all to come again, and I were sure
of faring ever so well here, I could not stay any longer.'
'You are right,' said her mistress; 'you shall do as you like;
and as you have worked for me so faithfully, I will myself
show you the way back again.' Then she took her by the
hand and led her behind her cottage, and opened a door,
and as the girl stood underneath there fell a heavy shower
of gold, so that she held out her apron and caught a great
deal of it. And the fairy put a shining golden dress over
her, and said, 'All this you shall have because you have
behaved so well;' and she gave her back the spindle too
which had fallen into the well, and led her out by another
door. When it shut behind her, she found herself not far
from her mother's house; and as she went into the court-
yard the cock sat upon the well-head and clapt his wings
and cried out,

'Cock a-doodle-doo!
Our golden lady's come home again.'

Then she went into the house, and as she was so rich she
was welcomed home. When her mother heard how she got
these riches, she wanted to have the same luck for her ugly

and idle daughter, so she too was told to sit by the well and spin. That her spindle might be bloody, she pricked her fingers with it, and when that would not do she thrust her hand into a thorn-bush. Then she threw it into the well and sprung in herself after it. Like her sister, she came to a beautiful meadow, and followed the same path. When she came to the oven in the cottage, the bread called out as before, 'Take me out! or I shall burn, I am quite done enough.' But the lazy girl said, 'A pretty story, indeed! just as if I should dirty myself for you!' and went on her way. She soon came to the apple-tree that cried, 'Shake me! shake me! for my apples are quite ripe!' but she answered, 'I will take care how I do that, for one of you might fall upon my head;' so she went on. At length she came to Mother Holle's house, and readily agreed to be her maid. The first day she behaved herself very well, and did what her mistress told her; for she thought of the gold she would give her; but the second day she began to be lazy, and the third still more so, for she would not get up in the morning early enough, and when she did she made the bed very badly, and did not shake it so that the feathers would fly out. Mother Holle was soon tired of her, and turned her off; but the lazy girl was quite pleased at that, and thought to herself, 'Now the golden rain will come.' Then the fairy took her to the same door; but when she stood under it, instead of gold a great kettle full of dirty pitch came showering upon her. 'That is your wages,' said Mother Holle as she shut the door upon her. So she went home quite black with the pitch, and as she came near her mother's house the cock sat upon the well, and clapt his wings, and cried out –

> 'Cock-a-doodle-doo!
> Our dirty slut's come home again!'

THE WATER OF LIFE

Long before you and I were born there reigned, in a country a great way off, a king who had three sons. This king once fell very ill, so ill that nobody thought he would live. His sons were very much grieved at their father's sickness; and as they walked weeping in the garden of the palace, an old man met them and asked what they ailed. They told him their father was so ill that they were afraid nothing could save him. 'I know what would,' said the old man; 'it is the Water of Life. If he could have a draught of it he would be well again, but it is very hard to get.' Then the eldest son said, 'I will soon find it,' and went to the sick king, and begged that he might go in search of the Water of Life, as it was the only thing that could save him. 'No,' said the king; 'I had rather die than place you in such great danger as you must meet with in your journey.' But he begged so hard that the king let him go; and the prince thought to himself, 'If I bring my father this water I shall be his dearest son, and he will make me heir to his kingdom.'

Then he set out, and when he had gone on his way some time he came to a deep valley overhung with rocks and woods; and as he looked around there stood above him on one of the rocks a little dwarf, who called out to him and said, 'Prince, whither hastest thou so fast?' 'What is that to you, little ugly one?' said the prince sneeringly, and rode on his way. But the little dwarf fell into a great rage at his behaviour, and laid a spell of ill luck upon him, so that, as he rode on, the mountain pass seemed to become narrower and narrower, and at last the way was so straitened that he could not go a step forward, and when he thought to have turned his horse round and gone back the way he came, the passage he found had closed behind also, and

shut him quite up; he next tried to get off his horse and
make his way on foot, but this he was unable to do, and so
there he was forced to abide spell-bound.

Meantime the king his father was lingering on in daily
hope of his return, till at last the second son said, 'Father, I
will go in search of this Water;' for he thought to himself,
'My brother is surely dead, and the kingdom will fall to me
if I have good luck in my journey.' The king was at first
very unwilling to let him go, but at last yielded to his wish.
So he set out and followed the same road which his brother
had taken, and met the same dwarf, who stopped him at
the same spot, and said as before, 'Prince, whither hastest
thou so fast?' 'Mind your own affairs, busy body!' answered the prince scornfully, and rode off. But the dwarf
put the same enchantment upon him, and when he came
like the other to the narrow pass in the mountains he could
neither move forward nor backward. Thus it is with proud
silly people, who think themselves too wise to take advice.

When the second prince had thus stayed away a long while,
the youngest said he would go and search for the Water of
Life, and trusted he should soon be able to make his father
well again. The dwarf met him too at the same spot, and
said, 'Prince, whither hastest thou so fast?' and the prince
said, 'I go in search of the Water of Life, because my father
is ill and like to die: – can you help me?' 'Do you know
where it is to be found?' asked the dwarf. 'No,' said the
prince. 'Then as you have spoken to me kindly and sought
for advice, I will tell you how and where to go. The Water
you seek springs from a well in an enchanted castle, and
that you may be able to go in safety I will give you an iron
wand and two little loaves of bread; strike the iron door of
the castle three times with the wand, and it will open: two
hungry lions will be lying down inside gaping for their
prey; but if you throw them the bread they will let you
pass; then hasten on to the well and take some of the Water

of Life before the clock strikes twelve, for if you tarry
longer the door will shut upon you for ever.'

Then the prince thanked the dwarf for his friendly aid,
and took the wand and the bread and went travelling on
and on over sea and land, till he came to his journey's end,
and found every thing to be as the dwarf had told him.
The door flew open at the third stroke of the wand, and
when the lions were quieted he went on through the castle,
and came at length to a beautiful hall; around it he saw
several knights sitting in a trance; then he pulled off their
rings and put them on his own fingers. In another room he
saw on a table a sword and a loaf of bread, which he also
took. Farther on he came to a room where a beautiful young
lady sat upon a couch, who welcomed him joyfully, and
said, if he would set her free from the spell that bound her,
the kingdom should be his if he would come back in a year
and marry her; then she told him that the well that held
the Water of Life was in the palace gardens, and bade him
make haste and draw what he wanted before the clock
struck twelve. Then he went on, and as he walked through
beautiful gardens he came to a delightful shady spot in
which stood a couch; and he thought to himself, as he felt
tired, that he would rest himself for a while and gaze on
the lovely scenes around him. So he laid himself down, and
sleep fell upon him unawares and he did not wake up till
the clock was striking a quarter to twelve; then he sprung
from the couch dreadfully frightened, ran to the well, filled
a cup that was standing by him full of Water, and hastened
to get away in time. Just as he was going out of the iron
door it struck twelve, and the door fell so quickly upon him
that it tore away a piece of his heel.

When he found himself safe he was overjoyed to think
that he had got the Water of Life; and as he was going on
his way homewards, he passed by the little dwarf, who
when he saw the sword and the loaf said, 'You have made a

noble prize; with the sword you can at a blow slay whole
armies, and the bread will never fail.' Then the prince
thought to himself, 'I cannot go home to my father without
my brothers;' so he said, 'Dear dwarf, cannot you tell me
where my two brothers are, who set out in search of the
Water of Life before me and never came back?' 'I have
shut them up by a charm between two mountains,' said the
dwarf, 'because they were proud and ill behaved, and
scorned to ask advice.' The prince begged so hard for his
brothers that the dwarf at last set them free, though unwillingly, saying, 'Beware of them, for they have bad
hearts.' Their brother, however, was greatly rejoiced to see
them, and told them all that had happened to him, how he
had found the Water of Life, and had taken a cup full of it,
and how he had set a beautiful princess free from a spell
that bound her; and how she had engaged to wait a whole
year, and then to marry him and give him the kingdom.
Then they all three rode on together, and on their way
home came to a country that was laid waste by war and a
dreadful famine, so that it was feared all must die for want.
But the prince gave the king of the land the bread, and all
his kingdom ate of it. And he slew the enemy's army with
the wonderful sword, and left the kingdom in peace and
plenty. In the same manner he befriended two other countries that they passed through on their way.

When they came to the sea, they got into a ship, and
during their voyage the two eldest said to themselves, 'Our
brother has got the Water which we could not find, therefore our father will forsake us, and give him the kingdom
which is our right;' so they were full of envy and revenge,
and agreed together how they could ruin him. They waited
till he was fast asleep, and then poured the Water of Life
out of the cup and took it for themselves, giving him bitter
sea-water instead. And when they came to their journey's
end, the youngest son brought his cup to the sick king, that

he might drink and be healed. Scarcely, however, had he tasted the bitter sea-water when he became worse even than he was before, and then both the elder sons came in and blamed the youngest for what he had done, and said that he wanted to poison their father, but that they had found the Water of Life and had brought it with them. He no sooner began to drink of what they brought him, than he felt his sickness leave him, and was as strong and well as in his young days; then they went to their brother and laughed at him, and said, 'Well, brother, you found the Water of Life, did you? you have had the trouble and we shall have the reward; pray, with all your cleverness why did not you manage to keep your eyes open? Next year one of us will take away your beautiful princess, if you do not take care; you had better say nothing about this to our father, for he does not believe a word you say, and if you tell tales, you shall lose your life into the bargain, but be quiet and we will let you off.'

The old king was still very angry with his youngest son, and thought he really meant to have taken away his life; so he called his court together and asked what should be done, and it was settled that he should be put to death. The prince knew nothing of what was going on, till one day when the king's chief huntsman went a-hunting with him, and they were alone in the wood together, the huntsman looked so sorrowful that the prince said, 'My friend, what is the matter with you?' 'I cannot and dare not tell you,' said he. But the prince begged hard and said, 'Only say what it is, and do not think I shall be angry, for I will forgive you.' 'Alas!' said the huntsman, 'the king has ordered me to shoot you.' The prince started at this, and said, 'Let me live, and I will change dresses with you; you shall take my royal coat to show to my father, and do you give me your shabby one.' 'With all my heart,' said the huntsman; 'I am sure I shall be glad to save you, for I could not have shot you.' Then he took the prince's coat, and gave him the shabby one, and went away through the wood.

Some time after, three grand embassies came to the old king's court, with rich gifts of gold and precious stones for his youngest son, which were sent from the three kings to whom he had lent his sword and loaf of bread, to rid them of their enemy, and feed their people. This touched the old king's heart, and he thought his son might still be guiltless, and said to his court, 'Oh! that my son were still alive! how it grieves me that I had him killed!' 'He still lives,' said the huntsman; 'and I rejoice that I had pity on him, and saved him, for when the time came, I could not shoot him, but let him go in peace and brought home his royal coat.' At this the king was overwhelmed with joy, and made it known throughout all his kingdom, that if his son would come back to his court, he would forgive him.

Meanwhile the princess was eagerly waiting the return of her deliverer, and had a road made leading up to her palace all of shining gold; and told her courtiers that whoever came on horseback and rode straight up to the gate upon it, was her true lover, and that they must let him in; but whoever rode on one side of it, they must be sure was not the right one, and must send him away at once.

The time soon came, when the eldest thought he would make haste to go to the princess, and say that he was the one who had set her free, and that he should have her for his wife, and the kingdom with her. As he came before the palace and saw the golden road, he stopt to look at it, and thought to himself, 'It is a pity to ride upon this beautiful road;' so he turned aside and rode on the right of it. But when he came to the gate, the guards said to him, he was not what he said he was, and must go about his business. The second prince set out soon afterwards on the same errand; and when he came to the golden road, and his horse had set one foot upon it, he stopt to look at it, and thought it very beautiful, and said to himself, 'What a pity it is that any thing should tread here!' then he too turned aside and rode on the left of it. But when he came to the gate the guards said he was not the true prince, and that he too must go away.

Now when the full year was come, the third brother left the wood, where he had laid for fear of his father's anger, and set out in search of his betrothed bride. So he journeyed on, thinking of her all the way, and rode so quickly that he did not even see the golden road, but went with his horse straight over it; and as he came to the gate, it flew open, and the princess welcomed him with joy, and said he was her deliverer and should now be her husband and lord of the kingdom, and the marriage was soon kept with great feasting. When it was over, the princess told him she had heard of his father having forgiven him, and of his wish to have him home again: so he went to visit him, and told him every thing, how his brothers had cheated and robbed him, and yet that he had borne all these wrongs for the love of his father. Then the old king was very angry, and wanted to punish his wicked sons; but they made their escape, and got into a ship and sailed away over the wide sea, and were never heard of any more.

PETER THE GOATHERD

In the wilds of the Hartz Forest there is a high mountain, where the fairies and goblins dance by night, and where they say the great Emperor Frederic Barbarossa still holds his court among the caverns. Now and then he shows himself and punishes those whom he dislikes, or gives some rich gift to the lucky wight whom he takes it into his head to befriend. He sits on a throne of marble with his red beard sweeping on the ground, and once or twice in a long course of years rouses himself for a while from the trance in which he is buried, but soon falls again into his former forgetfulness. Strange chances have befallen many who have strayed within the range of his court: – you shall hear one of them.

A great many years ago there lived in the village at the foot of the mountain, one Peter, a goatherd. Every morning he drove his flock to feed upon the green spots that are here and there found on the mountain's side, and in the evening he sometimes thought it too far to drive his charge home, so he used in such cases to shut it up in a spot amongst the woods, where an old ruined wall was left standing, high enough to form a fold, in which he could count his goats and rest in peace for the night. One evening he found that the prettiest goat of his flock had vanished soon after they were driven into this fold, but was there again in the morning. Again and again he watched, and the same strange thing happened. He thought he would look still more narrowly, and soon found a cleft in the old wall, through which it seemed that his favourite made her way. Peter followed, scrambling as well as he could down the side of the rock, and wondered not a little, on overtaking his goat, to find it employing itself very much at its ease in a cavern, eating corn, which kept dropping from some place above. He went into the cavern and looked about him to see where all this corn, that rattled about his ears like a hail storm, could come from: but all was dark, and he could find no clue to this strange business. At last, as he stood listening, he thought he heard the neighing and stamping of horses. He listened again; it was plainly so; and after a while he was sure that horses were feeding above him, and that the corn fell from their mangers. What could these horses be, which were kept thus in a mountain where none but the goat's foot ever trod? Peter pondered a while; but his won-

der only grew greater and greater, when on a sudden a little
page came forth and beckoned him to follow; he did so, and
came at last to a court-yard surrounded by an old wall.
The spot seemed the bosom of the valley; above rose on
every hand high masses of rock; wide branching trees threw
their arms over head, so that nothing but a glimmering twi-
light made its way through; and here, on the cool smooth
shaven turf, were twelve old knights, who looked very
grave and sober, but were amusing themselves with a game
of nine-pins.

Not a word fell from their lips; but they ordered Peter by
dumb signs to busy himself in setting up the pins, as they
knocked them down. At first his knees trembled, as he
dared to snatch a stolen sidelong glance at the long beards
and old-fashioned dresses of the worthy knights. Little by
little, however, he grew bolder; and at last he plucked up
his heart so far as to take his turn in the draught at the can,
which stood beside him and sent up the smell of the richest
old wine. This gave him new strength for his work; and as
often as he flagged at all, he turned to the same kind friend
for help in his need.

Sleep at last overpowered him; and when he awoke he
found himself stretched out upon the old spot where he had
folded his flock. The same green turf was spread beneath,
and the same tottering walls surrounded him: he rubbed
his eyes, but neither dog nor goat was to be seen, and when
he had looked about him again the grass seemed to be
longer under his feet, and trees hung over his head which he
had either never seen before or had forgotten. Shaking his
head, and hardly knowing whether he were in his right
mind, he wound his way among the mountain steeps,
through paths where his flocks were wont to wander; but
still not a goat was to be seen. Below him in the plain lay
the village where his home was, and at length he took the
downward path, and set out with a heavy heart in search of

his flock. The people who met him as he drew near to the
village were all unknown to him; they were not even drest
as his neighbours were, and they seemed as if they hardly
spoke the same tongue; and when he eagerly asked after
his goats, they only stared at him and stroked their chins.
At last he did the same too, and what was his wonder to
find that his beard was grown at least a foot long! The
world, thought he now to himself, is turned over, or at any
rate bewitched; and yet he knew the mountain (as he
turned round to gaze upon its woody heights); and he
knew the houses and cottages also, with their little gardens,
all of which were in the same places as he had always
known them; he heard some children, too, call the village
by its old name, as a traveller that passed by was asking his
way.

Again he shook his head and went straight through the
village to his own cottage. Alas! it looked sadly out of re-
pair; and in the court-yard lay an unknown child, in a
ragged dress, by the side of a rough, toothless dog, whom he
thought he ought to know, but who snarled and barked in
his face when he called him to him. He went in at an opening in the wall where a door had once stood, but found all so
dreary and empty that he staggered out again like a drunken man, and called his wife and children loudly by their
names; but no one heard, at least no one answered him.

A crowd of women and children soon flocked around the
long grey-bearded man, and all broke upon him at once
with the questions, 'Who are you?' 'Whom do you want?'
It seemed to him so odd to ask other people at his own door
after his wife and children, that in order to get rid of the
crowd he named the first man that came into his head; –
'Hans, the blacksmith!' said he. Most held their tongues
and stared, but at last an old woman said, 'He went these
seven years ago to a place that you will not reach to-day.'
'Frank the tailor, then!' 'Heaven rest his soul!' said an old

beldame upon crutches; 'he has laid these ten years in a house that he'll never leave.'

Peter looked at the old woman, and shuddered as he saw her to be one of his old friends, only with a strangely altered face. All wish to ask further questions was gone; but at last a young woman made her way through the gaping throng with a baby in her arms, and a little girl about three years old clinging to her other hand; all three looked the very image of his wife. 'What is thy name?' asked he wildly. 'Mary.' 'And your father's?' 'Heaven bless him! Peter! It is now twenty years since we sought him day and night on the mountain; his flock came back, but he never was heard of any more. I was then seven years old.' The goatherd could hold no longer. 'I am Peter,' cried he; 'I am Peter, and no other;' as he took the child from his daughter's arms and kissed it. All stood gaping, and not knowing what to say or think, till at length one voice was heard, 'Why, it is Peter!' and then several others cried, 'Yes, it is Peter! Welcome, neighbour, welcome home, after twenty long years!'

THE FOUR CLEVER BROTHERS

'DEAR children,' said a poor man to his four sons, 'I have nothing to give you; you must go out into the world, and try your luck. Begin by learning some trade, and see how you can get on.' So the four brothers took their walking-sticks in their hands, and their little bundles on their shoulders, and, after bidding their father good-bye, went all out at the gate together. When they had got on some way they came to four cross-ways, each leading to a different country. Then the eldest said, 'Here we must part; but this day four years we will come back to this spot; and in the mean time each must try what he can do for himself.' So each brother went his way; and as the oldest was hastening on, a man met him, and asked him where he was going and what he wanted. 'I am going to try my luck in the world, and should like to begin by learning some trade,' answered he. 'Then,' said the man, 'go with me, and I will teach you how to become the cunningest thief that ever was.' 'No,' said the other, 'that is not an honest calling, and what can one look to earn by it in the end but the gallows?' 'Oh!' said the man, 'you need not fear the gallows; for I will only teach you to steal what will be fair game; I meddle with nothing but what no one else can get or care any thing about, and where no one can find you out.' So the young man agreed to follow his trade, and he soon showed himself so clever that nothing could escape him that he had once set his mind upon.

The second brother also met a man, who, when he found out what he was setting out upon, asked him what trade he meant to learn. 'I do not know yet,' said he. 'Then come with me, and be a star-gazer. It is a noble trade, for nothing can be hidden from you when you understand the stars.' The plan pleased him much, and he soon became such a skilful star-gazer, that when he had served out his time, and wanted to leave his master, he gave him a glass, and said, 'With this you can see all that is passing in the sky and on earth, and nothing can be hidden from you.'

The third brother met a huntsman, who took him with him, and taught him so well all that belonged to hunting, that he became very clever in that trade; and when he left his master he gave him a bow, and said, 'Whatever you shoot at with this bow you will be sure to hit.'

The youngest brother likewise met a man who asked him what he wished to do. 'Would not you like,' said he, 'to be a tailor?' 'Oh no!' said the young man; 'sitting cross-legged from morning to night, working backwards and forwards with a needle and goose, will never suit me.' 'Oh!' answered the man, 'that is not my sort of tailoring; come with me, and you will learn quite another kind of trade from that.' Not knowing what better to do, he came into the plan, and learnt the trade from the beginning; and when he left his master, he gave him a needle, and said, 'You can sew any thing with this, be it as soft as an egg, or as hard as steel, and the joint will be so fine that no seam will be seen.'

After the space of four years, at the time agreed upon, the four brothers met at the four cross-roads, and having welcomed each other, set off towards their father's home, where they told him all that had happened to them, and how each had learned some trade. Then one day, as they were sitting before the house under a very high tree, the father said, 'I should like to try what each of you can do in his trade.' So he looked up, and said to the second son, 'At the top of this tree there is a chaffinch's nest; tell me how many eggs there are in it.' The star-gazer took his glass, looked up, and said, 'Five.' 'Now,' said the father to the eldest son, 'take away the eggs without the bird that is sitting upon them and hatching them, knowing any thing of what you are doing.' So the cunning thief climbed up the tree, and brought away to his father the five eggs from under the bird, who never saw or felt what he was doing, but kept sitting on at her ease. Then the father took the eggs, and put one on each corner of the table and the fifth in the middle, and said to the huntsman, 'Cut all the eggs in two pieces at one shot.' The huntsman took up his bow, and at one shot struck all the five eggs as his father wished. 'Now comes your turn,' said he to the young tailor; 'sew the eggs and the young birds in them together again, so neatly that the shot shall have done them no harm.' Then the tailor took his needle and sewed the eggs as he was told; and when he had done, the thief was sent to take them back to the nest, and put them under the bird, without its know-ing it. Then she went on setting, and hatched them; and in a few days they crawled out, and had only a little red streak across their necks where the tailor had sewed them to-gether.

'Well done, sons!' said the old man, 'you have made good use of your time, and learnt something worth the knowing; but I am sure I do not know which ought to have the prize. Oh! that a time might soon come for you to turn your skill to some account!'

Not long after this there was a great bustle in the coun-try; for the king's daughter had been carried off by a mighty dragon, and the king mourned over his loss day and night, and made it known that whoever brought her back to him should have her for a wife. Then the four brothers said to each other, 'Here is a chance for us; let us try what we can do.' And they agreed to see whether they could not set the princess free. 'I will soon find out where she is, how-ever,' said the star-gazer as he looked through his glass, and soon cried out, 'I see her afar off, sitting upon a rock in the sea, and I can spy the dragon close by, guarding her.' Then he went to the king, and asked for a ship for himself and his brothers, and went with them upon the sea till they came to the right place. There they found the princess sitting, as the star-gazer had said, on the rock, and the dragon was lying asleep with his head upon her lap. 'I dare not shoot at him,' said the huntsman, 'for I should kill the beautiful young lady also.' 'Then I will try my skill,' said the thief; and went and stole her away from under the dragon so quickly and gently that the beast did not know it, but went on snoring.

Then away they hastened with her full of joy in their boat towards the ship; but soon came the dragon roaring behind them through the air, for he awoke and missed the princess; but when he got over the boat, and wanted to pounce upon them and carry off the princess, the huntsman took up his bow and shot him straight at the heart, so that he fell down dead. They were still not safe; for he was such a great beast, that in his fall he overset the boat, and they had to swim in the open sea upon a few planks. So the tailor took his needle, and with a few large stitches put some of the planks together, and sat down upon them, and sailed about and gathered up all the pieces of the boat, and tacked them to-gether so quickly that the boat was soon ready, and they then reached the ship and got home safe.

When they had brought home the princess to her father, there was great rejoicing; and he said to the four brothers, 'One of you shall marry her, but you must settle amongst yourselves which it is to be.' Then there arose a quarrel be-tween them; and the star-gazer said, 'If I had not found the princess out, all your skill would have been of no use; therefore she ought to be mine.' 'Your seeing her would have been of no use,' said the thief, 'if I had not taken her away from the dragon; therefore she ought to be mine.' 'No, she is mine,' said the huntsman; 'for if I had not killed the dragon, he would after all have torn you and the princess into pieces.' 'And if I had not sewed the boat to-gether again,' said the tailor, 'you would all have been drowned; therefore she is mine.' Then the king put in a word, and said, 'Each of you is right; and as all cannot have the young lady, the best way is for neither of you to have her; and to make up for the loss, I will give each, as a re-ward for his skill, half a kingdom.' So the brothers agreed that would be much better than quarrelling; and the king then gave each half a kingdom, as he had said; and they lived very happily the rest of their days, and took good care of their father.

THE ELFIN-GROVE

'I HOPE,' said a woodman one day to his wife, 'that the children will not run into that fir-grove by the side of the river; who they are that have come to live there I cannot tell, but I am sure it looks more dark and gloomy than ever, and some queer-looking beings are to be seen lurking about it every night, as I am told.' The woodman could not say that they brought any ill luck as yet, whatever they were; for all the village had thriven more than ever since they came; the fields looked gayer and greener, and even the sky was a deeper blue. Not knowing what to say of them, the farmer very wisely let his new friends alone, and in truth troubled his head very little about them.

That very evening little Mary and her playfellow Martin were playing at hide and seek in the valley. 'Where can he be hid?' said she; 'he must have gone into the fir-grove,' and down she ran to look. Just then she spied a little dog that jumped round her and wagged his tail, and led her on towards the wood. Then he ran into it, and she soon jumped up the bank to look after him, but was overjoyed to see, instead of a gloomy grove of firs, a delightful garden, where flowers and shrubs of every kind grew upon turf of the softest green; gay butterflies flew about her, the birds sang sweetly, and, what was strangest, the prettiest little children sported about on all sides, some twining the flowers, and others dancing in rings upon the shady spots beneath the trees. In the midst, instead of the hovels of which Mary had heard, there was a palace that dazzled her eyes with its brightness. For a while she gazed on the fairy scene around her, till at last one of the little dancers ran up to her, and said, 'And you are come at last to see us? we have often seen you play about, and wished to have you with us.' Then she plucked some of the fruit that grew

near; and Mary at the first taste forgot her home, and
wished only to see and know more of her fairy friends.

Then they led her about with them and showed her all
their sports. One while they danced by moonlight on the
primrose banks; at another time they skipped from bough
to bough among the trees that hung over the cooling
streams; for they moved as lightly and easily through the
air as on the ground: and Mary went with them every
where, for they bore her in their arms wherever they

wished to go. Sometimes they would throw seeds on the turf, and directly little trees sprung up; and then they would set their feet upon the branches, while the trees grew under them, till they danced upon the boughs in the air, wherever the breezes carried them; and again the trees would sink down into the earth and land them safely at their bidding. At other times they would go and visit the palace of their queen; and there the richest food was spread before them, and the softest music was heard; and there all around grew flowers which were always changing their hues, from scarlet to purple and yellow and emerald. Sometimes they went to look at the heaps of treasure which were piled up in the royal stores; for little dwarfs were always employed in searching the earth for gold. Small as this fairy land looked from without, it seemed within to have no end; a mist hung around it to shield it from the eyes of men; and some of the little elves sat perched upon the outermost trees, to keep watch lest the step of man should break in and spoil the charm.

'And who are you?' said Mary one day. 'We are what are called elves in your world,' said one whose name was Gossamer, and who had become her dearest friend: 'we are told you talk a great deal about us; some of our tribes like to work you mischief, but we who live here seek only to be happy: we meddle little with mankind; but when we do come among them, it is to do them good.' 'And where is your queen?' said little Mary. 'Hush! hush! you cannot see or know her: you must leave us before she comes back, which will be now very soon, for mortal step cannot come where she is. But you will know that she is here when you see the meadows gayer, the rivers more sparkling, and the sun brighter.'

Soon afterwards Gossamer told Mary the time was come to bid her farewell, and gave her a ring in token of their friendship, and led her to the edge of the grove. 'Think of me,' said she; 'but beware how you tell what you have seen, or try to visit any of us again, for if you do, we shall quit this grove and come back no more.' Turning back, Mary saw nothing but the gloomy fir-grove she had known before. 'How frightened my father and mother will be!' thought she as she looked at the sun, which had risen some time. 'They will wonder where I have been all night, and yet I must not tell them what I have seen.' She hastened homewards, wondering however, as she went, to see that the leaves, which yesterday so fresh and green, were now falling dry and yellow around her. The cottage too seemed changed, and, when she went in, there sat her father looking some years older than when she saw him last; and her mother, whom she hardly knew, was by his side. Close by was a young man; 'Father,' said Mary, 'who is this?' 'Who are you that call me father?' said he; 'are you – no you cannot be – our long-lost Mary?' But they soon saw that it was their Mary; and the young man, who was her old friend and playfellow Martin, said, 'No wonder you had forgotten me in seven years; do not you remember how we parted seven years ago while playing in the field? We thought you were quite lost; but we are glad to see that some one has taken care of you and brought you home at last.' Mary said nothing, for she could not tell all; but she wondered at the strange tale, and felt gloomy at the change from fairy land to her father's cottage.

Little by little she came to herself, thought of her story as a mere dream, and soon became Martin's bride. Every thing seemed to thrive around them; and Mary called her first little girl Elfie, in memory of her friends. The little thing was loved by every one. It was pretty and very goodtempered; Mary thought that it was very like a little elf; and all, without knowing why, called it the fairy child.

One day, while Mary was dressing her little Elfie, she found a piece of gold hanging round her neck by a silken thread, and knew it to be of the same sort as she had seen in the hands of the fairy dwarfs. Elfie seemed sorry at its being seen, and said that she had found it in the garden. But Mary watched her, and soon found that she went every afternoon to sit by herself in a shady place behind the house: so one day she hid herself to see what the child did there; and to her great wonder Gossamer was sitting by her side. 'Dear Elfie,' she was saying, 'your mother and I used to sit thus when she was young and lived among us. Oh! if you could come and do so too! but since our queen came to us it cannot be; yet I will come and see you and talk to you, whilst you are a child; when you grow up we must part for ever.' Then she plucked one of the roses that grew around them and breathed gently upon it, and said, 'Take this for my sake. It will keep its freshness a whole year.'

Then Mary loved her little Elfie more than ever; and when she found that she spent some hours of almost every day with the elf, she used to hide herself and watch them without being seen, till one day when Gossamer was bearing her little friend through the air from tree to tree, her mother was so frightened lest her child should fall that she could not help screaming out, and Gossamer set her gently on the ground and seemed angry, and flew away. But still she used sometimes to come and play with her little friend, and would soon have done so perhaps the same as before, had not Mary one day told her husband the whole story, for she could not bear to hear him always wondering and laughing at their little child's odd ways, and saying he was sure there was something in the fir-grove that brought them no good. So to show him that all she said was true, she took him to see Elfie and the fairy; but no sooner did Gossamer know that he was there, (which she did in an instant,) than she changed herself into a raven and flew off into the fir-grove.

Mary burst into tears, and so did Elfie, for she knew she

should see her dear friend no more: but Martin was restless and bent upon following up his search after the fairies; so when night came he stole away towards the grove. When he came to it nothing was to be seen but the gloomy firs and the old hovels; and the thunder rolled, and the wind groaned and whistled through the trees. It seemed that all about him was angry; so he turned homewards frightened at what he had done.

In the morning all the neighbours flocked around, asking one another what the noise and bustle of the last night could mean; and when they looked about them, their trees looked blighted, and the meadows parched, the streams were dried up, and every thing seemed troubled and sorrowful; but they all thought that some how or other the fir-grove had not near so forbidding a look as it used to have. Strange stories were told, how one had heard flutterings in the air, another had seen the fir-grove as it were alive with little beings that flew away from it. Each neighbour told his tale, and all wondered what could have happened; but Mary and her husband knew what was the matter, and bewailed their folly; for they foresaw that their kind neighbours, to whom they owed all their luck, were gone for ever. Among the bystanders none told a wilder story than the old ferryman who plied across the river at the foot of the grove; he told how at midnight his boat was carried away, and how hundreds of little beings seemed to load it with treasures; how a strange piece of gold was left for him in the boat, as his fare; how the air seemed full of fairy forms fluttering around; and how at last a great train passed over that seemed to be guarding their leader to the meadows on the other side; and how he heard soft music floating around as they flew; and how sweet voices sung as they hovered over his head,

Fairy Queen!
Fairy Queen!

Mortal steps are on the green;
            Come away!
            Haste away!
      Fairies, guard your Queen!
Hither, hither, fairy Queen!
Lest thy silvery wing be seen;
            O'er the sky
            Fly, fly, fly!
Fairies, guard your lady Queen!
            O'er the sky
            Fly, fly, fly!
      Fairies, guard your Queen!

            Fairy Queen!
            Fairy Queen!
Thou hast pass'd the treach'rous scene;
            Now we may
            Down and play
      O'er the daisied green.
Lightly, lightly, fairy Queen!
Trip it gently o'er the green:
            .Fairies gay,
            Trip away
Round about your lady Queen!
            Fairies gay,
            Trip away
      Round about your Queen!

Poor Elfie mourned their loss the most, and would spend
whole hours in looking upon the rose that her playfellow
had given her, and singing over it the pretty airs she had
taught her; till at length when the year's charm had passed
away and it began to fade, she planted the stalk in her garden, and there it grew and grew till she could sit under the
shade of it and think of her friend Gossamer.

THE SALAD

As a merry young huntsman was once going briskly along through a wood, there came up a little old woman, and said to him, 'Good day, good day; you seem merry enough, but I am hungry and thirsty; do pray give me something to eat.' The huntsman took pity on her, and put his hand in his pocket and gave her what he had. Then he wanted to go his way; but she took hold of him, and said, 'Listen, my friend, to what I am going to tell you; I will reward you for your kindness; go your way, and after a little time you will come to a tree where you will see nine birds sitting on a cloak. Shoot into the midst of them, and one will fall down dead: the cloak will fall too; take it, it is a wishing-cloak, and when you wear it you will find yourself at any place where you may wish to be. Cut open the dead bird, take out its heart and keep it, and you will find a piece of gold under your pillow every morning when you rise. It is the bird's heart that will bring you this good luck.'

The huntsman thanked her, and thought to himself, 'If all this does happen, it will be a fine thing for me.' When he had gone a hundred steps or so, he heard a screaming and chirping in the branches over him, and looked up and saw a flock of birds pulling a cloak with their bills and feet; screaming, fighting, and tugging at each other as if each wished to have it himself. 'Well,' said the huntsman, 'this is wonderful; this happens just as the old woman said;' then he shot into the midst of them so that their feathers flew all about. Off went the flock chattering away; but one fell down dead, and the cloak with it. Then the huntsman did as the old woman told him, cut open the bird, took out the heart, and carried the cloak home with him.

The next morning when he awoke he lifted up his pillow, and there lay the piece of gold glittering underneath;

the same happened next day, and indeed every day when he arose. He heaped up a great deal of gold, and at last thought to himself, 'Of what use is this gold to me whilst I am at home? I will go out into the world and look about me.'

Then he took leave of his friends, and hung his bag and bow about his neck, and went his way. It so happened that his road one day led through a thick wood, at the end of which was a large castle in a green meadow, and at one of the windows stood an old woman with a very beautiful young lady by her side looking about them. Now the old woman was a fairy, and said to the young lady, 'There is a young man coming out of the wood who carries a wonderful prize; we must get it away from him, my dear child, for it is more fit for us than for him. He has a bird's heart that brings a piece of gold under his pillow every morning.' Meantime the huntsman came nearer and looked at the lady, and said to himself, 'I have been travelling so long that I should like to go into this castle and rest myself, for I have money enough to pay for any thing I want;' but the real reason was, that he wanted to see more of the beautiful lady. Then he went into the house, and was welcomed kindly; and it was not long before he was so much in love that he thought of nothing else but looking at the lady's eyes, and doing every thing that she wished. Then the old woman said, 'Now is the time for getting the bird's heart.' So the lady stole it away, and he never found any more gold under his pillow, for it lay now under the young lady's, and the old woman took it away every morning; but he was so much in love that he never missed his prize.

'Well,' said the old fairy, 'we have got the bird's heart, but not the wishing-cloak yet, and that we must also get.' 'Let us leave him that,' said the young lady; 'he has already lost his wealth.' Then the fairy was very angry, and said, 'Such a cloak is a very rare and wonderful thing, and I must and will have it.' So she did as the old woman told her, and set herself at the window, and looked about the country and seemed very sorrowful; then the huntsman said, 'What makes you so sad?' 'Alas! dear sir,' said she, 'yonder lies the granite rock where all the costly diamonds grow, and I want so much to go there, that whenever I think of it I cannot help being sorrowful, for who can reach it? only the birds and the flies, – man cannot.' 'If that's all your grief,' said the huntsman, 'I'll take you there with all my heart;' so he drew her under his cloak, and the moment he wished to be on the granite mountain they were both there. The diamonds glittered so on all sides that they were delighted with the sight and picked up the finest. But the old fairy made a deep sleep come upon him, and he said to the young lady, 'Let us sit down and rest ourselves a little, I am so tired that I cannot stand any longer.' So they sat down, and he laid his head in her lap and fell asleep; and whilst he was sleeping on she took the cloak from his shoulders, hung it on her own, picked up the diamonds, and wished herself home again.

When he awoke and found that his lady had tricked him, and left him alone on the wild rock, he said, 'Alas! what roguery there is in the world!' and there he sat in great grief and fear, not knowing what to do. Now this rock belonged to fierce giants who lived upon it; and as he saw three of them striding about, he thought to himself, 'I can only save myself by feigning to be asleep;' so he laid himself down as if he were in a sound sleep. When the giants came up to him, the first pushed him with his foot, and said, 'What worm is this that lies here curled up?' 'Tread upon him and kill him,' said the second. 'It's not worth the trouble,' said the third; 'let him live, he'll go climbing higher up the mountain, and some cloud will come rolling and carry him away.' And they passed on. But the huntsman had heard all they said; and as soon as they were gone, he climbed to the top of the mountain, and when he had sat there a short time a cloud came rolling around him, and caught him in a whirlwind and bore him along for some time, till it settled in a garden, and he fell quite gently to the ground amongst the greens and cabbages.

Then he looked around him, and said, 'I wish I had something to eat, if not I shall be worse off than before; for here I see neither apples nor pears, nor any kind of fruits, nothing but vegetables.' At last he thought to himself, 'I can eat salad, it will refresh and strengthen me.' So he picked out a fine head and ate of it; but scarcely had he swallowed two bites when he felt himself quite changed, and saw with horror that he was turned into an ass. However, he still felt very hungry, and the salad tasted very nice; so he ate on till he came to another kind of salad, and scarcely had he tasted it when he felt another change come over him, and soon saw that he was lucky enough to have found his old shape again.

Then he laid himself down and slept off a little of his weariness; and when he awoke the next morning he broke off a head both of the good and the bad salad, and thought to himself, 'This will help me to my fortune again, and enable me to pay off some folks for their treachery.' So he went away to try and find the castle of his old friends; and after wandering about a few days he luckily found it. Then he stained his face all over brown, so that even his mother would not have known him, and went into the castle and asked for a lodging; 'I am so tired,' said he, 'that I can go no farther.' 'Countryman,' said the fairy, 'who are you? and what is your business?' 'I am,' said he, 'a messenger sent by the king to find the finest salad that grows under the sun. I have been lucky enough to find it, and have brought it with me; but the heat of the sun scorches so that it begins to wither, and I don't know that I can carry it farther.'

When the fairy and the young lady heard of this beautiful salad, they longed to taste it, and said, 'Dear countryman, let us just taste it.' 'To be sure,' answered he; 'I have two heads of it with me, and will give you one;' so he opened his bag and gave them the bad. Then the fairy herself took it into the kitchen to be dressed; and when it was ready she could not wait till it was carried up, but took a few leaves immediately and put them in her mouth, and scarcely were they swallowed when she lost her own form and ran braying down into the court in the form of an ass. Now the servant maid came into the kitchen, and seeing the salad ready, was going to carry it up; but in the way she too felt a wish to taste it as the old woman had done, and ate some leaves; so she also was turned into an ass and ran after the other, letting the dish with the salad fall on the ground. The messenger sat all this time with the beautiful young lady, and as nobody came with the salad and she longed to taste it, she said, 'I don't know where the salad can be.' Then he thought something must have happened, and said, 'I will go into the kitchen and see.' And as he went he saw two asses in the court running about, and the salad lying on the ground. 'All right!' said he; 'those two have had their share.' Then he took up the rest of the leaves, laid them on the dish and brought them to the young lady, saying, 'I bring you the dish myself that you may not wait any longer.' So she ate of it, and like the others ran off into the court, braying away.

Then the huntsman washed his face and went into the court that they might know him. 'Now you shall be paid for your roguery,' said he; and tied them all three to a rope and took them along with him till he came to a mill and knocked at the window. 'What's the matter?' said the miller. 'I have three tiresome beasts here,' said the other; 'if you will take them, give them food and room, and treat them as I tell you, I will pay you whatever you ask.' 'With all my heart,' said the miller; 'but how shall I treat them?' Then the huntsman said, 'Give the old one stripes three times a day and hay once; give the next (who was the servant-maid) stripes once a day and hay three times; and give the youngest (who was the beautiful lady) hay three times a day and no stripes:' for he could not find it in his heart to have her beaten. After this he went back to the castle, where he found every thing he wanted.

Some days after the miller came to him and told him that the old ass was dead; 'the other two,' said he, 'are alive and eat, but are so sorrowful that they cannot last long.' Then the huntsman pitied them, and told the miller to drive them back to him, and when they came, he gave them some of the good salad to eat. And the beautiful young lady fell upon her knees before him, and said, 'O dearest huntsman! forgive me all the ill I have done you; my mother forced me to it, it was against my will, for I always loved you very much. Your wishing-cloak hangs up in the closet, and as for the bird's heart, I will give it you too.' But he said, 'Keep it, it will be just the same thing, for I mean to make you my wife.' So they were married, and lived together very happily till they died.

THE NOSE

DID you ever hear the story of the three poor soldiers, who, after having fought hard in the wars, set out on their road home begging their way as they went?

They had journeyed on a long way, sick at heart with their bad luck at thus being turned loose on the world in their old days, when one evening they reached a deep gloomy wood through which they must pass; night came fast upon them, and they found that they must, however unwillingly, sleep in the wood; so to make all as safe as they could, it was agreed that two should lie down and sleep, while a third sat up and watched lest wild beasts should break in and tear them to pieces; when he was tired he was to wake one of the others and sleep in his turn, and so on with the third, so as to share the work fairly among them.

The two who were to rest first soon lay down and fell fast asleep, and the other made himself a good fire under the trees and sat down by the side to keep watch. He had not sat long before all on a sudden up came a little man in a red jacket. 'Who's there?' said he. 'A friend,' said the soldier. 'What sort of a friend?' 'An old broken soldier,' said the other, 'with his two comrades who have nothing left to live on; come, sit down and warm yourself.' 'Well, my worthy fellow,' said the little man, 'I will do what I can for you; take this and show it to your comrades in the morning.' So he took out an old cloak and gave it to the soldier, telling him that whenever he put it over his shoulders any thing that he wished for would be fulfilled; then the little man made him a bow and walked away.

The second soldier's turn to watch soon came, and the first laid himself down to sleep; but the second man had not sat by himself long before up came the little man in the red jacket again. The soldier treated him in a friendly way as his comrade had done, and the little man gave him a purse, which he told him was always full of gold, let him draw as much as he would.

Then the third soldier's turn to watch came, and he also had the little man for his guest, who gave him a wonderful horn that drew crowds around it whenever it was played; and made every one forget his business to come and dance to its beautiful music.

In the morning each told his story and showed his treasure; and as they all liked each other very much and were old friends, they agreed to travel together to see the world, and for a while only to make use of the wonderful purse. And thus they spent their time very joyously, till at last they began to be tired of this roving life, and thought they should like to have a home of their own. So the first soldier put his old cloak on, and wished for a fine castle. In a moment it stood before their eyes; fine gardens and green lawns spread round it, and flocks of sheep and goats and herds of oxen were grazing about, and out of the gate came a fine coach with three dapple grey horses to meet them and bring them home.

All this was very well for a time; but it would not do to stay at home always, so they got together all their rich clothes and houses and servants, and ordered their coach with three horses, and set out on a journey to see a neighbouring king. Now this king had an only daughter, and as he took the three soldiers for kings' sons, he gave them a kind welcome. One day, as the second soldier was walking with the princess, she saw him with the wonderful purse in his hand; and having asked him what it was, he was foolish enough to tell her; – though indeed it did not much signify, for she was a witch and knew all the wonderful things that the three soldiers brought. Now this princess was very cunning and artful; so she set to work and made a purse so like the soldier's that no one would know one from the other, and then asked him to come and see her, and made him drink some wine that she had got ready for him, till he fell fast asleep. Then she felt in his pocket, and took away the wonderful purse and left the one she had made in its place.

The next morning the soldiers set out home, and soon after they reached their castle, happening to want some money, they went to their purse for it, and found something indeed in it, but to their great sorrow when they had emptied it, none came in the place of what they took. Then the cheat was soon found out; for the second soldier knew where he had been, and how he had told the story to the princess, and he guessed that she had betrayed him, 'Alas!' cried he, 'poor wretches that we are, what shall we do?'

'Oh!' said the first soldier, 'let no grey hairs grow for this mishap; I will soon get the purse back.' So he threw his cloak across his shoulders and wished himself in the princess's chamber. There he found her sitting alone, telling her gold that fell around her in a shower from the purse. But the soldier stood looking at her too long, for the moment she saw him she started up and cried out with all her force, 'Thieves! Thieves!' so that the whole court came running in and tried to seize him. The poor soldier now began to be dreadfully frightened in his turn, and thought it was high time to make the best of his way off; so without thinking of the ready way of travelling that his cloak gave him, he ran to the window, opened it, and jumped out; and unluckily in his haste his cloak caught and was left hanging, to the great joy of the princess, who knew its worth.

The poor soldier made the best of his way home to his comrades, on foot and in a very downcast mood; but the third soldier told him to keep up his heart, and took his horn and blew a merry tune. At the first blast a countless troop of foot and horse came rushing to their aid, and they set out to make war against their enemy. Then the king's palace was besieged, and he was told that he must give up the purse and cloak, or that not one stone should be left upon another. And the king went into his daughter's chamber and talked with her; but she said, 'Let me try first if I cannot beat them some other way.' So she thought of a cunning scheme to overreach them, and dressed herself out as a poor girl with a basket on her arm; and set out by night with her maid, and went into the enemy's camp as if she wanted to sell trinkets.

In the morning she began to ramble about, singing ballads so beautifully, that all the tents were left empty, and the soldiers ran round in crowds and thought of nothing but hearing her sing. Amongst the rest came the soldier to whom the horn belonged, and as soon as she saw him she

winked to her maid, who slipped slily through the crowd
and went into his tent where it hung, and stole it away.
This done, they both got safely back to the palace; the be-
sieging army went away, the three wonderful gifts were all
left in the hands of the princess, and the three soldiers were
as penniless and forlorn as when the little man with the red
jacket found them in the wood.

Poor fellows! they began to think what was now to be
done. 'Comrades,' at last said the second soldier, who had
had the purse, 'we had better part, we cannot live together,
let each seek his bread as well as he can:' So he turned to
the right, and the other two to the left; for they said they
would rather travel together. Then on he strayed till he
came to a wood; (now this was the same wood where they
had met with so much good luck before;) and he walked on
a long time till evening began to fall, when he sat down
tired beneath a tree, and soon fell asleep.

Morning dawned, and he was greatly delighted, at opening his eyes, to see that the tree was laden with the most
beautiful apples. He was hungry enough, so he soon
plucked and ate first one, then a second, then a third
apple. A strange feeling came over his nose: when he put
the apple to his mouth something was in the way; he felt it;
it was his nose, that grew and grew till it hung down his
breast. It did not stop there, still it grew and grew;
'Heavens!' thought he, 'when will it have done growing?'
And well might he ask, for by this time it reached the
ground as he sat on the grass, and thus it kept creeping on
till he could not bear its weight, or raise himself up; and it
seemed as if it would never end, for already it stretched its
enormous length all through the wood.

Meantime his comrades were journeying on, till on a sudden one of them stumbled against something. 'What can
that be?' said the other. They looked, and could think of
nothing that it was like but a nose. 'We will follow it and

find its owner, however,' said they; so they traced it up till
at last they found their poor comrade lying stretched along
under the apple tree. What was to be done? They tried to
carry him, but in vain. They caught an ass that was passing
by, and raised him upon its back; but it was soon tired of
carrying such a load. So they sat down in despair, when up
came the little man in the red jacket. 'Why, how now,
friend?' said he, laughing; 'well, I must find a cure for you,
I see.' So he told them to gather a pear from a tree that

grew close by, and the nose would come right again. No time was lost, and the nose was soon brought to its proper size, to the poor soldier's joy.

'I will do something more for you yet,' said the little man; 'take some of those pears and apples with you; whoever eats one of the apples will have his nose grow like yours just now; but if you give him a pear, all will come right again. Go to the princess and get her to eat some of your apples; her nose will grow twenty times as long as yours did; then look sharp, and you will get what you want of her.'

Then they thanked their old friend very heartily for all his kindness, and it was agreed that the poor soldier who had already tried the power of the apple should undertake the task. So he dressèd himself up as a gardener's boy, and went to the king's palace, and said he had apples to sell, such as were never seen there before. Every one that saw them was delighted and wanted to taste, but he said they were only for the princess; and she soon sent her maid to buy his stock. They were so ripe and rosy that she soon began eating, and had already eaten three when she too began to wonder what ailed her nose, for it grew and grew, down to the ground, out at the window, and over the garden, nobody knows where.

Then the king made known to all his kingdom, that whoever would heal her of this dreadful disease should be richly rewarded. Many tried, but the princess got no relief. And now the old soldier dressed himself up very sprucely as a doctor, who said he could cure her; so he chopped up some of the apple, and to punish her a little more gave her a dose, saying he would call to-morrow and see her again. To-morrow came, and of course, instead of being better, the nose had been growing fast all night, and the poor princess was in a dreadful fright. So the doctor chopped up a very little of the pear and gave her, and said he was sure that would do good, and he would call again the next day. Next day came, and the nose was to be sure a little smaller, but yet it was bigger than it was when the doctor first began to meddle with it.

Then he thought to himself, 'I must frighten this cunning princess a little more before I shall get what I want of her;' so he gave her another dose of the apple, and said he would call on the morrow. The morrow came, and the nose was ten times as bad as before. 'My good lady,' said the doctor; 'something works against my medicine, and is too strong for it; but I know by the force of my art what it is; you have stolen goods about you, I am sure, and if you do not give them back, I can do nothing for you.' But the princess denied very stoutly that she had any thing of the kind. 'Very well,' said the doctor, 'you may do as you please, but I am sure I am right, and you will die if you do not own it.' Then he went to the king, and told him how the matter stood. 'Daughter,' said he, 'send back the cloak, the ring, and the horn, that you stole from the right owners.'

Then she ordered her maid to fetch all three, and gave them to the doctor, and begged him to give them back to the soldiers; and the moment he had them safe he gave her a whole pear to eat, and the nose came right. And as for the doctor, he put on the cloak, wished the king and all his court a good day, and was soon with his two brothers, who lived from that time happily at home in their palace, except when they took airings in their coach with the three dapple grey horses.

THE FIVE SERVANTS

SOME time ago there reigned in a country many thousands of miles off, an old queen who was very spiteful and de-

lighted in nothing so much as mischief. She had one daughter, who was thought to be the most beautiful princess in
the world; but her mother only made use of her as a trap
for the unwary; and whenever any suitor who had heard
of her beauty came to seek her in marriage, the only answer
the old lady gave to each was, that he must undertake
some very hard task and forfeit his life if he failed. Many,
led by the report of the princess's charms, undertook these
tasks, but failed in doing what the queen set them to do.
No mercy was ever shown them; but the word was given at
once, and off their heads were cut.

Now it happened that a prince who lived in a country far
off, heard of the great beauty of this young lady, and said to
his father, 'Dear father, let me go and try my luck.' 'No,'
said the king; 'if you go you will surely lose your life.' The
prince, however, had set his heart so much upon the
scheme, that when he found his father was against it he fell
very ill, and took to his bed for seven years, and no art
could cure him, or recover his lost spirits: so when his
father saw that if he went on thus he would die, he said to
him with a heart full of grief, 'If it must be so, go and try
your luck.' At this he rose from his bed, recovered his
health and spirits, and went forward on his way light of
heart and full of joy.

Then on he journeyed over hill and dale, through fair
weather and foul, till one day, as he was riding through a
wood, he thought he saw afar off some large animal upon
the ground, and as he drew near he found that it was a man
lying along upon the grass under the trees; but he looked
more like a mountain than a man, he was so fat and jolly.
When this big fellow saw the traveller, he arose, and said,
'If you want any one to wait upon you, you will do well to
take me into your service.' 'What should I do with such a
fat fellow as you?' said the prince. 'It would be nothing to
you if I were three thousand times as fat,' said the man, 'so

that I do but behave myself well.' 'That's true,' answered the prince; 'so come with me, I can put you to some use or another I dare say.' Then the fat man rose up and followed the prince, and by and by they saw another man lying on the ground with his ear close to the turf. The prince said, 'What are you doing there?' 'I am listening,' answered the man. 'To what?' 'To all that is going on in the world, for I can hear every thing, I can even hear the grass grow.' 'Tell me,' said the prince, 'what you hear is going on at the court of the old queen, who has the beautiful daughter?' 'I hear,' said the listener, 'the noise of the sword that is cutting off the head of one of her suitors.' 'Well!' said the prince, 'I see I shall be able to make you of use; – come along with me!' They had not gone far before they saw a pair of feet, and then part of the legs of a man stretched out; but they were so long that they could not see the rest of the body, till they had passed on a good deal farther, and at last they came to the body, and, after going on a while farther, to the head; 'Bless me!' said the prince, 'what a long rope you are!' 'Oh!' answered the tall man, 'this is nothing; when I choose to stretch myself to my full length, I am three times as high as any mountain you have seen on your travels, I warrant you; I will willingly do what I can to serve you if you will let me.' 'Come along then,' said the prince, 'I can turn you to account in some way.'

The prince and his train went on farther into the wood, and next saw a man lying by the road side basking in the heat of the sun, yet shaking and shivering all over, so that not a limb lay still. 'What makes you shiver,' said the prince, 'while the sun is shining so warm?' 'Alas!' answered the man, 'the warmer it is, the colder I am; the sun only seems to me like a sharp frost that thrills through all my bones; and on the other hand, when others are what you call cold I begin to be warm, so that I can neither bear the ice for its heat nor the fire for its cold.' 'You are a queer fellow,' said the prince; 'but if you have nothing else to do, come along with me.' The next thing they saw was a man standing, stretching his neck and looking around him from hill to hill. 'What are you looking for so eagerly?' said the prince. 'I have such sharp eyes,' said the man, 'that I can see over woods and fields and hills and dales; – in short, all over the world.' 'Well,' said the prince, 'come with me if you will, for I want one more to make up my train.'

Then they all journeyed on, and met with no one else till they came to the city where the beautiful princess lived. The prince went straight to the old queen, and said, 'Here I am, ready to do any task you set me, if you will give your daughter as a reward when I have done.' 'I will set you three tasks,' said the queen; 'and if you get through all, you shall be the husband of my daughter. First, you must bring me a ring which I dropped in the red sea.' The prince went home to his friends and said, 'The first task is not an easy one; it is to fetch a ring out of the red sea, so lay your heads together and say what is to be done.' Then the sharp-sighted one said, 'I will see where it lies,' and looked down into the sea, and cried out, 'There it lies upon a rock at the bottom.' 'I would fetch it out,' said the tall man, 'if I could but see it.' 'Well!' cried out the fat one, 'I will help you to do that,' and laid himself down and held his mouth to the water, and drank up the waves till the bottom of the sea was as dry as a meadow. Then the tall man stooped a little and pulled out the ring with his hand, and the prince took it to the old queen, who looked at it, and wondering said, 'It is indeed the right ring; you have gone through this task well: but now comes the second; look yonder at the meadow before my palace; see! there are a hundred fat oxen feeding there; you must eat them all up before noon: and underneath in my cellar there are a hundred casks of wine, which you must drink all up.' 'May I not invite some guests to share the feast with me?' said the prince. 'Why, yes!' said the old woman with a spiteful laugh; 'you may ask one of your friends to breakfast with you, but no more.'

Then the prince went home and said to the fat man, 'You must be my guest to-day, and for once you shall eat your fill.' So the fat man set to work and ate the hundred oxen without leaving a bit, and asked if that was to be all he should have for his breakfast? and he drank the wine out of the casks without leaving a drop, licking even his fingers when he had done. When the meal was ended, the prince went to the old woman and told her the second task was done. 'Your work is not all over, however,' muttered the old hag to herself; 'I will catch you yet, you shall not keep your head upon your shoulders if I can help it.' 'This evening,' said she, 'I will bring my daughter into your house and leave her with you; you shall sit together there, but take care that you do not fall asleep; for I shall come when the clock strikes twelve, and if she is not then with you, you are undone.' 'Oh!' thought the prince, 'it is an easy task to keep my eyes open.' So he called his servants and told them all that the old woman had said. 'Who knows though,' said he, 'but there may be some trick at the bottom of this? it is as well to be upon our guard and keep watch that the young lady does not get away.' When it was night the old woman brought her daughter to the prince's house; then the tall man twisted himself round about it, the listener put his ear to the ground, the fat man placed himself before the door so that no living soul could enter, and the sharp-eyed one looked out afar and watched. Within sat the princess without saying a word, but the moon shone bright through the window upon her face, and the prince gazed upon her wonderful beauty. And while he looked upon her with a heart full of joy and love, his eyelids did not droop; but at eleven o'clock the old woman cast a charm over them so that they all fell asleep, and the princess vanished in a moment.'

And thus they slept till a quarter to twelve, when the charm had no longer any power over them, and they all awoke. 'Alas! alas! woe is me,' cried the prince; 'now I am lost for ever.' And his faithful servants began to weep over their unhappy lot; but the listener said, 'Be still and I will listen;' so he listened a while, and cried out, 'I hear her bewailing her fate;' and the sharp-sighted man looked, and said, 'I see her sitting on a rock three hundred miles hence; now help us, my tall friend; if you stand up, you will reach her in two steps.' 'Very well,' answered the tall man; and in an instant, before one could turn one's head round, he was at the foot of the enchanted rock. Then the tall man took the young lady in his arms and carried her back to the prince a moment before it struck twelve; and they all sat down again and made merry. And when the clock struck twelve the old queen came sneaking by with a spiteful look, as if she was going to say 'Now he is mine;' nor could she think otherwise, for she knew that her daughter was but the moment before on the rock three hundred miles off; but when she came and saw her daughter in the prince's room, she started, and said, 'There is somebody here who can do more than I can.' However, she now saw that she could no longer avoid giving the prince her daughter for a wife, but said to her in a whisper, 'It is a shame that you should be won by servants, and not have a husband of your own choice.'

Now the young lady was of a very proud, haughty temper, and her anger was raised to such a pitch, that the next morning she ordered three hundred loads of wood to be brought and piled up; and told the prince it was true he had by the help of his servants done the three tasks, but that before she would marry him some one must sit upon that pile of wood when it was set on fire and bear the heat. She thought to herself that though his servants had done every thing else for him, none of them would go so far as to burn themselves for him, and that then she should put his love to the test by seeing whether he would sit upon it himself. But she was mistaken; for when the servants heard this, they said, 'We have all done something but the frosty man; now his turn is come;' and they took him and put him on the wood and set it on fire. Then the fire rose and burnt for three long days, till all the wood was gone; and when it was out, the frosty man stood in the midst of the ashes trembling like an aspen-leaf, and said, 'I never shivered so much in my life; if it had lasted much longer, I should have lost the use of my limbs.'

When the princess had no longer any plea for delay, she saw that she was bound to marry the prince; but when they were going to church, the old woman said, 'I will never consent;' and sent secret orders out to her horsemen to kill and slay all before them and bring back her daughter before she could be married. However, the listener had pricked up his ears and heard all that the old woman said, and told it to the prince. So they made haste and got to the church first, and were married; and then the five servants took their leave and went away saying, 'We will go and try our luck in the world on our own account.'

The prince set out with his wife, and at the end of the first day's journey came to a village, where a swineherd was feeding his swine; and as they came near he said to his wife, 'Do you know who I am? I am not a prince, but a poor swineherd; he whom you see yonder with the swine is my father, and our business will be to help him to tend them.' Then he went into the swineherd's hut with her, and ordered her royal clothes to be taken away in the night; so that when she awoke in the morning, she had nothing to put on, till the woman who lived there made a great favour of giving her an old gown and a pair of worsted stockings. 'If it were not for your husband's sake,' said she, 'I would not have given you any thing.' Then the poor princess gave herself up for lost, and believed that her husband must indeed be a swineherd; but she thought she would make the best of it, and began to help him to feed them, and said, 'It is a just reward for my pride.' When this had lasted eight days she could bear it no longer, for her feet were all over wounds, and as she sat down and wept by the way-side, some people came up to her and pitied her, and asked if she knew what her husband really was. 'Yes,' said she; 'a swineherd; he is just gone out to market with some of his stock.' But they said, 'Come along and we will take you to him;' and they took her over the hill to the palace of the prince's father; and when they came into the hall, there stood her husband so richly drest in his royal clothes that she did not know him till he fell upon her neck and kissed her, and said, 'I have borne much for your sake, and you too have also borne a great deal for me.' Then the guests were sent for, and the marriage feast was given, and all made merry and danced and sung, and the best wish that I can wish is, that you and I had been there too.

CAT-SKIN

THERE was once a king, whose queen had hair of the purest gold, and was so beautiful that her match was not to be met with on the whole face of the earth. But this beautiful queen fell ill, and when she felt that her end drew near, she called the king to her and said, 'Vow to me that you will never marry again, unless you meet with a wife who is as beautiful as I am, and who has golden hair like mine.' Then when the king in his grief had vowed all she asked, she shut her eyes and died. But the king was not to be comforted, and for a long time never thought of taking another wife. At last, however, his counsellors said, 'This will not do; the king must marry again, that we may have a queen.' So messengers were sent far and wide, to seek for a bride who was as beautiful as the late queen. But there was no princess in the world so beautiful; and if there had been, still there was not one to be found who had such golden hair. So the messengers came home and had done all their work for nothing.

Now the king had a daughter who was just as beautiful as her mother, and had the same golden hair. And when she was grown up, the king looked at her and saw that she was just like his late queen: then he said to his courtiers, 'May I not marry my daughter? she is the very image of my dead wife: unless I have her, I shall not find any bride upon the whole earth, and you say there must be a queen.' When the courtiers heard this, they were shocked, and said, 'Heaven forbid that a father should marry his daughter! out of so great a sin no good can come.' And his daughter was also shocked, but hoped the king would soon give up such thoughts: so she said to him, 'Before I marry any one I must have three dresses; one must be of gold like the sun, another must be of shining silver like the moon, and a third must be dazzling as the stars: besides this, I want a mantle of a thousand different kinds of fur put together, to which every beast in the kingdom must give a part of his skin.' And thus she thought he would think of the matter no more. But the king made the most skilful workmen in his kingdom weave the three dresses, one as golden as the sun, another as silvery as the moon, and a third shining like the stars; and his hunters were told to hunt out all the beasts in his kingdom and take the finest fur out of their skins: and so a mantle of a thousand furs was made.

When all was ready, the king sent them to her; but she got up in the night when all were asleep, and took three of her trinkets, a golden ring, a golden necklace, and a golden brooch; and packed the three dresses of the sun, moon, and stars, up in a nut-shell, and wrapped herself up in the mantle of all sorts of fur, and besmeared her face and hands with soot. Then she threw herself upon heaven for help in her need, and went away and journeyed on the whole night, till at last she came to a large wood. As she was very tired, she sat herself down in the hollow of a tree and soon fell asleep: and there she slept on till it was mid-day: and it happened, that as the king to whom the wood belonged was hunting in it, his dogs came to the tree, and began to sniff about and run round and round, and then to bark. 'Look sharp,' said the king to the huntsmen, 'and see what sort of game lies there.' And the huntsmen went up to the tree, and when they came back again said, 'In the hollow tree there lies a most wonderful beast, such as we never saw before; its skin seems of a thousand kinds of fur, but there it lies fast asleep. 'See,' said the king, 'if you can catch it alive, and we will take it with us.' So the huntsmen took it up, and the maiden awoke and was greatly frightened, and said, 'I am a poor child that has neither father nor mother left; have pity on me and take me with you.' Then they said, 'Yes, Miss Cat-skin, you will do for the kitchen; you can sweep up the ashes and do things of that sort.' So they put her in the coach and took her home to the king's palace. Then they showed her a little corner under the staircase where no light of day ever peeped in, and said, 'Cat-skin, you may lie and sleep there.' And she was sent into the kitchen, and made to fetch wood and water, to blow the fire, pluck the poultry, pick the herbs, sift the ashes, and do all the dirty work.

Thus Cat-skin lived for a long time very sorrowfully. 'Ah! pretty princess!' thought she, 'what will now become of thee!' But it happened one day that a feast was to be held in the king's castle; so she said to the cook, 'May I go up a little while and see what is going on? I will take care and stand behind the door.' And the cook said, 'Yes, you may go, but be back again in half an hour's time to rake out the ashes.' Then she took her little lamp, and went into her cabin, and took off the fur skin, and washed the soot from off her face and hands, so that her beauty shone forth like the sun from behind the clouds. She next opened her nut-shell, and brought out of it the dress that shone like the sun, and so went to the feast. Every one made way for her, for nobody knew her, and they thought she could be no less than a king's daughter. But the king came up to her and held out his hand and danced with her, and he thought in his heart, 'I never saw one half so beautiful.'

When the dance was at an end, she curtsied; and when the king looked round for her, she was gone, no one knew whither. The guards who stood at the castle gate were called in; but they had seen no one. The truth was, that she had run into her little cabin, pulled off her dress, blacked her face and hands, put on the fur-skin cloak, and was Cat-skin again. When she went into the kitchen to her work, and began to rake the ashes, the cook said, 'Let that alone till the morning, and heat the king's soup; I should like to run up now and give a peep; but take care you don't let a hair fall into it, or you will run a chance of never eating again.'

As soon as the cook went away, Cat-skin heated the king's soup and toasted up a slice of bread as nicely as ever she could; and when it was ready, she went and looked in the cabin for her little golden ring, and put it into the dish in which the soup was. When the dance was over, the king ordered his soup to be brought in, and it pleased him so well, that he thought he had never tasted any so good before. At the bottom he saw a gold ring lying, and as he could not make out how it had got there, he ordered the cook to be sent for. The cook was frightened when she heard the order, and said to Cat-skin, 'You must have let a hair fall into the soup; if it be so, you will have a good beat-

ing.' Then she went before the king, and he asked her who
had cooked the soup. 'I did,' answered she. But the king
said, 'That is not true; it was better done than you could
do it.' Then she answered, 'To tell the truth, I did not cook
it, but Cat-skin did.' 'Then let Cat-skin come up,' said the
king: and when she came, he said to her, 'Who are you?' 'I
am a poor child,' said she, 'who has lost both father and
mother.' 'How came you in my palace?' asked he. 'I am
good for nothing,' said she, 'but to be scullion girl, and to
have boots and shoes thrown at my head.' 'But how did
you get the ring that was in the soup?' asked the king. But
she would not own that she knew any thing about the ring;
so the king sent her away again about her business.

After a time there was another feast, and Cat-skin asked
the cook to let her go up and see it as before. 'Yes,' said she,
'but come back again in half an hour, and cook the king
the soup that he likes so much.' Then she ran to her little
cabin, washed herself quickly, and took the dress out
which was silvery as the moon, and put it on; and when she
went in looking like a king's daughter, the king went up to
her and rejoiced at seeing her again, and when the dance
began, he danced with her. After the dance was at an end,
she managed to slip out so slily that the king did not see
where she was gone; but she sprang into her little cabin and
made herself into Cat-skin again, and went into the kitchen
to cook the soup. Whilst the cook was above, she got the
golden necklace, and dropped it into the soup; then it was
brought to the king, who ate it, and it pleased him as well
as before; so he sent for the cook, who was again forced to
tell him that Cat-skin had cooked it. Cat-skin was brought
again before the king; but she still told him that she was
only fit to have the boots and shoes thrown at her head.

But when the king had ordered a feast to be got ready for
the third time, it happened just the same as before. 'You
must be a witch, Cat-skin,' said the cook; 'for you always

put something into the soup, so that it pleases the king better than mine.' However, she let her go up as before. Then she put on the dress which sparkled like the stars, and went into the ball-room in it; and the king danced with her again, and thought she had never looked so beautiful as she did then: so whilst he was dancing with her, he put a gold ring on her finger without her seeing it, and ordered that the dance should be kept up for a long time. When it was at an end, he would have held her fast by the hand; but she slipt away and sprang so quickly through the crowd that he lost sight of her; and she ran as fast as she could into her little cabin under the stairs. But this time she kept away too long, and stayed beyond the half-hour; so she had not time to take off her fine dress, but threw her fur mantle over it, and in her haste did not soot herself all over, but left one finger white.

Then she ran into the kitchen, and cooked the king's soup; and as soon as the cook was gone, she put the golden brooch into the dish. When the king got to the bottom, he ordered Cat-skin to be called once more, and soon saw the white finger and the ring that he had put on it whilst they were dancing: so he seized her hand, and kept fast hold of it, and when she wanted to loose herself and spring away, the fur cloak fell off a little on one side, and the starry dress sparkled underneath it. Then he got hold of the fur and tore it off, and her golden hair and beautiful form were seen, and she could no longer hide herself: so she washed the soot and ashes from off her face, and showed herself to be the most beautiful princess upon the face of the earth. But the king said, 'You are my beloved bride, and we will never more be parted from each other.' And the wedding feast was held, and a merry day it was.

THE ROBBER-BRIDEGROOM

THERE was once a miller who had a pretty daughter; and when she was grown up, he thought to himself, 'If a seemly man should come to ask her for his wife, I will give her to him that she may be taken care of.' Now it so happened that one did come, who seemed to be very rich, and behaved very well; and as the miller saw no reason to find fault with him, he said he should have his daughter. Yet the maiden did not love him quite so well as a bride ought to love her bridegroom, but, on the other hand, soon began to feel a kind of inward shuddering whenever she saw or thought of him.

One day he said to her, 'Why do you not come and see my home, since you are to be my bride?' 'I do not know where your house is,' said the girl. ''Tis out there,' said her bridegroom, 'yonder in the dark green wood.' Then she began to try and avoid going, and said, 'But I cannot find the way thither.' 'Well, but you must come and see me next Sunday,' said the bridegroom; 'I have asked some guests to meet you, and that you may find your way through the wood, I will strew ashes for you along the path.'

When Sunday came and the maiden was to go out, she felt very much troubled, and took care to put on two pockets, and filled them with peas and beans. She soon came to the wood, and found her path strewed with ashes; so she followed the track, and at every step threw a pea on the right and a bean on the left side of the road; and thus she journeyed on the whole day till she came to a house which stood in the middle of the dark wood. She saw no one within, and all was quite still, till on a sudden she heard a voice cry,

'Turn again, bonny bride!
  Turn again home!
Haste from the robber's den,
  Haste away home!'

She looked around, and saw a little bird sitting in a cage that hung over the door; and he flapped his wings, and again she heard him cry,

> 'Turn again, bonny bride!
> Turn again home!
> Haste from the robber's den,
> Haste away home!'

However, the bride went in, and roamed along from one room to another, and so over all the house; but it was quite empty, and not a soul could she see. At last she came to a room where a very very old woman was sitting. 'Pray, can you tell me, my good woman,' said she, 'if my bridegroom lives here?' 'Ah! my dear child!' said the old woman, 'you are come to fall into the trap laid for you: your wedding can only be with Death, for the robber will surely take away your life; if I do not save you, you are lost!' So she hid the bride behind a large cask, and then said to her, 'Do not stir or move yourself at all, lest some harm should befall you; and when the robbers are asleep we will run off; I have long wished to get away.'

She had hardly done this when the robbers came in, and brought another young maiden with them that had been ensnared like the bride. Then they began to feast and drink, and were deaf to her shrieks and groans: and they gave her some wine to drink, three glasses, one of white, one of red, and one of yellow; upon which she fainted and fell down dead. Now the bride began to grow very uneasy behind the cask, and thought that she too must die in her turn. Then the one that was to be her bridegroom saw that there was a gold ring on the little finger of the maiden they had murdered; and as he tried to snatch it off, it flew up in the air and fell down again behind the cask just in the bride's lap. So he took a light and searched about all round the room for it, but could not find any thing; and another of the robbers said, 'Have you looked behind the large cask yet?' 'Pshaw!' said the old woman, 'come, sit still and eat your supper now, and leave the ring along till to-morrow; it won't run away, I'll warrant.'

So the robbers gave up the search, and went on with their eating and drinking; but the old woman dropped a sleeping-draught into their wine, and they laid themselves down and slept, and snored roundly. And when the bride heard this, she stepped out from behind the cask; and as she was forced to walk over the sleepers, who were lying about on the floor, she trembled lest she should awaken some of them. But heaven aided her, so that she soon got through her danger; and the old woman went up stairs with her, and they both ran away from the murderous den. The ashes that had been strewed were now all blown away, but the peas and beans had taken root and were springing up, and showed her the way by the light of the moon. So they walked the whole night, and in the morning reached the mill; when the bride told her father all that had happened to her.

As soon as the day arrived when the wedding was to take place, the bridegroom came; and the miller gave orders that all his friends and relations should be asked to the feast. And as they were all sitting at table, one of them proposed that each of the guests should tell some tale. Then the bridegroom said to the bride, when it came to her turn, 'Well, my dear, do you know nothing? come, tell us some story.' 'Yes,' answered she, 'I can tell you a dream that I dreamt. I once thought I was going through a wood, and went on and on till I came to a house where there was not a soul to be seen, but a bird in a cage, that cried out twice,

> "Turn again, bonny bride!
> Turn again home!
> Haste from the robber's den,
> Haste away home!"

– I only dreamt that, my love. Then I went through all the rooms, which were quite empty, until I came to a room where there sat a very old woman; and I said to her, "Does my bridegroom live here?" but she answered, "Ah! my dear child! you have fallen into a murderer's snare; your bridegroom will surely kill you;" – I only dreamt that, my love. But she hid me behind a large cask; and hardly had she done this, when the robbers came in, dragging a young woman along with them; then they gave her three kinds of wine to drink, white, red, and yellow, till she fell dead upon the ground; – I only dreamt that, my love. After they had done this, one of the robbers saw that there was a gold ring on her little finger, and snatched at it; but it flew up to the ceiling, and then fell behind the great cask just where I was, and into my lap; and here is the ring!' At these words she brought out the ring and showed it to the guests.

When the robber saw all this, and heard what she said, he grew as pale as ashes with fright, and wanted to run off; but the guests held him fast and gave him up to justice, so that he and all his gang met with the due reward of their wickedness.

———

THE THREE SLUGGARDS

THE king of a country a long way off had three sons. He liked one as well as another, and did not know which to leave his kingdom to after his death: so when he was dying he called them all to him, and said, 'Dear children, the laziest sluggard of the three shall be king after me.' 'Then,' said the eldest, 'the kingdom is mine; for I am so lazy that when I lie down to sleep, if any thing were to fall into my eyes so that I could not shut them, I should still go on sleeping.' The second said, 'Father, the kingdom belongs to me; for I am so lazy that when I sit by the fire to warm my-self, I would sooner have my toes burnt than take the trouble to draw my legs back.' The third said, 'Father, the kingdom is mine; for I am so lazy that if I were going to be hanged, with the rope round my neck, and somebody were to put a sharp knife into my hands to cut it, I had rather be hanged than raise my hand to do it.' When the father heard this, he said, 'You shall be the king; for you are the fittest man.'

THE SEVEN RAVENS

THERE was once a man who had seven sons, and last of all one daughter. Although the little girl was very pretty, she was so weak and small that they thought she could not live; but they said she should at once be christened.

So the father sent one of his sons in haste to the spring to get some water, but the other six ran with him. Each wanted to be first at drawing the water, and so they were in such a hurry that all let their pitchers fall into the well, and they stood foolishly looking at one another, and did not know what to do, for none dared go home. In the mean time the father was uneasy, and could not tell what made the young men stay so long. 'Surely,' said he, 'the whole seven must have forgotten themselves over some game of play;' and when he had waited still longer and they yet did not come, he flew into a rage and wished them all turned into ravens. Scarcely had he spoken these words when he heard a croaking over his head, and looked up and saw seven ravens as black as coals flying round and round. Sorry as he was to see his wish so fulfilled, he did not know how what was done could be undone, and comforted him-self as well as he could for the loss of his seven sons with his dear little daughter, who soon became stronger and every day more beautiful.

For a long time she did not know that she had ever had any brothers; for her father and mother took care not to speak of them before her: but one day by chance she heard the people about her speak of them. 'Yes,' said they, 'she is beautiful indeed, but still 'tis a pity that her brothers should have been lost for her sake.' Then she was much grieved, and went to her father and mother, and asked if she had any brothers, and what had become of them. So they dared no longer hide the truth from her, but said it was the will of heaven, and that her birth was only the innocent cause of it; but the little girl mourned sadly about it every day, and thought herself bound to do all she could to bring her brothers back; and she had neither rest nor ease, till at length one day she stole away, and set out into the wide world to find her brothers, wherever they might be, and free them, whatever it might cost her.

She took nothing with her but a little ring which her father and mother had given her, a loaf of bread in case she should be hungry, a little pitcher of water in case she should be thirsty, and a little stool to rest upon when she should be weary. Thus she went on and on, and journeyed till she came to the world's end: then she came to the sun, but the sun looked much too hot and fiery; so she ran away quickly to the moon, but the moon was cold and chilly, and said, 'I smell flesh and blood this way!' so she took herself away in a hurry and came to the stars, and the stars were friendly and kind to her, and each star sat upon his own little stool; but the morning-star rose up and gave her a little piece of wood, and said, 'If you have not this little piece of wood, you cannot unlock the castle that stands on the glass mountain, and there your brothers live.' The little girl took the piece of wood, rolled it up in a little cloth, and went on again until she came to the glass mountain, and found the door shut. Then she felt for the little piece of wood; but when she unwrapped the cloth it was not there, and she saw she has lost the gift of the good stars. What was to be done? she wanted to save her brothers, and had no key of the castle of the glass mountain; so this faithful little sister took a knife out of her pocket and cut off her little finger, that was just the size of the piece of wood she had lost, and put it in the door and opened it.

As she went in, a little dwarf came up to her, and said, 'What are you seeking for?' 'I seek for my brothers, the seven ravens,' answered she. Then the dwarf said, 'My masters are not at home; but if you will wait till they come, pray step in.' Now the little dwarf was getting their dinner ready, and he brought their food upon seven little plates, and their drink in seven little glasses, and set them upon the table, and out of each little plate their sister ate a small piece, and out of each little glass she drank a small drop; but she let the ring that she had brought with her fall into the last glass.

On a sudden she heard a fluttering and croaking in the air, and the dwarf said, 'Here come my masters.' When they came in, they wanted to eat and drink, and looked for their little plates and glasses. Then said one after the other, 'Who has eaten from my little plate? and who has been drinking out of my little glass?

'Caw! Caw! well I ween
Mortal lips have this way been.'

When the seventh came to the bottom of his glass, and found there the ring, he looked at it, and knew that it was his father's and mother's, and said, 'Oh that our little sister would but come! then we should be free.' When the little girl heard this, (for she stood behind the door all the time and listened,) she ran forward, and in an instant all the ravens took their right form again; and all hugged and kissed each other, and went merrily home.

ROLAND AND MAY-BIRD

THERE was once a poor man who went every day to cut wood in the forest. One day as he went along he heard a cry like a little child's; so he followed the sound till at last he looked up a high tree, and on one of the branches sat a very little girl. Its mother had fallen asleep, and a vulture had taken it out of her lap and flown away with it and left it on the tree. Then the wood-cutter climbed up, took the little child down, and said to himself, 'I will take this poor child home and bring it up with my own son Roland.' So he brought it to his cottage, and both grew up together! and he called the little girl May-bird, because he had found her on a tree in May; and May-bird and Roland were so very fond of each other that they were never happy but when they were together.

But the wood-cutter became very poor, and had nothing in the world he could call his own, and indeed he had scarcely bread enough for his wife and the two children to eat. At last the time came when even that was all gone, and he knew not where to seek for help in his need. Then at night, as he lay on his bed and turned himself here and there, restless and full of care, his wife said to him, 'Husband, listen to me, and take the two children out early to-morrow morning; give each of them a piece of bread, and then lead them into the midst of the wood where it is thickest, make a fire for them, and go away and leave them alone to shift for themselves, for we can no longer keep them here.' 'No, wife,' said the husband, 'I cannot find it in my heart to leave the children to the wild beasts of the forest, who would soon tear them to pieces.' 'Well, if you will not do as I say,' answered the wife, 'we must starve together:' and she let him have no peace until he came into her plan.

Meantime the poor children too were lying awake restless, and weak from hunger, so that they heard all that their mother said to her husband. 'Now,' thought May-bird to herself, 'it is all up with us:' and she began to weep. But Roland crept to her bed-side, and said, 'Do not be afraid, May-bird, I will find out some help for us.' Then he got up, put on his jacket, and opened the door and went out.

The moon shone bright upon the little court before the cottage, and the white pebbles glittered like daisies on the green meadows. So he stooped down, and put as many as he could into his pocket, and then went back to the house. 'Now, May-bird,' said he, 'rest in peace;' and he went to bed and fell fast asleep.

Early in the morning, before the sun had risen, the woodman's wife came and awoke them. 'Get up, children,' said she, 'we are going into the wood; there is a piece of bread for each of you, but take care of it and keep some for the afternoon.' May-bird took the bread and carried it in her apron, because Roland had his pocket full of stones, and they made their way into the wood.

After they had walked on for a time, Roland stood still and looked towards home, and after a while turned again, and so on several times. Then his father said, 'Roland, why do you keep turning and lagging about so? move your legs on a little faster.' 'Ah! father,' answered Roland, 'I am stopping to look at my white cat that sits on the roof, and wants to say good-bye to me.' 'You little fool!' said his mother, 'that is not your cat; 'tis the morning sun shining on the chimney top.' Now Roland had not been looking at the cat, but had all the while been staying behind to drop from his pocket one white pebble after another along the road.

When they came into the midst of the wood, the wood-man said, 'Run about, children, and pick up some wood, and I will make a fire to keep us all warm.' So they piled up a little heap of brush-wood, and set it a-fire; and as the flame burnt bright, the mother said, 'Now set yourselves by the fire and go to sleep, while we go and cut wood in the forest; be sure you wait till we come again and fetch you.' Roland and May-bird sat by the fire-side till the afternoon, and then each of them ate their piece of bread. They fancied the woodman was still in the wood, because they thought they heard the blows of his axe; but it was a bough which he had cunningly hung upon a tree, so that the wind blew it backwards and forwards, and it sounded like the axe as it hit the other boughs. Thus they waited till evening; but the woodman and his wife kept away, and no one came to fetch them.

When it was quite dark May-bird began to cry; but Roland said, 'Wait awhile till the moon rises.' And when the moon rose, he took her by the hand, and there lay the pebbles along the ground, glittering like new pieces of money, and marked the way out. Towards morning they came again to the woodman's house, and he was glad in his heart when he saw the children again; for he had grieved at leaving them alone. His wife also seemed to be glad; but in her heart she was angry at it.

Not long after there was again no bread in the house, and May-bird and Roland heard the wife say to her husband, 'The children found their way back once, and I took it in good part; but there is only half a loaf of bread left for them in the house; to-morrow you must take them deeper into the wood, that they may not find their way out, or we shall all be starved.' It grieved the husband in his heart to do as his wife wished, and he thought it would be better to share their last morsel with the children; but as he had done as she said once, he did not dare to say no. When the children had heard all their plan, Roland got up and wanted to pick up pebbles as before; but when he came to the door he found his mother had locked it. Still he comforted May-bird, and said, 'Sleep in peace, dear May-bird;

God is very kind and will help us.' Early in the morning a piece of bread was given to each of them, but still smaller than the one they had before. Upon the road Roland crumbled his in his pocket, and often stood still, and threw a crumb upon the ground. 'Why do you lag so behind, Roland?' said the woodman; 'go your ways on before.' 'I am looking at my little dove that is sitting upon the roof and wants to say good-bye to me.' 'You silly boy!' said the wife, 'that is not your little dove, it is the morning sun that shines on the chimney top.' But Roland went on crumbling his bread, and throwing it on the ground. And thus they went on still farther into the wood, where they had never been before in all their life. There they were again told to sit down by a large fire, and sleep; and the woodman and his wife said they would come in the evening and fetch them away. In the afternoon Roland shared May-bird's bread, because he had strewed all his upon the road; but the day passed away, and evening passed away too, and no one came to the poor children. Still Roland comforted May-bird, and said, 'Wait till the moon rises; then I shall see the crumbs of bread which I have strewed, and they will show us the way home.'

The moon rose; but when Roland looked for the crumbs, they were gone; for thousands of little birds in the wood had found them and picked them up. Roland, however, set out to try and find his way home; but they soon lost themselves in the wilderness, and went on through the night and all the next day, till at last they lay down and fell asleep for weariness: and another day they went on as before, but still did not reach the end of the wood, and were as hungry as could be, for they had nothing to eat.

In the afternoon of the third day they came to a strange little hut, made of bread, with a roof of cake, and windows of sparkling sugar. 'Now we will sit down and eat till we have had enough,' said Roland; 'I will eat off the roof for my share; do you eat the windows, May-bird, they will be nice and sweet for you.' Whilst May-bird, however, was picking at the sugar, a sweet pretty voice called from within:

'Tip, tap! who goes there?'

But the children answered;

'The wind, the wind,
That blows through the air;'

and went on eating; and May-bird broke out a round pane of the window for herself, and Roland tore off a large piece of cake from the roof, when the door opened, and a little old fairy came gliding out. At this May-bird and Roland were so frightened, that they let fall what they had in their hands. But the old lady shook her head, and said, 'Dear children, where have you been wandering about? come in with me; you shall have something good.' So she took them both by the hand, and led them into her little hut, and brought out plenty to eat, — milk and pancakes, with sugar, apples, and nuts; and then two beautiful little beds were got ready, and May-bird and Roland laid themselves down, and thought they were in heaven: but the fairy was a spiteful one, and had made her pretty sweetmeat house to entrap little children. Early in the morning, before they were awake, she went to their little bed, and when she saw the two sleeping and looking so sweetly, she had no pity on them, but was glad they were in her power. Then she took up Roland, and put him in a little coop by himself; and when he awoke, he found himself behind a grating, shut up as little chickens are: but she shook May-bird, and called out, 'Get up, you lazy little thing, and fetch some water; and go into the kitchen and cook something good to eat: your brother is shut up yonder; I shall first fatten him, and when he is fat, I think I shall eat him.'

When the fairy was gone, the little girl watched her time

and got up and ran to Roland, and told him what she had heard, and said, 'We must run away quickly, for the old woman is a bad fairy, and will kill us.' But Roland said, 'You must first steal away her fairy wand, that we may save ourselves, if she should follow.' Then the little maiden ran back, and fetched the magic wand, and away they went together; so when the old fairy came back, she could see no one at home, and sprang in a great rage to the window, and looked out into the wide world, (which she could do far and near,) and a long way off she spied May-bird running away with her dear Roland; 'You are already a great way off,' said she; 'but you will still fall into my hands.' Then she put on her boots, which walked several miles at a step, and scarcely made two steps with them, before she overtook the children: but May-bird saw that the fairy was coming after them, and by the help of the wand turned her dear Roland into a lake, and herself into a swan which swam about in the middle of it. So the fairy set herself down on the shore, and took a great deal of trouble to decoy the swan, and threw crumbs of bread to it; but it would not come near her, and she was forced to go home in the evening, without taking her revenge. And May-bird changed herself and her dear Roland back into their own forms once more, and they went journeying on the whole night until the dawn of day; and then the maiden turned herself into a beautiful rose, which grew in the midst of a quickset hedge, and Roland sat by the side and played upon his flute.

The fairy soon came striding along. 'Good piper,' said she, 'may I pluck the beautiful rose for myself?' 'Oh yes,' answered he; 'and I will play to you meantime.' So when she had crept into the hedge in a great hurry to gather the flower (for she well knew what it was), he began to play upon his flute; and, whether she liked it or not, such was the wonderful power of the music that she was forced to dance a merry jig, on and on without any rest. And as he did not

cease playing a moment, the thorns at length tore the
clothes from off her body, and pricked her sorely, and there
she stuck quite fast.

Then May-bird was free once more; but she was very
tired, and Roland said, 'Now I will hasten home for help,
and by and by we will be married.' And May-bird said, 'I
will stay here in the mean time and wait for you; and, that
no one may know me, I will turn myself into a stone and lie
in the corner of yonder field.' Then Roland went away, and
May-bird was to wait for him. But Roland met with
another maiden, who pleased him so much that he stopped
where she lived, and forgot his former friend; and when
May-bird had stayed in the field a long time, and found he
did not come back, she became quite sorrowful, and turned
herself into a little daisy, and thought to herself, 'Some one
will come and tread me under foot, and so my sorrows will
end.' But it so happened that as a shepherd was keeping
watch in the field he found the flower, and thinking it very
pretty, took it home, placed it in a box in his room, and
said, 'I have never found so pretty a flower before.' From
that time every thing throve wonderfully at the shepherd's
house: when he got up in the morning, all the household
work was ready done; the room was swept and cleaned; the
fire made, and the water fetched: and in the afternoon,
when he came home, the table-cloth was laid and a good
dinner ready set for him. He could not make out how all
this happened; for he saw no one in his house: and although
it pleased him well enough, he was at length troubled to
think how it could be, and went to a cunning woman who
lived hard by, and asked her what he should do. She said,
'There must be witchcraft in it; look out to-morrow morning early, and see if any thing stirs about in the room; if it
does, throw a white cloth at once over it, and then the
witchcraft will be stopped.' The shepherd did as she said,
and the next morning saw the box open and the daisy

come out: then he sprang up quickly and threw a white cloth over it: in an instant the spell was broken, and May-bird stood before him; for it was she who had taken care of his house for him; and as she was so beautiful he asked her if she would marry him. She said 'No,' because she wished to be faithful to her dear Roland; but she agreed to stay and keep house for him.

Time passed on, and Roland was to be married to the maiden that he had found; and according to an old custom in that land, all the maidens were to come and sing songs in praise of the bride and bridegroom. But May-bird was so grieved when she heard that her dearest Roland had for-gotten her, and was to be married to another, that her heart seemed as if it would burst within her, and she would not go for a long time. At length she was forced to go with the rest; but she kept hiding herself behind the others until she was left the last. Then she could not any longer help coming forward; and the moment she began to sing, Ro-land sprang up, and cried out, 'That is the true bride; I will have no other but her;' for he knew her by the sound of her voice; and all that he had forgotten came back into his mind, and his heart was opened towards her. So faithful May-bird was married to her dear Roland, and there was an end of her sorrows; and from that time forward she lived happily till she died.

THE MOUSE, THE BIRD, AND
THE SAUSAGE

ONCE upon a time a mouse, a bird, and a sausage took it into their heads to keep house together: and to be sure they managed to live for a long time very comfortably and happily; and beside that added a great deal to their store, so as to become very rich. It was the bird's business to fly every day into the forest and bring wood; the mouse had to carry the water, to make the fire, and lay the cloth for dinner; but the sausage was cook to the household.

He who is too well off often begins to be lazy and to long for something fresh. Now it happened one day that our bird met with one of his friends, to whom he boasted greatly of his good plight. But the other bird laughed at him for a poor fool, who worked hard, whilst the two at home had an easy job of it: for when the mouse had made her fire and fetched the water, she went and laid down in her own little room till she was called to lay the cloth; and the sausage sat by the pot, and had nothing to do but to see that the food was well cooked; and when it was meal time, had only to butter, salt, and get it ready to eat, which it could do in a minute. The bird flew home, and having laid his burden on the ground, they all sat down to table, and after they had made their meal slept soundly until the next morning. Could any life be more glorious than this?

The next day the bird, who had been told what to do by his friend, would not go into the forest, saying, he had waited on them, and been made a fool of long enough; they should change about, and take their turns at the work. Although the mouse and the sausage begged hard that things might go on as they were, the bird carried the day. So they cast lots, and the lot fell upon the sausage to fetch wood, while the mouse was to be cook, and the bird was to bring the water.

What happened by thus taking people from their proper work? The sausage set out towards the wood, the little bird made a fire, the mouse set on the pot, and only waited for the sausage to come home and bring wood for the next day. But the sausage kept away so long that they both thought something must have happened to him, and the bird flew out a little way to look out for him; but not far off he found a dog in the road, who said he had met with a poor little sausage, and taking him for fair prey, had laid hold of him and knocked him down. The bird made a charge against the dog of open robbery and murder; but words were of no use, for the dog said, he found the sausage out of its proper work, and under false colours; and so he was taken for a spy and lost his life. The little bird took up the wood very sorrowfully, and went home and told what he had seen and heard. The mouse and he were very much grieved, but agreed to do their best and keep together.

The little bird undertook to spread the table, and the mouse got ready the dinner; but when she went to dish it up, she fell into the pot and was drowned. When the bird came into the kitchen and wanted the dinner to put upon the table, no cook was to be seen; so he threw the wood about here, there, and every where, and called and sought on all sides, but still could not find the cook. Meantime the fire fell upon the wood and set it on fire; the bird hastened away to get water, but his bucket fell into the well, and he after it; and so ends the story of this clever family.

THE JUNIPER TREE

A LONG while ago, perhaps as much as two thousand years, there was a rich man who had a wife of whom he was very fond; but they had no children. Now in the garden before the house where they lived there stood a juniper tree; and one winter's day as the lady was standing under the juniper tree, paring an apple, she cut her finger, and the drops of blood trickled down upon the snow. 'Ah!' said she, sighing deeply and looking down upon the blood, 'how happy should I be if I had a little child as white as snow and as red as blood!' And as she was saying this, she grew quite cheerful, and was sure her wish would be fulfilled. And after a little time the snow went away, and soon afterwards the fields began to look green. Next the spring came, and the meadows were dressed with flowers; the trees put forth their green leaves; the young branches shed their blossoms upon the ground; and the little birds sung through the groves. And then came summer, and the sweet-smelling flowers of the juniper tree began to unfold; and the lady's heart leaped within her, and she fell on her knees for joy. But when autumn drew near, the fruit was thick upon the trees. Then the lady plucked the red berries from the juniper tree, and looked sad and sorrowful; and she called her husband to her, and said, 'If I die, bury me under the juniper tree.' Not long after this a pretty little child was born; it was, as the lady wished, as red as blood, and as white as snow; and as soon as she had looked upon it, her joy overcame her, and she fainted away and died.

Then her husband buried her under the juniper tree, and wept and mourned over her; but after a little while he grew better, and at length dried up his tears, and married another wife.

Time passed on, and he had a daughter born; but the child of his first wife, that was as red as blood, and as white as snow, was a little boy. The mother loved her daughter very much, but hated the little boy, and bethought herself how she might get all her husband's money for her own child; so she used the poor fellow very harshly, and was always pushing him about from one corner of the house to another, and thumping him one while and pinching him another, so that he was for ever in fear of her, and when he came home from school, could never find a place in the house to play in.

Now it happened that once when the mother was going into her store-room, the little girl came up to her, and said,

'Mother, may I have an apple?' 'Yes, my dear,' said she, and gave her a nice rosy apple out of the chest. Now you must know that this chest had a very thick heavy lid, with a great sharp iron lock upon it. 'Mother,' said the little girl, 'pray give me one for my little brother too.' Her mother did not much like this; however, she said, 'Yes, my child; when he comes from school, he shall have one too.' As she was speaking, she looked out of the window and saw the little boy coming; so she took the apple from her daughter, and threw it back into the chest and shut the lid, telling her that she should have it again when her brother came home. When the little boy came to the door, this wicked woman said to him with a kind voice, 'Come in, my dear, and I will give you an apple.' 'How kind you are, mother!' said the little boy; 'I should like to have an apple very much.' 'Well, come with me then,' said she. So she took him into the store-room and lifted up the cover of the chest, and said, 'There, take one out yourself;' and then, as the little boy stooped down to reach one of the apples out of the chest, bang! she let the lid fall, so hard that his head fell off amongst the apples. When she found what she had done, she was very much frightened, and did not know how she should get the blame off her shoulders. However, she went into her bed-room, and took a white handkerchief out of a drawer, and then fitted the little boy's head upon his neck, and tied the handkerchief round it, so that no one could see what had happened, and seated him on a stool before the door with the apple in his hand.

Soon afterwards Margery came into the kitchen to her mother, who was standing by the fire, and stirring about some hot water in a pot. 'Mother,' said Margery, 'my brother is sitting before the door with an apple in his hand; I asked him to give it me, but he did not say a word, and looked so pale, that I was quite frightened.' 'Nonsense!' said her mother; 'go back again, and if he won't answer you, give him a good box on the ear.' Margery went back, and said, 'Brother, give me that apple.' But he answered not a word; so she gave him a box on the ear; and immediately his head fell off. At this, you may be sure she was sadly frightened, and ran screaming out to her mother, that she had knocked off her brother's head, and cried as if her heart would break. 'O Margery!' said her mother, 'what have you been doing? However, what is done cannot be undone; so we had better put him out of the way, and say nothing to any one about it.'

When the father came home to dinner, he said, 'Where is my little boy?' And his wife said nothing, but put a large dish of black soup upon the table; and Margery wept bitterly all the time, and could not hold up her head. And the father asked after his little boy again. 'Oh!' said his wife, 'I should think he is gone to his uncle's.' 'What business could he have to go away without bidding me good-bye?' said his father. 'I know he wished very much to go,' said the woman; 'and begged me to let him stay there some time; he will be well taken care of there.' 'Ah!' said the father, 'I don't like that; he ought not to have gone away without wishing me good-bye.' And with that he began to eat; but he seemed still sorrowful about his son, and said, 'Margery, what do you cry so for? your brother will come back again, I hope.' But Margery by and by slipped out of the room and went to her drawers and took her best silk handkerchief out of them, and tying it round her little brother's bones, carried them out of the house weeping bitterly all the while, and laid them under the juniper tree; and as soon as she had done this, her heart felt lighter, and she left off crying. Then the juniper tree began to move itself backwards and forwards, and to stretch its branches out, one from another, and then bring them together again, just like a person clapping hands for joy: and after this, a kind of cloud came from the tree, and in the middle of the cloud was a burning fire, and out of the fire came a pretty bird, that flew away into the air, singing merrily. And as soon as the bird was gone, the handkerchief and the little boy were gone too, and the tree looked just as it had done before; but Margery felt quite happy and joyful within herself, just as if she had known that her brother had been alive again, and went into the house and ate her dinner.

But the bird flew away, and perched upon the roof of a goldsmith's house, and sang,

> 'My mother slew her little son;
> My father thought me lost and gone:
> But pretty Margery pitied me,
> And laid me under the juniper tree;
> And now I rove so merrily,
> As over the hills and dales I fly:
> O what a fine bird am I!'

The goldsmith was sitting in his shop finishing a gold chain; and when he heard the bird singing on the house-top, he started up so suddenly that one of his shoes slipped off; however, without stopping to put it on again, he ran out into the street with his apron on, holding his pincers in one hand, and the gold chain in the other. And when he saw the bird sitting on the roof with the sun shining on its bright feathers, he said, 'How sweetly you sing, my pretty bird! pray sing that song again.' 'No,' said the bird, 'I can't sing twice for nothing; if you will give me that gold chain, I'll try what I can do.' 'There,' said the goldsmith, 'take the chain, only pray sing that song again.' So the bird flew down, and taking the chain in its right claw, perched a little nearer to the goldsmith, and sang:

> 'My mother slew her little son;
> My father thought me lost and gone:
> But pretty Margery pitied me,
> And laid me under the juniper tree;
> And now I rove so merrily,

As over the hills and dales I fly:
O what a fine bird am I!'

After that the bird flew away to a shoemaker's, and sitting upon the roof of the house, sang the same song as it had done before.

When the shoemaker heard the song, he ran to the door without his coat, and looked up to the top of the house; but he was obliged to hold his hand before his eyes, because the sun shone so brightly. 'Bird,' said he, 'how sweetly you sing!' Then he called into the house, 'Wife! wife! come out here, and see what a pretty bird is singing on the top of our house!' And he called out his children and workmen; and they all ran out and stood gazing at the bird, with its beautiful red and green feathers, and the bright golden ring about its neck, and eyes which glittered like the stars. 'O bird!' said the shoemaker, 'pray sing that song again.' 'No,' said the bird, 'I cannot sing twice for nothing; you must give me something if I do.' 'Wife,' said the shoemaker, 'run up stairs into the workshop, and bring me down the best pair of new red shoes you can find.' So his wife ran and fetched them. 'Here, my pretty bird,' said the shoemaker, 'take these shoes; but pray sing that song again.' The bird came down, and taking the shoes in his left claw, flew up again to the house-top, and sang:

'My mother slew her little son;
My father thought me lost and gone:
But pretty Margery pitied me,
And laid me under the juniper tree;
And now I rove so merrily,
As over the hills and dales I fly:
O what a fine bird am I!'

And when he had done singing, he flew away, holding the shoes in one claw and the chain in the other. And he flew a long, long way off, till at last he came to a mill. The mill was going clipper! clapper! clipper! clapper! and in the mill were twenty millers, who were all hard at work hewing a millstone; and the millers hewed, hick! hack! hick! hack! and the mill went on, clipper! clapper! clipper! clapper!

So the bird perched upon a linden tree close by the mill, and began its song:

> 'My mother slew her little son;
> My father thought me lost and gone:

here two of the millers left off their work and listened:

> 'But pretty Margery pitied me,
> And laid me under the juniper tree;'

now all the millers but one looked up and left their work;

> 'And now I rove so merrily,
> As over the hills and dales I fly:
> O what a fine bird am I!'

Just as the song was ended, the last miller heard it; and started up, and said, 'O bird! how sweetly you sing! do let me hear the whole of that song; pray, sing it again!' 'No,' said the bird, 'I cannot sing twice for nothing; give me that millstone, and I'll sing again.' 'Why,' said the man, 'the millstone does not belong to me; if it was all mine, you should have it and welcome.' 'Come,' said the other millers, 'if he will only sing that song again, he shall have the millstone.' Then the bird came down from the tree: and the twenty millers fetched long poles and worked and worked heave, ho! heave, ho! till at last they raised the millstone on its side; and then the bird put its head through the hole in the middle of it, and flew away to the linden tree, and sang the same song as it had done before.

And when he had done, he spread his wings, and with the chain in one claw, and the shoes in the other, and the millstone about his neck, he flew away to his father's house.

Now it happened that his father and mother and Mar-

gery were sitting together at dinner. His father was saying,
'How light and cheerful I am!' But his mother said, 'Oh, I
am so heavy and so sad, I feel just as if a great storm was
coming on.' And Margery said nothing, but sat and cried.
Just then the bird came flying along, and perched upon the
top of the house; 'Bless me!' said the father, 'how cheerful
I am; I feel as if I was about to see an old friend again.'
'Alas!' said the mother, 'I am so sad, and my teeth chatter
so, and yet it seems as if my blood was all on fire in my
veins!' and she tore open her gown to cool herself. And
Margery sat by herself in a corner, with her plate on her
lap before her, and wept so bitterly that she cried her plate
quite full of tears.

And the bird flew to the top of the juniper tree and sang:

> 'My mother slew her little son; –'

Then the mother held her ears with her hands, and shut her
eyes close, that she might neither see nor hear; but there
was a sound in her ears like a frightful storm, and her eyes
burned and glared like lightning. 'O wife!' said the father,

> 'My father thought me lost and gone: –'

'what a beautiful bird that is, and how finely he sings; and
his feathers glitter in the sun like so many spangles!'

> 'But pretty Margery pitied me,
> And laid me under the juniper tree; –'

At this Margery lifted up her head and sobbed sadly, and
her father said, 'I must go out, and look at that bird a little
nearer.' 'Oh! don't leave me alone,' said his wife; 'I feel
just as if the house was burning.' However, he would go out
to look at the bird, and it went on singing:

> 'But now I rove so merrily,
> As over the hills and dales I fly:
> O what a fine bird am I!'

As soon as the bird had done singing, he let fall the gold

chain upon his father's neck, and it fitted so nicely that he went back into the house and said, 'Look here, what a beautiful chain the bird has given me; only see how grand it is!' But his wife was so frightened that she fell all along on the floor, so that her cap flew off, and she lay as if she were dead. And when the bird began singing again, Margery said, 'I must go out and see whether the bird has not something to give me.' And just as she was going out of the door, the bird let fall the red shoes before her; and when she had put on the shoes, she all at once became quite light and happy, and jumped into the house and said, 'I was so heavy and sad when I went out, and now I'm so happy! see what fine shoes the bird has given me!' Then the mother said, 'Well, if the world should fall to pieces, I must go out and try whether I shall not be better in the air.' And as she was going out, the bird let fall the mill-stone upon her head and crushed her to pieces.

The father and Margery hearing the noise ran out, and saw nothing but smoke and fire and flame rising up from the place; and when this was past and gone, there stood the little boy beside them; and he took his father and Margery by the hand, and they went into the house, and ate their dinner together very happily.

G. Cruikshank fect

And so, Gentle Reader, craving thy kind acceptance, I wish thee as much willingness to the reading as I have been forward on the printing, and so I end – Farewell.

Preface to 'Valentine and Orson ... with new pictures lively expressing the history.' – 1677.

THE STORY OF PENGUIN CLASSICS

Before 1946 ...'Classics' are mainly the domain of academics and students, without readable editions for everyone else. This all changes when a little-known classicist, E. V. Rieu, presents Penguin founder Allen Lane with the translation of Homer's *Odyssey* that he has been working on and reading to his wife Nelly in his spare time.

1946 *The Odyssey* becomes the first Penguin Classic published, and promptly sells three million copies. Suddenly, classic books are no longer for the privileged few.

1950s Rieu, now series editor, turns to professional writers for the best modern, readable translations, including Dorothy L. Sayers's *Inferno* and Robert Graves's *The Twelve Caesars*, which revives the salacious original.

1960s 1961 sees the arrival of the Penguin Modern Classics, showcasing the best twentieth-century writers from around the world. Rieu retires in 1964, hailing the Penguin Classics list as 'the greatest educative force of the 20th century'.

1970s A new generation of translators arrives to swell the Penguin Classics ranks, and the list grows to encompass more philosophy, religion, science, history and politics.

1980s The Penguin American Library joins the Classics stable, with titles such as *The Last of the Mohicans* safeguarded. Penguin Classics now offers the most comprehensive library of world literature available.

1990s Penguin Popular Classics are launched, offering readers budget editions of the greatest works of literature. Penguin Audiobooks brings the classics to a listening audience for the first time, and in 1999 the launch of the Penguin Classics website takes them online to an ever larger global readership.

The 21st Century Penguin Classics are rejacketed for the first time in nearly twenty years. This world famous series now consists of more than 1,300 titles, making the widest range of the best books ever written available to millions – and constantly redefining the meaning of what makes a 'classic'.

The Odyssey continues ...

The best books ever written

PENGUIN CLASSICS

SINCE 1946

TEACH YOURSELF BOOKS

ITALIAN

The purpose of this book is to enable the reader
to teach himself Italian without any help other
than that which it provides. It is intended for
those who do not know the language and, while
not being a formal grammar, all essential grammatical points are explained one by one in easy
stages and illustrated by sentences; and anyone
who works carefully through it should be able
to read, write and speak Italian with a very
considerable degree of success.

'Italian without tears' would have been an appropriate sub-title for this carefully and attractively composed primer . . . To devise hundreds of simple sentences from a very limited vocabulary taxes the imagination to the utmost. Miss Speight avoids the necessity of straining her inventive genius to the breaking point by an ingenious and yet simple method: the bulk of the reading matter is offered in the form of a journey to Italy.

The Times Literary Supplement

TEACH YOURSELF BOOKS

ITALIAN

KATHLEEN SPEIGHT
M.A., M.Litt., Dott.Lett.(Florence)

TEACH YOURSELF BOOKS
ST PAUL'S HOUSE   WARWICK LANE   LONDON EC4

First printed 1943
New Edition 1962
This impression 1971

NEW EDITION
COPYRIGHT © 1962
The English Universities Press Ltd.

ISBN 0 340 05798 x

Printed in Great Britain for The English Universities Press, Ltd.,
by Richard Clay (The Chaucer Press), Ltd., Bungay, Suffolk

PREFACE

THE title of this book explains itself: its purpose is to enable the reader to teach himself Italian without any help other than that which it provides. It is intended for those who do not know the language and, while not being a formal grammar, all essential grammatical points are explained one by one in easy stages and illustrated by sentences; and anyone who works carefully through it should be able to read, write and speak Italian with a very considerable degree of success.

The study of Italian has, unhappily, been neglected in this country, which is a great pity, seeing how easy it is to acquire a working knowledge of the language, and considering the vast and interesting treasure house of literature which is open to him who learns how to unlock the door. *Teach Yourself Italian* aims at providing a key to that door, by giving the student the essentials of Italian, so that he may be in a position to enter and explore the treasure-house unaided. Being planned with an eye to the needs of the person intending or hoping to travel in Italy, the sentences and exercises are conversational in tone and practical, everyday things form their subject-matter; while the short extracts of Italian prose for translation give a hint of some of the many delights that await the visitor to that country and afford a glimpse—although a very brief one—of the character of its people.

It is hoped that the chapter on pronunciation will be found useful. It cannot be claimed that it will give the student a faultless Italian accent—that can only be acquired by contact with Italians—but it should at least prevent him from making many blunders, such as asking a waiter for roast dog (*cane* is the word for dog, and *carne* for meat); or talking about riding on cabbages (*càvoli*—pronounced cà-volee) when he means horses (*cavàlli*—pronounced cavàllee); or like a tall, thin, gaunt American lady who once caused much merriment in a Florentine tram by stressing the wrong syllable in a word: she wanted a ticket to Gràssina (stress on the Gràss)—a little village outside Florence—but what she said was: *Una, grassìna* (grasséena), which means " One, small and fat ".

This book follows in the main the method of *Teach Yourself*

French and *Teach Yourself Spanish* published in the same series, and I am grateful to the author of those two books, Mr. Norman Scarlyn Wilson, for some very useful suggestions he made for this one. I should also like to thank my friend Dottoressa Antonietta Pettoello for very kindly reading some of the passages for translation, and Professor Bullock of Manchester University for reading through the proof.

KATHLEEN SPEIGHT

Manchester University
1943.

NOTE TO REVISED EDITION

In this revised edition the bibliography on pages 151–154 has again been brought up to date, as have also the Italian passages for translation, particularly as regards post-war hotel prices, etc. A comprehensive index has also been added, referring to both parts of the book, so that information on specific grammatical points may be found more readily.

KATHLEEN SPEIGHT

Manchester
1961.

INTRODUCTION

In order to use this book to the best advantage the following points should be noted:

There are two parts: Part I contains most of the actual instruction and a series of exercises; and Part II is the key to the exercises in Part I and, in addition, it offers notes on any difficulties arising from them. The two parts should be used in conjunction. Study the lesson and then attempt the exercise *before* looking at Part II. Then turn to Part II and correct your effort. After the first three lessons the exercises marked (*a*) are always translation from Italian into English, and those marked (*b*) are translation the other way about: from English into Italian. Most benefit will be derived from the instruction if you do exercise (*a*) and *correct* it by means of Part II before you do exercise (*b*) for that lesson, and having corrected exercise (*a*), you will find (*b*) all the easier to do. Whenever uncertain how to express an English sentence in Italian, look back at previous lessons, where you will nearly always find a model from which to work.

It would be a good thing to revise after every *three* lessons; in fact, the lessons are so arranged that revision will be found most convenient after lessons 3, 9, 12, etc. When revising, turn back and again study each lesson in Part I; but for the exercises turn straight to the corresponding section in Part II, and do those sentences as exercises, using Part I as a key to correct them. In this way you will have done a fresh lot of exercises, as what was in the first place Italian–English is now English–Italian, and vice versa.

Memorize each new word and phrase as it appears. Try to remember the Italian word for the various things you see about you during the day, and get into the habit of repeating sentences in Italian over and over again. If you can get native help for the pronunciation, so much the better; if not, try to imitate the wireless. The oftener you repeat sentences over to yourself, the more quickly will you learn the language and the sooner will you begin to think in Italian. They need not be long nor difficult sentences; the shorter and simpler the better. "I get up", "I open the door", "I enter the room", and such like will do excellently to start with; when performing simple actions such as these, try to remember to say to yourself in Italian what you are doing.

The vocabulary at the end is Italian–English only, to give you the necessary help in translating from Italian to English, when you will be meeting new words. In translating from English into Italian you will be using words which you have already met—words which should therefore be in your memory; if they are not, they will usually be found without much trouble by consulting previous lessons.

Two words of advice and warning: First, use the key sensibly. Never turn to it until you have made some attempt at the exercise yourself. Always write down something *before* you see what the key says. Having to put right a wrong effort of your own is a hundred times more useful than merely copying down a correct version of someone else's, for in the latter case no impression is left on the mind. An Italian saying is very apt in this connection: *Sbagliando s'impara* ("By making mistakes one learns"); so don't be discouraged at the number of mistakes you make; correct them, and resolve not to make the same mistakes again. Secondly, while teaching yourself Italian, try to do some regularly each day. A short time, even only half an hour, each day will be far more beneficial than a huge spurt every now and then with long periods in between of no study at all. You cannot teach yourself a language by fits and starts; you must make up your mind to go slowly and steadily, always being sure of one lesson before passing on to the next, and you will soon surprise yourself with the progress you are making.

CONTENTS

PART II

PART I

ITALIAN PRONUNCIATION

It is not easy to learn from a book how to pronounce a language; but Italian is simpler than some other languages to learn this way, for it is almost entirely phonetic: the same letter or combination of letters is nearly always used for the same sound. Therefore once we have become acquainted with the various sounds an Italian makes, and learnt which letters represent them, there will be little difficulty in pronouncing new words met in reading, or in spelling words heard spoken for the first time.

The following rules for pronunciation should be studied, and the words given as examples might be read aloud. It would be a good plan to read aloud the Italian words and sentences as we do each exercise. During the first few lessons this will involve some looking back to this preliminary chapter; but gradually there will be less looking back as the words become familiar. While teaching ourselves Italian we should make a point of hearing it spoken as much as possible. If we have no Italian acquaintances and no possibility of hearing lectures in Italian, there is always the wireless to fall back on. The news bulletins, talks and plays will seem rather difficult at first; but very soon we shall be able to distinguish words, then phrases, then whole sentences, and all the time we shall unconsciously be acquiring a correct intonation and a good accent.

Alphabet.—The Italian alphabet has twenty-one letters. These are the same as ours, except that there is no *j, k, w, x* or *y*.

Pronunciation of the Vowels.—The five vowel signs represent seven sounds which are pronounced approximately as follows:

a as *a* in *father*	carta = paper	sala = room
e as *a* in *mate* (called the close *e*)	mele = apples	vedere = to see
e as *e* in *pet* (called the open *e*)	bello = fine, beautiful	tenda = tent
i as *i* in *machine*	vini = wines	spilli = pins
o as *o* in *rope* (close *o*)	sole = sun	colore = colour

11

o as *o* in *soft* (open *o*)	porta = door	toro = bull
u as *oo* in *moon*	fumo = smoke	luna = moon

The following points should be noted:

1. Each vowel must be distinctly sounded, whatever its position in a word. In English unstressed vowels are often slurred; in Italian the unstressed vowels, although pronounced more rapidly and more lightly than the stressed ones, keep their pure sound.

2. They do not tend to become diphthongs, as in English. For instance, we pronounce the *a* in the word *mate* almost as *ay-ee*, and the *o* in rope is nearly *oh-oo*. The Englishman, when speaking Italian, must remember to avoid drawling the vowels.

3. The voice should be carried farther forward in the mouth when speaking Italian. The mouth should be opened well for the vowels *a*, *open e* and *open o*; in pronouncing *i* it should be nearly closed, with the lips drawn well back. The mouth, lips and jaw may be moved more than when speaking English; an Italian does not mind what sort of a face he is making so long as he produces clear and correct sounds. If we wish to speak his language correctly, we must try to imitate him.

Bearing these points in mind, let us return for a moment to the Italian words just given as examples and read them aloud. The consonants are more or less the same as in English, except that the *r* is strongly trilled, with the point of the tongue vibrating against the back of the top teeth. In each word the stress falls on the syllable next to the last:

carta	(cárr-tah)*	sala	(sáh-lah)
mele	(máy-lay)	vedere	(vay-dáy-rray)
bello	(béll-loh)	tenda	(tén-dah)
vini	(vée-nee)	spilli	(spée-lee)
sole	(sóh-lay)	colore	(coh-lóh-rray)
porta	(páwrr-tah)	toro	(táw-rroh)
fumo	(fóo-moh)	luna	(lóo-nah)

Stress in Pronunciation.—In Italian words one syllable is always more stressed than the others. The majority of words have the stress on the vowel in the syllable next to the last; but there are some which have the final vowel, and others which have the vowels in the third-last or fourth-last syllable,

* The division of words for pronunciation is not always syllabically correct. See Appendix, page 214. It will also be realized that these pronunciations in brackets can only be approximate.

stressed. When the *final vowel* is stressed it has a written accent to show that this is the case:

> virtú = virtue (pronounced veer-tóo)
> portò = he carried (pronounced pawrr-taw)
> città = town (pronounced chee-táh)

but there is normally no accent to indicate when the stress falls on the third-last or fourth-last syllables. To help the student, this book adopts the following device: words which have the stress on any syllable *before* the next to the last will have the vowel in that syllable printed in dark type, as: camera = bedroom (pronounced cáh-may-rah), sedici = sixteen (sáy-dee-chee). Therefore a word which has no written accent on its last vowel and no vowel printed in dark type will have the stress in the normal position: on the syllable next to the last.

Open and close *e* and *o*.—*E* and *o* each have two sounds: the open and the close. When these two vowels are in an unstressed position, they have the close sound; but when stressed, they may have either. It is important to distinguish between the open and close sounds, as important as, for example, our distinguishing between our words *pen* and *pain* and *not* and *note*. But, in writing, these sounds are not differentiated, so the student needs some guide to enable him to know when the vowel is open and when close. In this book we are adopting special printing in dark type to denote the OPEN sounds of *e* and *o*:

> bello   tenda   porta   toro

The CLOSE *e* and *o* in a stressed position will therefore be printed in ordinary printing.*

The special printing and the dark type will appear in the grammar rules and examples and in the vocabularies, but not in the exercises. In this way the student will be guided as to how to pronounce each new word as he comes across it, and at the same time, when doing the exercises, he will be getting used to reading Italian as it is normally written.

Pronunciation of Two or More Vowels.—*A*, *e* and *o* are called strong vowels, and *i* and *u* weak vowels. When two strong vowels come together we have what is called *hiatus*, and they are pronounced as two separate syllables:

---

* They may or may not be in dark type according to whether the stressed position is normal or not. See preceding paragraph.

soave = sweet, gentle (pronounced soh-áh-vay)
beato = happy (pronounced bay-áh-toh)

Hiatus also occurs when a strong and a weak vowel come together and the weak one is stressed:

via   = road   (vée-ah)
pio   = pious (pée-oh)
due   = two   (dóo-ay)
paura = fear   (pah-oó-rah)

When a strong and weak vowel come together and the strong is stressed, they count as one syllable, the weak one being lightly and rapidly pronounced, and this is called a diphthong:

piɛde = foot   (peeáy-day)
fiore = flower (feeóh-rray)
buɔno = good   (bwáw-noh)
guɛrra = war   (gwáy-rrah)
rauco = hoarse (ráh-oo-coh)

Two weak vowels together also form a diphthong:

guida = guide (gwée-dah)
piú   = more   (like English word *pew*)

There are a few cases in which three vowels come together and are pronounced as one syllable: this is called a triphthong. The three vowel combinations used in Italian are: *iuɔ*, *uɔi*, *iɛi*:

barcaiuɔlo = boatman (barr-cah-yoo-óll-loh)
suɔi = his (masc. plural) (swóh-ee)
miɛi = my (masc. plural) (mee-áyee)

In pronouncing a triphthong, remember that the stress is always on the strong vowel. You will have noticed that, when making an effort to produce the three vowels as one syllable, the first weak one almost loses vowel force and becomes a consonant, the *i* has the force of English *y* and the *u* of our *w*.

Pronunciation of Consonants.—The sixteen consonant signs are used to represent the following sounds: *b, d, f, l, m, n, p, q, t* and *v* are pronounced as in English, except that *d, l, n* and *t* are pronounced farther forward in the mouth, the tongue pressing just behind the top teeth, instead of touching the roof of the mouth;

c has two sounds. Followed by *e* or *i*, it is like the English *ch* in *church*, otherwise it has the hard sound of *k*:

centro = centre (chén-trroh)
vicino = near (vee-chée-noh)
comprare = to buy (kohm-práh-rray)

g also has two sounds. Followed by *e* or *i*, it has the sound of *g* as in *general* or *j* as in *July*; otherwise it has the hard sound as in *go*:

gigante = giant (gee-gán-tay)
generale = general (jay-nay-rráh-lay)
gatto = cat (gáh-toh)

h is never sounded, and, except with *c* and *g* (see groups of consonants below), appears in only two or three words:

ha = he has (pronounced ah)

n followed by a hard *c*, hard *g* or *q* is like the English *n* in *ing*:

banca = bank (báng-ka)
lungo = long (lúng-goh)

r is always trilled with the point of the tongue against the upper teeth:

caro = dear (cáh-rroh)

s has two sounds: like *s* in *taste*, called unvoiced; and like *s* in *rose*, called voiced:

unvoiced: spillo = pin   casa   = house
voiced: viso = face   smemorato = forgetful

z also has two sounds: unvoiced like a sharp *ts*; and voiced, which is pronounced *dz*:

unvoiced: *ts*: azione   = action   zio   = uncle
voiced: *dz*: romanzo = novel   mezzo = half

To help the student to determine whether to give the *s* and *z* the voiced or the unvoiced sound, the *voiced s* and *z* will in future be distinguished in the text and in the vocabularies by a small dot printed beneath them as: viṣo, romanẓo.

Double Consonants are pronounced as prolonged single ones. They always represent a single sound; never two different ones, as in the English *accept*:

accento = accent (ah-chén-toh)
vacca = cow   (váh-cah)

Groups of Consonants.—The following five groups each represent a single sound:

ch (used only before *e* and *i*) is pronounced as *k*:

chiesa = church (keeáy-zah)*
perché = because (pair-káy)

gh (only before *e* and *i*) is like the hard *g*:

ghiaccio = ice (g [as in *gear*] eeáh-cho)

gl followed by *i* has a very liquid sound, as in the word *million*:

figlio = son (féel-yo)

(There are a few exceptions to this rule when *g* and *l* are pronounced as separate letters; but these are mostly unusual words, with which we do not need to concern ourselves.)

gn is like the *ni* of our word *onion*:

bagno = bath (báhn-yoh)

sc before *e* and *i* is like the English *sh*; before any other vowel or a consonant it is like *k*:

uscire = to go out (oo-shée-rray)
oscuro = dark (oh-skóo-rroh)

It would be a good plan to put these rules into practice by reading aloud and learning by heart the numbers from one to twenty. Here they are, with approximate English pronunciation. Note which syllable carries the stress in each word:

1.	uno (masc.)	oó-noh
	una (fem.)	oó-nah
2.	due	dóo-ay
3.	tre	tray
4.	quattro	kwát-trroh
5.	cinque	cheéng-kway
6.	sei	sáy-ee
7.	sette	sét-tay
8.	otto	áwt-toh
9.	nove	náw-vay
10.	dieci	deeáy-chee
11.	undici	oón-dee-chee

* It should be emphasized that these approximations in English are only *very* approximate. It is, for instance, not possible to indicate the "open" quality of the ε here.

12.	dodici	dóh-dee-chee
13.	tredici	tráy-dee-chee
14.	quattordici	kwat-tórr-dee-chee
15.	quindici	kwéen-dee-chee
16.	sedici	sáy-dee-chee
17.	diciassette	dee-cheeah-sét-tay
18.	diciotto	dee-cheeáwt-toh
19.	diciannove	dee-cheeah-náw-vay
20.	venti	váyn-tee

For those who would like more practice, here are the days and the months; a capital letter is not required in Italian:

Monday, etc.	lunedí	(loo-nay-dée)
	martedí	(mahrr-tay-dée)
	mercoledí	(mairr-coh-lay-dée)
	giovedí	(joh-vay-dée)
	venerdí	(vay-nayrr-dée)
	sabato	(sáh-bah-toh)
	domenica	(doh-máy-nee-cah)
January, etc.	gennaio	(jay-náhee-oh)
	febbraio	(fay-bráhee-oh)
	marzo	(máhrr-tso)
	aprile	(ah-prrée-lay)
	maggio	(máh-jeeoh)
	giugno	(jeeóon-yoh)
	luglio	(lóo-leeoh)
	agosto	(ah-góh-stoh)
	settembre	(say-tém-brray)
	ottobre	(oht-tóh-brray)
	novembre	(noh-vém-brray)
	dicembre	(dee-chém-brray)

Written Accents.*—It will be noticed in the paragraph on stress on page 13 that the examples had different accents over the final vowel. Those who have learnt French are familiar with the use of three accents: the acute (´), the grave (`) and the circumflex (ˆ). These accents are also used in Italian, but

* The use of the grave and acute accents is not uniform throughout Italy. Many writers always use the grave to denote the stressed vowel, irrespective of whether the sound may be open or close. Others differentiate only with the vowel E. The system here followed, if written accents are to indicate pronunciation as well as stress, is the most logical, and it has the authority of many of the chief publishers in Italy, as: Mondadori, Einaudi, S.E.I., Laterza, etc.

not to serve quite the same purpose. In Italian the acute and grave accents are stress marks. They are primarily used to indicate that the vowel over which they are placed is the one to be stressed, and only in the cases of the open and close *e* and *o* are they concerned with pronunciation, for then they are distinguishing signs as well as stress marks, the acute being used for the close sounds and the grave for the open. These two accents must not be placed over the other vowels just as one wishes: the acute is over *i* and *u*, and the grave over *a*. The third accent, the circumflex, is very rarely used, and has a different function: it denotes that a word has been abbreviated by the omission of a letter or syllable.

Examples:

Acute: lunedí; virtú; credé (he believed).

Grave: portò; onestà (honesty); caffè (coffee, café).

Circumflex: studî—studies (the plural of studio—study, a shortened form of studii, the accent denoting that one *i* has been omitted).

As we learn each new word we must note where the stress falls and remember that all words of more than one syllable which have the final vowel stressed must have the accent over that vowel.

The *acute* and *grave* accents are also used:

1. On certain words of one syllable to distinguish them from other words of the same spelling and pronunciation, but of different meaning:

ché	= because	che	= which, that, who (rel. pronoun)
dà	= he gives	da	= by, from
dí	= day	di	= of
è	= is	e	= and
là	= there	la	= the (fem. sing.)
lí	= there	li	= them (masc.)
né	= nor	ne	= of it
sé	= himself	se	= if
sí	= yes	si	= himself
tè	= tea	te	= thee

2. And on the following five short words:

ciò	= that, this
già	= already
giú	= down
piú	= more
può	= he can

Additional notes on pronunciation and syllabication are to be found in the Appendix, page 212.

Preliminary Exercise

1. Place the correct accent on each of the final vowels of the following words: virtu, porto, perche, mercoledi, crede, onesta, caffe, citta (town), sincerita (sincerity).

2. Pronounce the following words with a true Italian accent and *not* as we say them in English. Then turn to the Key to this Exercise, where you will find approximate pronunciations in English, from which to check your effort: arena, cupola, incognito, pianoforte, vermicelli, terra cotta, ultimatum, Galli-Curci, Marco Polo, Medici.

LESSON I

INDEFINITE ARTICLE—GENDER

WHEN learning the numbers from 1 to 20 you will have noticed that there are two words for "one": *uno* and *una*. *Uno* is used with persons and things of masculine gender and *una* with persons and things which are feminine. In English we have three genders: masculine, feminine and neuter, gender being equivalent to sex; a man is masculine, a cow feminine, an apple neuter. In Italian there is no neuter; therefore things, not only persons and animals, are also masculine and feminine.

Uno and *una* also mean *a* and *an*: *uno* for the masculine and *una* for the feminine: *uno zio* = an uncle; *una zia* = an aunt. In English we have two forms for the indefinite article: *a* for words beginning with a consonant and *an* for words beginning with a vowel: *a* man, *an* apple; and in Italian *uno* and *una* have different forms according to what letter comes at the beginning of the word which follows them. But in Italian the matter is a little more complicated:

Masculine		*Feminine*	
un uno		una un'	
un ragazzo	= a boy	una ragazza	= a girl
un albero	= a tree	un'ora	= an hour
uno spillo	= a pin	una strada	= a street
uno zio	= an uncle	una zia	= an aunt

Of the two masculine forms, *un* is the more usual: *uno* is used only before words beginning with *s impure* (*s* followed by another consonant) and *z*; and of the feminine forms *una* is to be used before any consonant and *un'* before a word beginning with a vowel.

Look again at the nouns given as examples. You will see that all the masculine nouns end in *-o*, and all the feminines in *-a*. ALL ITALIAN NOUNS END IN A VOWEL: those in *-o* are masculine, except one: *mano* (hand), which is feminine. "A hand" is therefore *una mano*. Nouns ending in *-a* are mostly feminine. Before doing Exercise I, read through this vocabulary and decide the gender of the various nouns.

Vocabulary

(Words which have already appeared in the text are not included in these vocabularies.)

Maria	= Mary	hanno	= they have
Piero	= Peter		
donna	= woman	a	= at, to
figlia	= daughter	anche	= also
finestra	= window	che?, che cosa?	= what?, what thing?
fratello	= brother	chi?	= who?, whom?
libro	= book	dove?	= where? (dov'è? = where is?)
sbaglio	= mistake	ecco	= here is, here are, there is, there are
sorella	= sister		
specchio	= mirror	in	= in
uomo	= man		

Exercise 1

a. Supply the indefinite article in the blank spaces in the following sentences:

1. Maria è   donna e Piero è   uomo.
2. Maria e Piero hanno   casa.
3. Piero e Maria hanno   figlio e   figlia.
4. Chi ha   fratello? Maria ha   fratello e anche   sorella.
5. Ha Piero   zio? Sí, Piero ha   zio e anche   zia.
6. Dov'è   porta? E dov'è   finestra?
7. Chi ha   libro? Piero ha   libro? Che cosa ha Maria? Maria ha   specchio.
8. Dov'è   sbaglio? Ecco   sbaglio in   libro.

b. Translate the preceding sentences into English.

c. Translate into Italian:

1. Mary has a house and Peter has a house.
2. Peter has a son and * daughter.
3. Has Mary an aunt? Yes, Mary has an aunt and also an uncle.
4. Where is a mistake? Here is a mistake.
5. Who has a book? Mary has a book. Mary gives a book to Peter.
6. Mary has a brother and * sister.
7. What has Peter in one hand? Peter has a book in one hand.
8. Has Mary a mirror? Yes, Mary has a mirror.

LESSON II

VERBS AND PRONOUNS

IN Italian, changes in the meaning of words are often indicated by changes in their endings, particularly in the case of verbs. We met some verbs in the preliminary chapter. Among these were: *comprare*, *credere* and *uscire*. The Infinitive, which gives the general idea of the verb without saying who is doing the action or when it is done, is indicated in English by the word *to* and in Italian by the endings *-are*, *-ere* and *-ire*. Italian verbs are divided into three groups, called conjugations, according to these three infinitive endings. First conjugation verbs end in *-are*; second in *-ere* (some verbs in this conjugation have the stress on the infinitive ending: as *vedere*; others, like *credere*, have the stress on an earlier syllable), and the third in *-ire*. If we cut off these endings we have left what is known as the *stem*, the part of the verb which does not usually change: *compr-*, *cred-*, *usc-*, and it is to this part that other endings are added which denote the *person* (that is, *who* is doing the action) and the *tense* (that is, *when* it is taking place).

Let us take the first two conjugations and study their present indicative tense, using *comprare* and *credere* as models. The present indicative makes a plain statement about some action which is going on at the present time.

* Repeat article before each noun.

comprare, 1st conjugation   *credere*, 2nd conjugation

Sing.

1st person	compr-o *	I buy	cred-o	I believe
2nd ,,	compr-i	thou buyest	cred-i	thou believest
3rd ,,	compr-a	he buys	cred-e	he believes

Plur.

1st ,,	compr-iamo	we buy	cred-iamo	we believe
2nd ,,	compr-ate	you buy	cred-ete	you believe
3rd ,,	compr-ano	they buy	cred-ono	they believe

Note where the stress falls. It comes on the *stem* in all three persons singular and in the third person plural: COMPR-, and CRED-, and on the *ending* (the syllable next to the last) in the first and second persons plural: compriAMO, comprATE, crediAMO, credETE.

Note, in the second place, that where in English we have only three different endings: buy, buyest and buys; in Italian there are six, a different one for each person. In Italian, therefore, we always know which person is meant by the ending of the verb: *compriamo* is always *we* buy, for *-iamo* is the ending for *we*, and so no word for *we* is required. Normally no subject pronoun of a verb—I, thou, he, etc.—is necessary in Italian, and it is omitted.

And thirdly we must note that this present tense also translates the other two English present tenses: the emphatic: *I do buy*, and the continuous or progressive: *I am buying*.

Subject pronouns are sometimes required for emphasis or for clearness. In such a sentence as: "I am learning Italian and he is learning French", the pronouns are necessary to indicate the contrast between the two subjects. It would be useful, therefore, to learn these pronouns at this point, and we may then practise them while making ourselves familiar with the present indicative. They are as follows:

	Singular		*Plural*	
First person	†io	= I	noi	= we
Second ,,	tu	= thou	voi	= you
Third ,,	lui	= he	loro	= they (masc.)
	egli	= he	. . . . .	
	esso	= he, it	essi	= they (masc.)

* The division of words in these tables is made to help you to memorize the verb endings and is syllabically incorrect. For correct syllabication, see Appendix, page 214.

† Capital letter not required except at beginning of a sentence.

Third Person	lɛi = she	loro = they (fem.)
	ella = she	. . . . .
	essa = she, it	esse = they (fem.)

Third person pronouns may seem a little confusing, but they are really quite simple. *Egli* and *ella* are used only in writing, in literary style; never in conversation. They refer only to persons, not to things or animals. *Lui* and *lɛi* are used in conversation and in familiar or intimate style when writing; we shall use these mostly in this book: they are also only for persons. *Esso* and *essa* are used both in literary and conversational style and for things, animals and persons; but they are more often used for things than for persons. There is no plural of *egli* or *ella*, the plurals of *esso* and *essa* being used instead.

This all boils down to a simple solution: we shall use *lui* and *lɛi* mostly in this book with their plural *loro* when speaking of persons, and *esso* and *essa* when speaking of things. But at the same time we must know the literary forms; for although we may not aspire to write literary Italian, we may very easily feel bold enough to read some, and therefore we must be able to recognize these forms.

Interrogative Sentences.—In the first lesson we saw that in Italian one asks a question as we do in English, by inverting the order of the verb and its subject: *Ha Maria una zia?* But this inversion is not so frequent as in English; we might as well have said: *Maria ha una zia?* the question being indicated merely by the tone of voice. What Italian *never* does is employ an auxiliary (or helping) verb to form a question, as we do in English. "Does Mary speak Italian?" is: *Parla Maria italiano?* or *Maria parla italiano?*

Vocabulary

foglio = sheet of paper	guardare = to look at	con = with
inchiostro = ink	leggere (irreg.)* = to read	
lettera = letter	scrivere (irreg.)* = to write	mentre = while
penna = pen		oggi = today
tavola = table	trovare = to find	quando = when
	usare = to use	(pronounce:
	vendere = to sell	kwándoh)

* All verbs not regular will be so indicated in these vocabularies, and they are listed in the appendix, with their irregular parts shown. Take no notice of this "irreg." at present.

Exercise 2

a. Continue the following, throughout all persons, singular and plural:

1. Vendo una vacca e compro un gatto.
2. Mentre scrivo uso una penna, inchiostro e un foglio.
3. Quando leggo guardo un libro.

b. Continue the following through all the persons, including the subject pronouns in each case:

Io parlo con Piero.

c. Translate into English:

1. Chi trova un libro? Io trovo un libro.
2. Maria e Piero parlano? Sí, parlano.
3. Scrive Maria una lettera a Piero?
4. Sí, e mentre lei scrive, io guardo un libro.
5. Che cosa compra Piero oggi?
6. Oggi Piero compra un libro.

d. Translate into Italian:

1. Where is a table?
2. She is selling a cow and buying a cat.
3. They are writing a letter to Mary.
4. While she reads I write.
5. What do you see? I see a woman and a man, a boy and a girl.
6. She is buying a mirror and I am buying a book.
7. Do Peter and Mary speak Italian? Yes, they speak Italian.
8. He is looking at Mary while she writes a letter.

LESSON III

DEFINITE ARTICLE—NUMBER

Just as there are various forms of the indefinite article, according to its gender and to the initial letter of the word which follows it, so the definite article—translating "the"—has various forms in Italian:

Masculine

Singular: il	*Plural*: i
lo	gli
l'	gli, gl'

il libro   (the book)   i libri
lo studio   (the study)   gli studî
lo zio   (the uncle)   gli zii
l'insetto   (the insect)   gl'insetti
l'accento   (the accent)   gli accenti

From these examples it will be seen that *il*, plural *i*, is used before a masculine word beginning with a consonant (except *s impure* and *z*); that *lo*, plural *gli*, is used before masculine words beginning with *s impure* and *z*; that *l'* is used before a word beginning with a vowel, and its plural *gli* drops the *i* before another *i*.

It must be emphasized that it is the initial letter of the word *immediately* following the article which determines the form to be used. If any other word comes between the article and its noun, then it is this other word which determines the form of the article:

Example: il libro, l'altro libro (the other book), lo stesso libro (the same book).

Feminine

Singular: la   *Plural*: le
          l'   le, l'
la porta   le porte
l'altra porta   le altre porte
l'entrata (the entrance)   l'entrate

The feminine forms are not so complicated. There is only one form for the singular: *la*, which becomes *l'* before a word beginning with a vowel; and one form for the plural: *le*, which becomes *l'* before another *e*.

Number.—By studying the endings of the nouns in the foregoing examples we can learn something about the formation of their plurals. In English we usually form the plural by adding -*s* or -*es* to the singular; but when we remember that we cannot say *sheeps, mouses* or *childs*, we realize that it is not so easy in English. In Italian, too, there are various ways of forming the plural. The first important rule is that nouns ending in -*o* form their plural by changing the *o* to *i*, and that *feminine* nouns ending in -*a* change the *a* to *e*. Words which go with or qualify the noun, such as *stesso* and *altro*, must also take the noun's gender and number. Adjectives which end in -*o* (there are some which end in -*e*) have a feminine form in -*a*, and they form their plural like the nouns in -*o* and -*a*:

lo stesso libro   la stessa porta
gli stessi libri   le stesse porte

il cappɛllo rosso = the red hat
i cappɛlli rossi = the red hats

la cravatta rossa = the red tie
le cravatte rosse = the red ties

Some adjectives precede their nouns, usually short ones of very common use; but more often they follow, as in the example just given. The student is advised to place them as he finds them in the examples, and if in any doubt, to put them *after* the noun to which they refer. An adjective must also agree in number and gender with its noun when it comes in a different part of the sentence:

Il cappɛllo è rosso, ma le cravatte sono gialle.—The hat is red, but the ties are yellow.

Vocabulary

calzino = sock	alto = tall, high	sono = are (they)
ɛrba = grass	azzurro = blue	
giardino = garden	basso = low	molto = very, much
muro = wall	bellino = pretty	c'è = there is
tetto = roof	bɛllo = beautiful, fine, lovely	ci sono = there are
	nuɔvo = new	non = not
	piccolo = small	
	questo = this	

Exercise 3

a. Supply the definite article where missing in the following sentences:

1. Dov'è   donna?   donna è a casa.
2.   fratelli e   sorelle di Maria sono in città. Comprano   cappelli e   cravatte.
3.   zio di Pietro è alto, ma   zia è molto piccola.
4. Ecco   casa nuova.   Dov'è   entrata?
5.   tetto è rosso, e   muri sono gialli.
6. Questo muro è alto, ma   altro è basso.
7.   giardino è bellino;   erba è bella e ci sono molti alberi.
8. Piero guarda   zio, perché ha un cappello giallo, una cravatta azzurra e   calzini sono rossi.
9. Maria non è in casa; è in città e compra   specchi.

From the last sentence it will be seen that a sentence is made negative by placing *non* (not) before the verb. Note also that possession is expressed by the preposition *di* (of). Peter's uncle is tall = *Lo zio di Piero è alto*.

b. Translate into English the sentences in Exercise 3 (*a*). (Note that *a casa* or *in casa* means "at home").

c. Translate into Italian:

1. The trees are very high.
2. The new house has a red roof and yellow walls. It is in a very pretty garden.
3. The windows are very high, but the door is low.
4. Uncle is at home, but Aunt is in town. She is buying a hat. (Say: *the* uncle, *the* aunt.)
5. He is very tall, but Aunt is small.
6. This boy is buying a pen, but the other boy is buying socks and a tie.
7. The house has five doors and seventeen windows.
8. They are not writing the letters, they are looking at Peter's yellow hat and red socks.

LESSON IV

MORE VERBS—THE POLITE PRONOUN

VERBS of the third conjugation are divided into two groups according to whether they add *-isc* to their stem in certain persons of the present indicative, present subjunctive and imperative. We are now concerned only with the present indicative: and as the majority of verbs add the *-isc*, we will call these the first group, and those which do not, the second*. The present tense of verbs of the third conjugation is as follows:

1st group: *finire* = to finish	2nd group: *partire* = to depart
fin-isc-o	part-o
fin-isc-i	part-i
fin-isc-e	part-e
fin-iamo	part-iamo
fin-ite	part-ite
fin-isc-ono	part-ono

* Indication as to which group a verb belongs is to be found in the vocabularies.

The -*isc* is added in the first group throughout the singular and in the third person plural. Except for this addition of -*isc*, the verbs of both groups are exactly alike.

Note where the stress falls. Note also, in regard to group I, that in the first person singular and in the third person plural the *c* being followed by an *o* has the hard sound, but in the second and third persons singular it is soft (*finisco* is pronounced fee-née-skoh, *finisci* fee-née-shee).

The Polite Pronoun

We now come to an important point about the translation of "you". Italian has three different ways of saying *you*. In the verbs conjugated above we have used two forms: *tu* = thou, and *voi* = you; the third form is the same as the word for *she*: *lɛi*, but it is often spelt with a capital letter. Of these forms, *tu* is singular, and is used when speaking to a near relative, a very close friend or to a child; *voi*, besides being the plural of *tu*, is also used for the singular when speaking to acquaintances or to strangers; but as it carries with it a slight indication that the person to whom one is speaking is an inferior, or at any rate no better than oneself, the third form, *Lɛi* (originally from an expression meaning Your Grace, and which infers special courtesy towards the person addressed), is more generally used between persons not on intimate terms. *Lɛi* is the form we shall mostly use in this book, and if and when you go to Italy it is the form you should use when speaking to Italians.

Lɛi, although meaning *you*, is always third person; the verb used with it must be THIRD PERSON SINGULAR. The plural of *Lɛi* is *Loro* (the same form as the word for "they") and it requires the verb in the THIRD PERSON PLURAL.

While learning the present indicative of two more verbs, we might insert these pronouns for practice. These two verbs, *ɛssere* = to be and *avere* = to have, are called auxiliary verbs, for, like the corresponding English verbs, they help to form compound tenses; and as they do not conform to any of the models of the three conjugations, they are called irregular verbs.

Present Indicative

ɛssere = to be		*avere* = to have	
io sono	I am	io hɔ	I have
tu sɛi	{thou art {you are	tu hai	{thou hast {you have
lui, lɛi, esso, essa, ɛ	he, etc., is	lui, etc., ha	he, etc., has
Lɛi ɛ	you are	Lɛi ha	you have

noi siamo	we are	noi abbiamo	we have
voi siete	you are	voi avete	you have
loro sono	they are	loro hanno	they have
Loro sono	you are	Loro hanno	you have

The following sentences will help to clarify the uses of the three forms of address. We will translate the sentence *You are very tall* into Italian in three ways: first as if addressing a child, secondly a social equal or inferior, and thirdly as one would speak to a stranger; then we will put all three sentences into the plural:

Singular	Plural
Tu sei molto alto	Voi siete molto alti
Voi siete molto alto	Voi siete molto alti
Lei è molto alto	Loro sono molto alti

As *lei* and *loro* mean respectively *she* and *they* as well as *you*, it might be thought that confusion would arise. But one nearly always knows from the tone of the speaker's voice whether he is talking *to* you or *about* her; if there should be any doubt, this is overcome by adding *Signore* (Sir), *Signora* (Madam) or *Signorina* (Miss) when using the polite form. Note that these three words: *signore*, *signora* and *signorina*, also mean respectively: (1) "gentleman", "lady" and "young lady"; and (2) "Mr.", "Mrs." and "Miss". A capital letter is required in the latter case only when used in direct address, not otherwise

Nouns and Adjectives in -e.—Many Italian nouns end in *-e*, and some are masculine and some feminine. They form their plural by changing the *-e* to *-i* (except those ending in *-ie*: see page 42).

Singular	Plural
il padre = the father	i padri
la madre = the mother	le madri

Many adjectives also end in *-e*; they have the same form in the masculine and the feminine, and they form their plural in the same way as the nouns ending in *-e*: *L'albero è verde* = the tree is green; *Gli alberi sono verdi* = the trees are green.

Vocabulary

balcone (m.) = balcony	aprire (irreg.) (2nd group) = to open
bambino = child	
cucina = kitchen	capire (1st group) = to understand
parola = word	

piano = floor

al pianterreno = on the ground floor

al piano superiore = on the upper floor

sala da pranzo = dining room

salotto = drawing room

sedia = chair

soprabito = overcoat

stanza = room

terrazza = terrace

dormire (2nd group) = to sleep

preferire (1st group) = to prefer

comodo = comfortable

facile = easy

grande = large

spagnuolo = Spanish

troppo = too, too much

domani = tomorrow

per = for

Exercise 4 (a)

1. La madre apre la finestra mentre il bambino dorme.
2. Non capisco perché la signora parte oggi e non domani.
3. Capiamo questa parola ma non l'altra.
4. Questa casa ha dodici stanze.
5. La sala da pranzo ha una terrazza e le due stanze grandi hanno balconi.
6. La sala da pranzo e la terrazza sono belle, ma la cucina è troppo piccola.
7. Apriamo la finestra e vediamo il giardino.
8. Noi abbiamo un giardino molto bello.
9. Dov'è la sorella di Piero? È in cucina.
10. Aprono la porta e vedono la terrazza.
11. Il salotto non è piccolo e le sedie sono comode.
12. Il salotto è al pianterreno ma lo studio è al piano superiore.
13. Dove dormite voi, Maria e Lucia? Noi dormiamo in una camera al piano superiore.
14. Lei trova facile l'italiano,* Signorina?
15. Sí, trovo facile l'italiano. È facile anche lo spagnuolo; ma preferisco l'italiano.

Exercise 4 (b)

1. This chair is very comfortable, but I prefer the other.
2. I do not understand this word.
3. Do you understand this book?
4. Where are the young ladies? Are they leaving today?
5. Yes, they are leaving today. They are in the kitchen with Peter. (Say: *in kitchen*.)
6. Peter sleeps on the ground floor.

* A small letter, except when speaking of the people: Gl'Italiani = the Italians. The article is required, except after the verb parlare and certain prepositions (see page 117).

7. Mary's bedroom is on the upper floor.
8. Is Peter at home? No, he is in town.
9. Are Peter and Mary in town? Yes, they are buying apples.
10. Why are they leaving today? I do not understand why.
11. The kitchen is small, but the dining-room is large.
12. They are buying a new house with a garden.
13. We prefer a house in town.
14. Here is the study. Peter opens the door and we see Uncle.
    (Say: *the* uncle.) Uncle is sleeping.
15. While Uncle is sleeping, Aunt is in town. She is in town
    with Mary. They are buying ties, socks, hats and an
    overcoat for Uncle.

LESSON V

CONTRACTIONS OF WORDS—THE PARTITIVE

ITALIAN is a very melodious language It avoids harsh and
ugly sounds and sounds that are difficult to pronounce. It cuts
words short or runs them together, or sometimes changes their
form so as to produce agreeable sounds and a pleasing and
harmonious rhythm. Some examples of this we have already
met in the different forms of the article, when, to avoid an ugly
hiatus, *lo* and *la* become *l'* before a following vowel. Something
of the same kind occurs when the definite article is preceded by
certain prepositions, some of which we have met, such as *a*, *di*
and *in*. These prepositions, together with one or two more
when used with the definite article, often join with it and form
one word. For example, *di* when followed by *il* becomes *del*,
so avoiding the hiatus between *di—il*. Seven of the common
prepositions are written together with the article, and they
may be studied from this table:

	il	i	lo	gli	la	le	l'
a = to, at	al	ai	allo	agli	alla	alle	all'
con = with	col	coi	collo	cogli	colla	colle	coll'
	or con il	con i	con lo	con gli	con la	con le	con l'
da = by, from	dal	dai	dallo	dagli	dalla	dalle	dall'
di = of	del	dei	dello	degli	della	delle	dell'
in = in, into	nel	nei	nello	negli	nella	nelle	nell'
per = for	pel	pei	per lo	per gli	per la	per le	per l'
	or per il	per i					
su = on	sul	sui	sullo	sugli	sulla	sulle	sull'

Study the following sentences. After which, practise the prepositions and articles by taking some nouns that you already know, such as *libro, albero, zio, casa*, etc., and place the correct form of the preposition and article before them. That is: find out how to say *to the uncle, with the uncle, from the uncle*, etc. Then change your expressions from the singular to the plural. Your effort can always be checked by referring to the preceding table. Practise with every kind of noun—*i.e.*, one that begins with a consonant, one with a vowel, one with *s impure*, etc.

Maria è nel giardino ma lo zio è nello studio.

Pietro dà una mela all'uomo e un'arancia (orange) alla donna.

Pietro dà i calzini al ragazzo.

Lui dà i calzini allo stesso ragazzo.

Capisco le parole dello zio.

La cravatta è sulla tavola nella sala da pranzo.

Il cappello della zia è sulla sedia nell'altra camera.

Translation of "Some" and "Any".—There are different ways of saying *some* and *any* in Italian. One is to use the preposition *di* with the definite article (the partitive construction):

Còmpra del pane = He is buying some (of the) bread.

Ha delle rose rosse = He has some red roses.

Ha dei calzini gialli, per favore? = Have you any yellow socks, please?

Another way is the use of *alcuno* or *qualche*, both meaning *some* and *any*:

Hanno alcuni libri nuovi? Sí: hanno alcuni libri nuovi.

Hanno qualche libro nuovo? Sí: hanno qualche libro nuovo.

Have they any new books? Yes, they have some new books.

Alcuno, an adjective in *-o*, has a feminine form in *-a* and the two plurals *alcuni* and *alcune*; but *qualche* (pronounced kwahl-kay) *never* changes for gender, nor for number. Also it is curious that it must ALWAYS BE FOLLOWED BY ITS NOUN IN THE SINGULAR. *Qualche libro* therefore means either *some books* or *some book*.

Leggeva qualche libro = He was reading some book.

Compra qualche libro = He is buying some books.

Negative Sentences.—*Some* and *any* mean the same thing in English, but we use *some* in affirmative sentences and *any* in negative and interrogative sentences. In Italian the partitive construction is used in all three kinds of sentences:

> Ha del pane = He has some bread.
> Ha del pane? = Has he any bread?
> Non ha del pane = He hasn't any bread.*

There are other ways of translating *any* in a negative sentence. If *any* is followed by a word in the plural, it may simply be omitted:

> Non ha libri = He hasn't any books.

If *any* is followed by a noun in the singular, which has a plural, like book, garden, etc. (but *not* bread, flour, etc.), another word, *nessuno*, which means *no*, *not one*, is used. *Nessuno* has forms like the indefinite article *un*: *nessun*, *nessuno*, *nessuna* and *nessun'*:

> Non ha nessun libro = He hasn't any book.

In this last sentence *nessuno* is an adjective, qualifying *libro*, but it can also be used as a pronoun, meaning "nobody", "no one":

> Non vedo nessuno = I see nobody, I don't see anybody.

There are, you will notice, two negatives in the Italian sentence, *non* and *nessuno*, but together they convey a *single* negative idea, and not an affirmative as is the case in English. Two negatives, also conveying a single negative idea, are used with other words:

> Piero non scrive mai lettere = Peter never writes letters.
> Maria non vede nulla = Mary doesn't see anything.
> Non capisce niente = He understands nothing.
> Non trovo né la borsa né il denaro = I don't find either the money or the purse.

From these sentences we learn that never is *non . . . mai*; nothing—*non . . . niente* or *non . . . nulla*; neither . . . nor—*non . . . né . . . né*. In each case the final word is a negative in itself, and may be used without *non* if it precedes the verb:

> Non scrive mai, *or* mai scrive = He never writes.
> Non vede nulla, *or* nulla vede = He sees nothing.

In the second version of the sentences, great emphasis is laid on the negative words *mai*, *niente*, etc.

* Also: *Non ha pane.*

B

Vocabulary

fazzoletto = handkerchief	bianco = white
fiume (m.) = river	pigro = lazy
guanto = glove	povero = poor
macchina = car	
ospite (m. & f.) = guest, host	cercare = to look for
scarpa = shoe	
tasca = pocket	poi = then

Exercise 5 (a)

1. Maria è nel giardino e la zia è nella sala da pranzo.
2. Giovanni (John) dà delle mele agli ospiti e poi parte per la città nella macchina dello zio.
3. Lo zio è coi bambini nel salotto.
4. Che cosa hai nella tasca, Piero? Ho due fazzoletti e una cravatta dello zio.
5. Dov'è Piero? È nello studio con la ragazza.
6. Le sedie della sala da pranzo sono sul balcone.
7. Guardano nello specchio. Che cosa vedono?
8. Vedono il cappello e i guanti della zia. Essi sono sulla tavola.
9. Dov'è il cappello giallo dello zio? Il cappello giallo dello zio è nel fiume.
10. Povero zio! Giovanni e Piero comprano un nuovo cappello per lo zio.
11. Non abbiamo del pane? Sí, è sulla tavola nella cucina.
12. Che cosa c'è nel fiume? Io non vedo niente.
13. Ha delle cravatte gialle, per favore?
14. No, Signore, ma ho qualche cravatta bianca e azzurra.
15. È molto pigro Giovanni! Non scrive mai a nessuno.

Exercise 5 (b)

1. Mary is in the study with Uncle. They are writing letters.
2. Peter is buying socks, handkerchiefs and ties from a boy in the street.
3. John is buying a hat and gloves from the same boy.
4. He is a very poor boy; he has no shoes.
5. What have you in the pocket? I have three handkerchiefs and a tie.
6. What do you see in the river, John? I don't see anything.
7. I am looking in the mirror. I see the three children with the cat.
8. Mary is looking for the cat in the garden.
9. Where is the bread? We have no bread.
10. The man in the drawing-room is John's brother.

11. Where is John's tie? It is on the table in the dining-room
    with Aunt's gloves (of *the* aunt).
12. I see neither the tie nor the gloves.
13. Haven't you any ink? Yes, it is on the table in the study.
14. This chair is for the guest. But it isn't very comfortable.
15. The book that you are looking for is in the study.

LESSON VI

PAST DEFINITE—POSITION OF ADJECTIVES

THREE past tenses in Italian correspond to the following
English past tenses:

The Past Definite translates the English simple past tense
(example: *I bought*), and the emphatic past (*I did buy*);

The Imperfect translates our imperfect (*I was buying*), and
the habitual tense (*I used to buy*);

The Present Perfect, a compound tense, as the English
tense it translates (*I have bought*).

These three tenses are used more or less as the English tenses
mentioned above, except that we often substitute our simple
past tense for the imperfect and the present perfect, while
Italian is much more particular in using each of these tenses
on the occasion for which it is meant, particularly in the
written language; in conversation we may sometimes take
liberties with the past definite and use the present perfect
instead.

The Past Definite makes a statement about something which
happened at a definite time in the past, without any connection
with or reference to the present; it is a narrative or historic
tense: I *bought* the book last week; They *caught* the thief when
he was climbing through the window; Columbus *discovered*
America. In Italian this tense is formed by adding certain
endings to the stem, as will be seen from the following table:

1st Conj. *comprare*	2nd Conj. *vendere*	3rd Conj. *finire*
compr-ai = *I bought*, etc.	vend-ei (-etti) = *I sold*, etc.	fin-ii = *I finished*, etc.
compr-asti	vend-esti	fin-isti
compr-ò	vend-é (ette)	fin-í
compr-ammo	vend-emmo	fin-immo
compr-aste	vend-este	fin-iste
compr-arono	vend-erono (-ettero)	fin-irono

Note the following points about this tense:

1. In all regular verbs the third person singular has the stress on the final vowel, and *must* have the written accent. A stressed final *o* has always the open sound, therefore a *grave* accent is required; final *e*, with very few exceptions, is close, and requires the *acute*, and *i* always takes an acute. Therefore the first conjugation has a grave accent: *compr-ò*, and the second and third an acute: *vendé, finì*. This does not apply to verbs which are irregular in this tense, for in that case the final vowel of the third person is NOT stressed.

2. The stress is on the syllable next to the last in all the other persons with the exception of the third plural, where it falls on the third from the end.

3. If we take the three characteristic vowels: *a* for the first conjugation (*-are*), *e* for the second (*-ere*) and *i* for the third (*-ire*), we see that—with the exception of the third person singular of the first conjugation—the characteristic vowel appears throughout the tense in each case, otherwise the endings are the same for all three conjugations.

4. The second conjugation has alternative forms for the first and third persons singular and the third person plural. Some verbs do not have this alternative form, and many which *do*, prefer the form which is here given first, for this is the one most commonly used.

Past Definite of the Auxiliary Verbs

ɛssere = to be	avere = to have
fui = I was, etc.	ɛbbi = I had, etc.
fosti	avesti
fu	ɛbbe
fummo	avemmo
foste	aveste
furono	ɛbbero

Note that these two irregular verbs have *no* written accent on the third person singular; and in the pronunciation of the past definite of *avere* the initial *e* of the three irregular persons is an open *e*, while the *e* of the second syllable of the regular persons is a close *e*.

Position of Adjectives.—We have seen that adjectives generally follow the noun they qualify. An Italian says "a table round" = *una tavola rotonda*, "a carpet green" = *un tappeto verde*. But some adjectives usually precede their noun.

The commonest of these are: *bɛllo* = beautiful, *buɔno* = good, *grande* = big, *lungo* = long, *giɔvane* = young, *nuɔvo* = new, with their opposites: *brutto, cattivo, piccolo, brɛve, vɛcchio, antico.* All these adjectives *may* come after their noun; when they do, special stress is laid on the idea in the adjective: *è un brutto affare* = It's an ugly business; *è una ragazza brutta* = She's an *ugly* girl.

One or two adjectives, having both a literal and figurative meaning, change their meaning according to their position. When they precede the noun they may be taken in the figurative sense; when they follow they have the literal meaning:

Example: *pɔverɔ* = poor. Literal meaning "not rich":

è una famiglia pɔvera, il padre è disoccupato.
They are (it is) a poor family, the father is out of work.

and figurative meaning, "miserable", "unfortunate":

Pɔvero ragazzo, non ha né padre né madre.
Poor boy, he has neither father nor mother.

Another adjective, *grande*, sometimes has the figurative sense of "great" when preceding its noun: *Un grand'uɔmo* = a great man; but *Un uɔmo grande* = a big, therefore a tall, man.

Note that before a word beginning with a vowel, *grande* drops its final -*e*. Three adjectives: *bɛllo, buɔno* and *grande*, undergo certain changes when they precede the noun.* *Bɛllo* imitates the definite article *il* and *lo*:

un bɛl concɛrto = a fine concert
i bɛi teatri = the fine theatres
un bɛllo spɛcchio = a beautiful mirror
i bɛgli spɛcchi = the beautiful mirrors
un bɛll'anɛllo = a lovely ring
i bɛgli alberi = the beautiful trees
una bɛlla donna = a beautiful woman
una bɛll'idɛa = a fine idea
due bɛlle rɔse rosse = two lovely red roses

* *Santo* (= saint) undergoes similar changes.
San Giɔrgio, Sant'Antɔnio, Santo Stɛfano;
Sant'Anna, Santa Caterina.

Buono, in the singular, has forms similar to those of the indefinite article *un, uno, una* and *un'*:

> un buon cavallo = a good horse
> un buon amico = a good friend (masc.)
> una buon'amica = a good friend (fem.)
> un buono stipendio = a good salary
> una buona cuoca = a good cook

Grande becomes *gran* before a masculine singular word beginning with a consonant (other than *s* impure or *z*), *grand'* before any singular word beginning with a vowel, and it keeps its full form before *s* impure and *z*:

> un gran fuoco = a big fire
> un grande sbaglio = a big mistake
> un grand'armadio = a large wardrobe
> una grand'anima = a great soul

These adjectives always have their full forms when they follow the noun they qualify and when they are separated from their noun by the verb *essere*:

> il gran fuoco   but   il fuoco è grande
> una buon'idea   „   l'idea è buona

Note, too, that when any of these adjectives are qualified by an adverb such as "very" (= *molto*), they always follow their noun, and therefore have their full forms: a very large house = *una casa molto grande*.

Vocabulary

avvocato = lawyer
cartolina = postcard
dottore (m.) = doctor
francobollo = stamp
giorno = day
pacco = parcel
posta = post office
postino = postman
ricevuta = receipt
sala di scrittura = writing-room
settimana = week

raccomandato = registered

firmare = to sign
incontrare = to meet
offrire (irreg.) = to offer (2nd group)
perdere (irreg.) = to lose
portare = to bring, carry, wear
ricevere = to receive

fa = ago
ieri = yesterday
scorso = past, last (in expressions of time as "last week", etc.)

Exercise 6 (a)

1. Vendé i due bei cavalli la settimana scorsa.
2. Tre settimane fa perdetti un bell'anello nel giardino.
3. Due giorni fa ricevei una lettera raccomandata e un pacco
   e firmai una ricevuta.
4. La cuoca offrí del tè al postino.
5. La settimana scorsa il postino portò una bella rosa rossa
   per la cuoca.
6. Il postino ha un buono stipendio ma è di una famiglia
   molto povera.
7. Dove fu * la cuoca ieri? Fu * alla posta e incontrò il postino.
   È una buon'amica del postino.
8. Io fui * anche alla posta e all'entrata incontrai il dottore.
9. Il dottore è un buon amico dell'avvocato.
10. Poi incontrammo anche l'avvocato nella sala di scrittura.
11. Comprai dodici cartoline e venti francobolli; finii una lettera
    e poi fummo * a un caffè.
12. Il postino portò due cartoline dalla zia in America ieri.
13. È un bell'uomo il postino, e la cuoca non è brutta.

Exercise 6 (b)

1. I sold a fine ring yesterday and bought these books.
2. She lost a lovely ring three weeks ago.
3. Where did she lose the ring? In the garden.
4. Aunt received a registered parcel yesterday and she signed
   a receipt.
5. Mary went with cook (with *the* cook) to the post office.
   They bought stamps and some postcards.
6. Mary's brother is a very handsome man.
7. I received a long letter from Uncle yesterday and also two
   postcards and a large parcel.
8. Didn't you receive anything yesterday, Mr. Pazzi?
9. No, I didn't receive anything yesterday.
10. The theatres in this town are very fine.
11. Yes, we went to the theatre last week.
12. The lawyer received a postcard from the doctor yesterday.
13. Last year he bought a car, two horses, a cow and a house
    with a large garden; now he is very poor.

* The past definite of *essere* may be used to translate "went".

LESSON VII

IMPERFECT—INVARIABLE NOUNS—DEMONSTRATIVE ADJECTIVES

THE Imperfect expresses an incomplete or habitual action in the past. It states what was going on or what used to happen when something else also happened. It is also a descriptive tense. The difference between the imperfect and the past definite is seen in this sentence: They *caught* the thief when he *was climbing* through the window: *caught* is the single complete action in the past; *was climbing* is incomplete (the thief never finished his climbing, for they caught him before he got through the window). Again, in this sentence: "The thief *used to climb* through the window but one day they caught him," *used to climb* indicates habitual action: the thief found he could take what he wanted and then escape through the window, so he did this regularly—until they caught him, which put a stop to it, once and for all.

Read the following extract (referring to the translations for help as to its meaning) and note the use of the tenses in Italian. The verbs in the imperfect are all in italics. Note how the imperfect describes the scene, while the past definite carries on the narrative. The subject-matter of the piece is briefly: Renzo, a poor young peasant engaged to Lucia, a girl of his village, learns on his wedding morning that the priest refuses to marry them because of the threats of a rich and powerful lord who has his eye on Lucia. He is on his way to break the dreadful news to the bride, who, knowing nothing at all about it, is busy dressing for the wedding.

"Predominato da questi pensięri Ręnzo passò davanti alla sua casa che *era* pòsta nel męzzo del villaggio, e attraversatolo, si avviò a quella di Lucia che *stava* all'estremità opposta. *Aveva* quella casetta un piccolo cortile davanti, che la *separava* dalla via, ed *era* cinto con un muretto. Ręnzo entrò nel cortile, e intese un misto e continuo gridío che *veniva* da una stanza superiore. S'immaginò che sarębbero amiche e comari venute a far cortęo a Lucia; e non si volle mostrare a quel mercato, con quella novęlla in cǫrpo e sul volto. Una fanciulletta che si *trovava* nel cortile, gli corse incontro gridando: lo spǫso! lo spǫso!"

Literal translation. Predominated by these thoughts, Renzo passed in front of his own house, which was situated in the middle of the village, and having crossed it (the village) himself he directed to that of Lucia, which was standing at the end opposite. Had that little house a small yard in front, which it separated from the road, and it was surrounded with a little wall. Renzo entered into the yard, and heard a mixed and continuous shouting which was coming from a room upper. Himself he imagined that they would be the girl friends and neighbours come to make procession to Lucia; and not himself did he wish to show to that market, with that news in body and on the face. A little girl who herself was finding in the yard, to him ran against shouting: "The bridegroom, the bridegroom!"

Free translation. With these thoughts uppermost in his mind, Renzo went right past his own house, which was situated in the centre of the village and going straight on he directed his steps to Lucy's home, which stood at the opposite end. Her little house had a small yard in front, which separated it from the road and which was enclosed by a low wall. Renzo entered the yard and heard a continual hubbub and shouting coming from one of the upstairs rooms. He imagined that it must be Lucy's friends and neighbours who had come to attend her to church; and he didn't want to show himself to that noisy party with sadness in his heart and bad news written all over his face. But a little girl who was in the yard ran to meet him shouting "The bridegroom, the bridegroom!"

It would be useful to pick out the verbs which are in the past definite. Note those which are regular and the three of the second conjugation which are irregular: *intese* (intendere), *volle* (volere) and *corse* (correre). Then study the imperfects and notice their endings, which may be learnt from this table:

I bought	I sold	I finished
was buying	was selling	was finishing
used to buy	used to sell	used to finish
compr-avo	vend-evo	fin-ivo
compr-avi	vend-evi	fin-ivi
compr-ava	vend-eva	fin-iva
compr-avamo	vend-evamo	fin-ivamo
compr-avate	vend-evate	fin-ivate
compr-avano	vend-evano	fin-ivano

It will be noted (with satisfaction) that this tense is an easy one to learn, for, except for the characteristic vowel, the endings are the same for all three conjugations.

Another reason for being satisfied with this tense is that,

with the exception of εssere, all verbs are regular: all other Italian verbs are conjugated in the imperfect like one or other of the models just given.

Imperfect of the Auxiliary Verbs

εssere	avere
εro = I was, was being, used to be	avevo = I had, was having, used to have
εri	avevi
εra	aveva
eravamo	avevamo
eravate	avevate
εrano	avevano

Note where the stress in pronunciation comes in both these tables; and, with regard to εssere, note that the initial e of the singular and of the third person plural is an open e.

Invariable Nouns.—The nouns we have met so far ended in -a, -o or -e; and they formed their plurals by changing the final vowel: -a to -e; and -o and -e to -i. The greatest number of Italian nouns end in one or other of these three vowels, but there are a few which end in -i and -u, and a few words borrowed from other languages which end in a consonant. None of these nouns change for the plural, and the only indication as to whether we are speaking of one or more than one is given by the article used with them or by the context. A few other nouns are also invariable in the plural: the complete list is as follows:

1. Those ending in -i (nearly all feminine): la crisi (crisis), le crisi.

2. Those ending in -u (always accented on the final u, and nearly all feminine): la virtú, le virtú.

3. Those ending in any accented vowel: la città, le città; il caffè, i caffè.

4. Those ending in -ie (always feminine): la sεrie (series), le sεrie.

5. Those ending in a consonant: il bar, i bar (where one drinks!).

6. Words of one syllable, whatever their ending: il re (king), i re.

7. Certain compound nouns formed by a noun + a verb: il portacenere (ash-tray), i portacenere.

Demonstrative Adjectives.—We have met the word *questo*, meaning "this". Like other adjectives ending in -o, *questo* has a feminine form in -a and the two corresponding plurals: *questo libro*, *questa casa*, *questi cavalli*, *queste tavole*. When *questo* comes before a *singular* word beginning with a vowel, it elides the final vowel and becomes *quest'*: *quest'uomo*, *quest'aria* ("this air"), but *questi alberi*.

There are two words for "that": *codesto*, which refers to something near to the person addressed, and *quello*. *Codesto* changes for the feminine and the plural, just as *questo*, and, like *questo*, it drops its final vowel before a singular noun beginning with a vowel; but *quello* needs a little more attention, for, like *bello*, it has various changes:

> quel medico = that doctor
> quell'albero = that tree
> quello specchio = that mirror
> quei ragazzi = those boys
> quegli uccelli = those birds
> quegli stessi alberi = those same trees
> quella signorina = that young lady
> quelle donne = those women

Vocabulary

biblioteca = library	scaffale (m.) = book-shelf	andare (irreg.) = to go
carne (f.) = meat		
giornale (m.) = news-paper	scrivania = desk	
	storia = story, history	che! = what! what a!
lampada = lamp		
legume (m.) = vege-table	volta = time, turn	
		tutto = whole (plural, = all)
libreria = bookshop	elegante = smart	
mattina = morning	ricco = rich	

Exercise 7 (a)

1. Quando era a * Firenze andava tutti i giorni alla biblioteca.
2. Dove andavate voi? Andavamo a un caffè in Via Torna-buoni.
3. Via Tornabuoni era una delle vie eleganti di quella città.
4. Incontrai l'avvocato in città ieri. Era in Via Tornabuoni e guardava i nuovi libri nella libreria.
5. Cercava quel libro sulla storia d'Italia che vedemmo a Roma la settimana scorsa.

* Before names of towns English "in" is usually *a* in Italian, unless the meaning within is emphasized.

6. Vede Lei quella vecchia * senza scarpe? Una volta era molto ricca ma ora è molto povera.
7. Stamattina (short for *questa mattina*) cercavo la cuoca. Dov'era? Non era in cucina?
8. No, era in città; comprava carne e legumi al mercato.
9. Ieri incontrai il fratello di Maria e il postino in città; parlavano con quella ragazza della libreria.
10. Che bello studio aveva il signor Pazzi! Era una stanza grande con un balcone e due finestre.
11. La scrivania era davanti al balcone e sulla tavola rotonda vicino alla porta c'era una bella lampada.
12. Aveva anche un bel tappeto verde e un grande scaffale con molti libri.

Exercise 7 (b)

1. Did she go to church every day when she was in Florence?
2. Yes, she used to go with Aunt every morning.
3. She used to write to John every week.
4. I was looking for Mary's brother. Where was he?
5. He was in the bookshop and he was talking to the lawyer.
6. The doctor entered while they were talking.
7. The lawyer was finishing a letter when they entered the study.
8. He was looking at the lawyer, who was near the desk.
9. They were looking for that newspaper which those women were reading.
10. Was cook at the market this morning, Mrs. Pazzi?
11. Yes, she was buying meat and vegetables, bread and wine.
12. Have they good wines at the market? No, they are not very good.

LESSON VIII

POSSESSIVES—INTERROGATIVES

FOLLOWING is a table of possessive adjectives and pronouns. Note that each word has four forms: masculine singular and plural and feminine singular and plural, and that the definite article is used with them; an Italian usually says *the* my hat and *the* mine = *il mio cappello, il mio*. Note, too, that the same word is used for *my* and *mine*, etc.; for in Italian these words

* *Vecchio* is used as a noun as well as an adjective; in the masculine it means *old man*, in the feminine *old woman*.

may either be used with a noun or they may stand alone: they are both adjectives and pronouns.

Masculine		Feminine		
Singular	Plural	Singular	Plural	
il mio	i miei	la mia	le mie	my, mine
il tuo	i tuoi	la tua	le tue	thy, thine
				your, yours
il suo	i suoi	la sua	le sue	his, her, hers,
				its
il Suo (suo)	i Suoi	la Sua	le Sue	your, yours
il nostro	i nostri	la nostra	le nostre	our, ours
il vostro	i vostri	la vostra	le vostre	your, yours
il loro	i loro	la loro	le loro	their, theirs
il Loro	i Loro	la Loro	le Loro	your, yours

An important difference between English and Italian possessive pronouns and adjectives is that in Italian the possessive word refers to the thing that is possessed, and not to the possessor:

il mio giardino = my garden   la mia casa = my house

These Italian forms would be the same whether the person referred to in the "my" were a man or a woman, *mio* agreeing with *giardino*, and *mia* with *casa*. Similarly if two men shared a car they would talk about *la nostra macchina*, as *macchina* is feminine.

il suo giardino = his, her or its garden, or your garden
la sua casa = his, her, its or your house

Note that *il suo* and *la sua* may refer to four persons; his, her, its and your (polite form, sometimes spelt with a capital letter). Usually one can tell which person is meant; but if there is any doubt, a phrase meaning *of him, of her*, etc. must be used instead of the possessive. The possessive normally refers to the subject of the sentence, therefore in such a sentence as: *Lui legge il suo giornale, il suo* naturally refers to *lui*, so we know that it is his own newspaper. But should we wish to say: "He is reading *her* newspaper," the possessive cannot be used, and the sentence is written: *Lui legge il giornale di lei*.

Using the definite article "the" with the possessive seems strange to us at first, but one quickly becomes used to it. There is one important occasion when it is not used, and that is when one is speaking of a near relative in the singular, such as mother, father, etc.: *mia madre, mio padre*. But when this near relative is qualified by an adjective, it *does* require the article;

and the article is also required if the possessive is *loro*, or if the relation is in the plural. Study these examples:

mia madre = my mother
il mio caro padre = my dear father
mia sorella = my sister
la mia piccola sorella = my little sister
i miei fratelli = my brothers
la loro sorella = their sister

Just as we can use the definite article before the possessive and say *the* my book, so we can use the indefinite article and say *a* my book (meaning: "one of my books"). And we can go farther, and say *that* my book, *two* my books, *many* my books and even *some* my books:

un mio libro = one of my books
quel mio libro = that book of mine
due miei libri = two of my books
molti miei libri = many of my books
dei, *or* alcuni miei libri = some of my books

The "of" in the English phrase is therefore not translated in Italian; although one might say *uno dei miei libri*, this is not usual, the more concise form is preferred.

Interrogatives.—We have used some of the more common interrogative words: *Chi? Che?* or *Che cosa? Dove?* and *Perché?* (*Perché* also means "because": *Perché non compra un nuovo cappello? Perché non ho denaro.* = Why don't you buy a new hat? Because I've no money.) These words may be governed by prepositions: to whom?—*a chi?* by whom?—*da chi?* with what?—*con che?* and they are all invariable. Two other interrogative words change their endings: *quale?* = which? and *quanto?* = how much? *Quale* becomes *quali* in the plural; *quanto?* has the feminine *quanta?* and in the plural (when it means "how many?") *quanti?* and *quante?* Study the following interrogative sentences:

Chi c'è nella stanza da bagno? = Who is there in the bathroom?
Chi vedo nella cucina? = Whom do I see in the kitchen?
A chi scrive quella lunga lettera? = To whom are you writing that long letter?
Di chi parlate? = Of whom are you speaking?
Di chi è questo fazzoletto bianco? = Whose is this white handkerchief?
Che cosa vende? = What is he selling?

Per chi è quel gran pacco? = For whom is that large parcel?

Da chi è quel libro? = By whom is that book?

Che (or quale) libro compraste ieri? = What (which) book did you buy yesterday?

Quali porte sono aperte? = Which doors are open?

Quante chiese ci sono in questa città? = How many churches are there in this town?

Vocabulary

autorimessa = garage	bere (irreg.) = to drink
barba = beard	mangiare = to eat
baule (m.) = trunk	
bottiglia = bottle	sempre = always
vestito = dress (woman's)	qui = here
suit (man's)	

Exercise 8 (a)

1. Chi è quel signore? È un amico mio.
2. Scrivo a una mia amica a Roma.
3. Per chi è quel pacco raccomandato? È per mio padre.
4. Quanto pane c'è in cucina, Maria?
5. Non c'è pane. Quel ragazzo mangiò tutto il nostro pane ieri.
6. Perché non compra uno scaffale per i suoi libri?
7. Che buon vino! Bevono vino Loro tutti i giorni?
8. Quella loro cuoca è molto buona.
9. Che bel fuoco è quello! Sí, la cuoca ha sempre un bel fuoco.
10. Quanto vino beve quell'uomo al giorno? * Generalmente beve cinque o sei bottiglie al giorno.
11. Quell'armadio è per i miei vestiti e questo è per i suoi.
12. Qual'è il suo baule, Signorina? Questo qui è il mio, codesto è di mia madre e quello là è di quel signore dalla † barba.

* Note that an Italian says "How much do you drink *at the* day?" The definite article is also used in Italian where we would use the indefinite in such phrases as: two shillings *a* pound—due scellini *la* libbra.

† An idiomatic use of the preposition *da*. This preposition is used where we in English use "with" to denote a special characteristic in the appearance of someone: Il ragazzo dal naso lungo = the boy with the long nose; but: The coat with the yellow belt = l'abito con la cintura gialla.

Exercise 8 (b)

1. Who is that man with the beard? He is a friend of my father's.
2. My father and mother went to town yesterday. They met that friend of yours in the bookshop.
3. Whose is this trunk? It is my mother's.
4. How many books are there in that bookcase?
5. We have many good wines, sir; which do you prefer, white or red?
6. One of my friends bought that car yesterday. Which? That car there in the garage.
7. What is that old woman selling? She is selling handkerchiefs and socks.
8. Where do you buy your hats? That new hat of yours (translate either "that your hat new", or: "that your new hat") is very smart.
9. Which dress do you prefer? I prefer that blue one. (Omit "one".)
10. That green hat of his is very old. Didn't he buy a new one last week?
11. Many of my books are in my trunk.
12. How many trunks have you, sir? I have two trunks. This one is mine and that one there is also mine.

LESSON IX

FUTURE AND CONDITIONAL—NOUNS IN -*IO*

THE future and conditional, translating respectively "I shall" and "I should", are formed in Italian from the infinitive. They take the infinitive as a stem and add to it certain endings. Before adding the endings the final vowel of the infinitive is dropped, and the first conjugation makes a further alteration by changing the -*a* of the -*are* to -*e*.

I shall buy, etc.	I shall sell, etc.	I shall finish, etc.
comprer-ò	vender-ò	finir-ò
comprer-ai	vender-ai	finir-ai
comprer-à	vender-à	finir-à
comprer-emo	vender-emo	finir-emo
comprer-ete	vender-ete	finir-ete
comprer-anno	vender-anno	finir-anno

Note that the *first* and *third persons singular* of all three conjugations have the stress on the final vowel, and therefore must have the written accent. There are no irregularities in any future endings, so when we have learnt these endings we shall be able to form the future of any verb—with the exception of a few which have slightly irregular forms in their stem (as *andare* = to go, *andrò* = I shall go). The same applies to the endings of the conditional:

I should buy, etc.	I should sell, etc.	I should finish, etc.
comprer-ɛi	vender-ɛi	finir-ɛi
comprer-esti	vender-esti	finir-esti
comprer-ɛbbe	vender-ɛbbe	finir-ɛbbe
comprer-emmo	vender-emmo	finir-emmo
comprer-este	vender-este	finir-este
comprer-ɛbbero	vender-ɛbbero	finir-ɛbbero

Future of ɛssere and avere

I shall be, etc.	I shall have, etc.
sarò	avrò
sarai	avrai
sarà	avrà
saremo	avremo
sarete	avrete
saranno	avranno

Conditional of ɛssere and avere

I should be, etc.	I should have, etc.
sar-ɛi	avr-ɛi
sar-esti	avr-esti
sar-ɛbbe	avr-ɛbbe
sar-emmo	avr-emmo
sar-este	avr-este
sar-ɛbbero	avr-ɛbbero

Uses of the Future.—The future is used, as in English, to denote what is going to happen, and it is also used in some cases where we use the present. In the sentence "When I sell the horse I shall buy a cow", an Italian would say: "When I *shall* sell the horse I shall buy a cow"—*Quando venderò il cavallo comprerò una vacca*. Strictly speaking the Italian is more correct, for both actions are really future. Subordinate sentences of this kind are introduced by "if" (*se*) or by a word denoting time, such as "when" (*quando*). So when translating into Italian be on the lookout for subordinate clauses beginning with "if" or "when" in the present tense, followed by a main clause which has its verb in the future, and make both verbs future in Italian. The future is also used in Italian to denote probability: She may be a clever girl, but she doesn't seem so = *Sarà una ragazza intelligente, ma non sembra.*

We must add a word about our English "shall" and "will". The English future tense is: I shall buy, thou wilt buy, he will, we shall, you will, they will buy; but if we mix up the "shalls" and "wills", using *will* instead of *shall* and *shall* instead of *will*, these auxiliaries have a special meaning. "I will buy" means "I want to buy" or "I insist on buying", and "He shall buy" means "He must buy" or "He is to buy". These are therefore not the simple future and cannot be translated into Italian by the future tense, or the ideas of *want* and *must* will be lost. We shall learn later how to turn into Italian *shall* meaning *must* and *will* meaning *want* (pages 83, 147); for the moment remember that *shall* and *will* are not always the simple future, and that when translating the Italian future tense into English we must be sure to use the correct English word.

Uses of the Conditional.—The conditional, like English *should* and *would*, is used in direct speech after a verb of saying (also thinking and believing) in the past. It is the tense which in direct speech would be future: "He said he would write the letter"; what he actually said was in the future: "I shall write the letter". It is also used for the conclusion of a conditional sentence: If I had enough money, I should buy a car. These sentences are dealt with in a later lesson, page 146.

Italian also uses the conditional to express what is said on the authority of someone else. There is usually some word or phrase in the sentence to indicate that the person who is reporting what was said is not sure of the truth of the statement and disclaims responsibility for it. Such a sentence is: According to the judge, the girl is not guilty = *Secondo il giudice, la ragazza non sarebbe colpevole.*

Nouns ending in -io may present uncertainty in the formation of their plural, for sometimes they have double *i*, and sometimes they merely drop the *o* of the singular. This depends on what use the *i* has in the word: if the *i* is stressed, as in *mormorio* (murmur) and *rio* (brook) there are two *i*'s in the plural: *mormorii, rii*; if the *i* is pronounced as a separate syllable, but not stressed, the plural usually keeps one *i* only, but may have a circumflex accent to show the abbreviation: *studio, studî*; and lastly, if the *i* hardly counts as a letter, but is merely to influence the pronunciation of a preceding consonant, as in *figlio, viaggio* (journey), the plural is formed by dropping the final *o* of the singular: *figli, viaggi.* Adjectives follow the same rule: *il vestito grigio* (= the grey dress), *i vestiti grigi*; and in the feminine if the *i* is not accented in the singular, it disappears in the plural: *la sciarpa grigia* (= the grey scarf), *le sciarpe grige.*

Nouns ending in *-aio* (only a few) should be noted. They form their plural by dropping the final *o* of the singular: *cucchiaio* (= spoon), plural: *cucchiai.*

Useful Expressions of Time.—We have already met the word *ora* = hour (also meaning *now*). An Italian asks not "What *time* is it?" but "What *hour* is it?" or "What hours are they?" and the corresponding reply is equivalent to: "It is the one" (hour understood), "They are the three", etc.:

Che ora è? } = What time is it?
Che ore sono? }

è l'una = It is one o'clock (*ora* understood).
Sono le quattro meno un quarto = It is a quarter to four (quattro *ore* understood, *meno* = less).
Sono le undici e mezzo = It is half-past eleven.
Sono le cinque meno venti = It is twenty to five.
Sono le otto e dieci = It is ten minutes past eight.
È mezzanotte = It is midnight.
È mezzogiorno = It is midday.
A che ora? = At what time? Alle tre = At three o'clock.
Stamane, stamani or stamattina = This morning.
Stasera = This evening.
Stanotte = Last night.

Vocabulary

stazione (f.) = station
tempo = time, weather
treno = train

arrivare = to arrive
mandare = to send
prendere (irreg.) = to take

ancora = yet, still, again
prima di = before

sicuro = sure, certain
generalmente = generally

Exercise 9 (a)

1. Quando venderò la casa, comprerò una macchina.
2. A che ora arriverà il treno?
3. Arriverà alle cinque e mezzo. Avremo il tempo per prendere il tè prima di andare (translate: "going") alla stazione.
4. Prendiamo il tè alle cinque generalmente.

5. A che ora arriverà suo figlio, Signora? Arriverà col treno delle otto meno venti.
6. Quando partiranno? Giovanni partirà stasera a mezzanotte, ma i suoi fratelli partiranno domani mattina per Firenze.
7. Noi mangiamo all'una generalmente, ma domani mangeremo a mezzogiorno e mezzo e prenderemo il treno alle due.
8. Sono le undici e la cuoca è ancora al mercato.
9. Che cosa comprerà al mercato? Al mercato comprerà molte cose e parlerà con le sue amiche.
10. Secondo mio padre la cuoca sarebbe una donna intelligente, ma non sembra.
11. Sono sicuro che mio figlio non firmerebbe questa lettera.
12. I viaggi in treno non sono sempre comodi.

Exercise 9 (b)

1. What time is it? It is half-past three.
2. At what time does the train arrive? At a quarter to eight.
3. How many hats has that woman? She has nine, I think. (She *will* have.)
4. When we sell the horses we shall buy a car.
5. I am sure that my mother would not buy that hat.
6. We generally take tea at half-past four, but tomorrow we shall take tea at four o'clock before going to the station. (Before *to go*.)
7. The lawyer will send the letter to the judge tomorrow.
8. When will he arrive at home? Not before midnight.
9. This evening her four sons will be at home.
10. She bought a grey hat yesterday and tomorrow she's going to buy (she will buy) a grey scarf and grey gloves. (Say: a scarf and some gloves grey; "grey" being masculine plural.)
11. It is a quarter to four, and cook is still at the market.
12. According to Mrs. Pazzi, our cook is lazy.

LESSON X

COMPOUND TENSES

So far we have learnt only *Simple* tenses of verbs; now we come to *Compound* tenses, which are formed with the help of the auxiliary verbs, *avere* and *essere*. These tenses are formed with the past participle (the part of the verb which in English goes with "I have", "I had", *e.g.*, I had *spoken*) and the various tenses of the auxiliary. Five compound tenses correspond to the five simple tenses we already know:

1. Present Perfect (Present indicative of the auxiliary verb and the past participle), translates: I have spoken.
2. Past Perfect (Imperfect of the auxiliary and the past participle), translating: I had spoken.
3. Second Past Perfect (Past definite of the auxiliary and the past participle), also: I had spoken.
4. Future Perfect (Future of the auxiliary and past participle): I shall have spoken.
5. Conditional Perfect (Conditional of auxiliary and past participle): I should have spoken.

To be able to form the compound tenses we must know the past participles; here they are:

1st Conjugation	2nd Conjugation	3rd Conjugation
compr-ato (bought)	vend-uto (sold)	fin-ito (finished)

Auxiliary verbs

stato (been)　　　　　　　　avuto (had)

The past participle of verbs of the first conjugation end in *-ato* (there is only one exception: *fatto* from *fare* = to make); those of the second in *-uto* (generally, but we shall come across some irregular endings); and the third (with a very few exceptions) in *-ito*.

A participle, as its name implies, participates in two parts of speech, it is partly a verb and partly an adjective. Sometimes it is more of a verb than an adjective—in this case its ending never varies; at other times it is more of an adjective, and then it changes like the adjectives ending in *-o*.

Some Italian verbs use *avere* to form their compound tenses and others *essere*. *Avere* is used by verbs which are *transitive*, that is by verbs which have a direct object, as for example the verb "to buy". In the sentence "I buy a house", "house" is the direct object of "buy"; "I have bought a house" is in Italian = *ho comprato una casa*. *Avere* is also used for a very few *intransitive* verbs * (verbs which cannot take an object), as "to sleep" (*dormire*): I have slept = *ho dormito*; but most intransitive verbs, such as *arrivare* = to arrive, *partire* = to depart, take *essere* as their helping verb: I have arrived = *sono*

* Noted in the vocabulary.

arrivato (literally "I *am* arrived"). ɛssere is also used with reflexive verbs (see page 73), and it is the auxiliary used to form the passive voice (just as in English we use the verb "to be"): *e.g.*, active voice: I buy a house = *compro una casa*; passive voice: a house is bought by me = *una casa è comprata da me*. ɛssere is also used to form its own compound tenses: an Italian says: *Sono stato* (lit. "I *am* been"); ɛro stato ("I *was* been"); *siamo stati* ("we *are* been").

Note in the last example, and in the example of the passive: *la casa è comprata*, that we have agreement of the past participle with the subject of the sentence. WHEN THE VERB IS CONJUGATED WITH ɛssere, THE PAST PARTICIPLE AGREES WITH THE SUBJECT; WHEN THE VERB IS CONJUGATED WITH *avere*, THERE IS NO AGREEMENT BETWEEN THE LAST PARTICIPLE AND THE SUBJECT; the past participle then usually agrees with the direct object if it precedes the verb, but the writer may please himself. (See also page 61.)

Consider the two past participles in the following sentence, and you will realize why one agrees with the subject and the other does not: She has fallen and broken all the glasses = *è caduta e ha rotto tutti i bicchiɛri* (*caduta*, from *cadere* = to fall; *rotto*, from *rompere* (irreg.) = to break). "Fallen" indicates a state or condition; it is more of an adjective than a verb, and *cadere* is intransitive; therefore we have the auxiliary ɛssere and agreement of the past participle with the subject. But "broken" is more of a verb than an adjective, it governs an object "glasses"; *rompere* is a transitive verb, conjugated with *avere*; therefore we have no agreement of the past participle with the subject. As the object follows the verb, there is no agreement at all; but in such a sentence as: "The glasses which she has broken", we might have agreement in Italian with the preceding direct object: *I bicchiɛri che lɛi ha rotto*, or *I bicchieri che lei ha rotti* (*bicchiɛri* is plural of *bicchiɛre*, masculine).

The following compound tenses should be completed in all persons, singular and plural; remember that the past participle must change for the feminine and for the plural when the verb is conjugated with ɛssere:

Present Perfect

I have bought, etc. = ho comprato
I have sold, etc. = ho venduto
I have finished, etc. = ho finito
I have arrived, etc. = sono arrivato -a
I have fallen, etc. = sono caduto -a

I have departed, etc. = sono partito -a
I have been, etc. = sono stato -a
I have had, etc. = ho avuto

Past Perfect

I had bought = avevo comprato
I had sold = avevo venduto
I had finished = avevo finito
I had arrived = ɛro arrivato -a
I had fallen = ɛro caduto -a
I had departed = ɛro partito -a
I had been = ɛro stato -a
I had had = avevo avuto

Second Past Perfect

I had bought = ɛbbi comprato
I had sold = ɛbbi venduto
I had finished = ɛbbi finito
I had arrived = fui arrivato -a
I had fallen = fui caduto -a
I had departed = fui partito -a
I had been = fui stato -a
I had had = ɛbbi avuto

Future Perfect

I shall have bought = avrɔ comprato
I shall have sold = avrɔ venduto
I shall have finished = avrɔ finito
I shall have arrived = sarɔ arrivato -a
I shall have fallen = sarɔ caduto -a
I shall have departed = sarɔ partito -a
I shall have been = sarɔ stato -a
I shall have had = avrɔ avuto

Conditional Perfect

I should have bought = avrɛi comprato
I should have sold = avrɛi venduto
I should have finished = avrɛi finito
I should have arrived = sarɛi arrivato -a
I should have fallen = sarɛi caduto -a
I should have departed = sarɛi partito -a
I should have been = sarɛi stato -a
I should have had = avrɛi avuto

Uses of the Compound Tenses.—The *present perfect* states something which happened in the past that has reference to the present; it is often introduced by a word expressing time in the present: This morning I bought a new hat = *Stamane ho comprato un nuovo cappɛllo*; or it expresses something which happened in the past the effects of which are lasting into the present: He has seen that famous picture = *Ha veduto quel quadro famoso*. This tense is often used in conversation in place of the past definite when the event is not very remote past: Yesterday I went to the theatre = *Iɛri sono stato al teatro*. The *future perfect* and *conditional perfect* are used as in English (but see the lesson on the conditional sentences, page 146). The two *past perfects* denote, as in English, what had happened; but the *second past perfect* is used only after certain conjunctions of time in a subordinate clause which is followed by a main sentence which has its verb in the past definite. These conjunctions are: *quando* = when, *appena* = as soon as, *dopo che* = after, *subito che* = immediately after; *e.g.*, *Appena ɛbbe finito la lɛttera, partì* = As soon as he had finished the letter, he left.

Vocabulary

camerigra = maid, waitress
coltɛllo = knife
forchetta = fork
piatto = plate
piattino = saucer
poliziɔtto = policeman
pranzo = dinner
tazza = cup
vassɔio = tray

aiutare = to help
apparecchiare = to lay (a table)
invitare = to invite
lavare = to wash
lasciare = to leave, to let
pulire (1st group) = to clean, polish
tornare = to return
tardi = late

Exercise 10 (a)

1. Oggi abbiamo ospiti a pranzo.
2. La cuoca è andata al mercato per comprare carne e legumi e la cameriera ha lavato i piatti, le tazze e i bicchieri.
3. Maria aiuterà la donna ad apparecchiare e a pulire le forchette, i cucchiai e i coltelli.
4. Quando avrà aiutato la donna andrà alla stazione per incontrare gli ospiti.
5. La donna aveva lavato tutti i piatti ma non aveva pulito i coltelli.
6. Quando vedrà il dottore, avrà già venduto la macchina.

7. Appena ebbe rotto una tazza lasciò cadere anche una bottiglia.
8. Ha rotto tutte le cose che erano sul vassoio? Sí, tutte.
9. Erano stati alla casa del dottore quando incontrarono l'avvocato.
10. Saranno già arrivati quando Carlo tornerà a casa? Sí, saranno già in casa.
11. Sarà intelligente quella cameriera ma non sembra. Ha già rotto dodici piatti e due bicchieri. Ha lasciato cadere anche tre bottiglie e abbiamo perduto del buon vino.
12. A che ora è tornata la cuoca dal mercato oggi? È arrivata molto tardi a casa, credo. Avrà incontrato il postino per la via.

Exercise 10 (b)

1. We have invited Mr. and Mrs. Pazzi to dinner today.
2. The maid has already laid the table for twelve.
3. She had already cleaned the knives and forks when cook returned from the market.
4. Cook had been at the market a long time ("much time") because she had lost her purse.
5. As soon as she had lost her purse she spoke to the policeman ("with the policeman").
6. She also met the postman this morning.
7. There were many things on the tray: plates, glasses, cups and saucers.
8. Has she broken many things? Yes, two cups, three saucers and five plates.
9. As soon as she had laid the table the guests arrived.
10. Will he have seen Mary, do you think?
11. She lost her purse in the train this morning.
12. All my books were in that trunk that I have sent to Naples (say "all the my books").

LESSON XI

CONJUNCTIVE PRONOUNS—IMPERATIVE

THERE are two kinds of pronouns: *disjunctive* and *conjunctive*—emphatic and unemphatic. The pronouns we already know—the subjects of the verb—are emphatic pronouns; they are required only for emphasis, and they are also known as disjunctive pronouns—disjunctive or separated, for they may stand alone, independent of the verb: *Chi è la? io.* = Who is there? I. Disjunctive pronouns may also stand alone as objects of a preposition: *A chi dà quel denaro? a me.* = Who's he giving that money to? To me. In both sentences the pronoun is the most emphatic word.

But in sentences and phrases such as: He sees me; I find them; seeing us; to help you; the *object* pronouns (me, them, us, you) are not emphatic; they are very closely connected with the verb, and are almost joined to it, hence the name *conjunctive*. We shall deal with these pronouns first. They are always used in close connection with the verb; they cannot stand alone, and they are always direct, indirect or reflexive objects of a verb. (A verb is called reflexive when the object and the subject are the SAME person; in English the reflexive objects are myself, himself, etc.)

Conjunctive Personal Pronouns

Direct object	Indirect object	Reflexive object
mi = me	mi = to me	mi = myself
ti = thee, you	ti = to thee, to you	ti = thyself, yourself
lo = him, it (m.)	gli = to him, to it (m.)	si = himself, herself, itself, yourself
la = her, it (f.), you	le = to her, to it (f.), to you	
ci = us	ci = to us	ci = ourselves
vi = you	vi = to you	vi = yourself, yourselves
li = them, you (m.)	loro = to them, to you	si = themselves, yourselves
le = them, you (f.)		

The first and second persons singular and plural are the same for the three different kinds of objects. Learn carefully the forms of the third person which are used in the polite form of address. They may be seen more clearly from the following:

	Direct	Indirect	Reflexive
Addressing one person:	La = you	Le = to you	Si = yourself
Addressing more than one man, or men and women:	Li = you	Loro = to you	Si = yourselves
Addressing more than one woman:	Le = you	Loro = to you	Si = yourselves

Position of the Conjunctive Pronouns.—In English the conjunctive pronouns FOLLOW the verb; but in Italian they PRECEDE (except in certain cases which we shall learn later). An Italian says: *Lui la trovò* = He her found; *Lei gli scriverà* = She to him will write. Study the following sentences:

Non lo capisco = I don't understand it.
Ci mandò la lettera ieri = He sent us the letter yesterday.
Gli ho parlato = I have spoken to him.
Mi ha, *or* m'ha veduto = He has seen me.
L'ho finito = I have finished it.
Io mi lavo = I wash myself.
Noi ci laviamo = We wash ourselves, we wash one another.
Manderò loro la lettera = I shall send them the letter.

And now the following points should be noted: Some conjunctive pronouns drop their final vowel before a word beginning with a vowel or an *h*; *lo* and *la* nearly always do so, and *mi*, *ti* and *si* quite often. The reflexive pronouns in the plural may mean *one another* and *each other* as well as *ourselves, themselves*, etc.; and one conjunctive pronoun (*loro*) always FOLLOWS the verb.

The conjunctive pronoun *ne* is a very useful one; it means "of it", "of them", "some of it", "some of them", "any of it", "any of them". It precedes the verb:

Ne avevo tre = I had three of them.
Ne ho molto = I have a lot of it.
Non ne abbiamo = We haven't any.

Ne is inserted in a sentence where we in English do not always need to say "of it". It always refers to something that has just been mentioned, and it must not be omitted when a number or an adjective of quantity comes after the verb, if the noun itself is not repeated.

The Imperative.—When asking or commanding anyone to do anything, we are using the imperative. A true imperative exists only in the second person (singular and plural); but when speaking to someone in the polite form in Italian it would be very rude to change suddenly to the second person to ask him to do something. Therefore a polite form of the imperative is supplied from the third persons singular and plural of the present subjunctive. A first person plural is also supplied from this tense, which translates the English: "Let us . . ." We have, therefore, five persons to learn as used for the imperative:

	1st conj.	2nd conj.
(tu)	compr-a = buy	vend-i = sell
(Lei)	compr-i = buy	vend-a = sell
(noi)	compr-iamo = let us buy	vend-iamo = let us sell
(voi)	compr-ate = buy	vend-ete = sell
(Loro)	compr-ino = buy	vend-ano = sell

	3rd conj. (1st group)	(2nd group)
(tu)	fin-isc-i = finish	part-i = depart
(Lei)	fin-isc-a = finish	part-a = depart
(noi)	fin-iamo = let us finish	part-iamo = let us depart
(voi)	fin-ite = finish	part-ite = depart
(Loro)	fin-isc-ano = finish	part-ano = depart

Essere	*avere*
sii = be	abbi = have
sia = be	abbia = have
siamo = let us be	abbiamo = let us have
siate = be	abbiate = have
siano = be	abbiano = have

Imperative Negative

non comprare = don't buy
non compri = don't buy
non compriamo = don't let us buy
non comprate = don't buy
non comprino = don't buy

To form the imperative negative of the second person singular (*tu*), Italian uses the *infinitive*; the other persons remain the same as in the affirmative:

Compra quella macchina = Buy that car.
Non comprare quel fazzoletto = Don't buy that handkerchief.
Compri un bel fiore, signora = Buy a beautiful flower, lady.
Non compri quella carne = Don't buy that meat.

And now let us study a few sentences in the imperative which have conjunctive pronouns as objects instead of nouns:

Comprala = Buy it (referring to *macchina*).
Compratela = Buy it (referring to *macchina* but using *Voi*).
Lo compri, Signora = Buy it, lady.
Compriamolo = Let's buy it.
Parlate loro = Speak to them.

Non lo comprare⎱
Non lo comprate⎰ = Don't buy it.

Non la compri = Don't buy it (referring to *carne* (f.)).

Non lo compriamo = Don't let's buy it.

It will be seen that with the imperative *affirmative* conjunctive pronouns used with the *second person singular* and *first and second persons plural* FOLLOW the verb, and they are joined to it, forming one word. When they do this, the word does not change its stress; the same syllable carries the stress as was the case before the unemphatic pronoun was added; LORO, however, is *never* joined to the verb. The polite form of the imperative takes the conjunctive pronouns (except *loro*) BEFORE the verb, both in the negative and in the affirmative.

Three other forms of the verb have the conjunctive pronouns after them in the same way as the imperative affirmative: the infinitive, the past participle used without an auxiliary verb and the present participle (which corresponds to our form of the verb ending in -*ing*):

> Andava a vederla = he was going to see her.
> Parlandone loro = speaking of it to them.
> Parlatoci = (having) spoken to us.

Note that the infinitive loses its final vowel when it combines with the pronoun.

One more point about conjunctive pronouns. It has been noted that the past participle of a verb conjugated with *avere* may agree with a preceding direct object; * when that object is a conjunctive pronoun, the best writers always make the past participle agree with it. In fact, sometimes this agreement is necessary in the case of the third person singular pronoun to distinguish between *him* and *her*, as will be seen from these examples:

L'ho veduto al teatro = I saw *him* at the theatre.

L'abbiamo veduta per la strada = We saw *her* along the road.

Ci avrà veduti nel treno = He will have seen *us* on the train.

Hai comprato quella macchina? Sí, l'ho comprata = Have you bought that car? Yes, I have.

Vocabulary

albergo = hotel	facchino = porter
biglietto = ticket	finestrino = small window,
burro = butter	carriage window

* See page 54.

carrozza = carriage
prosciutto = ham
ristorante (m.) = restaurant
sala d'aspetto = waiting-room
salame (m.) (no plural) = sausage, sausage meat
salsiccia (pl. salsicce) = small sausage
valigia = suitcase

frutta = fruit
pronto = ready
un po' di = a little

addio = good-bye!
dappertutto = everywhere
finalmente = at last
forse = perhaps

Exercise 11 (a)

1. Ho perduto il mio baule, l'ha veduto Lei?
2. No, io ho perduto la valigia, l'ho cercata dappertutto ma non l'ho ancora trovata.
3. Il facchino non l'ha portata al treno?
4. No, l'avrà lasciata all'albergo.
5. Non è già nella carrozza? No, l'ho cercata nella carrozza, forse l'ho lasciata nella sala d'aspetto.
6. Ha comprato i biglietti, Signora? No, non li ho ancora comprati.
7. La cuoca ha portato il pane e burro e la frutta? Sí, li ha portati; ha portato anche del salame e un po' di prosciutto.
8. Dov'è quel facchino? Non l'hai trovato Giovanni? Ma il treno parte e noi partiremo senza bauli.
9. Ecco arriva il facchino. Eccolo: * Andiamo a incontrarlo. Ma ha delle rose rosse in mano! † [Note andare a—go to meet, translate "go and meet."]
10. Dio mio! rose rosse! Ma i bauli ! Dove sono? Dove sono i bauli? Eccoli, eccoli finalmente.
11. Ora siamo pronti. Ma dov'è Maria? Corri, corri Maria, il treno parte. Finalmente partiamo, addio, addio.
12. Ma per chi erano quelle rose rosse? Erano per la cuoca.
13. Povera cuoca ! Abbiamo perduto le sue belle rose rosse. Maria le ha lasciate cadere dal finestrino del treno.

Exercise 11 (b)

1. We have lost our suitcases. Have you seen them, porter?
2. No, madam, I have not seen them.
3. I have looked for them everywhere in the carriage.
4. Buy the tickets, please, John.

* *Ecco* takes the conjunctive pronouns after it.
† *in mano.* No possessive is necessary in Italian; we know it must be *his own* hand.

5. John and Mary, go and buy the tickets.
6. Have you any fruit? No, I haven't any.
7. Shall I go and buy some fruit? Yes, go * and buy fruit and a little ham.
8. Does she sell sausage too? Yes, she does.
9. Let us buy some fruit, bread and butter and a little ham.
10. Have you brought the sausages, too? Yes, here they are.
11. Why has he not brought the trunk? He has left it in the restaurant.
12. Shall we go and look for it?
13. No, children, stay here; you will miss the train. (Stay = remain.)

LESSON XII

CONJUNCTIVE PRONOUNS (*CONTD.*)—PRESENT PARTICIPLE

IN the preceding lesson each sentence contained only a single conjunctive pronoun; but two often come together, as direct and indirect objects of the same verb: He gives it to me. In Italian the indirect pronoun comes before the direct, and both pronouns either precede or follow the verb, according to the rules we have just learnt: *Lui me lo dà* = He to me it gives. But it will be said: There is a mistake: *me* should be *mi*. No, there is no mistake; for indirect pronouns change their form slightly when followed by the direct *lo, la, li, le* and *ne*:

Me lo danno = They give it to me (danno, from *dare* = to give, irreg.).
Te li danno = They give them to you.
Se lo dà = He gives it to himself.
Glielo daremo = We shall give it to him.
Glielo daremmo = We should give it to her.
Parlatecene = Speak to us of it.
Parlandovene = Speaking of it to you.
Parlatogliene = (Having) spoken to him of it.
Va' a dargliene = Go and give him some.
Lo daremo loro = We shall give it to them.

Note that *loro*, as before, always follows the verb. From the preceding we may learn that: before the direct pronouns *lo, la, li, le* and *ne*, the indirect change as follows: *mi, ti, si, ci* and *vi*

---

* *andare* has an irregular second person singular imperative—*va'*.

change the final *i* to *e*; and *gli* and *le* become *glie* and are written as one word with the following pronoun: *glielo* = it (masc.) to him, or to her, or to you (polite form); *glieli* = them (masc.) to him, or to her or to you; *gliene* = some to him, some to her, some to you.

Conjunctive Adverbs.—You will have noticed that *ci* (= us) is the same word as *ci* (= there, in the phrases "there is", *c' è*, etc.). *Ci* is both a pronoun and an adverb. *Vi*, too, means "there" as well as "you": *vi è* = there is; and *ne*, besides being a pronoun (= of it, some), is also an adverb meaning "thence". These three conjunctive adverbs are used to denote a place already mentioned when no special emphasis is required, and they precede or follow the verb, according to the rules given for the pronouns; *ci* and *vi*, as adverbs, also change to *ce* and *ve* when followed by *lo, la, li, le* or *ne*:

Vi andò ieri = He went there yesterday.

Spera di arrivarci alle due = He hopes to arrive there at two.

Ne arrivano oggi = They are arriving from there today.

Present Participle.—The forms for the three conjugations and the auxiliary verbs are as follows:

Compr-ando = buying   vend-endo = selling
fin-endo = finishing   essendo = being   avendo = having

Perfect Participle

avendo comprato = having bought
avendo venduto = having sold
avendo finito = having finished
essendo stato = having been   avendo avuto = having had

The endings *-ando* and *-endo* correspond to the English ending *-ing*; but we cannot always use the Italian present participle for every occasion when English uses *-ing*, for the present participle in Italian is more truly a verb, and cannot be used as a noun or an adjective. In the sentence: "On opening the drawer she saw the box", the word "opening" is a verb, describing an action; therefore this can be rendered in Italian by a word in *-endo*: *Aprendo il cassetto vide la scatola* (the preposition "on" is not required). But in "I like riding" or "She spoke without hesitating", the word in *-ing* is more of a noun than a verb; while in phrases like "boiling water", "following chapter", the words in *-ing* are adjectives. In neither of these cases does Italian use a present participle; the way to render them will be dealt with later (Lesson XXVI, page 124, and Lesson XIX, Part II, page 183). For the moment we will concern ourselves only with the Italian present participle (remember that it never changes its endings); it is used in the following cases:

1. When it is preceded by one of the following prepositions (which are not translated in Italian): "by", "in", "on", "through":

Combattendo vinciamo = Through fighting we win.

2. Instead of a subordinate clause of time, cause or condition, which is introduced in English by "as", "while", "since", "if" (none of these words being translated into Italian, for they are understood in the present participle):

Camminando per Via Tornabuoni incontrai il dentista = As I was walking down Tornabuoni Road I met the dentist.
Andando per quella strada non la vedremo = If we go that way we shan't see her.

When the present participle is so used, however, it always agrees with the subject of the main sentence. For instance, the present participle could not be used in this sentence: "As I was walking down Tornabuoni Road a policeman stopped me"; this would be in Italian: *Mentre camminavo per via Tornabuoni un poliziotto mi fermo.*

3. It forms the progressive tenses with the verb *stare* (to stand, to be) as an auxiliary. There are two progressive or continuous tenses: the present, formed by the present indicative of *stare* and the present participle; and the past, formed by the imperfect of *stare* and the present participle:

Sto leggendo = I am reading.
Stavano dormendo = They were sleeping.

It should be noted that these two tenses are specially emphatic in Italian; they lay particular stress on the continuity of the action; we have seen that our continuous present and past tenses can often be rendered by the Italian ordinary present and imperfect respectively. There are no other progressive tenses in Italian; our other continuous tenses are usually rendered in Italian by the simple tense: "I shall be going" = *andro.*

C

Vocabulary

autobus (m.) = bus
cantonata = corner
farmacia = chemist
mancia = tip
passaporto = passport
piazza = square

aspettare = to wait for
domandare = to ask for

a piedi = on foot (piede (m.) = foot)
volentieri = willingly, gladly

Exercise 12 (a)

1. Uscendo dalla posta, incontrai il dentista.
2. Signora, dov'è la farmacia per favore? Ce n'è una alla cantonata, Signorina: eccola.
3. Mentre attraversava la piazza, un poliziotto lo fermò e gli domandò il passaporto. (Note the construction with *domandare*: to ask something *to* someone.)
4. Che belle rose rosse! Datemene una, per favore.
5. Non sono le mie; sono della cuoca, ma ve ne darò una molto volentieri.
6. Parlandogliene, perdette l'autobus e andò a casa a piedi.
7. Non c'è autobus, prendiamo una carrozza. Vedi, ce n'è una nella piazza, che aspetta.
8. Mentre apriva la scatola tutti la guardavano.
9. Sono stati a Firenze Loro? Sí, Signore, ne arriviamo ora.
10. È stata a Milano Lei, Signora? Sí, Signore, ci sono stata.
11. Aspettami, aspettami. Ma non aspettiamo nessuno. Il treno parte. Hai dato la mancia al facchino? Sí, gliel'ho data.
12. Ci hanno dato i biglietti? Sí, ce li hanno dati. E ha avuto la mancia il facchino? Sí, l'ha avuta.

Exercise 12 (b)

1. When coming out of the church they met the dentist and the doctor.
2. There was a large box in that drawer. Has she found it?
3. Yes, she has given it to him.
4. Why doesn't she give it to me? She has already given it to them.
5. While walking along Tornabuoni Road, Cook met the postman.
6. She has lost her passport. Have you seen it?
7. No, but the porter has found it; he will give it to her.
8. Give him some; but I haven't any more. (The polite form of the imperative, *i.e.*, the present subjunctive of *dare* is irregular: *dia*.)

9. Where is that famous church? At the corner. Don't you
    see it?
10. Has the dentist given you a receipt? Yes, he has given it to
    me.
11. Have you bought the tickets? Yes, I have bought them, and
    I have given them to Mary.
12. Has he given them to you? I have given them to him.
    Why didn't you (*voi*) give them to them? Because he
    hadn't given any to us. And why hadn't he given any to
    you? Because he hadn't any.

LESSON XIII

DISJUNCTIVE PRONOUNS—MORE PLURALS

WE know the disjunctive pronouns as subjects of the verb; as
objects of the verb they have these forms:

	Singular	Plural
First person	me = me	noi = us
Second ,,	te = thee, you	voi = you
Third ,,	lui = him	loro = them (m. and f.)
	lɛi = her	
	esso = him, it	essi = them (m.)
	essa = her, it	esse = them (f.)
	Lɛi = you	Loro = you
	se = himself,	se = themselves
	herself, itself	

With the exception of the first and second persons singular, the
disjunctive or emphatic pronouns as subjects and as objects
are the same; and again *lui*, *lɛi* and *loro* are used only for persons, *esso*, *essa*, etc., may refer to things and to animals.

The most common use of disjunctive pronouns is after a
preposition:

Il mɛdico ɛ con lei = The doctor is with her.
Il bambino cammina da sé ora = The baby walks by himself
    now.

They are also used after "than" (= *di*) with a comparative:

Giovanni ɛ piú alto di me = John is taller (more tall) than I.

When a verb has two pronoun *direct* objects, disjunctives are
required:

Ho veduto te e lui in città stamane = I saw you and him in
    town this morning

and with two pronoun *indirect* objects:

Ne dò a lui e a lɛi = I'm giving some to him and to her

Sometimes when special emphasis is laid on the pronoun, a disjunctive is used:

Lo darò a lui = I'll give it to *him*;

and again when two objects are contrasted:

Lo darò a lui ma non a lɛi = I'll give it to him, but not to her.

In such phrases as the following the emphatic pronoun is required:

Felice lui ma povero me! = Happy he, but poor me!

and lastly, when the pronoun stands alone in the predicate:

Se io fossi te = If I were you (fossi = past subjunctive of *ɛssere*).

More Plurals.—The nouns ending in -*a* we have learnt so far have all been feminine. But there are a few in -*a* which are masculine, and they form their plural by changing the -*a* to -*i*. They mostly end in -*ma*, -*ta*, -*ca* and -*ga*:

Singular	Plural
il telegramma (the telegram)	i telegrammi
il poɛta (the poet)	i poɛti

Some words ending in -*a* may be either masculine or feminine, and then they have two plural forms. The most usual are nouns ending in -*ista*:

Singular	Plural
il pianista (m.) (the pianist)	i pianisti
la pianista (f.) (the pianist)	le pianiste
l'artista (m.) (the artist)	gli artisti
l'artista (f.) (the artist)	le artiste

Slight irregularities are found in the formation of the plural of nouns and adjectives ending in -*co*, -*go*, -*ca*, -*ga*, -*cia* and -*gia*:

-co and **-go.**—Words which have the stress on the syllable before the last add an *h* to keep the hard sound in the plural:

Singular	Plural
fuɔco (fire)	fuɔchi
antico (ancient)	antichi
lago (lake)	laghi
albɛrgo (hotel)	albɛrghi

but if the stress is on a syllable before the next to the last, they
do not keep the hard sound in the plural:

Singular	Plural
medico (doctor)	medici
monaco (monk)	monaci
magnifico (magnificent)	magnifici

There are, however, a few exceptions to this rule. The following
should be remembered: *amico* (= friend), *nemico* (= enemy),
porco (= pig), *greco* (= Greek), which, although having the
next to the last syllable stressed, form their plurals in -*ci*:
amici, nemici, porci, greci; and *carico* (= laden or load), with
the stress on the *a*, puts in an *h* in the plural to keep the hard
sound: *carichi*.

-ca and -ga.—Nouns and adjectives keep the hard sound of
the *c* and *g* in the plural:

Singular	Plural
la barca (the boat)	le barche
il duca (the duke)	i duchi
lunga (long)	lunghe
magnifica (magnificent)	magnifiche

Note that an adjective ending in -*co* in the masculine and -*ca* in
the feminine may preserve the hard sound in the feminine
plural and not in the masculine:

Singular	Plural
il cavallo magnifico	i cavalli magnifici
la statua magnifica	le statue magnifiche

Note, too, the word for friend in both genders:

Singular	Plural
amico	amici
amica	amiche

-cia and -gia.—In a previous lesson (page 51) we noted that
the word *grigio* became *grige* in the feminine plural. Like *grigia*,
nouns and adjectives ending in -*cia* and -*gia* drop the *i* before
the ending -*e* of the plural, provided the *i* is not stressed:

Singular	Plural
la guancia = the cheek	le guance
la pioggia = the rain	le piogge
la spiaggia = the shore	le spiagge
but la farmacia = the chemist's	le farmacie
la bugia = the lie	le bugie

There are a few exceptions to this rule, usually words which have a vowel immediately preceding the *-cia* or *-gia*: *valigia* (= suitcase), *valigie*.

Irregular Nouns.—A few masculine nouns ending in *-o* have an irregular plural in *-a* which is feminine. Some of the commonest are:

Singular	Plural
il braccio = the arm	le braccia
il ciglio = the eyelash	le ciglia
il dito = finger	le dita
il frutto = fruit	le frutta
(also la frutta = fruit, collectively)	
il ginocchio = the knee	le ginocchia
il labbro = the lip	le labbra
il lenzuolo = the sheet	le lenzuola
il muro = wall	le mura or i muri
il membro = limb, member	le membra (limbs), i membri (members of society, club, etc.)
il miglio = mile	le miglia
l'osso = bone	le ossa
il paio = pair	le paia
l'uovo = egg	le uova

The following have irregular plurals: *il bue* (= ox), *i buoi*; *l'uomo* (= man), *gli uomini*; and *la moglie* (= wife), *le mogli*.

Vocabulary

acqua = water
asciugamano (m.) = towel
capelli = hair (m. plur.)
pesce (m.) = fish
portamonete (m.) = purse
porto = port

alpino = alpine
calmo = calm
fortunato = happy, fortunate

Exercise 13 (a)

1. Non lo date a lui, datelo a lei.
2. Ho incontrato lei in città oggi ma non lui.
3. Avete veduto il lago voi? Sí, ci siamo andati oggi. L'acqua era molto calma, e c'erano molte barche.
4. Queste lenzuola sono molto vecchie, non sono per l'ospite, cerchiamone delle nuove.
5. Questo telegramma è per te, non è per me.
6. Le barche arrivarono al porto cariche di pesce.

7. Non sono aperte le farmacie oggi? Sí, Signora, sono aperte.
8. Ha già imparato a scrivere la bambina? Sí, ha scritto una lettera da sè. (*scritto* irreg. past participle of *scrivere*.)
9. Il duca ha una lunga barba bianca e i capelli bianchi. È vecchio ma sua moglie è piú vecchia di lui.
10. La vecchia stava dormendo; aveva ancora quel libro in mano e sulle ginocchia c'era il gatto che dormiva anch'esso.
11. I membri del club alpino di Torino sono arrivati oggi.
12. Che ragazza è quella! Ha perduto ieri due paia di guanti nel treno; e oggi in cucina ha lasciato cadere sei uova.
13. Mi dia un asciugamano pulito, per favore.

Exercise 13 (b)

1. Give it to me, not to him.
2. Those two men with the oxen will arrive tomorrow.
3. I met them in town this morning, but I did not see her.
4. That book was written by him.
5. This letter is for me, not for him.
6. Bring me those sheets, please. Here they are.
7. Those boats were laden with fish when they arrived at the port.
8. How many eggs have you bought?
9. That old man is very smart; he has a clean shirt every day.
10. That old woman has twenty pairs of shoes.
11. Lucky she! She had left her purse in the train, and the porter found it.
12. I have lost two new pairs of socks. I had them with me last week when I was carrying all those eggs from town. I have probably left them in the bus.
13. He was going to see her when I met him.

LESSON XIV

RELATIVE PRONOUNS—REFLEXIVE VERBS

WE have often used the relative pronoun *che*; it is the commonest, and it translates "who", "whom", "which" and "that". It is invariable, used as subject or object of a verb and for persons and for things. It cannot be left out of a sentence, as such words are in English:

Il libro che è sulla scrivania = The book which is on the desk.
I dolci che abbiamo mangiati = The sweets we have eaten.

Il giornale che ho trovato nel trɛno = The newspaper I found in the train.

Che is not used when the relative is an indirect object or when it is governed by a preposition: then we have another form, also invariable and also used for persons and for things: *cui*.

La signora a cui mandiamo il pacco = The lady to whom we are sending the parcel.

Il film di cui parlo = The film of which I am speaking.

Il poɛta da cui era scritta questa poesia = The poet by whom this poem was written.

A third relative pronoun, also referring to persons and things, but which is variable, is *il quale* (fem. *la quale*; plurals: *i quali, le quali*). This may be used in place of either *che* or *cui*, and when it is governed by a preposition, this preposition and article join together: *del quale* = of whom, whose. Note, too, that it agrees in gender and number with the noun coming before it, to which it refers. *Il quale* is not used very often, but it is sometimes necessary, to avoid ambiguity, as in this sentence: *La moglie del dottore, la quale mi mandɔ quella lɛttera* = The doctor's wife, who sent me that letter. Had we used *che* it would presumably have been the doctor, not his wife, who had sent the letter, for *che* usually refers to the noun immediately preceding it; but if it had been the doctor, and not his wife, it would still have been better to use *il quale*, to be quite sure of not being misunderstood.

Del quale is one way of translating whose; but it is not the most usual. A commoner word is *cui* (invariable). It is preceded by the article (*il, i, la, le*) which agrees with the noun which follows *cui*:

Quel ristorante, i cui piatti sono famosi = That restaurant, whose dishes are celebrated.

Il fornaio, il cui pane ɛ̀ molto buɔno = That baker, whose bread is very good.

Quella signora, il cui indirizzo ho perduto = That lady, whose address I have lost.

Had we used *del quale* in these sentences, it would have agreed with the preceding noun in each case: *Quel ristorante del quale i piatti . . . Quella signora della quale ho perduto l'indirizzo. . . .*

Other relative pronouns are: "he who", "him who" = *chi* (invariable) and *colui che* (fem. *colɛi che*, plural both genders: *coloro che*).

Chi dorme non piglia pesci = He who sleeps doesn't catch fish. (Italian version of "The early bird . . .")

Coloro che hanno tegole di vetro non tirino sassi al vicino = Those who have glass roofs (lit. tiles) let them not throw stones at their neighbour.

Colei che entrerà per quella porta è la pianista famosa = She who will come in by that door is the famous pianist.

"That which" or "what" is *quel che, quello che* or *ciò che*:

Prendermo quel che troveremo = We shall take what we find.

(It should be noted that in a sentence such as: It is I who have left the door open, Italian does not use the impersonal construction *it is*; instead we have: *I am I who have . . .* = Sono io che ho lasciato aperta la porta. Similarly: "Who is there? It is I", is in Italian: *Chi c'è? Sono io*: "It is we" = *Siamo noi*; "It is you" = *Siete voi*, etc.).

Reflexive Verbs.—A verb is reflexive when its subject and object are the same person: I wash myself = *Io mi lavo*. The present indicative of a reflexive verb is as follows:

Lavarsi (1st conj.), *to wash oneself*

mi lavo = I wash myself, etc.

ti lavi	ci laviamo
si lava (lui)	vi lavate
si lava (lei)	si lavano

All reflexive verbs are conjugated with *essere*; the present perfect of *alzarsi* (= to get up) is therefore:

mi sono alzato -a = I have got up, etc.
ti sei alzato -a
si è alzato -a
ci siamo alzati -e
vi siete alzati -e
si sono alzati -e

Some verbs are reflexive in Italian which are not so in English. You will always be able to recognize a reflexive verb in the vocabulary, for its infinitive will have the reflexive pronoun *-si* joined to it. One or two reflexive verbs are followed by the preposition *di*, instead of the direct object as in English; such a verb is *ricordarsi* = to remember. I remember that day = *Io mi ricordo di quel giorno*, and I remember it = *me ne ricordo* (*ne* = of it). For practice let us conjugate the past definite of this verb with *it* as an object:

me ne ricoardai = I remembered it, etc.
te ne ricordasti
se ne ricordò
ce ne ricordammo
ve ne ricordaste
se ne ricordarono

Italian uses reflexive verbs in some cases where English has a different construction: In the first place, instead of the possessive "my", "your", "his", etc., when speaking of clothes and of parts of the body (when we know from the context whose clothes or whose body is being referred to):

Lui si mette il capotto = He is putting on his overcoat (lit.: He to himself puts on the overcoat).

Povero Pinocchio! Si toccò il naso. Era lungo quasi un metro = Poor Pinocchio! He touched his nose! It was almost a yard long.

Secondly, when a verb in English is in the passive without any agent expressed, the third person singular or plural of the reflexive is used in Italian. This will be seen more clearly from the examples:

Si parla inglese = English is spoken (lit.: English speaks itself).

Molte storie si narravano = Many stories were told (lit.: Many stories were telling themselves).

In neither of the above sentences have we any agent expressed: we do not know by whom English is spoken nor by whom the stories were told; had an agent been expressed, the passive would have been used in Italian as in English (see pages 54 and 107).

Thirdly, the third person singular of the reflexive is also used to translate English impersonal sentences beginning "one", "you", "they", etc., meaning people in general:

Qui si vede bene = The light is good here, or You see well here (lit.: Here itself it sees well).

Come si sta bene sulla spiaggia! = How lovely it is on the beach! (lit.: How it stands itself well on the beach!).

Sì, qui si è contenti, Signora = Yes, here one is happy, madam.

Note the last example, where we have a singular verb and pronoun, and a plural adjective which goes with them. This is a peculiarity of the verbs *essere*, *restare* (= to stay), *rimanere*, *diventare* (= to become), *divenire* (= to become), which may take the following adjective in the *plural* when the verb is *singular* with this reflexive construction standing for "one", "we", meaning people in general.

One brief admonition before we do the exercises. In English "myself", "himself", etc., are not always reflexive; they are sometimes used to give emphasis to another pronoun, as: "I will give it to him myself". Here "myself" merely emphasizes the "I", and is not the object of a verb as in: "I am buying myself a pair of shoes". This last sentence is reflexive in Italian, as in English: *Mi compro un paio di scarpe*; but in the first sentence "myself" is rendered in Italian by the word *stesso*: *Io stesso glielo darɔ* (*stesso* has fem. *stessa*, and the two plurals *stessi*, *stesse*). Note that *stesso* immediately follows the pronoun with which it is used, and if it is put at the end of the sentence for further emphasis, this pronoun must be repeated: *Io glielo darɔ, io stesso*.

Vocabulary

caldo (adj. and noun) = warm, hot
faccia = face
montagna = mountain
professore (m.) = professor
università = university
veduta = view
come! = what!

chiamarsi = to call oneself (come si chiama = what is your name?)
lavorare = to work
pagare = to pay for
passare = to pass
scusare = to excuse
presto = early
prossimo = next

Exercise 14 (a)

1. Mangeremo a pranzo il pesce che abbiamo pigliato stamane.
2. La signorina con cui parlavo ieri è mia sorella.—È una bella ragazza! Come si chiama?
3. Lo studio in cui lavoro è molto comodo. È una stanza grande con tre finestre, dalle quali ho una bella veduta del lago e delle montagne.
4. L'uomo a cui ha venduto la macchina è partito. Come! Partito! E non me l'ha ancora pagata (*pagare* takes a direct object: he has not yet paid it to me).
5. Come si chiama questa piazza? La piazza per cui passiamo ora è piazza Vittorio Emanuele.
6. Il signore, la cui figlia abbiamo veduta in città stamane, è professore d'università (supply in English "a" professor).

7. La figlia del dottore, alla quale Lei ha scritto oggi, è un'amica mia.
8. A che ora si alza Lei la mattina, Signora? Io mi alzo presto, generalmente alle sei; ma mia sorella è pigra e si alza molto tardi.
9. Che bel sole! Come si sta bene qui al caldo!
10. Sí, qui sulla spiaggia si è sempre contenti.
11. Scusi, Signora, la signorina il cui anello si perdette sulla spiaggia è alla porta.
12. Ti ricordi di quel bel giorno sulla spiaggia l'anno scorso? E come! Me ne ricordo molto bene.

Exercise 14 (b)

1. That woman to whom you were speaking is Cook's sister.
2. That book of which you were speaking is not in the library.
3. The girl from whom I have received this letter will arrive next week.
4. That man who has bought your car has already left for Italy (*the* Italy).
5. The cook whose dishes were so famous has left that restaurant. (Cook may also be masculine—*il cuoco*.)
6. What time does your father get up? He generally gets up at eight, but yesterday he got up at seven, and left by the eight o'clock train for Rome.
7. He was putting on his overcoat when his sister arrived.
8. That girl hasn't washed herself! What hands! and what a face!
9. Excuse me, sir. What is the name of this square?
10. The street I am looking for is near to this square.
11. Did you remember that book? Yes, I went to that bookshop where they speak English.
12. Is Uncle going already? Yes, he's putting on his hat. Where are those new gloves I bought for him? Here they are; he never remembers them.

LESSON XV

CONJUGATION OF REGULAR VERBS

As we are nearly half-way through this little book, it would be well to look back for a moment over what we have learnt, and revise particularly any points which seemed difficult or any rules which we do not seem to remember easily. It would be a good plan to look over the exercises and see which mistakes have been the most frequent; and also to turn back to tables and lists and run through some of them again. It is very likely that the conjunctive and disjunctive pronouns would benefit by a little revision. But probably it will be verbs that need the most attention; so it will be profitable at this point to show in tabular form the conjugations of the three types of regular verbs. The tenses we have already learnt are shown here together, where the different endings of the conjugations may be compared, and the tenses of the subjunctive mood—which we have not yet studied—are here also; they will be useful for reference later.

When studying the formation of the various tenses, the following points should be remembered:

1. The future and conditional are formed by adding the given endings to a shortened form of the infinitive (the first conjugation changing its -a to -e): comprer-, vender-, finir-.

2. All other parts of the verb are formed by adding certain endings to the stem: compr-, vend-, fin-.

3. The characteristic vowels, -a, -e and -i, mark the only difference between the three conjugations in the second person plural of the present indicative, in the whole imperfect indicative and imperfect subjunctive tenses, and in all persons of the past definite except the third singular.

4. The first person plural ending -iamo is the same for the present indicative, present subjunctive and imperative of all three conjugations.

5. Three persons only in each conjugation have a written accent: the first and third persons singular of the future (always a grave); and the third person singular of the past definite (grave on the final -ò of the first conjugation and acute on the final -é and -i of the other two).

CONJUGATION OF REGULAR VERBS
SIMPLE TENSES

I	II	III
	Infinitive	
compr-are = to buy	vend-ere = to sell	fin-ire = to finish
	Present Participle	
compr-ando = buy-ing	vend-endo = sell-ing	fin-endo = finish-ing
	Past Participle	
compr-ato = bought	vend-uto = sold	fin-ito = finished

Indicative Mood

I	II	III

Present

I buy, do buy, am buying	I sell, do sell, am selling	I finish, do finish, am finishing
compr-o	vend-o	fin-isc-o *
compr-i	vend-i	fin-isc-i
compr-a	vend-e	fin-isc-e
compr-iamo	vend-iamo	fin-iamo
compr-ate	vend-ete	fin-ite
compr-ano	vend-ono	fin-isc-ono

* Verbs of the second group of the third conjugation: part-o, parti-, part-e, part-ono; see page 27.

Imperfect

I was buying, used to buy	I was selling, used to sell	I was finishing, used to finish
compr-avo	vend-evo	fin-ivo
compr-avi	vend-evi	fin-ivi
compr-ava	vend-eva	fin-iva
compr-avamo	vend-evamo	fin-ivamo
compr-avate	vend-evate	fin-ivate
compr-avano	vend-evano	fin-ivano

Past Definite

I bought	I sold	I finished
compr-ai	vend-ei (-ɛtti)	fin-ii
compr-asti	vend-esti	fin-isti
compr-ò	vend-é (-ɛtte)	fin-í
compr-ammo	vend-emmo	fin-immo
compr-aste	vend-este	fin-iste
compr-arono	vend-erono (-ɛttero)	fin-irono

Future

I shall buy	I shall sell	I shall finish
comprer-ò	vender-ò	finir-ò
comprer-ai	vender-ai	finir-ai
comprer-à	vender-à	finir-à
comprer-emo	vender-emo	finir-emo
comprer-ete	vender-ete	finir-ete
comprer-anno	vender-anno	finir-anno

Subjunctive Mood

I	II	III

Present

(that) I (may) buy	(that) I (may) sell	(that) I (may) finish
compr-i	vend-a	fin-isc-a *
compr-i	vend-a	fin-isc-a
compr-i	vend-a	fin-isc-a
compri-amo	vend-iamo	fin-iamo
compr-iate	vend-iate	fin-iate
compr-ino	vend-ano	fin-isc-ano

* Verbs of the second group: part-a, part-a, part-a, part-ano.

Imperfect

(that) I (might) buy	(that) I (might) sell	(that) I (might) finish
compr-assi	vend-essi	fin-issi
compr-assi	vend-essi	fin-issi
compr-asse	vend-esse	fin-isse
compr-assimo	vend-essimo	fin-issimo
compr-aste	vend-este	fin-iste
compr-assero	vend-essero	fin-issero

Conditional Mood

I should buy	I should sell	I should finish
comprer-ɛi	vender-ɛi	finir-ɛi
comprer-esti	vender-esti	finir-esti
comprer-ɛbbe	vender-ɛbbe	finir-ɛbbe
comprer-emmo	vender-emmo	finir-emmo
comprer-este	vender-este	finir-este
comprer-ɛbbero	vender-ɛbbero	finir-ɛbbero

Imperative

Buy	Sell	Finish
compr-a	vend-i	fin-isc-i *
compr-ate	vend-ete	fin-ite

* Verbs of the second group: part-i.

COMPOUND TENSES

parlare = to speak	partire = to depart
(conjugated with *avere*)	(conjugated with *ɛssere*)

Perfect Infinitive

avere parlato = to have
spoken

ɛssere partito = to have departed

Perfect Participle

avɛndo parlato = having
spoken

essɛndo partito = having departed

Indicative Mood
Present Perfect

ho parlato = I have spoken

sono partito = I have departed

Past Perfect

avevo parlato = I had spoken

ɛro partito = I had departed

Second Past Perfect

bbi parlato = I had spoken

fui partito = I had departed

Future Perfect

avrɔ parlato = I shall have
spoken

sarɔ partito = I shall have
departed

Subjunctive Mood
Present Perfect

abbia parlato = I (may) have
spoken

sia partito = I (may) have
departed

Past Perfect

avessi parlato = I (might) have
spoken

fossi partito = I (might) have
departed

Conditional Mood
Perfect

avrɛi parlato = I should have
spoken

sarɛi partito = I should have
departed

Before doing the following exercise we should give ourselves
some verb drill by taking, one after another, the stem of
several verbs we know and substituting them for *compr-*, *vend-*
or *fin-* (according to which conjugation they belong) in all the
forms and tenses in the preceding table. The more often we do

this, the better, and when choosing verbs we must be sure not to take any marked "irregular" in the vocabularies.

Vocabulary

grazie = thanks
letto = bed
minuto = minute
momento = moment
notte (f.) = night
occhiali (m. pl.) = spectacles
polizia = police
sera = evening
telefono = telephone
occupato = engaged, busy

piacere (irreg.) = to please
telefonare = to telephone
viaggiare = to travel

male = badly
naturalmente = of course
neppure = not even
proprio = just
sotto = under, beneath

Exercise 15 (a)

1. L'uomo di cui parliamo è stato qui stamane. Non l'hai veduto, Zio?
2. Naturalmente lo zio non l'ha veduto, perché era a letto.
3. Ma a che ora si alza tuo zio?—Mai prima delle dieci.
4. E tu? A che ora ti sei alzato stamane?—Ma se io non sono neppure andato a letto? Ho viaggiato in treno tutta la notte, e ho dormito molto male.
5. Che cosa sta cercando, Signore? I miei occhiali; mi sono caduti dal naso proprio in questo momento. Povero me, non vedo niente.
6. Lasci fare a me, Signore, li cercherò * io (lasci fare = let to do; that is: "leave it to me").
7. Eccoli, eccoli, li ho trovati; erano sotto quella sedia. Grazie Signorina.
8. Ho comprato questo vestito quando ero a Milano la settimana scorsa, Le piace? (lit.: does it please you?).
9. Sí, mi piace molto; quel colore Le sta molto bene. (Stare bene = to suit; also: "to be well" (of health).)
10. La casa aveva un piccolo giardino davanti, che la separava dalla via, dove lavorava ogni sera quel vecchio dalla barba bianca.
11. È arrivato l'avvocato? No, arriverà col treno delle sette e mezzo. Andremo a incontrarlo alla stazione.
12. Appena che ebbe finito la lettera, chiamò Giovanni per telefono, ma il numero era occupato.

* Verbs of the first conjugation in -care insert h after the c whenever it precedes -e or -i.

Exercise 15 (b)

1. I don't like Mary's new dress. Where did she buy it?
2. That colour doesn't suit her; I prefer the dress she had last year.
3. Aunt is always losing her spectacles. She never remembers where she has left them.
4. Last Monday she was looking for them for hours, and they were on her nose all the time. (Say: to her they were standing on the nose.)
5. Are we near Florence, please? Yes, we shall be there in five minutes.
6. The lady of whom you are speaking has just left. Yes, I met her as I came in.
7. This isn't a very comfortable bed. How is yours?
8. Did you sleep well, sir? No, I slept very badly.
9. I am leaving for Florence this evening.
10. I shall travel in the train all night and arrive there at six o'clock in the morning. (Say: of the morning.)
11. Whose is that overcoat? Is it yours or his?
12. As soon as the professor had finished the letter, the lawyer telephoned the police.

LESSON XVI

FIRST READING LESSON

I T is now time to attempt the translation of continuous Italian prose. So far we have done only sentences containing words and phrases already learnt; now we must be prepared to meet strange words and look them up in the vocabulary. We shall often find that we can guess the meaning of new words and get the hang of a sentence before referring to the vocabulary. Each new word should be memorized as we look it up, so that we do not have to waste time looking up the same word twice. Those who have studied a foreign language have had experience of dictionaries, and know that they do not give every single word we meet, particularly in the case of verbs, for only the infinitive is given, not the various parts. For instance, take the word *pɔsso* in the first sentence of the piece we are going to translate on page 84; we may guess that it must mean "can I". But we shall not find *pɔsso* in any dictionary, as it is part of an irregular verb, *potere*. We shall often meet verbs whose infinitives we do not know; if the verbs are regular, the infinitive is easily found, for the verb-ending tells us to which conjugation it belongs; but if they are irregular, the thing to do is to turn to the list of irregular verbs in the Appendix, page 214. Suppose we are hunting down *pɔsso*, then looking through all the verbs beginning with *pɔ-*, we shall soon find *potere* ("to be able"), with its irregular tenses, among which *pɔsso* stands out as the first person singular of the present indicative: our guess, "I can" or "can I" was correct.

Translation may be done in two ways: literal or free. A literal translation gives the meaning of the Italian, word for word, in English, and this results in English which reads very awkwardly—sometimes it will hardly make sense. A free translation is one which considers the meaning of the Italian sentence as a whole and then expresses that meaning in good English. When making our own translation it would be better to be rather literal at first, and not trouble too much about the sound of the English; after a little practice we shall soon be able to make our translation freer and pay more attention to the English style.

Before doing the translation we might learn some tenses of three of the irregular verbs which occur in it: *dovere*, *potere* and *volere*. These verbs are very often in use, for besides being main verbs—when they mean, respectively, "to owe", "to be able" and "to wish"—they are also used as a kind of auxiliary before an infinitive, when they have these meanings:

dovere = to be obliged to, to have to, must, ought;
potere = to be able (the idea of capability), can, could; and (the idea of possibility), may, might;
volere = to be willing, to want, will, would.

Each verb has an irregular present indicative:

dovere	*potere*	*volere*
I must, am obliged to, have to	I can, may, am able	I want, will, am willing
dɛvo or dɛbbo	pɔsso	vɔglio
dɛvi	puɔi	vuɔi
dɛve	puɔ	vuɔle
dobbiamo	possiamo	vogliamo
dovete	potete	volete
dɛvono or dɛbbono	pɔssono	vɔgliono

Note that *vuɔle* may drop its final *-e* before words beginning with a vowel or a consonant (except *s* impure): *vuɔl andare*, *vuɔl rimanere*, but *vuɔle studiare*.

Note, too, that each verb has a shortened infinitive stem to which the future and conditional endings are added: *dovrò, potrò, vorrò; dovrɛi, potrɛi, vorrɛi.*

Translation I

—Buɔn giorno, Signore, in che cɔsa pɔsso servirla? *—mi domandò l'impiegato quando entrai nell'ufficio del turismo italiano a Londra.

Non risposi subito, perché, sebbɛne † avessi studiato l'italiano, non l'avevo mai parlato, e la parɔle non mi venivano prontamente alle labbra. Ma, contento dell'occasione di esercitarmi nella lingua prima del mio viaggio in Italia, gli dissi in italiano, un po' timidamente:

—Buɔn giorno. Avrɛi bisogno di qualche informazione. Vorrɛi andare in Italia per le vacanze quest'estate, ma ho pɔco tɛmpo e denaro a mia disposizione.

—ɛ la prima vɔlta che va ‡ in Italia, Signore?—

—Sí, non ci sono mai stato.—

—Hɔ capito. Ma, prima di tutto, mi dica, ha il passapɔrto in rɛgola?—

—Sí, ɛ in rɛgola. Vɛngo or ora dall'ufficio passapɔrti e il cɔnsole italiano m'ha detto che non ɛ necessario un visto speciale.—

—Benissimo. Allora, quali città vorrɛbbe visitare? Lɛi s'interɛssa di arte? Dunque vorrà vedere Firɛnze, forse anche Pisa e Siɛna o Venɛzia? O ha l'intenzione di andare a Roma a visitare le antichità? Oppure di fare un giro per i laghi? O forse preferisce fermarsi in qualche stazione balneare? o in qualche luɔgo di villeggiatura in montagna? Agl'Inglesi piacciono molto le bellezze naturali, lo sɔ; e in Italia ci sono tanti bɛi posti . . . quali sono i Suɔi progɛtti, Signore?—

—Lɛi mi dovrɛbbe consigliare. Di arte non me ne intɛndo molto, dɛbbo confessarlo, e bɛn pɔco di antichità romane. Desideravo soprattutto visitare Firɛnze dove ɛra nata mia madre, e forse altre città di Toscana, e mi piacerɛbbe moltissimo vedɛr Venɛzia se c'ɛ tɛmpo e se il viaggio non costa trɔppo. Roma ɛ un po' trɔppo lontana; sarà per un'altra vɔlta.—

* The same punctuation marks are used in Italian as in English except that in Italian a dash is generally employed to denote conversation instead of quotation marks.

† *sebbɛne* (= although) is followed by the subjunctive.

‡ *va*—look up *andare* (irreg.).

When you have translated literally the foregoing passage, compare your version with the two in Part II, page 174, and after you have studied the notes given there, you will do the following exercise without much difficulty.

Vocabulary

gruccia (f.) = clothes-hanger   spesso = often
mare (m.) = sea
musica = music

Exercise 16

1. Where is he going for his holidays this summer?
2. He will go to Italy if the journey does not cost too much.
3. Does he speak Italian? Yes, he speaks it very well; he was born in Rome.
4. Do you want to go to the theatre today or tomorrow?
5. Tomorrow, please. I can't go today because Uncle arrives this evening and I shall have to go and meet him.
6. Good morning, madam. What can I do for you?
7. I should like to see some scarves, please.
8. Certainly, madam (say: very willingly). What colour would you like?
9. He often goes to the concert, but he is no judge of music.
10. When will you have finished with that book? I shall need it for next week. (Note: aver bisogno di.)
11. *We* are going to the sea this year for our holidays; and *you*, aren't you going? (Supply "there".)
12. No, this year we are going to spend our holidays in the mountains.
13. I need a coat-hanger. Can you give me one?
14. I am very thirsty ("I have much thirst"). Give me a glass of water, please.

LESSON XVII

IRREGULAR VERBS

IRREGULAR verbs are apt to worry people, for they seem to herald a long list of tiresome tenses to be learnt, when it would have been so much kinder of these verbs if they had made an effort to conform to the types we already know. A list of irregular verbs in an Italian grammar does seem rather long, as often between 200 and 300 verbs are given; but many of these are rare, and others are compounds from a shorter irregular verb conjugated like them. There are about fifty irregular verbs which must be learnt; but of these many are not original or unique—they have similarities with other irregular verbs: similarities which, if not of such a kind as to allow of the verbs being grouped together, are at any rate helpful when we have to commit them to memory. There is, too, the consoling thought that only one verb—*essere*—is irregular in all its tenses, and other irregular verbs—with the exception of four: *dare* (= to give), *fare* (= to do, to make), *stare* (= to stand, to be), and *dire* (= to say)—are *always* regular in certain parts. Therefore of the fifty or so which we must learn as we work through this book, we shall often be learning only a few parts, probably one tense only—the past definite—which will be irregular.

The parts which are always regular (except in *essere* and the four verbs just mentioned) are: the present participle, imperfect indicative, imperfect subjunctive, second person plural of the present indicative and of the imperative, and the second person singular and the first and second persons plural of the past definite. These will be seen from the conjugation of *porre* (= to put) which follows. The parts always regular are shown in italics; the changeable parts in ordinary printing.

Infinitive and Participles

| Porre | *ponendo* | posto |

Indicative Mood

Present	Imperfect	Past definite	Future
pongo	*ponevo*	posi	porrò
poni	*ponevi*	*ponesti*	porrai
pone	*poneva*	pose	porrà
poniamo	*ponevamo*	*ponemmo*	porremo
ponete	*ponevate*	*poneste*	porrete
pongono	*ponevano*	posero	porranno

Subjunctive Mood / Conditional / Imperative

Present	Imperfect (Past)	Conditional	Imperative
ponga	*ponessi*	porrei	
ponga	*ponessi*	porresti	poni
ponga	*ponesse*	porrebbe	
poniamo	*ponessimo*	porremmo	
poniate	*poneste*	porreste	*ponete*
pongano	*ponessero*	porrebbero	

Note that the infinitive of this verb *porre* is irregular, as it is a contracted form of *ponere*. In verbs with a contracted infinitive the present participle keeps the regular stem, in this case *pon-*. *Condurre* (= to lead) from *conducere* is a similar verb: it has *conducɛndo* for the present participle and *conducevo* is the imperfect. *Fare* and *dire* are contracted from *facere* and *dicere* respectively, and they have changed their conjugations: if you remember these points, the irregularities become more understandable.

The following notes may be of help in learning irregular verbs:

Future and Conditional.—The only irregularity is the contracted form of the infinitive to which the usual endings are added. The contracted form is always given in the list in the Appendix; where there is no form given, these tenses are quite regular.

Imperative.—The same form as the present indicative, except in the following verbs: three which have a form like the present subjunctive—*avere* (*abbi*, *abbiate*), *sapere* (*sappi*, *sappiate*) and *volere* (*vɔgli*, *vogliate*)—and five which have an irregular singular —*andare* (*va'*), *dare* (*da'*), *fare* (*fa'*), *stare* (*sta'*) and *dire* (*di'*).*

Past Definite.—The tense which is most frequently irregular, but only in three persons: first and third persons singular and third plural. The irregular endings are the SAME for all irregular verbs: first singular, *-i*; third singular, *-e*; and third plural, *-ero*. When given the first person singular of this tense, you can form the other two irregular persons by changing the *-i* to *-e* for the third singular, and adding *-ro* to the third singular to form the third plural.

Example: Porre: posi, pose, posero.

Except in the three verbs ɛssere, dare and stare, the other persons of this tense are always regular.

Examples of the past definite:

Sapere = to know	*Fare* = to make
(stem *sap-*)	(stem *fac-*)
Past def. *sɛppi*	Past def. *feci*
sɛppi	feci
sapesti	facesti
sɛppe	fece
sapemmo	facemmo
sapeste	faceste
sɛppero	fecero

* Conjunctive pronouns, except *gli*, double their initial consonant when added to any form of a verb ending in an accented vowel. These irregular imperatives are such forms:

dammi = give me   *fàllo* = do it   *dillo* = say it

Decidere = to decide	*Vedere* = to see
(stem *decid-*)	(stem *ved-*)
Past def. *decisi*	Past def. *vidi*
decisi	vidi
· decidesti	vedesti
decise	vide
decidemmo	vedemmo
decideste	vedeste
decisero	videro

The majority of verbs of the second conjugation are irregular
only in this tense and the past participle. It would be a good
plan to practise with some more verbs, such as *chiudere,
giungere, leggere, mettere, rimanere* and *scendere*. Look up their
past definite tense (first person) in the Appendix, and then
continue the whole tense, as in the examples above; at the same
time note their past participles.

Translation II

—Bene, Signore. Lei decide dunque per Firenze,—continuò
l'impiegato, mentre apriva un cassetto e tirava fuori diversi
fogli e libri e un'enorme carta geografica.

—E sarebbe possibile andare a Firenze—chiesi,—passando
per Genova e Pisa, e poi tornare per un'altra strada?—

—Possibilissimo.—

—Che direbbe se andassi * da Firenze a Venezia, poi da
Venezia a Milano, e nel viaggio di ritorno facessi * un giro per i
laghi? So che il biglietto di andata e ritorno è piú a buon
mercato; ma con quel giro, dovrei spendere molto di piú?—

—No, no. Ecco qui la cosa che fa per lei; un biglietto circolare turistico, valevole per 45 giorni; e le conviene, perché le dà
una riduzione del cinquanta per cento, purché si fermi in Italia
per un periodo di almeno dodici giorni.—

—Va proprio bene per me, perché mi fermerò almeno due
settimane, forse anche tre.—

—Vediamo un po' la carta geografica per fissare piú precisamente il suo itinerario. Dunque, partendo da Londra la
mattina presto, lei arriva a Parigi la sera verso le sei. Lí avrà
il tempo di mangiare prima di ripartire col rapido Parigi-Roma:
proprio la sua strada: Modane-Torino-Genova-Pisa. È un ottimo
treno. Arriva alla frontiera italiana all'alba, e a Pisa nel
pomeriggio. E col biglietto circolare lei può fermarsi quando e

---

* A condition uncertain in the future; this use of the subjunctive is
explained on page 146.

dove vuole, e può viaggiare con qualsiasi treno: quindi lasciar Pisa quando vuole e fermarsi a Firenze quanto le pare, naturalmente sempre nel termine dei quarantacinque giorni.—

—Capisco.—

—Dopo Firenze il suo percorso è questo: Bologna, Venezia, Milano e poi Como e Lugano dove prenderà il direttissimo per Parigi. Così entra in Italia per il passo del Moncenisio ed esce per il San Gottardo. Va bene così?—

—Grazie, va benissimo. Vorrebbe prepararmi il biglietto? Partirò venerdí prossimo e viaggerò in seconda.—

—ecco fatto. Questo è il biglietto; e qui c'è anche un libro che forse le sarà utile: "Annuario alberghi d'Italia", e una rivista turistica con altre indicazioni interessanti.—

—Ben gentile, mille grazie.—

—Niente, Signore prego. Buon viaggio e buon divertimento.—

Learn, from the Appendix, the irregular verbs *andare* and *dare* and then do the following exercise:

Vocabulary

cane (m.) = dog
cinema (m.), cinematografo = cinema
colletto = collar
striscia = stripe

marino = of the sea; blu marino = navy blue
scuro = dark
terzo = third
solo = alone, only

Exercise 17

1. As he was speaking he opened a drawer and took out a large map.

2. Couldn't you come with us to the cinema? They say there is a very good film.

3. A return ticket to London, please—second class. Must I buy a ticket for the dog, too? Yes, madam, the dog must have a ticket.

4. He didn't want to come and talk to you yesterday; today he is glad to. (Say: to do it.)

5. Did you put Uncle's collars in this drawer? No, he put them there himself.

6. Have you ever been to London, madam? Yes, I have been there many times.

7. Has he not arrived yet? No, Mary went to meet him, but she came back alone.

8. Perhaps he has gone by another road? Yes, it is possible.

9. Yesterday he got up at seven o'clock, but remained in his room reading (say: to read = *a leggere*) the newspaper, and only came down at ten for his coffee. (Say: for to take his coffee.)

10. Give me the map a moment, please; I want to look for Siena.

11. Good morning. I want a tie to wear with this suit. I have just the thing for you, sir. This navy blue with yellow stripe will go very well with the dark green of your suit.

12. You ought to buy a circular ticket. It is the cheapest; and you can stop where and when you like and for as long as you like.

LESSON XVIII

COMPARATIVES AND SUPERLATIVES

WHEN we wish to compare two persons or two things, we use the comparative. In English we form the comparative by adding a suffix *-r* or *-er* to the adjective, or by putting the words "more" or "less" in front of it: great, greater; beautiful, more beautiful. Italian uses the second way, and puts the words *piú* (= more) and *meno* (= less) before the adjective.

Il poliziotto è piú intelligente della cuoca = The policeman is cleverer than the cook.

Il poliziotto è meno furbo del postino = The policeman is less cunning than the postman.

The translation of "than" into Italian may present difficulty: it is *di* or *che*. *Di* before a noun (as in the above sentences), before a pronoun and before a number:

Tu sei piú alto di me = You are taller than I.

Hai delle mele? Sí, ne ho piú di dieci = Have you any apples? Yes, I've more than ten.

But if two nouns which are both subjects or objects of the same verb are compared, "than" is *che*:

C'erano piú signori che signore = There were more gentlemen than ladies.

"Than" is *che* before all other parts of speech:

Before an adjective:

La ragazza è piú bella che intelligente = The girl is more beautiful than clever.

Before an adverb:

Meglio tardi che mai = Better late than never.

Before an infinitive:

Lui ama piú leggere che scrivere = He likes reading better than writing.

Before a preposition:

C'è piú acqua nel bicchiere che nella bottiglia = There's more water in the glass than in the bottle.

If "than" is preceded by *piuttosto* (= rather), it is also *che*:

Piuttosto la morte che il disonore = Rather death than dishonour.

And, finally, if "than" introduces a whole clause, it is either *di quel* or *che non*, and is followed by the subjunctive if implying uncertainty.*

La lezione è piú facile che non si pensi = The lesson is easier than one thinks.

In English we also compare things by "as . . . as" and "so . . . as". In Italian *cosí . . . come* and *tanto . . . quanto* both mean "as . . . as" and "so . . . as" (our "so . . . as" is simply the negative form of "as . . . as", and the two Italian expressions may be either affirmative or negative):

Lui è tanto alto quanto lei = He is as tall as she.
Il postino non è cosí ricco come il poliziotto = The postman is not so rich as the policeman.
Non parla l'inglese tanto bene quanto l'italiano = He doesn't speak English as well as Italian.

The first part of the comparison *cosí* and *tanto* may be omitted:

Lui è alto quanto lei.

In all these sentences *tanto* and *quanto* are adverbs; but they may also be adjectives, qualifying nouns, and in this case they mean: "as much as", "as many as", "so much as", "so many as":—

* See page 143, clause type no. 7.

Ho tanto denaro quanto Lɛi = I have as much money as you.

Non ho scritto tante lɛttere quante Lɛi = I have not written so many letters as you.

In Italian there are two superlatives: the relative, a comparison of more than two things, as in English, and the absolute, which has no corresponding form in English and which we must translate by "very" or "exceedingly". The relative superlative is formed by placing the definite article before the comparatives *piú* and *meno*:

Questa torre è la piú alta della città = This tower is the highest in the town.

Questa è la piú alta torre ⎫ = ⎰This is the highest (or
Questa è la torre piú alta ⎭   ⎱ higher) tower.

Note.—1. There is no difference in form between the comparative with the definite article and the relative superlative, but the meaning is always clear, for the speaker always knows whether he is comparing one thing with another or one thing with many others.

2. When the superlative follows a noun which already has a definite article, no other article is required (see the third sentence).

3. After the superlative "in" is rendered by *di*.

We have already met the absolute superlative in the words *benissimo* and *possibilissimo*. It is formed by adding *-issimo* to the adjective or adverb after the last vowel has been dropped.

Lui è poverissimo = He is extremely poor.

A word ending in *-co* or *-go* preserves the hard sound of the *c* or *g* before the ending *-issimo* by inserting an *h*: *ricco, ricchissimo*; and five adjectives ending in *-re* or *-ro* have an irregular ending in *-ɛrrimo* instead of *-issimo*:

acre = sour	acɛrrimo
cɛlebre = famous	celebɛrrimo
integro = righteous	integɛrrimo
misero = wretched	misɛrrimo
salubre = healthful	salubɛrrimo

To finish our lesson on the comparison we must learn the following irregular comparisons:

Positive	Comparative	Rel. Superlative	Abs. Superlative
buono = good	migliore	il migliore	ottimo
cattivo = bad	peggiore	il peggiore	pessimo
grande = big	maggiore	il maggiore	massimo
piccolo = small	minore	il minore	minimo
alto = tall	superiore	il superiore	supremo
basso = low	inferiore	l'inferiore	infimo

These six adjectives also have the regular comparatives and superlatives. Slight differences of meaning in regular and irregular forms should be noted: *più grande* and *più piccolo* mean "larger" and "smaller", and *maggiore* and *minore* usually "older" and "younger"; *più alto* and *più basso* have the literal meaning "higher" and "lower", while *superiore* and *inferiore* the figurative: "superior" and "inferior" (although they, too, may have the literal sense).

Study the two irregular verbs *fare* and *stare*.

Translation III

Di solito non dormo bene in treno: ma forse perché questa volta ero stanco o avevo mangiato troppo bene al ristorante della stazione di Parigi (ci si mangia divinamente, ma si paga anche, profumatamente); o forse perché ero tutto solo nello scompartimento e mi ero potuto sdraiare sui cuscini come in un letto; il fatto sta che, tolte le scarpe, la cravatta e la giacchetta, appena posi il capo sul guanciale—noleggiato per cento franchi alla stazione,— m'addormentai profondamente e continuai a dormire come un ghiro tutta la notte.

Mi svegliai che era già giorno; il treno andava rallentando e finalmente si fermò. Guardando fuori del finestrino vidi sul marciapiede di una stazione intermedia un piccolo gruppo d'impiegati della ferrovia, facchini e soldati, con due carabinieri e diverse altre guardie, che ridevano e scherzavano fra di loro, con l'aria di non far nessum caso di noi e del nostro treno. Ma un fischio acuto emesso dal rapido Parigi—Roma sciolse quel gruppo. Uno di loro, il capostazione (lo si riconosceva dal berretto rosso) andò a parlare col macchinista, mentre tutti gli altri, sempre parlando e ridendo, salirono sul treno. L'orologio della stazione segnava le cinque. Soltanto le cinque del mattino e già faceva caldo e c'era un bel sole, un cielo azzurro e sereno e l'aria era così mite e dolce! Tirai fuori l'orologio per regolarlo, ma in quel momento, qualcuno aprì bruscamente la porta del mio scompartimento, e gridò con una voce rauca ma forte: —Signori, la dogana italiana, preparino il bagaglio.— Tre uomini in uniforme mi stavano davanti sulla porta.

Vocabulary

carrozza-letti = sleeping-car
orologio = clock
orologio da tasca = watch
passeggiata = walk

fare una passeggiata = to go for a walk
fare male (followed by *a*) = to hurt, harm, pain
presentare = to introduce, to present

Exercise 18

1. Good morning, sir. And how are you today? Thank you, today I am not very well; I am very tired.
2. Did you sleep well in the train yesterday? Yes, thanks, I slept very well indeed. I travelled in a sleeping-car. (I *have* travelled . . .)
3. Is the food good at that restaurant where you went yesterday? Yes, it is very good, but a bit dear. (Say: "Does one eat well at . . .")
4. Are you going to the station already? But the train only arrives at ten.
5. We have had a very good journey. (Say: "We have made . . .") There was nobody in our compartment, and we slept very well.
6. What lovely weather it is! Shall we go for a walk along the beach?
7. He closed the door and windows of the compartment, took off his tie, jacket and shoes, put his money, passport and watch under the pillow, and having stretched himself out on the seat, he fell asleep in a moment.
8. Where are you getting out, madam? I am getting out at Florence; I got in the train at Paris.
9. You are taller than I; but John is taller than you.
10. Who is the cleverest in that family? The cook; she's cleverer than you think.
11. That is the richest man in town! Is he a friend of yours? Will you introduce me to him?
12. I have not as much money as he, but I have more than you.
13. I do not want to go for a walk; my foot hurts (to me hurts the foot).

LESSON XIX

NUMERALS

WE have learnt the cardinal numbers up to 20. After refreshing our memory (pp. 16–17), we may continue with the following:

21 = ventuno		50 = cinquanta	
22 = ventidue		60 = sessanta	
23 = ventitré		70 = settanta	
24 = ventiquattro		80 = ottanta	
25 = venticinque		90 = novanta	
26 = ventisei		100 = cento	
27 = ventisette		101 = cento uno or centuno	
28 = ventotto		102 = cento due or centodue	
29 = ventinove		180 = cento ottanta	
30 = trenta		200 = duecento or dugento	
31 = trentuno		1,000 = mille	
32 = trentadue		2,000 = due mila	
38 = trentotto		100,000 = cento mila	
40 = quaranta		1,000,000 = un milione	

Note the following points:

1. *Venti, trenta*, etc., drop the final vowel when combining with *uno* and *otto*.

2. The accent is used on the final *e* of any number ending in *-tre* except *tre* itself: *cinquantatré*.

3. When a noun immediately follows *ventuno* and compounds of *-uno*, it must be in the singular, unless preceded by an adjective: *quarantuna lira* (= 41 lire); *trentun cavallo* (= 31 horses); but *trentun buoni cavalli*.

4. Eleven hundred, twelve hundred, etc., are always translated one thousand one hundred, one thousand two hundred, etc.; *mille novecento* = nineteen hundred.

5. No article is required before *cento* and *mille*.

6. *Milione* is a noun, and has the preposition *di* before the noun to which it refers:

tre milioni di tonnellate = three million tons.

7. In compound numbers no conjunction is required:

eighteen hundred and eighty six = mille ottocento ottantasei.

Dates are expressed as follows: the article *il* with the cardinal number (except for the 1st of the month, when *primo* (= first) is used), then the month, then the year. Never translate *on*:

il tre giugno mille novecento trentanove = on the 3rd of June, 1939.

If the month is not mentioned, the article is used with the year: 1494 = *il* 1494 (*mille quattrocento novantaquattro*); in 1910 = *nel* 1910. We might look back a moment to page 17 to revise the days and the months; and also learn the seasons: spring, etc. *la primavera, l'estate, l'autunno, l'inverno*. Note that a capital letter is not required for the days, nor for the months, nor the seasons:

Qual' è la data di oggi? Oggi è lunedí il 28 aprile = What is the date today? Today is Monday the 28th April.

Age is expressed by the verb *avere*:

Quanti anni hai? (lit.: How many years have you?) = How old are you?
Ho dodici anni (lit.: I have twelve years) = I am twelve.

The word for birthday is either *giorno natalizio* or *compleanno*, the second word being the more usual. This means the day on which one finishes one's year, from the verb *compiere* = to fulfil, to complete, and *anno* = year. This verb is also used to express age:

Il tre luglio compirà venticinque anni = On the third of July he'll be twenty-five.
Ha compiuto vent'anni il sedici del mese scorso = He was twenty on the 16th of last month.

Measurements are expressed by the verb *essere*, but the adjective comes before the measurement:

La torre è alta sessanta piedi = The tower is 60 feet high.

If the measurement is expressed by a noun: "The tower is 60 feet in height", the Italian equivalent is: *La torre è dell'altezza di* 60 *piedi*, or *La torre ha l'altezza di* 60 *piedi*, or again: *è di* 60 *piedi di altezza*. Long is *lungo*; wide = *largo*, deep = *profondo*, thick = *spesso*; and the nouns corresponding to these adjectives are: *lunghezza, larghezza, profondità* and *spessore* (m.).

Study the irregular verbs *dovere, potere* and *volere* (all tenses).

Translation IV

—Lɛi,— mi chiɛse il piú vicino dei tre, —Ha spedito il bagaglio?—

—No, l'ho tutto qui,— risposi prontamente, tirando giú dalla rete la mia unica valigia. Siccome ɛro venuto in Italia per poco tɛmpo, non avevo bisogno di bauli.

—Ha soltanto bagaglio a mano questo signore,— allora due dei doganiɛri se ne andarono, sɛnza dubbio a cercare altre vittime, mentre il tɛrzo, rimasto solo con me, riprese:

—Ha qualchecosa da dichiarare, Signore?—

—No, niɛnte.—

—Proprio niɛnte? Niɛnte tabacco, sigarette, sigari, cioccolata. . . .— una pausa —. . . articoli di seta? . . . profumi?—

Abbozzai un sorriso.

—Ma che, diamine; che cosa me ne farɛi io, di profumi?—

Eh, Signore, non si sa mai! Non si sa mai! Un regalino per qualche amica italiana forse?— suggerí; poi, con un grosso pezzo di gesso bianco segnò qualche sua linea misteriosa sulla mia valigia.

—No, Signore, lasoi stare,— disse, quando io feci per aprirla. —Non importa.—

—Mille grazie,— risposi io, contɛnto di non dover aprire la valigia e mettere tutto in disordine.

—Viɛne a passare le vacanze in Italia, non è vero? Bɛne. Bravo. Si divɛrta! Buon giorno.— E se ne andò finalmente anche lui.

Ma appena fuori nel corridoio, fece un passo indiɛtro e, tutto sorridɛnte, s'affacciò ancora una volta alla porta dicɛndo:

—E buona fortuna . . . a quel profumo!—

Ascoltando quel burlone d'un doganiɛre non mi ɛro accorto che il trɛno ɛra di nuovo in moto, e con sorpresa, guardando fuori del finestrino, vidi che già si passava velocemente fra alte montagne. Mi accomodai nel mio posto d'angolo a contemplare il paesaggio. La strada ferrata, fiancheggiata da una parte e dall'altra da precipizî rocciosi, seguiva il corso di un torrɛnte; uno di quei tanti corsi d'acqua che, sorgɛndo dalle Alpi si rovɛsciano in cascatɛlle giú per i ripidi declivi delle lunghe valli strette per sboccare in quelli piú grandi, tributarî del Po. Questo ɛra un torrɛnte impetuoso; ogni tanto s'udiva lo scroscio delle sue acque al di sopra del rumore del trɛno; e ci scorreva allato, come se volesse dire: —Arriverò io prima di voi.—

D

Vocabulary

capra = goat
carbone (m.) = coal
contadino -a = peasant
metro quadrato = sq. metre

mondo = world
pecora = sheep
superficie (f.) = surface, area
scoprire (irreg.) = to discover

Exercise 19

1. Have you sent three trunks or four for that gentleman with the beard?
2. Three only; I shall have to forward the other tomorrow.
3. There was once upon a time (*c'era una volta*) a peasant woman who had a hundred sheep, twenty-eight cows, fifty-five pigs, nineteen goats, a dog and a cat, and she was very happy.
4. What is the date today? It is the 4th of July 1940.
5. In what year did Columbus * discover America? In 1492, wasn't it? (Say: is it not true?)
6. How old are you, child? I shall be six next Monday, miss.
7. When is your birthday? On the 9th of May.
8. Have my luggage taken up to my room immediately, please.
9. Six million tons of coal pass through this port every week (through = *per*).
10. The largest church in the world is St. Peter's at Rome; it has an area of 15,160 square metres, and its dome is more than 130 metres high. (Say: *the* dome.)

LESSON XX

NUMERALS (*CONTD.*)

Ordinal Numbers

1st = primo	13th = tredicesimo
2nd = secondo	14th = quattordicesimo
3rd = terzo	15th = quindicesimo
4th = quarto	20th = ventesimo
5th = quinto	21st = ventunesimo
6th = sesto	22nd = ventiduesimo
7th = settimo	30th = trentesimo
8th = ottavo	101st = centesimo primo
9th = nono	102nd = centesimo secondo

* Without any article.

10th = dɛcimo	111th = centundicɛṣimo
11th = undicɛṣimo or dɛcimo primo	1000th = millɛṣimo
	2000th = duemillɛṣimo
12th = dodicɛṣimo or dɛcimo secondo	

Note the following:

1. After the first ten ordinal numbers the others can be formed by dropping the last vowel of the cardinal number and adding -ɛṣimo. But the last vowel of 23, 33, etc., being stressed, it is kept: *ventitréɛṣimo* = 23rd.

2. After the first ten there is a second form: *dɛcimo primo* (lit.: 10th 1st, *i.e.*, 11th) which may be used for any number: *ventɛṣimo ̵ɛrzo* = 23rd.

3. Ordinal numbers are adjectives, and agree as such: *la seconda lezione.*

4. They are used, without any article, after names of rulers and the words chapter, volume, canto, book, etc.: *Carlo quinto* = Charles the fifth; *Capitolo quarto* = the fourth chapter.

5. The ordinal number is used for the *first* of the month in dates: *il primo maggio* = on the first of May.

6. It is used when speaking of centuries: *Il sɛcolo quarto* = the 4th century. After the 10th century (*il sɛcolo dɛcimo*) the form *dɛcimo primo*, etc., is employed rather than *undicɛṣimo.* But from the 13th century onwards it is more usual to find the following expressions, instead of the ordinal numbers:

13th century	= il duecɛnto	17th century	= il seicɛnto
14th „	= il trecɛnto	18th „	= il settecɛnto
15th „	= il quattrocɛnto	19th „	= l'ottocɛnto
16th „	= il cinquecɛnto	20th „	= il novecɛnto

Collective Numerals.—Study the following: *un paio* = a pair (irregular plural: *due paia*); *una doẓẓina* = a dozen, *una decina* = about ten, *una quindicina* = about fifteen, *una ventina* = a score, *una trentina* = about thirty (forty, fifty, etc., have in Italian a corresponding collective number formed with the ending -*ina*); *un centinaio* = about 100, un *migliaio* = about 1000 (the last two have irregular plurals: *centinaia* = hundreds, *migliaia* = thousands). Note that all these words are nouns, and therefore require *di* before the following noun: *un paio di scarpe, una cinquantina di persone.*

Fractions are expressed as in English, a cardinal for the numerator and an ordinal for the denominator: *due quinti* = two-fifths. Half (noun) is *la metà,* (adjective) *mɛẓẓo.*

Useful Phrases of Time

Fra un'ora = In an hour.

Il mio orologio fa le cinque e mezzo = It is 5.30 by my watch.

Il mio orologio va bene = My watch is right.

Quest'orologio è avanti e quello è indietro = This watch is fast and that is slow.

Il mio orologio va avanti cinque minuti al giorno = My watch gains five minutes a day.

Quell'orologio rimane indietro dieci minuti al giorno = That clock loses ten minutes a day.

oggi a otto = today week, oggi a quindici = today fortnight.

Una settimana fa = A week ago.

Domani a quindici = Tomorrow fortnight.

Una quindicina di giorni = A fortnight.

Suonano le undici (*ore*, "hours", is understood) = Eleven is striking.

L'orologio batte le undici = The clock is striking eleven.

è un'uomo sulla cinquantina = He is a man nearing fifty.

Sapere and *Conoscere*. Both these verbs mean "to know"; but *conoscere* means to know in the sense of "being acquainted with", and *sapere* "to know a fact", and also "to know how to":

Conosci quella signorina dai capelli biondi? = Do you know that young lady with the fair hair?

Lui conosce l'Italia molto bene, c'è stato diverse volte = He knows Italy very well, he's been there many times.

Sa parlare bene italiano? = Can he speak Italian well?

Sa Lei chi è quella signora, per favore? = Do you know who that lady is, please?

Sa che Giovanni è tornato? = Do you know that John has come back?

Study the following irregular verbs: *conoscere, crescere, morire, nascere* and *sapere*.

Translation V

Ora la valle si allargava: montagne nude e rocciose davano luogo a colline coperte di pini e di abeti; poi queste alla pianura coi suoi vigneti, con le case coloniche, e i campi biondi di grano e di granturco già maturo. Ciò che mi sorprendeva di piú era il poco terreno tenuto a pascolo; quasi tutto era coltivato: un succedersi di campi gialli, svariati qua e là dalle ombre degli ulivi e di loppi, coi loro festoni di viti. M'interessava molto la coltivazione della vite. I tralci si arrampicavano su per il tronco e per i rami di alberi bassi, quali i loppi e gli olmi, e penzolavano in bei festoni da un albero all'altro; di sotto cresceva qualche pianta verde, che non potevo distinguere bene. —Dev'essere molto fertile questo terreno,— pensai, —E la gente lo vuol sfruttare il piú possibile.— Ma quanto diverso questo paesaggio dal nostro! Da princípio i colori e la luce mi sembravano troppo forti; sentivo la mancanza del bel verde dei pascoli inglesi. —E dove sono le vacche?—pensai. —Ah, eccole.— In lontananza ce n'erano due bianche; e mi alzai per vedere meglio; ma mi maravigliai che, invece di stare tranquillamente a ruminare, le due bestie lavorassero. —Ma che vacche!— Erano due enormi buoi aggiogati a un carro carico di fieno. —Allora il bue s'adopra qui come animale da soma,— pensai; —E anche il mulo!— perché, passando vicino a un'autostrada, vidi parecchi carri tirati da muli; e non tardarono ad apparire automobili, autobus, case alte e fabbriche. Ci s'avvicinava a qualche grande città.

—Giornali, riviste, Domenica del Corriere!— Aprii il finestrino, e, chiamato il giornalaio, comprai un giornale per trentacinque lire e una rivista per centocinquanta. era ancora presto, ma nella stazione c'era molta gente. —Forse vanno già a lavorare,— pensai, ricordandomi che in Italia si comincia il lavoro piú presto che da noi, perché col gran caldo che fa nei mesi estivi hanno bisogno di riposarsi durante il giorno. Cosí molti negozi e uffici sono aperti dalle otto al mezzogiorno, e poi chiudono per riaprire solamente alle tre o alle quattro, e rimangono aperti la sera fino alle otto, e in alcuni casi, anche piú tardi. Le ore dei pasti sono quindi alquanto diverse che da noi. Si può dire che gl'Italiani mangiano due volte al giorno: pranzano all'una e cenano alle otto. I piú non mangiano la mattina presto; la loro prima colazione consiste di caffè e latte e nient'altro; ma mangiano bene al pranzo e alla cena. Ciò non toglie però che vadano spessìssimo ai caffè, tanto di mattino che di sera, come io venni a sapere piú tardi.

Vocabulary

chilometro = kilometre	produrre (irreg.) = to produce
domanda = question	stare (irreg.) per = to be about to, to be going to
est = east	
ovest = west	
persona = person	improvvisamente = suddenly
Adriatico = Adriatic	magro = thin

Exercise 20

1. That gentleman has received three trunks, but not the fourth.
2. The river Po is the longest river in Italy; it is more than 600 km. long.
3. It rises in the Piedmontese Alps, crosses a very fertile plain, and, flowing from west to east, it has its mouth in the Adriatic Sea.
4. Petrarch (say: *the* Petrarch, *il Petrarca*) was born in 1304 and died in 1374; he was only seventeen in 1321 when Dante (without article) died. Dante was born in 1265.
5. Do you know who that lady is? No, sir. You are the third person who has asked me that question. (Say: the third person to make me that question.)
6. Have you bought me two dozen eggs? No, I couldn't buy two dozen; I got only about twenty. (Say: *found* about twenty.)
7. How much does your watch gain in a day? It doesn't gain; it loses ten minutes a day.
8. What was yesterday's date? It was the 10th of June, 1941.
9. The year begins on the 1st of January and finishes on the 31st of December.
10. Henry VIII had six wives; but not all at the same time.
11. What a lovely vineyard! Yes, it produces thousands and thousands of bottles of wine a year.
12. It was striking twelve a year ago this evening, and I was just about to go to bed, when suddenly the door of my room was opened, and that tall thin man stood before me.

LESSON XXI

ADVERBS—ORTHOGRAPHIC CHANGES IN VERBS

WE are already familiar with every kind of adverb, for we have used the following:

Adverbs of manner: come, già, molto, così, bene, quasi;
Adverbs of place: dove, vi, ci, davanti, dappertutto, lí, là;
Adverbs of time: quando, sempre, oggi, mai;
Adverbs of quantity: molto, tanto, troppo, poco, soltanto;
Adverbs of affirmation and negation: sí, no, non;
Adverbial expressions: appena, di solito, da principio.

Position of Adverbs.—Looking back over the previous exercises, we see that unless the adverb begins a clause, it is generally placed immediately after the verb—with the exception of *non*, which always precedes a verb. When the verb is a compound tense, the adverb nearly always follows the past participle, with the exception of the following: (1) the conjunctive adverbs *vi* and *ci*, which precede both parts of the verb; and (2) *già, mai, più, sempre* and sometimes *ancora*, which may come *between* both parts of the verb:

Non l'ho mai veduto = I have never seen it.
Ha sempre parlato così = He has always spoken like that.

Having gathered together these few points, we may add the following:

Adverbs of Place.—*Qui* and *qua*, both meaning "here", refer to something near the person who speaks: *costì* and *costà*, "there", to something near the person addressed, and *lì* and *là*, "there", to something far away from both. (Note the connection between these and the three demonstrative adjectives: *questo, codesto* and *quello*, see page 43.)

Adverbs of Quantity.—*Solo*, besides being an adjective meaning "only", "alone", is also an adverb meaning "only", used in place of *soltanto* or *solamente*. "Only" can also be rendered by *non* before the verb and *che* after it:

Non ne abbiamo che due = We have only two.

Adverbs of Manner are also formed by adding *-mente* to the feminine singular of an adjective or a participle (as we add "-ly": slow, slowly):

fortunato = lucky	fortunatamente = luckily
felice = happy	felicemente = happily
deciso = decided (resolute)	decisamente = decidedly (resolutely)

Adjectives ending in *-le* or *-re*, preceded by a vowel, drop the final vowel before adding *-mente*: *regolare* = regular, *regolarmente*. When the *-le* and *-re* are preceded by a consonant, they keep the final vowel in the ordinary way: *acre* = harsh, *acremente* = harshly.

The form in *-mente* should not be used too often, from the point of view of style and the unpleasant sound many "*-mente's*" will produce. Instead a phrase such as *in un modo* or *in una maniera* ("in a way", "in a manner") is used with an adjective: *in un modo corraggioso* = courageously; or else *con* with a noun: *con corraggio*.

To avoid too often a recurrence of long words in *-mente*, an adjective (masculine singular form) is sometimes used instead of an adverb:

> Parlare chiaro = to speak distinctly
> Parlare forte = to speak loudly
> Parlare piano = to speak softly
> Andar diritto = to walk straight on
> Guardare fisso = to stare fixedly
> Veder chiaro = to see clearly

Comparison of Adverbs.—Adverbs are compared like adjectives:

Lui corre piú rapidamente di me = He runs faster than I.

Ma lei corre il piú rapidamente di tutti = But she runs the fastest of all.

There is also an absolute superlative of adverbs, which is not very much used: *-mente* is added to the feminine singular superlative of the adjective: *ricco, ricchissimo, ricchissimamente*.

Four adverbs have irregular comparatives and superlatives:

Positive	Comparative	Rel. Superlative	Abs. Superlative
bene = well	meglio	il meglio	ottimamente / benissimo
male = badly	peggio	il peggio	pessimamente / malissimo
molto = very	piú	il piú	moltissimo
poco = little	meno	il meno	pochissimo

Orthographic Changes in Certain Verbs.—Certain letters—*c* and *g*, for example—vary in their pronunciation according to the vowel which follows them. This must be remembered when dealing with certain verbs. A verb like *cercare*, for example, which has the hard *c* in the infinitive, must add an *h* to its stem before endings which begin with *e* or *i*, if it is to preserve this hard sound. Thus the present indicative becomes: *cerco, cerchi, cerca, cerchiamo, cercate, cercano,* and the future *cercherò*, etc. The same thing happens in verbs ending in *-gare*: *paghi, paghiamo, pagherò*. The rule is therefore that verbs ending in *-care* and *-gare* insert an *h* after the *c* and *g* whenever these letters come before *e* and *i*. Verbs in *-ciare* and *-giare* drop the *i* before an *e* or another *i*:

lasciare = to let, leave   lasci, lasciamo, lasceremo
mangiare = to eat   mangi, mangiamo, mangeremo

while verbs in *-iare* drop the *i* before another *i* only:

pigliare = to catch: pigli, pigliamo; but: piglieremo.

All these verbs are first conjugation verbs. Other conjugations are not so particular about the preservation of the sound of the infinitive; look up, for example, the present indicative of l*ɛggere*, which has the soft sound in four persons and the hard sound in two. The *only* orthographic change in verbs of the second conjugation is this: verbs in *-cere* or *-gere* insert an *i* before the *u* of the past participle: *piacere* = to please, *piaciuto* = pleased. There are no such changes in the third conjugation.

Study these irregular verbs: *rimanere*, *vedere*, *venire* and *vivere*.

Translation VI

—In carrozza, Signori, in carrozza!— e di nuovo si partí. Questa volta non ɛro piú solo. Due uomini, uno giovane, l'altro sulla cinquantina vennero a sedersi nel mio scompartimento. Il piú vecchio, di colorito molto scuro, aveva gli occhi e i capɛlli neri; il giovane invece, con capɛlli biondi e occhi azzurri, poteva ɛssere inglese. Erano commessi viaggiatori, a quanto sembrava, e parlavano ad alta voce e animatamente; ma sɛmpre in piemonteṣe, dialetto cosí divɛrso dall'italiano, che io non li potei capire. Lɛssi un po' il giornale; non c'ɛra niɛnte di speciale e in poco piú di due ore eravamo a Gɛnova.

—Gelati, biscotti, caramɛlle, uva fresca, cestini da viaggio!— Mi affacciai al finestrino. Che rumore! Che folla! Gɛnte che saliva; gɛnte che scendeva; gɛnte venuta a salutare chi arrivava o a dare gli ultimi addii a chi partiva; e nella calca facchini con bagagli sulle spalle, facɛntisi * avanti a forza di spinte, non meno dei giornalai, dei gelatiɛri e dei venditori di dolci e di bibite. Finalmente riuscii a richiamare l'attenzione di uno di questi e a comprare un cestino, molto a buon mercato, in verità, perché lo pagai solo 500 lire, e dentro c'ɛra un piatto di maccheroni caldi, due fettone di vitɛllo arrosto, prosciutto, formaggio, frutta, biscotti, due panini e perfino un fiaschettino di vino rosso. Avevo una fame da lupi; ma ɛra ancora un po' prɛsto per far colazione.

—Buon appetito, Signore,—mi disse con un sorriso colui che occupava il posto di faccia (il trɛno ɛra oramai complɛto e nel

* Verbal adjective from *farsi*.

mio scompartimento non c'erano piú posti liberi). —Grazie,
altrettanto,—risposi, vedendo che cominciava a mangiare
anche lui. Facevano altrettanto i miei altri compagni di viaggio,
alcuni dei quali, indovinando che ero forestiere, m'indicavano
tutto ciò che potesse interessarmi. —Questo è il golfo della
Spezia, dove morí affogato il poeta Shelley;— mi dissero. In
distanza biancheggiavano le montagne di Carrara con le
famose cave di marmo. Piú tardi, mentre si passava per una
bella pineta, mi chiesero se amassi la musica e mi dissero che lí
c'era la casa e la tomba del compositore Giacomo Puccini.

Vocabulary

pollo = chicken	mancare = to lack
radio (f.) = wireless	trasmettere (irreg.) = to transmit
	voltarsi = to turn
calvo = bald	
corto = short	a destra = to the right
grasso = fat	cortesemente = politely
	fino a = as far as, up to

Exercise 21

1. Do not take any notice of what she says; she has always
   spoken like that.
2. Yesterday he was a bit better, but today he is worse. Have
   they called a doctor?
3. Which is the shortest way to the station, please? (Say: for
   to go to . . .)
4. Keep straight on, sir, as far as the church, and there you
   turn to the right, and you will find the station opposite.
5. Speak quietly; can't you see that they are listening to us?
   (If you use progressive tense, put pronoun object before
   the auxiliary.)
6. What time do you have breakfast? At eight, usually; but I
   don't take much—only coffee and milk.
7. What time do they have lunch here? Generally at one
   o'clock, sir. Good! there's only ten minutes more. (Say:
   lack only ten minutes.) I'm ravenous.
8. Did you have a good meal on the train? Yes, very, thank
   you. I bought a luncheon basket, and in it there were so
   many good things: chicken, ham, biscuits, cheese and
   fruit.
9. There were so many people, and there wasn't a place empty
   (free). But a gentleman there near the door got up saying
   very politely: "Take this seat, madam, please."

10. Another traveller came and sat down in my compartment. He was a man nearing sixty, small and fat, bald and with a white beard (say: *the* white beard).

11. Didn't the boys come with you to the theatre? No, they remained at home; they wanted to hear the wireless; they were broadcasting a good concert from the Scala.

12. What did you do yesterday? Nothing in particular. I stayed at home.

LESSON XXII

PASSIVE VOICE—IMPERSONAL VERBS—IDIOMATIC USE OF CERTAIN TENSES

Passive Voice.—We have noted that the auxiliary of the passive voice is *essere*: *La casa è comprata da me* = "The house is bought by me", and if the verb is in a compound tense, we have the compound tense of *essere*: *La casa è stata comprata da me* = "The house has been bought by me", both past participles therefore agreeing with the subject. Instead of *essere* the following verbs are sometimes used as auxiliaries in the SIMPLE tenses of the passive voice; *venire, rimanere, restare* and *andare*. *Andare* implies a special meaning of duty or obligation:

I ladri vennero arrestati dal poliziotto = The thieves were arrested by the policeman.

Quella chiave non va toccata = That key must not be touched.

Impersonal Verbs.—A verb without a definite subject is impersonal. A real impersonal verb is one which is used only in the third person singular. The following are the most frequently met: *piove* = it rains, *nevica* = it snows, *tuona* = it thunders, *lampeggia* = it lightens, *grandina* = it hails, *gela* = it freezes.

But there are many other verbs which are used impersonally. The most common are:

bisogna = it is necessary   basta = it is enough
conviene = it is profitable   pare, sembra = it seems
ci vuole = it is necessary   succede = it happens
(ci—"there" = "for that", "for it")

mi piace = I like it (lit.: it pleases me)
mi dispiace = I am sorry (lit.: it displeases me)
mi preme: = I am anxious (lit.: it presses me)
mi riesce = I succeed, I can (lit.: it succeeds to me)

There are also some impersonal expressions formed by *fare*, *essere* and one or two other verbs:

fa caldo = it is hot	fa freddo = it is cold
fa bɛl tɛmpo = it is fine	fa cattivo tɛmpo = it is bad
che tɛmpo fa? = what sort of weather is it?	weather
	c'ɛ della nɛbbia = it is foggy
tira vɛnto = it is windy	ɛ umido = it is damp
(tirare = to pull, also = to throw)	vale la pena = it is worth while (lit.: it is worth the trouble; (valere = to be worth))

Note that in all these expressions the pronoun "it" is always understood in the verb.

When these impersonal expressions are followed by an infinitive there is no intervening preposition, except in the case of the verbs *parere* and *sembrare*, which may be used with or without the preposition *di* and the verbs *piacere* and *dispiacere* which take *di*:

Bişogna vederlo subito = It is necessary to see him at once.
Mi dispiace di doverle dire = I am sorry to have to tell you.
Mi pare di vedere del fumo laggiú = I think I see smoke down there.

In the above Italian sentences there is no personal subject in the dependent clause; when there is, this clause has its verb in the subjunctive:

Bişogna vederlo BUT Bişogna che *io* lo veda = *I* must see him.
Mi dispiace di non ɛssere venuto piú prɛsto = I am sorry not to have come sooner BUT Mi dispiace che *lui* non sia venuto piú prɛsto = I am sorry that *he* didn't come sooner.

Auxiliary Verbs with Impersonals.—Compound tenses of impersonal verbs are formed with *ɛssere* in the case of true impersonal verbs: *ɛ piovuto* = it has rained; and also when an intransitive verb is used impersonally: *ɛ succɛsso* = it has happened; but *avere* is used when a transitive verb forms the impersonal expression: *Ha tirato vɛnto tutta la nɔtte* = It has blown wind all night.

It would be helpful at this point to list the common verbs which take the auxiliary *ɛssere* (excluding the impersonals mentioned above). This will be revision, as most of these verbs have already been used in the exercises. Note, too, that they are marked, both in the list of irregular verbs in the Appendix when irregular, *and* in the vocabulary as taking *ɛssere*:

andare	morire	salire
arrivare	nascere	scendere
cadere	partire	stare
correre	restare	uscire
entrare	tornare	venire

Idiomatic Use of Certain Tenses.—In English when we indicate how long something has been going on and is still continuing, we use the present perfect: *I have been* in Italy five years. But this tense in Italian would not mean the same thing. Translated literally: *Sono stato in Italia cinque anni*, it means, "I have been in Italy for five years" BUT I AM NO LONGER THERE, for the present perfect indicates that the action is over in the past, though its results may be felt in the present. To render the meaning of the English tense—"I have been in Italy"—and am STILL THERE, Italian uses the simple present: *Sono in Italia da cinque anni* (= I am in Italy since five years), or *Sono cinque anni che sono in Italia* (= There are five years that I am in Italy).

Similarly when speaking of something which has been going on in the past with respect to a time in the past as: I had been in Italy five years when I met your sister in Florence = *ero in Italia da cinque anni quando incontrai tua sorella a Firenze*. And similarly with the future: On the fifteenth of next month I shall have been in Italy five years = *Il 15 del mese prossimo sarò in Italia da cinque anni*, or *Il 15 del mese prossimo saranno cinque anni che sono in Italia*.

This use of the tenses seems strange to us; just as our use of these perfects bewilders the Italian. The student would do well to learn by heart the literal English equivalent to each of the above sentences, so as to become familiar with the turn of the Italian phrase.

Study the verbs: *parere, piacere, piovere, valere*.

Translation VII

A Pisa riuscii a liberarmi con difficoltà da quella folla di commissionari di alberghi, di ciceroni e di fiaccherai che ingombrano l'uscita della stazione; ma, lasciata la valigia al deposito, una volta fuori con la pianta della città in mano, m'incamminai verso la piazza del duomo. In meno di una mezz'oretta ci arrivai.

Han * chiamato questa piazza il prato dei miracoli; e c'è

* *Hanno* may be thus abbreviated before a past participle which does not begin with *s* impure.

davvero del meraviglioso nella visione di quei quattro monumenti candidi che s'innalzano maestosi in mezzo a un campo, e che risaltano con tanta grazia sul verde del prato e sull'azzurro del cielo. Costruiti in epoche diverse, fra il secolo decimo primo e il dugento, quando Pisa era una potente repubblica marinara, i quattro edifizi—battistero, chiesa, cimitero, e torre pendente— sono tuttavia legati in armonia mirabile. Di stile romanico, hanno un loro carattere tipico e originale specialmente nelle decorazioni esterne di arcate cieche e di ordini di loggiati, le quali danno a queste moli marmoree leggiadria ed eleganza. Nel battistero ammirai il pulpito di Nicola Pisano e anche mi divertii a udire la famosa eco. Cantando una sola nota quella cupola conica ci rimanda l'eco in un accordo musicale perfetto; cantando poi tutta una canzone, è come se ci fosse lí un organo che suonasse in pieno. L'interno della cattedrale è impressionante con le enormi colonne monolitiche, e siccome piove molta luce dai finestroni della navata centrale potevo vedere molto bene le numerose opere d'arte. Mi mostrarono anche la lampada di Galileo (il quale era pisano) e la tradizione vuole che lo scienziato, osservandone le oscillazioni, scoprisse le leggi del pendolo. Pagai poi centocinquanta lire per entrare nel Campo Santo a verdere gli affreschi; e si paga anche per salire la torre pendente (cento lire). Ne vale la pena per il magnifico panorama e anche per provar la sensazione singolare che si ha su una torre che strapiomba (ha una deviazione di piú di quattro metri dalla verticale). Ci vuole un cuore forte, però e anche due buone gambe: ci sono quasi trecento scalini!

Sceso dalla torre, mi sedetti un momento sull'erba. C'era altra gente lí, per lo piú pisani venuti a far merenda all'ombra dei loro monumenti. Il sole tramontava; l'aria mite e serena era piena di voli di rondini; quel bianco dei marmi si era mutato in un color di rosa. Che pace! Che tranquillità! Riprendendo il cammino per la stazione, pensai che questo era il mio primo giorno in Italia: e mi pareva impossibile, già mi sembrava di essere lí da tanto tempo.

Vocabulary

caduta = fall
esperimento = experiment
grave (m.) = weight (adj. = heavy)
sommità = top

strano = strange

cominciare = to begin
iniziare = to begin

Exercise 22

1. Just as he was about to open the door, that thief was arrested by the policeman.
2. The cathedral of Pisa was begun in the year 1063.
3. The leaning tower is among the strangest in the world.
4. How long have you been in Italy?
5. I have been in Italy for three years.
6. Is it worth while visiting the tower? Yes, certainly, there is a magnificent view.
7. But let us not go today, it is cold and windy. We ought to wait for a day when it is fine, or we shall not see anything. (Use the subjunctive "it may be fine" to imply uncertainty.) *
8. How long does it take to go from here to the church, sir? (Say: How much time for it is necessary? using *volere*.)
9. Hasn't he come down for his breakfast yet? What shall we do? The train doesn't wait for anyone. We shall have to leave tomorrow.
10. That book was bought by me and I don't want to give it to anyone.
11. I am very sorry but I shall not be able to come; a friend of mine should (trans. *deve*) arrive today.
12. They say that Galileo did his famous experiments on the fall of heavy weights from the top of the leaning tower.

LESSON XXIII

DEMONSTRATIVES (*CONTD.*)—INDEFINITE ADJECTIVES AND PRONOUNS

WE must now add some other demonstrative words to those we already know: *questo*, *codesto* and *quello*. These words are both adjectives and pronouns, meaning "this" and "that" when used with a noun, and "this one", "that one" when standing alone. As adjectives they have the various shortened forms we have already learnt; as pronouns they always have their full forms, though they change for gender and number:

Questi mi piacciono piú di quelli = I like these better than those.

* See page 135.

Other demonstratives are:

1. *Ciò*, invariable, "this" or "that" referring to a whole sentence or an idea, not a single word:

Ciò non è vero = That's not true.

2. *Quegli* = "that man", *questi* = "this man" (there is no feminine form and no plural, and these words can be used only for persons and not for things and as subject of a verb). They also mean "former" and "latter":

Questi è italiano e quegli è inglese = This man is Italian and that man English.

Note that *quello* and *questo* also mean the "former" and the "latter":

Maria e Luisa sono partite oggi; questa tornerà stasera, quella domani = Mary and Lucy left today; the latter will come back this evening, the former tomorrow.

3. *Costui* = "this man", *costɛi* = "this woman", *costoro* = "those people" or "those men", "those women": all these convey a slight idea of contempt:

Chi è costui? = Who is that fellow?
Non vado a sedermi vicino a costoro = I'm not going to sit near to those people.

4. *Colui* = "that man", *colɛi* = "that woman", *coloro* = "those people" or "those men", "those women":

Parlo di coloro = I'm speaking of them, of those people.

Indefinite Adjectives and Pronouns.—On pages 32 and 33 we met some indefinite adjectives and pronouns. There are many such words in Italian, and as we add them to our vocabulary we must distinguish which are pronouns, which adjectives, and which may be used as both. Study the following tables:

1. "Each", "every", "each one", "everyone".

> *ogni* (invariable), adj.
> *ognuno*, -*a* (no plural), pron.
> *ciascuno*, -*a* (no plural), adj. and pron.
> *tutto*, -*a*, -*i*, -*e*, adj. and pron.

Examples :

Ogni uomo prese uno per sé = Each man took one for himself.

Ciascuno prese uno per sé = Each one took one for himself.
Ciascuna donna prese uno per sé = Each woman took one for herself.

Ognuno, ciascuno lo dice⎫
Tutti lo dicono   ⎬ = Everyone says so.

Ciascuno as a pronoun is used only of persons; as an adjective it may be used for things also, but *ogni* is preferable. *Ciascuno* lays more emphasis on the partitive sense of the word, and *ognuno* and *ogni* on the collective; it is better to use *ciascuno* for "each" and *ogni* and *ognuno* for "every", "everybody".

2. "None", "no one", "nobody", "nothing".

> *nessuno, -a* (no plural), adj. and pron.
> *alcuno, -a* (with *non* has no plural), adj. and pron.
> *nulla* (invariable), pron.
> *nullo, -a, -i, -e*, adj.
> *niɛnte* (invariable), pron.

Examples:

Nessuno ti crede   ⎫
Non ti crede nessuno⎬ = Nobody believes you.

Non ho alcun amico, nessun amico = I have no friend.
Non ho nulla = I have nothing (also means: I've nothing the matter with me).
Le sue speranze sono nulle = His hopes are vain.

3. "Anybody", "anyone", "anything", "any".

> *alcuno, -a, -i, -e*, adj. and pron.
> *qualcuno, -a* (no plural), pron.
> *qualche* (invariable), adj.
> *qualcheɔsa* (invariable), pron.

Examples:

Conosce alcuni di questi uɔmini? = Does he know any of these men?
Conoscete alcuno qui? = Do you know anybody here?
Hai qualche libro da darmi = Have you any book to give me?

Note that *qualche* is always followed by its noun in the singular, and *alcuno* when affirmative has a plural.

4. "Somebody", "someone", "something", "some", are the same words as for "any", etc., see previous paragraph.

5. "Whoever", "whatever", "however".

chiunque (invariable), pron., whoever, whosoever.
chicchessia (plural: *chicchesiano*), pron., whoever, whosoever
qualunque (invariable), adj. and pron., however, whichever
per quanto (*-ti*), adj., however much, however many
checché (invariable), pron., whatever
qualsiasi (*qualsiansi*), adj., whatever

Examples (note that these indefinite words are followed by
the subjunctive (see also page 138)):

Chiunque tu sia = Whoever you may be.
Datemi qualunque libro = Give me any book whatever.

Note too that *per quanto* may also be an adverb, in which case
it is invariable: *Per quanto cari siano* = However dear they
may be.

6. "Some . . . others", "the one . . . the other". *Chi . . . chi*;
altri . . . altri; *alcuni . . . alcuni*; translate "some . . . others";
l'uno . . . l'altro (plural: *Gli uni . . . gli altri*) "the one . . . the
other". Note that *alcuni* used in this sense is always plural;
but the verb with *chi* and *altri* used in this sense is in the
singular:

Alcuni camminano, alcuni corrono ⎱
Altri cammina, altri corre   ⎰
Chi cammina, chi corre   ⎬ Some walk, others run
Gli uni camminano, gli altri corrono ⎰

7. Finally, an indefinite pronoun meaning "of others": *altrui*
(pronounce al-tróo-ee) which is invariable, and can *never* be
subject of a verb; it is really an inflection of *altri*, and does not
require any preposition before it:

Bisogna rispettare i diritti altrui = The rights of others must
be respected.

Study the verbs: *dire*, *salire* and *uscire*.

Translation VIII

Firenze, per la sua storia, per l'arte, e anche per la bellezza
della sua posizione, è fra le città piú celebri. Il mio soggiorno
colà fu troppo breve per permettermi piú di uno sguardo
rapido ad alcune cose d'importanza artistica e storica, ma bastò
per darmi un'idea delle numerose bellezze naturali e artistiche
di quella città in riva all'Arno e per farmene sentire il fascino,
cosí da decidermi di ritornarvi al piú presto.

Il primo mattino mi svegliai di buon'ora. La mia pensione
era all'ultimo piano di un vecchio palazzo, al pianterreno del
quale c'erano dei negozi, da una parte un fioraio, e dall'altra un
venditore di antichità e di oggetti d'arte. Scesi le scale (non
c'era ascensore), passai per il corridoio oscuro, fresco e pro-
fumato dai fiori e dalle piante che stavano lí esposti, e, data
un'occhiata ai vecchi quadri, mobili e gioielli della vetrina
dell'antiquario, uscii sulla via. Con la pianta in mano mi diressi
verso la piazza del duomo. Anche a Firenze, come a Pisa e
come in tante città d'Italia, il duomo, il battistero e il campanile
sono tre edifizi staccati l'uno dall'altro, ma legati in intima
unità dallo stile architettonico. Qui a Firenze il marmo è di un
altro colore, un colore piú caldo, quasi rosa, con linee di un
verde tanto scuro da sembrare nero. Il duomo fu iniziato
nell'anno 1296. L'interno è grandioso e solenne, molto chiaro e
sobrio, perché quasi privo di elementi decorativi. Ammirai
l'altare di puro argento, ma le due famose cantoríe, l'una di
Donatello e l'altra di Luca della Robbia, le quali erano prima
nella cattedrale, bisogna cercarle ora nel museo lí accanto. Il
battistero è un edifizio a pianta ottagonale e dentro è ornatissimo
di marmi e di mosaici. Quando entrai battezzavano un
bambino; e guardando quel piccolo gruppo intorno al fonte mi
ricordai che era qui, in questo stesso luogo, che Dante ricevette
il battesimo quasi sette secoli fa. Lí vidi anche le belle porte in
bronzo * del Ghiberti; quelle che Michelangelo disse degne di
esser le porte del Paradiso: rappresentano scene del Vecchio
Testamento, incorniciate da un fregio in cui si alternano
statuette di profeti e tondi con teste. Il terzo monumento di
questo gruppo, il campanile di Giotto è una torre alta, quadrata,
di forma semplice e salda, ma elegante; anche qui bisogna
ammirare i bassorilievi nella parte inferiore, dovuti ai discepoli
di Giotto, su disegni del maestro.

Vocabulary

opinione (f.) = opinion
peccato = pity
   Che peccato! = What a pity!
pianoforte (m.) = piano
violino = violin

ripetere = to repeat
suonare = to sound, to ring
   (bell); to play (piano, etc.).
tutti e due = both (lit.: all
   and two)

---

* The Baptistery doors are now gilded, having been restored, since
World War II, to their original state.

Exercise 23

1. I have seen both of those pictures; I like the latter better than the former.
2. Who is that woman? Does she always shout with that voice?
3. Mary and Lucy both play very well: the latter the violin, the former the piano.
4. Every time I go there that man follows me to the door.
5. It is a great pity to sell that flower shop; everyone says so. (Say: that shop of flowers.)
6. Have you seen anyone on the road? No, I have not seen anyone.
7. However rich she is, it doesn't make any difference to me (to matter = *importare*). I do not want her for my wife.
8. Whoever you may be I cannot let you in here.
9. Some were going to see the pictures; others to be admired by the rest (say: the others) (*farsi ammirare* = to be admired); all were walking along towards the museum.
10. Whatever has happened? (Whatever? interrogative = *che cosa mai?*) Some are running, others walking, but they are all going along towards the church.
11. You should not repeat other people's opinions; you should have some of your own. (Use *bisognare*, say: *non bisogna ripetere . . .*)
12. Are you going out this morning? Yes, I'm going out in a little while (*fra poco*); do you want anything?

LESSON XXIV

USE OF THE ARTICLES

THE definite and indefinite articles are used in Italian on many occasions exactly as in English; but there are some differences between the two languages. One we know already: the use in Italian of the definite article with the possessive: *il mio libro*; and when doing the exercises you have sometimes been told to add the *definite* article and to omit the *indefinite*. We must now learn the following rules:

A. *The Definite Article, il, lo,* etc., is used in Italian when we do *not* use "the" in the following cases:

1. Before a noun used in a general sense, or before an abstract noun:

L'erba è verde = Grass is green.
I libri sono utili = Books are useful.

2. Before the name of a language (though it may be omitted after *parlare*) and the prepositions *in* and *di*:

Studio l'italiano = I am studying Italian.
Si parla inglese = English spoken.

3. Before a surname, used without a Christian name: *

Il Boccaccio nacque a Parigi = Boccaccio was born in Paris.

But:

Dante Alighieri era fiorentino = Dante Alighieri was a Florentine.

4. Before a surname preceded by a title:

Il signor Bianchi è in città = Mr. Bianchi is in town.
Il dottor Viani viene oggi = Dr. Viani is coming today.

(Note that titles ending in *-ore*, such as *signore*, *professore*, drop their final *-e* when followed by another title, or by a name.)
When the title is used in direct address, however, the article is not used:

Buon giorno, Signor Bianchi = Good morning, Mr. Bianchi.

5. Before names of countries, continents, provinces and large islands:

l'America   La Toscana = Tuscany
l'Inghilterra   La Sardegna = Sardinia

Exception to rule 5: No article is used with feminine names after the prepositions *in* or *di*, if the noun is not modified:

in Francia = in France   d'Italia = of Italy

But:

negli Stati Uniti = in the United States
del Canadà = of Canada
La storia dell'Italia meridionale = The history of Southern Italy.

* A few famous surnames may have no article: Garibaldi, Colombo.

Note that when the preposition *di* with the name of the country is not equivalent to an adjective of nationality, the article is used:

La Germania è piú grande dell'Italia = Germany is larger than Italy.

6. The definite article is used instead of the possessive when the latter is not absolutely necessary for clearness:

Mise la mano in tasca = He put his hand in his pocket.

B. *The Definite Article is omitted* in Italian where we would use it in English in these cases:

1. Before a noun in apposition to another:

Roma, capitale d'Italia = Rome, the capital of Italy.

2. Before an ordinal used with a proper noun:

Vittorio Emanuele terzo = Victor Emanuel the third.

C. *The Indefinite Article is omitted* in Italian, and used in English, in the following cases:

1. Before a noun in apposition:

Toscana, provincia d'Italia = Tuscany, a province of Italy.

2. Before a noun in the predicate which is unqualified:

Lui è dottore = He is a doctor.
Io sono forestiero = I am a foreigner.

But:

Il dottor Rossi è un buon medico = Dr. Rossi is a good doctor.

3. In exclamations after *che!* and *quale!*

Che peccato! = What a pity!

4. Before *cento* and *mille*:

Centocinquanta = One hundred and fifty.

5. After the preposition *da* used in the idiomatic sense of "like", "in the manner of":

Parla da sciocco = He talks like a fool.

Study the irregular verbs: *cadere*, *sedere*, *tacere* and *tenere*.

Translation IX

Dal centro religioso m'incamminai al centro storico della città, cioè alla Piazza della Signoría. è molto pittoresca, con il

maestoso Palazzo Vecchio a un lato, costruito come una fortezza
con mura merlate, e accanto c'è la Loggia dei Lanzi, dove una
volta venivano a parlare i Signori della città, e dove ora la
gente ammira alcune delle statue piú conosciute del mondo.
Dalla piazza si entra nel lungo piazzale degli Uffizi, che si apre
fra il Palazzo e la Loggia. è circondato da tre lati dall'enorme
Palazzo degli Uffizi, cosí chiamato perché destinato a sede di
uffizi amministrativi: oggi è un museo e contiene la piú importante collezione di pitture in Italia. I giorni feriali bisogna
pagare cento lire d'entrata, quindi rimandai la mia visita alla
domenica. Quando vi andai, vi trovai con mia grande sorpresa,
una folla d'Italiani in abiti festivi, che passeggiavano su e giú
per i lunghi corridoi luminosi, o, seduti sulle panche fra l'uno e
l'altro monumento, chiacchieravano e guardavano i visitatori.
Sembravano indifferenti alle bellezze d'arte che li circondavano;
ma se domandi a uno, come feci io, dove si trovi un certo
capolavoro, o a quale scuola appartenga un certo maestro, ti
sanno quasi sempre rispondere lí per lí correttamente. La
passeggiata domenicale negli Uffizi è per loro un'abitudine;
quelle pitture fanno parte della loro vita.

Passando sotto la loggia in fondo al Piazzale, si sale sul
Lungarno, una delle strade che costeggiano il fiume, e voltando
a destra, poco dopo si giunge al Ponte Vecchio. Questo, il ponte
piú antico della città, è molto pittoresco, con le piccole botteghe
degli orefici che si aggrappano ai lati, appoggiate all'esterno del
ponte da mensole in legno. Cosí piccole sono queste botteghe
che si direbbe che non si possano entrare piú di cinque o sei
persone alla volta; invece ci entrano in gran numero specialmente donne e turisti: per chi ama belle collane, orecchini,
fermagli, cammei e anelli, è difficilissimo resistere alla tentazione
di quelle vetrine, o meglio bacheche, che fiancheggiano la via
strettissima del ponte e che sono disposte con tanto gusto al
livello degli occhi dei passanti.

Traversato il fiume, camminai dapprima per straducole scure
e strette, fra palazzi antichi; poi, salendo per viali e vie di
campagna, su per le pendici di un colle, giunsi al Piazzale
Michelangelo. Di là si vede tutta Firenze entro la cerchia delle
sue colline; colline amene e ridenti al sole, coperte di vigne e di
uliveti e sparse qua e là di ville e di case, su cui a tratti si leva
un albero piú alto e piú scuro degli altri—l'albero tipico della
campagna toscana: il cipresso. Ora uno isolato; ora una bella
fila che disegna la linea di un viale o i contorni di un poggio.
Distinsi in lontananza il colle di Fiesole con in cima il monastero
che volevo visitare. era assai lontano ma l'aria limpida e chiara

lo faceva parer vicino. Suonò mezzogiorno. Come batteva il sole! Tutto quel che si toccava scottava. Mi guardai intorno sulla piazza. Non c'era anima viva, e nessun rumore fuorché l'interminabile canto di miriadi di cicale.

Vocabulary

patria = fatherland, country
pittore (m.) = painter
scrittrice (f.) = woman writer

negare = to deny
sacrificare = to sacrifice
Cristoforo = Christopher

Exercise 24

1. Green is a nice colour. (nice = *bello*)
2. He is studying Italian; he can already speak French.
3. Christopher Columbus discovered America.
4. Mrs. Bianchi is at home. Who wants her?
5. He has fallen from the tree and broken his leg. When will Dr. Rossi arrive?
6. He is a great painter; he who denies it, talks like a fool.
7. Florence is one of the most beautiful cities in Italy.
8. Grazia Deledda, a famous Italian woman writer, was born in Sardinia.
9. He sacrificed his life for his country.
10. My father is a lawyer and my uncle a doctor.
11. Good morning, Doctor. Would you come up, please?
12. Necklaces, earrings, brooches, cameos and rings are all sold in those little shops on Ponte Vecchio. (Say: "sell themselves".)

LESSON XXV

SUFFIXES

ITALIANS often add a particular ending to a word to express size or quality instead of using another word. (We have the same thing in English: *e.g.*, Johnny, piggy, doggie, streamlet.) There are many such suffixes in Italian added to nouns, adjectives, adverbs and, very occasionally, to verbs. A noun thus modified usually keeps its original gender, but sometimes a masculine suffix is added to a feminine noun and the word becomes masculine: *la finestra* = window; *il finestrino* = the little window; *il finestrone* = the large window. It will be seen from these examples that when adding a suffix, the final vowel of the word is dropped; and when the final vowel is preceded by

a *c* or *g*, the original sound of that letter is kept, by the addition
of an *h* or an *i*: *barca* = boat, *barchetta* = little boat; *sɛmplice* =
simple, *semplicione* = very simple, a simpleton.

The commonest suffixes are these:

1. *-issimo* (= very), added to adjectives and adverbs.

buɔno   buonissimo
pɔco   pochissimo
piccolo   piccolissimo

2. *-one*, fem. *-ona* (= large). The feminine form is used only
with nouns and adjectives which have a masculine and feminine
form; in other cases the feminine noun takes the masculine
suffix and becomes masculine:

il libro   il librone
la casa   il casone
il ragazzo   il ragazzone
la ragazza   la ragazzona
la donna   il donnone (= big woman)

3. *-etto*, *-ɛllo*, *-cɛllo*, *icɛllo*, *-arɛllo*, *-erɛllo*, *-uɔlo* and *-ɔlo* all
denote smallness, and all have feminine forms in *-a*:

la piazza   la piazzetta
la donna   la donnetta
il fiume = river   il fiumicɛllo = stream

4. *-ino*, *-cina*, *-icino*, with feminine form in *-a*, mean small
(often with the idea of "nice", "dear"):

il gatto   il gattino = little cat, kitten
caro = dear   carino = darling
la casa   la casina = little house
Giovanni = John   Giovannino = dear little John

5. *-uccio*, *-uzzo*, *-ucolo*, feminine forms in *-a*, mean small (with
the idea of affection if used with the name of a person; with the
idea of pity or contempt if used with a common noun):

Maria = Mary   Mariuccia = dear little Mary
la donna   la donnuccia = silly little woman
la strada   la straducola = back street, poor street

6. *-ɔtto*, fem. *-a*, gives the idea of strength, sturdiness,
vigour:

la contadina (peasant woman)   la contadinɔtta = sturdy
                                  peasant woman

il giovane = the youth   il giovanotto = the grown
                          up or strong young man

7. -accio, fem. -a, means worthless, bad:

Che tempo! = what weather!   Che tempaccio! = what foul
                              weather!
la casa = the house   la casaccia = the awful,
                              dreadful house
povero = poor   poveraccio = poor wretch

These suffixes may not be used just as one likes; that is, not
by a foreigner, whose ear would not be sufficient guide for him
to choose the right one; some words take one, other words
another. The student is advised to use a suffix with any word
only if he has already met that word and suffix together. There
is also another danger in making words by adding a suffix:
many words have been employed so often with a certain suffix
that they have taken on special meanings, as:

scala = stair; scalino = stair; scaletta = ladder, staircase;
casa = house; casina = nice little house; casino = club,
    casino; casella = pigeon-hole;
cavalla = mare; cavallina = nice little mare; cavaletta =
    locust.

A word may sometimes have two suffixes added at once:
fiasco = flask or bottle, *fiaschetto* = little bottle, *fiaschettino* =
very small bottle, nice little bottle; *tovaglia* = table-cloth,
tovagliolo = serviette, *tovagliolino* = very small serviette, or
bib.

In very rare cases suffixes are joined to verbs: *-ello*, *-arello* and
-erello are joined to the stem, and they lose their final *-o* before
the infinitive ending: *cantare* = to sing, *canterellare*, *cantarellare*
= to hum continually; *saltare* = to jump; *saltellare*, *salterellare*
= to keep on giving little jumps.

Study the verbs: *chiedere, chiudere, perdere, prendere, ridere,
rispondere*.

Translation X

—Pronto! Parlo con la Pensione Primavera? No? Oh, mi
dispiace, ho sbagliato numero. Pronto! Centrale! Mi dia per
favore il numero 25,054 (venti-cinque zero cinque quattro).
Grazie. Pronto! Parlo con la Pensione Primavera? Bene. C'è
il signore inglese, che è arrivato poco tempo fa? Si chiama. . . .—
—Mi dispiace, Signora, non c'è . . . oh, aspetti, torna proprio
adesso. Lo vado a chiamare. Un momento.—

—Signore, scusi.— mi disse il portiere al momento che rientravo per mangiare. —La vogliono al telefono.—

—Dio mio, al telefono,— pensai, —Chi può essere? e come farò a farmi capire in italiano?—

Ma mi riuscí facile. Era una vecchia signora inglese, sposata a un italiano, la quale aveva conosciuto mia madre, e m'invitava a visitarla nella sua villa a Fiesole. Molto volentieri ci andai.

Si può salire a Fiesole col tram e coll'autobus; ma io preferivo andarci a piedi. Partii una sera verso le cinque. Faceva ancora caldo ma non troppo; c'era un bel venticello fresco che veniva dalle montagne. Traversata la piazza del Duomo e fatta tutta una strada lunga e stretta entrai in un'altra bella piazza grande e armoniosa, circondata in tre lati da bei portici, e in mezzo alla quale c'erano una statua equestre e due fontane ornatissime. Sopra ciascuna colonna dei portici notai un tondo in terra cotta con quel famoso putto in fasce su fondo celeste, opera di uno dei della Robbia; allora compresi dove mi trovavo; ero nella Piazza della Santissima Annunziata e quell'edifizio era l'Ospedale degli Innocenti. Proseguii per altre vie e piazze finché mi trovai in piena campagna e, sempre salendo ora fra gli alti muri di ville fiorite, ora fra boschi di cipressi e di ulivi—che offrivano qua e là alla vista il panorama della città—giunsi finalmente alla piazza di Fiesole.

Era giorno di mercato e la piazza presentava uno spettacolo molto vivace. All'ombra degli alberi (la piazza ha due belle file di castagni e di tigli) e degli edifizi in pietra grigia, i venditori avevano disposto le loro baracche e i loro banchi sul marciapiede e li avevano coperti di tende, sotto le quali gridavano la loro merce. Vendevano per lo piú oggetti di paglia: cappelli, ceste, cestini, borse di colori e di disegni vivacissimi, per i quali la cittadina è famosa; e anche oggetti in cuoio che si fabbricano a Firenze, anch'essi con bei disegni a colori: e poi, tante altre cose come scarpe, libri, cartoline, calze, gioie di poco valore, panno, rosarii, crocefissi, biscotti, caramelle e frutta. Vidi grosse ceste piene d'uva, di pere e di fichi, posate in terra. Siccome dovevo aspettare la signora inglese e alcuni suoi amici mi sedetti a una delle tavole di fuori, sotto gli alberi, a bere un vermut col ghiaccio mentre guardavo quella folla animata e allegra.

Vocabulary

campanello = bell (of door)   villino = small villa, cottage
parco = park
tavolino = small table   regalare = to give a present

Exercise 25

1. He eats very little indeed, that boy.
2. They are rich, those foreigners. They have an enormous house in the middle of a park.
3. Have you any kittens? What little ones! Poor little things! (Suffix *-ino* for both nouns.)
4. Dear little Mary, will you go to the door? Didn't you hear the bell? Somebody has rung.
5. Will you help me carry some water from the well? I haven't time; that sturdy peasant girl will help you.
6. But of whom are you speaking? Of that little woman who came yesterday to help Cook?
7. I left all those papers in my trunk, which will now be closed, and I have lost the key. Haven't you asked the porter? He will perhaps have the key.
8. Have you replied to that girl (*signorina*) who gave you that large book? Yes, I replied the day after.
9. What did that silly little woman reply when you told her that she shouldn't hum like that all the time? She didn't say anything, she only laughed. ("Shouldn't"—use *bisognare*.)
10. He went up the stairs and entered the little bedroom. There was nobody there. He put the parcel and the flowers on the little table near to the window.
11. What an awful house! Who lives there? Some poor wretch!
12. They have a small villa on one of those little country roads which go up the hill. ("To go up the hill" = *andare su per il colle*.)

LESSON XXVI

THE INFINITIVE

Infinitive as a Verbal Noun.—When the English present participle in *-ing* is more of a noun than a verb it is rendered in Italian by the infinitive. The infinitive as a *verbal noun* may be subject or object or predicate; in the first two cases it usually takes the article:

Mi piace il ballare = I like dancing
Amo il viaggiare = I like travelling

but not as predicate (*i.e.*, after the verb "to be"):

è facile ṣbagliarsi = It is easy to make mistakes.

It is also used after prepositions (except "by", "on", "in" and "through"; refer back to page 65). It usually takes the definite article in this case too, except after *di, dopo di, invece di, prima di, senza* and *oltre*:

Parlò senza eṣitare = She spoke without hesitating.
Votò contro il dare tanto a uno solo = He voted against giving so much to only one.

Conjunctive Pronouns with Certain Verbs and the Infinitive.

Dovere, potere and *volere* have a kind of auxiliary function when followed by an infinitive; and a pronoun object, which is really the object of the infinitive, may either precede both verbs or follow and be joined on to the infinitive (see Part II, page 173). Two other verbs have a similar construction: *oṣare* (= to dare) and *sapere*:

Non mi oṣa dire ciò, *or* Non oṣa dirmi ciò = He daren't tell me that.
Lo sa parlare bene, *or* Sa parlarlo bene = He can speak it well.

Five verbs, however, when followed by the simple infinitive, take *all* the object pronouns, even when these belong to the infinitive: *fare, lasciare, sentire, udire* and *vedere*:

Glielo fanno spedire ora = They are having it sent to him now.
L'ho sentito dire mille volte = I've heard it said a thousand times.
Glielo vedo dare = I see it given him.

Note that in these constructions the Italian *infinitive* translates an English *past participle*.

In the above examples, of the two pronoun objects one was direct and the other indirect; but each verb may govern a direct object in English. In this case, in Italian, the direct object of the main verb becomes indirect and the object of the infinitive remains direct:

Gliela feci scrivere = I made him write it (letter, understood) (lit.: to him it I made to write).

When the object of either verb is a noun, it follows both verbs in Italian; but again when there are two direct objects, the one belonging to the main verb becomes indirect:

Feci scrivere la lettera = I had the letter written.

Feci scrivere la lettera a quella ragazza = I made that girl write the letter (lit.: I made to write the letter to that girl).

Infinitive Governed by a Preposition.—One or two other verbs take the infinitive after them without any intervening preposition, as: *desiderare* = to desire, *preferire* = to prefer, *solere* = to be accustomed, in addition to the impersonal verbs already mentioned (pp. 107–108); but certain verbs require a preposition after them before a following infinitive: some *a*; others *di*; *essere* and *avere* may be followed by *da* to express duty or necessity; and when the English "to" means "in order to" it is rendered by *per*:

è abituato *ad* alzarsi presto = He is used to getting up early.

Ha cercato *di* farlo = He has tried to do it.

Non ho niente *da* fare = I have nothing to do.

è tornato *per* vederla = He has come back to see her.

The following verbs require *a* after them before an infinitive: verbs meaning accustoming, beginning or continuing, compelling, helping, hastening, inviting, learning, preparing, teaching and verbs of motion or rest in a place. The most common are:

abituarsi, aiutare, cominciare, continuare, destinare (= to destine), *costringere* (= to compel), *imparare* (= to learn), *insegnare* (= to teach), *invitare, riuscire.*

Andrò a vederla domani = I will go and see her tomorrow.

è riuscito a vincere il concorso = He has succeeded in winning the competition.

Most other verbs take *di.* We may note the following:

cercare (= to try), *credere* (= to believe), *dire, finire, maravigliarsi, permettere* (= to permit), *pregare* (= to beg), *proibire* (= to prohibit), *promettere* (= to promise), *rifiutare* (= to refuse), *sperare* (= to hope).

Ha finito di scrivere quel capitolo = He has finished writing that chapter.

Prometto di venire subito = I promise to come at once.

The infinitive preceded by *di* is often used after some of these verbs where we in English would use a noun clause, when the subject of the principal sentence and the dependent clause is the same:

Credo di dover andare fra poco = I think I shall have to go in a little while.

Disse di averlo finito tutto = He said he had finished it all.

With verbs denoting command, permission or prohibition, this same construction may be used in Italian when the subject of the main clause is different from that of the dependent clause (when no doubt or uncertainty is implied—see lesson on the subjunctive, page 136):

Ti proibisco di parlare = I forbid you to speak.

Mi prega di andare a vederlo = He begs me to go and see him.

Gli ho detto di venire alle sei = I have told him to come at six.

Study these verbs: *aprire, offrire* and *udire*. When translating the following passage, note verbs which are followed by an infinitive, whether they take any preposition, and if so, which.

Translation XI

Eravamo seduti sulla terrazza del villino della signora inglese dopo un'ottima cena, a godere la veduta della città di notte—tutto uno scintillio di luci laggiú nella valle—quando i miei ospiti decisero di condurmi a Signa a vedere il Palio.* —Noi si va ogni anno,— mi dissero, —è uno spettacolo bellissimo e divertente. Vedrà che le piacerà.—Avevano ragione; mi divertii proprio immensamente.

Si prese la littorina.† Fra parentesi, non raccomanderei questo trenino automobile a persone nervose, ma è il mezzo piú

* Name given to a horse-race run in the city square: a competition between the different wards, the winner receiving as a prize a special banner, beautifully embroidered, called the "Palio". This race dates from mediaeval times.

† A train which came into service just before World War II. It runs along the ordinary track, but instead of an engine, it has a motor driven on petrol. Small, light and very stream-lined, it develops a high speed, but is meant for short journeys only; it holds less than 100 passengers and heavy luggage is not allowed. The main Italian railway system is electrified; the *littorina* is to take the place of the old steam trains which served (and in some few cases still serve) the less important local lines.

rapido. Va tanto veloce che sembra volare sul binario senza toccarlo; ma quando lo tocca, dà una tale scossa che i viaggiatori balzano sui cuscini; e i pacchetti che stanno ballando nella rete cascano in testa alla gente. Cosí s'arrivò alla graziosa e pulita stazioncina di Signa; modernissima e da far convertire allo stile novecento, tanto belle e armoniose ne sono la forma e le proporzioni.

E poi, dopo una scarrozzata per una strada ripida, mi trovai entro le mura della città medioevale, la quale, dai suoi tre monti, domina tutto il paesaggio circostante. I maestosi palazzi gotici, di pietra grigia, alcuni con merli, e i vicoli scuri e stretti (qualchevolta non ci passa nemmeno la carrozza), mi parvero dapprima austeri e freddi. Ma vennero i giorni del Palio. Che trasformazione! Tutto appariva inondato di gioia: abitanti, strade, palazzi. Da quegli edifizi solenni pendevano bandiere, arazzi, panni—ogni finestra dava il suo contributo; le strade erano uno sventolio di bandiere; e i senesi, a qualunque ora del giorno o della notte, passeggiavano su e giú a braccetto, cantando e ridendo, tutti allegri. Questa corsa di cavalli, che celebra un'antica festa religiosa, è la piú strana del mondo. Ha luogo in mezzo alla città, cioè nella Piazza del Campo, e tutti i partecipanti sono vestiti in costumi medioevali di colori vivaci bene armonizzati. Non sapendo io niente del significato religioso e non avendo fatto nessuna scommessa, non potevo partecipare a quell'entusiasmo frenetico per la corsa; nondimeno quello fu per me come uno spettacolo teatrale interessantissimo, di cui mi colpirono di piú le scene seguenti:

Atto primo.—Una chiesetta di una delle contrade. Personaggi—un cavallo, un prete, un fantino (tutti vicino all'altare); una folla che ride e chiacchiera tutt'il tempo. Il prete, ripetendo una certa preghiera asperge il naso del cavallo. Grida e risa della folla. —Bravo! bravo! Viva la lupa *!— Escono tutti ridendo. Sipario.

Atto secondo.—Una piazza grande, che ha la forma di una conchiglia o di un ventaglio. è affollatissima. A tutte le finestre, gente; su tutti i tetti, gente. Un pigia pigia nella piazza stessa, fuorché nello spazio riservato per la corsa tutt'intorno. Un urlo tremendo della folla; la corsa pazza di dieci cavalli; mentre per un minuto e mezzo l'aria è in tempesta per il gridare e il fischiare

---

* Each district or ward has its own flag and emblem, and is represented in the race by horse and jockey wearing its colours. Each has, too, its own small church in which the ceremony of blessing the horse takes place. The *contrada* in question was that of the *lupa* or "She-wolf".

di diecine di migliaia di persone, per il rullio di tamburi, lo squillo di trombe, i colpi di mortaretto, e il suonare delle campane di piú di venti chiese. Sipario.

Atto terzo.—La strada principale della contrada vincitrice, a notte inoltrata. Ad una lunga tavola cenano all'aperto parecchie centinaia di persone; la scena è illuminata dagli antichi torchietti che pendono dalla facciata dei vetusti palazzi. E in capo alla tavola sta l'attore principale, il cavallo vincitore, con la sua propria mangiatoia dentro la quale ci sono—fra altre cose—maccheroni. Esso sta mangiando. Fine. Sipario.

Exercise 26

1. He gave me that book before leaving for Rome.
2. Why has he said that? He speaks without thinking.
3. I hear that said a thousand times a day.
4. Have they had that door opened?
5. Yes, Cook opened it, and now we cannot close it.
6. Instead of reading a novel he ought to study that lesson.
7. Yes, *I* would make him study it, and at once.
8. The motor-train leaves at eleven, I think. Could you reserve me a seat?
9. I told him to buy the tickets yesterday.
10. Yes, he tried to (. . . to do it), but he couldn't—everything was closed.
11. He had promised to go immediately, but he can't—there isn't a train before tomorrow.
12. I forbid you to go to that house.

LESSON XXVII

PREPOSITIONS

THESE short invariable words, which connect a noun, pronoun or infinitive to a word preceding them, sometimes present difficulties, for corresponding prepositions in English and Italian are often used on different occasions and with very different meanings. Also some verbs which take a direct object in Italian require a preposition in English, and vice versa.

Only a few Italian verbs require a preposition which in English take a direct object. The most common are: *entrare IN*, *credere A* (when the object is a person), *ricordarsi DI*, and *fidarsi DI* (= to trust):

E

Entrò nella camera = He entered the room.

Non credere a quell'uomo, è bugiardo = Don't believe that man, he's a liar.

Ti ricordi di quel giorno? = Do you remember that day?

There are more Italian verbs which govern a direct object which in English require a preposition: for example, *fischiare* (= to hiss AT), *guardare* (= to look AT), *aspettare* (= to wait FOR), *pagare* (= to pay FOR), *cercare* (= to look FOR).

Lui me la pagherà = He'll pay me *for* it.

Sta cercando quel libro = He's looking *for* that book.

The following verbs require a preposition in both languages, but a different one:

adornare di = to adorn with
approfittare di = to profit by, to take advantage of
caricare di = to load with
maravigliarsi di = to wonder at
occuparsi di = to busy oneself with, look after, see to, attend to
ridere di = to laugh at
vivere di = to live on
dipendere da = to depend on

Lei si occupa anche del giardino? = Do you look after the garden too?

Ride sempre di me = He always laughs at me.

Note the constructions with the following verbs:

chiedere = to ask (Italian: to ask something to someone).
Chiedo il conto al cameriere = I ask the waiter for the bill.
pensare (followed by *a* = to think of).
Hai pensato a me? = Have you thought of me?
pensare (followed by *di* = to have an opinion about).
Che cosa pensa di quel romanzo? = What do you think about that novel?
perdonare (Italian: to pardon a thing to a person).
Non vuoi perdonare quello a tua sorella? = Aren't you going to pardon your sister for that?

We must not get the impression that the use of the prepositions in Italian is never the same as in English; many verbs take the same in both languages; on the other hand, it must not be thought that the above list of words is by any means exhaustive. Only by continuous reading and careful observation can the student hope to master the use of the prepositions thoroughly.

We have often met the preposition *di* after an adjective or past participle doing the service of our "with". Note the following, which are always followed by *di*:

> abbondante di = abundant in
> carico di = laden with
> contento di = contented with
> fornito di = provided with
> povero di = poor in
> pratico di = experienced in
> ricco di = rich in
> soddisfatto di = satisfied with
> sorpreso di = surprised at
> vestito di = dressed in

and three which take *a*, where we use "for: *adatto a* = fit for," *buono a* = good for, *diretto a* = bound for.

The prepositions *a*, *di*, *da* are *simple* prepositions. Others (some of which also exist as adverbs) are: *in, con, su, per, tra* or *fra, senza, verso, sopra, sotto, dentro, dopo, dietro, contro*; others again are phrases made up of another word and a true preposition, as *fuori di* = outside of. The following when governing a personal pronoun take *di* after them, and thus become prepositional phrases: *contro, dietro, dopo, senza, sopra, sotto* and —sometimes—*fra* and *verso*.

> senza di te = without you
> verso di loro = towards them

We must now gather together idiomatic uses we have already met and add a few others to them. We will begin with *da*, which has the most varied meanings:

DA, besides meaning "by" and "from", also means:

1. "at", "at the house of", "with", "in the district":

Non può venire da me oggi? No, mi dispiace, devo andare dal medico = Can't you come to me today? No, I'm sorry I have to go to the doctor's.

2. "like", "in the manner of":

Ho una fame da lupi = I am ravenous (lit.: I have hunger like wolves).

3. "of such a kind as to":

Non è uomo da fare ciò = He's not the man to do that.

4. It describes a personal or characteristic quality:

Quell'uomo dal naso lungo = That man with the long nose.

5. It indicates the purpose for which something is intended:

la sala da pranzo = the dining-room
la stanza da bagno = the bathroom
una bottiglia da vino = a wine-bottle
una tazza da tè = a tea-cup

(Note that a bottle *of* wine is *una bottiglia di vino*, a cup *of* tea = *una tazza di tè*.)

6. Before the word "parte" it means "on":

da questa parte = on this side

DI = "of", and the partitive "some", is also used before adverbs to mean "from":

è lontano di qua = It is far from here,

and it also indicates certain times of the day or year, rendered in English by "in" or "by":

di mattina, di sera, di notte, di giorno = in the morning, in the evening, by night, by day
di primavera, d'inverno = in spring, in winter.

A = "to", and "at", is also:

1. "in" before the name of a town:

Mia moglie è a Roma = My wife is in Rome.

2. It indicates the way a thing is done in certain idiomatic phrases:

chiudere a chiave = to shut with a key (= to lock)
andare a piedi = to go on foot
andare a cavallo = to ride
alla romana = in the Roman fashion (*maniera* understood)

Note: *pagare alla romana* means "to pay one's own share".

3. It also forms compound nouns:

una barca a vela = a sailing boat
una macchina a vapore = a steam engine

IN translates "to" before the name of a country:

è andato in Francia = He has gone to France

FRA = "among", translates "in" when expressing future time:

Sarà pronto fra un'ora = He'll be ready in an hour.

Study the irregular verbs: *cogliere, scegliere* and *sciogliere*.

Translation XII

Oltre a essere una delle città piú romantiche e pittoresche, Venezia è anche fra le piú originali del mondo. Chi non l'abbia veduta non può figurarsi questa città di marmo e di acqua. Vi manca la vegetazione, o quasi; non ci sono né erbe, né piante, né alberi, eccetto che in pochi giardini. Mancano strade larghe; le vie di Venezia sono canali e rii; quindi né automobili, ne autobus, né carrozze. Il taxi di Venezia è la gondola o il vaporetto. In questo luogo singolare l'occhio deve abituarsi a un panorama del tutto diverso da quello di ogni giorno: un panorama di palazzi, acqua e cielo: palazzi candidi, palazzi gialli, palazzi color di rosa, tutti scintillanti nella luce purissima e forte, e tutti lambiti a pianterreno dal mare. L'orecchio nota l'assenza dei soliti rumori; la prima impressione è di un gran silenzio, rotto ogni tanto dal grido melanconico del gondoliere che s'avvicina all'angolo di una strada o dal lontano fischio del vaporino che fa servizio alle isole vicine.

Questi e altri pensieri mi passavano per la mente, una sera, seduto a un tavolino in piazza San Marco. C'erano con me parecchi amici (conoscenze fatte al Lido, dove andavo a bagnarmi tutti i giorni) venuti a sentire la serenata sul Canal Grande.

—E pensa, Carlo,— mi diceva uno di loro, —che questa città fantastica è costruita in mezzo a una laguna, sopra un arcipelago di quasi centoventi isole, e ha centosessanta canali e quattro-cento ponti.—

—La sua storia dev'essere molto interessante,— dissi io.

—Avanti, Luigi, lo storico— gridarono tutti.

—Bene, bene,— rispose Luigi. —Era fondata nel quinto secolo— mi pare —dai profughi dalle invasioni barbariche, e andò sempre acquistando maggior importanza e potere con le sue relazioni commerciali coll'oriente. I veneziani, sapete, erano un popolo pratico e intraprendente: seppero approfittare di ogni occasione per arricchirsi e per estendere la loro potenza. Nel medioevo si erano acquistato il monopolio del commercio del sale, un prodotto allora molto scarso e caro; ai tempi delle crociate con le loro navi trasportarono in oriente le truppe cristiane e naturalmente da quei furbi mercanti che erano fecero pagar cari quei viaggi. Nel dugento Venezia era già una potenza importante nel Mediterraneo, con colonie nell'Egeo e nell'Asia Minore, e nel trecento cominciò a farsi paladina del cristianesimo contro i Turchi, e fu allora, se mi ricordo bene, che le sue navi raggiunsero i porti della lontana Inghilterra. Avendo conquistato molta parte dell'Italia settentrionale, questa repubblica marittima divenne poi uno dei cinque grandi stati italiani. La decadenza data dal cinquecento coll'aprirsi di nuove vie marittime alle Indie e col principio di lunghe guerre contro la Turchia. Oggi può sembrare una città morta; ma è un ricchissimo museo e un paradiso per i turisti . . . e per studenti in vacanza.— soggiunse, con un sorriso.

—Bravo Luigi!— —Trenta con lode!—

—Grazie, Luigi,— dissi io, e mi guardai intorno sulla piazza.

Ci stava di fronte nella lontananza la facciata della basilica, e ai due lati i bei portici con i negozi di cristallerie e di pizzi, dove andava su e giú a passi lenti la folla (era l'ora della passeggiata serale). L'orchestra suonava una musica sentimentale, e tutt'intorno volavano quegli abitanti sfrontati della piazza—i piccioni—i quali venivano ogni tanto sul marciapiede o a posarsi sulle tavole per cercarvi delle briciole. —Venga pur qui a Venezia chi ha bisogno di riposarsi— pensai. —Cullandosi al ritmo lento della gondola, un senso di calma e di pace gl'invaderà l'anima come in nessun altro luogo. Qui si è pigri, qui nessuno ha fretta, c'è tempo per tutto, perchè il tempo stesso pare che si sia arrestato.—

Vocabulary

adriatico = Adriatic

fedele = faithful (adj. and noun)

marinaro = seafaring

nord (m.) = north

orientale = eastern

patriottico = patriotic

sentimento = feeling

abbellire (1st group) = to beautify

animare = to animate

attestare a = to bear witness to

fare guerra a = to make war on

Exercise 27

1. He is a cheeky boy: he was looking at me all the time.
2. Haven't you paid for that ticket yet?
3. He will not allow me to see those books; he has locked the door of his room.
4. What do you think of that man? He is a liar; I do not believe what he says.
5. The bottle of wine is on the table in the dining-room; that new maid with the red hair has left it there.
6. Venice was one of the largest and most important cities of the Middle Ages. Built on an archipelago of 120 islands in a lagoon at the north of the Adriatic, it was destined to become a maritime power. The Venetians were a practical and enterprising people. They acquired the monopoly of the salt trade and charged a high price for that commodity. In the times of the Crusades they knew how to take advantage of the opportunity of enriching themselves and of extending their power in the Eastern Mediterranean, and their ships carried thousands of the faithful who were making war on the Turks. On the return journeys to their own country, those same ships came laden with rich marble and mosaics, which that seafaring people used to beautify their city. The beautiful Venetian monuments and buildings which we admire today bear witness to the strong patriotic feeling which animated the sons of this famous maritime republic of the Middle Ages.

(Note: In the times . . . translate *at* the times; *on* the return . . . *in* the journeys of return; their own country . . . is *their own* necessary if you use *patria*?)

LESSON XXVIII

THE SUBJUNCTIVE

THE Subjunctive Mood has almost disappeared from English, and except for an occasional "Long live!" and an "If I were you", we no longer use it. Italian, however, observes the mood strictly, and we must learn to use it correctly.

The *indicative* makes a plain statement about something which is an actual fact; the *subjunctive* expresses something which is possible but uncertain, some action which is dependent upon another action, sometimes resulting from emotion or thought expressed in that other action. It is chiefly found in subordinate clauses, though it appears, too, in principal sentences, to express a wish:

Voglia il cielo che torni in tempo = Heaven grant he returns in time!

and we have met it as supplying the third persons of the imperative:

Mi dia quel libro per favore = Give me that book, please.

In this lesson we will confine ourselves to the *Present Subjunctive*. The three model verbs are conjugated on page 76. Note that the three persons singular are identical for all verbs; that the first person plural is the same as that of the present indicative; and that the third conjugation verbs which have the *-isc* in the present indicative also have it in the present subjunctive. We might also study at this point the irregular present subjunctive of the following verbs: *andare, dare, dire, fare, potere, sapere, stare, venire* and *volere*. These will be found in the appendix, where it will be seen that the three persons singular are identical and that the endings are the same for all these verbs (i.e., *-a, -iamo, -iate* and *-ano*). The same remarks apply to the auxiliary verbs, which are conjugated as follows: *essere*: sia, sia, sia, siamo, siate, siano; and *avere*: abbia, abbia, abbia, abbiamo, abbiate, abbiano.

Uses of the Subjunctive

The subjunctive is used in clauses depending on verbs which express:

1. desire, will, preference:

   Voglio che *veniate* voi tutti = I want you all to come.

2. request, command, prohibition, hindering or preventing:

   Il capitano *comanda* che tu *venga* subito = The captain orders you to come at once.

3. doubt, uncertainty, ignorance:

   Dubito che quella *sia* vero = I doubt that that is true.

4. belief, opinion, supposition:

   Credo che *sia* già partito = I think he's already gone.

(Where there is no doubt, but simply a future idea with *credere*, the indicative is used: *Credo* che *partirà* alle nove.)

5. a negative idea:

Non sɔ se *sia* già partito = I don't know whether he's already left.

Non c'è *nessuno* che essa *conosca* = there is no one she knows.

6. emotion (joy, sorrow, fear, wonder, shame, expectancy):

Sono tanto *contɛnto* che *sappiano* ogni cɔsa = I'm so glad that they know everything.

Mi *dispiace* che tu *abbia* lɛtto quello = I'm sorry that you have read that.

7. It is also used after an impersonal expression, except when that expression denotes something clear and evident, an actual fact:

Bisogna che ci *vada* = I must go there.

BUT:

ɛ *vero* che ci *sono* stato = It's true that I've been there.

All the dependent clauses quoted above are noun clauses; they stand as subject, object or predicate of a verb. Note that the subject of the main clause and of the dependent clause is always different; if the subject is the same in both clauses, the subordinate clause would not require the subjunctive, but the infinitive (see page 127).

Another type of subordinate clause is the adjectival clause, modifying a noun or pronoun, and introduced by a relative pronoun = who, which, that. They have their verbs in the subjunctive:

1. After a relative superlative and the words *primo, ultimo, solo* and *unico,* in the main clause:

ɛ *la piú grande* chiɛsa che *abbia* mai vista = It's the largest church I've ever seen.

2. After a negative or an interrogative:

Non ha chi lo *pɔssa* aiutare = He has nobody who can help him.

Non c'è nessuno che lo possa aiutare? = Isn't there anyone who can help him?

3. When the subordinate clause expresses purpose:

Scelgono dieci volontari che *prendano* d'assalto la fortezza = They are choosing ten volunteers to take the fort by assault.

4. When the relative pronoun has an indefinite antecedent:

Cerco *una giacca* che *vada* bene con questa gonna = I'm looking for a coat (jacket) to match this skirt (uncertain as to whether there will be one).

BUT:

Cerco *la giacca* che *va* con questa gonna = I'm looking for the short coat that goes with this skirt (a definite coat).

5. After the indefinite words: *chiunque, qualunque, checché, dovunque, per quanto*:

Chiunque tu *sia*, non puoi entrare = Whoever you are, you cannot go in.

Study the irregular verbs: *leggere, muovere, scrivere*.

Translation XIII

A Venezia la vita della città si svolge intorno alla Piazza San Marco, e piú precisamente intorno a quei tavolini di caffè; a Milano il centro vitale è la Piazza del Duomo con la contigua galleria Vittorio Emmanuele, anch'essa coi suoi tavolini occupati a tutte le ore del giorno. La galleria, tradizionale luogo di ritrovo dei milanesi, è enorme. Dalla Piazza del Duomo ci si entra per una maestosa arcata, e, attraversata tutta la galleria, si esce nella Piazza della Scala dove c'è il famoso teatro di quel nome. Per tutta la sua lunghezza la galleria è fiancheggiata da eleganti negozi e da molti caffè, e io certo ho passato ore molto gradevoli seduto con amici a un tavolino a guardare e a criticare la folla che passava e a mangiar gelati, che sono davvero squisiti!

Un giorno, dopo una visita al convento di Santa Maria delle Grazie in compagnia di due turisti americani per vedere la celebre Ultima Cena di Leonardo da Vinci, tornai alla galleria per riposarmi. Sedutomi alla mia solita tavola, chiesi un vermut al cameriere e mi misi a guardare i passanti. Mi rimanevano soltanto pochi giorni di vacanze, e pensavo che sarei dovuto andare al teatro almeno una volta. Chiamato il cameriere, che mi era già amico—tante volte mi aveva aiutato e consigliato, gli chiesi un giornale, per leggervi la rubrica dei teatri.

—Molto volentieri, Signore,— rispose, —a momenti passerà il giornalaio col Corriere della Sera, e glielo comprerò io, Signore. Ma in quanto ai teatri, temo che ci sia ben poco ora perché si è fuori di stagione. La maggior parte dei teatri son chiusi e gli artisti sono via in vacanza. Ma ci sono moltissimi cinema; non vorrebbe vedere qualche buona pellicola?— Ma sapevo già che ai cinema non c'era gran che.

Mentre aspettavo il giornalaio comprai carta da scrivere e francobolli dal cameriere, e lí, al mio tavolino scrissi ai miei in Inghilterra per annunciare la data del mio ritorno a casa. Stavo mettendo i francobolli da settanta lire alla mia lettera quando tornò il cameriere col giornale. Egli lo aveva già consultato e me lo porse dicendo:

—C'è una cosa che fose le andrà a genio, Signore. Le place la musica?— Alla mia risposta affirmativa continuò:

—Allora, c'è una recita straordinaria di beneficenza, la bellissima opera di Puccini, Madame Butterfly—Lei la conosce certamente, Signore—con un tenore bravissimo e una cantante giapponese con una voce divina. Vale la pena di sentirla. Ma la danno in un teatro piccolo, un po' fuori del centro, vicino a casa mia,—

—Benissimo, Beppino— risposi (cosí si chiamava quel brav'uomo); —se è vicino a casa sua, venga con me stasera a sentire Madame Butterfly, eh?—

Vocabulary

affari (m.pl.) = business

movimento = movement, bustle

penisola = peninsula

speranza = hope

tregua = respite

bancario (adj.), of banks, banking

industriale = industrial

discutere (irreg.) = discuss

Exercise 28

1. Give me some of that writing-paper, please; I want to write to my people at home (omit "some").
2. He wants you all to go away immediately; he cannot see anybody.
3. I doubt whether they will come now; it is so late.
4. He is glad you know it now; but he did not dare tell you himself.
5. Do you know whether they have gone or not?
6. He is the naughtiest boy I know.
7. Isn't there anyone here who can play the piano?

8. Milan is one of the largest towns in Italy, with more than a
   million inhabitants. It is the most important city of
   northern Italy, and the largest industrial, commercial and
   banking centre in the whole of the peninsula. When I am
   in Milan I go to the Victor Emanuel Arcade every day.
   It is the traditional meeting-place for the Milanese, and
   there are some smart shops and very many cafés there.
   I sit down at one of the little tables and ask the waiter for
   a vermouth or a coffee, and while I am there drinking
   I watch the crowd go by. Some come here to walk up and
   down, some to chat, some to meet their friends, and others
   to discuss business; but they all come in the hope of
   having a moment's peace and respite from the noise and
   bustle of the large modern industrial town. (Say: of the
   large town industrial modern. "whole" = tutto.)

LESSON XXIX

THE SUBJUNCTIVE (*CONTD.*)

ON page 76 the *Imperfect Subjunctive* of regular verbs is given.
Note that the double *ss* appears in all persons except the second
person plural; that the second person plural is the same as that
of the past definite; and that, except for the characteristic
vowel, the endings are the same for all three conjugations.
Study also the irregular imperfect subjunctives (in the Appendix) of: *dare, fare, stare* and *dire*; and of the auxiliary *essere*;—
fossi, fossi, fosse, fossimo, foste, fossero. (*avessi* from *avere* is
regular.)

Use of the Tenses of the Subjunctive

In our last lesson we translated the Italian present subjunctive into English by the present indicative, by the infinitive
or by "may" and "might". Where Italian requires the subjunctive, if the English verb is in the *present* indicative, in
Italian it will often be in the *present* subjunctive; and if the
English verb is a *past* tense, Italian will on most occasions
employ the *imperfect* subjunctive. But we cannot take the
English equivalents as a basis to decide which tense of the
subjunctive to use in every case in Italian; our "may" and
"might" are sometimes interchangeable, and the infinitive in
English is sometimes rendered by the Italian present and sometimes by the imperfect subjunctive:

Vuɔle che tu *vɛnga* subito = He wants you to come at once.
Voleva che tu *venissi* subito = He wanted you to come at once.

The tense of the subjunctive in the subordinate clause is determined by what tense of the indicative is to be found in the main clause. The two sentences just quoted show that a present subjunctive follows a present indicative, and an imperfect subjunctive follows an imperfect indicative. We may formulate the rules as follows:

1. When the verb in the main clause is in the present indicative or the future or the imperative, the verb in the subordinate clause is in the present subjunctive or in the present perfect subjunctive:

Temo che non *vɛnga* ɔggi = I'm afraid he won't come today.
Crederà che tu *sia uscito* = He'll think you've gone out.

2. When the verb in the main clause is in any other tense of the indicative (except the present perfect), the verb in the dependent clause is in the imperfect subjunctive, or in the past perfect subjunctive:

Credeva che tu *scherzassi* = He thought you were joking.
Credeva che tu *fossi uscito* = He thought you had gone out.

3. When the verb in the main clause is in the present perfect, the verb in the subordinate clause may be either present or imperfect subjunctive, according as to whether it expresses a present or a past action:

Ha scritto che tu *dɛbba* tornare subito = He has written that you should return at once.
Ha voluto che tu *rimanessi* a casa = He wanted you to stay at home.

The imperfect or past perfect subjunctive is also used in clauses expressing a condition,* and in independent sentences to express a wish that cannot be fulfilled:

Avesse dato rɛtta a me! = Had he only listened to me! (Dare rɛtta a = to pay attention to.)

and occasionally it is used instead of the present in such sentences as:

Volesse il ciɡlo! = Would to heaven!

* See page 146.

Further Uses of the Subjunctive

The third type of subordinate clause, the adverbial clause, modifying a verb and introduced by a conjunction (as *sebbɛne*, or *benché*), has its verb in the subjunctive after certain of these conjunctions. These may best be listed under the different types of clause they introduce:

1. Purpose: perché   } = so that, in order that
               affinché }
               di mɔdo = in such a way that

2. Time: prima che } = before
              avanti che }
              finché, finché . . . non = until, as long as (only followed by subjunctive when it contains the idea of doubt, uncertainty or possibility).

3. Condition: purché = provided that
              a meno che . . . non = unless
              nel caṣo che = in case
              dato che = given that
              se mai, se pure, se anche = even if

4. Concession: benché, sebbɛne = although
               non ostante che = in spite of the fact that
               per quanto = however much

5. Manner: come se, quasi = as if

6. Negation: sɛnza che, sɛnza che . . . non = without

7. Than-clause, introducing a comparison when implying uncertainty: di quel che, che non = than.

Examples:

1. *Purpose.*

Studia molto *affinché pɔssa* vincere un prɛmio = He's studying a great deal so as to win a prize.

2. *Time.*

Voglion partire *prima che* lɛi *vɛnga* = They want to go before she comes.

Aspettate *finché* io *tɔrni* = Wait till I come back.

But:

Finché l'autobus non si fɛrma, non si puɔ̀ scɛndere = Until the bus stops, you cannot get off.

3. *Condition.*

Glielo venderò *purché* mi *paghi* bɛne = I'll sell it to him so long as he pays me well.

4. *Concession.*

Benché abbia ricevuto tante lɛttere, non è contɛnto = Although he's received so many letters, he's not satisfied.

5. *Manner.*

Trasalí *come se avesse visto* uno spɛttro = He started as if he had seen a ghost.

6. *Negation.*

Aprite la porta *sɛnza che* lui se ne *accɔrga* = Open the door without his noticing. (Accɔrgersi *di* = to notice.)

7. *Than-clause.*

Quel ragazzo lavora meglio *che* tu *non pensi,* or: meglio *di quel che pensi* = That boy works better than you think.

Two further uses of the subjunctive remain to be considered: the indirect question and the indirect statement. The verb of an indirect question is in the subjunctive if it depends on a verb in the past tense or in the conditional, when there is uncertainty in the indirect statement:

Ci *chiɛse* se *potesse* venire = He asked us if he might come.
Avrɛbbe voluto sapere dove tu *fossi stato?* = Would he have wanted to know where you had been?

The verb of an indirect statement—that is, the verb in a clause depending on a verb of saying—is also in the subjunctive if the main verb is (1) negative, (2) interrogative or (3) in a past tense or the conditional, unless, in the case of (3), the speaker wishes to indicate that the indirect statement is true:

Non dico che non *sia* intelligɛnte = I don't say that he's not clever.
Ha chiɛsto che *andasse* anche lo zio? = Has he asked for uncle to go too?
Dissero che il re *fosse mɔrto* = They said that the king was dead.

In this last sentence the person who is repeating the statement is not absolutely certain that it is true: in the one that follows he is:

Dissero che il re morí ieri sera alle undici = They said the king died at eleven o'clock last night.

Study the verbs: *correre*, *giungere*, *piangere* and *rompere*.

Translation XIV

—Grazie, Signore, Lei è troppo gentile,— continuò Beppino. —Oggi per l'appunto sono libero, e se le fa veramente piacere. . . .—

Cosí finí per venire al teatro con me non solamente Beppino, ma anche tutta la sua numerosa e simpatica famiglia—la moglie, la sorella, il fratello, il nonno e quattro bambini. Ma che buona gente! Non vollero in nessun modo che io pagassi i biglietti, neppure il mio, malgrado tutte le mie proteste. E che ressa! Poche volte in vita mia ho visto tanto entusiasmo. Non era possibile prenotare i posti, tanta era la gente; anzi si dovette fare la coda. Ma all'aprirsi delle porte ci fu un pigia pigia e fra risa e grida ognuno si precipitò per entrare per primo, e io mi sentii trasportare su per le scale e a un buon posto nella galleria. Beppino perdette di vista alcuni membri della sua famiglia, ma non pareva preoccuparsene molto; era un po' piú ansiosa però, la moglie, che aveva perso una scarpa, ma fortunatamente la trovò piú tardi.

Non dimenticherò mai quel pubblico italiano: critico, persin severo; fischiò senza complimenti un cantante che non gli piaceva e non gli permise di continuare. Tutti conoscevano l'opera nota per nota, e le arie molto famose le cantava anche il pubblico, il che mi infastidí. Se il cantante era veramente buono, però, e l'esecuzione musicale eccellente, c'era nel pubblico un tal rapimento e silenzio che pareva tutti trattenessero il respiro, fino all'ultima nota, poi scoppiò una tempesta di applausi e di "bis" che non finivano piú. Per una certa aria di quel tenore cosí bravo gridarono "bis" sette volte! E per accontentarli il pover'uomo tornò a cantarlo sette volte!

Come si può imaginare era molto tardi quando uscimmo da teatro; due bimbi già si erano addormentati e noi tutti eravamo stanchi ma tanto soddisfatti. Io dovetti affrettarmi all'albergo per fare la valigia, perché partivo il giorno dopo. Tutti m'accompagnarono al tram, e dopo tante strette di mano e "addio" e "torni presto", lasciai finalmente quella brava gente.

Vocabulary

ciao = good-bye! so long!   accompagnare = to accompany
fischio = whistle   lagnarsi = to complain
saluto = greeting   raccontare = to relate, to tell

insieme = together

Exercise 29

1. I was glad that they had gone.
2. I thought that you were all in Italy.
3. If only he had never seen her!
4. Although she had not been the one to break the Venetian mirror, she kept on crying. (Say: Although it had not been she who had . . .; to keep on = to continue.)
5. Did your wife ask where you had been last night?
6. No, I got in without her seeing me.
7. Dear John,

   Do you know where I have come to spend my holidays? My father has always wanted me to see Italy, and now here I am at last! I have visited various famous cities: Pisa, Florence, Siena, Venice, and now I am in Milan, where I have met some of my Italian friends. Yesterday they took me to the theatre (accompanied me to . . .) to hear the opera. They all sang very well; but what interested me most was the Italian audience. What enthusiasm! If only you had seen it. (Omit "it" in translating.) What encores! (How many times encore!) A very good tenor had to come back and sing one of the songs they liked seven times. Seven times! On the other hand (*d'altra parte*), what whistling and shouts when there was one that couldn't sing! What a pity that you weren't here too with me! We would have had a good laugh together! (We would have laughed so much!)
   Don't reply to this; I may have to leave for England in a short time. And excuse this short letter; I'll have heaps of things to tell you (. . . a thousand things . . .); at least you can't complain that I haven't written. My greetings to your people. So long! Yours, Charles.

(Note: Use *tu* throughout this letter, which is obviously to an intimate friend.)

LESSON XXX

THE CONDITIONAL—NOTE ON *DOVERE* AND AUXILIARY VERBS

THE conditional is used to express future time in relation to a verb of saying, thinking and believing in the past; for example:

Direct statement: Scriverò la lɛttera = I will write the letter.
Indirect statement present: Dice che scriverà la lɛttera = He says he will write the letter.
Indirect statement past: Disse che scriverɛbbe la lɛttera = He said he would write the letter.

If the indirect statement in the conditional tense has not yet come true, the *conditional perfect* is used in Italian. The last example therefore implies that he has already written the letter, as he said he would; had he not done so the sentence would be:

Disse che *avrɛbbe scritto* la lɛttera.

It is often clear from the sentence that the action in the dependent clause has not yet been performed:

Risposi che avrɛi fatto tutto il possibile per aiutarlo = I replied that I would do everything possible to help him.

In such cases, therefore, when translating from English, it must be remembered that Italian requires the conditional perfect where we would use the simple conditional.

The most common use of the conditional is in conditional sentences; sentences stating that *if* such a thing happened, something else depending on it *would* come about. The use of the tenses in such sentences is as follows:

1. When a condition is contrary-to-fact in the present, or doubtful in the future, the if-clause (stating the condition) is in the imperfect subjunctive, and the would-clause (drawing the conclusion) in the conditional:

Se avessi abbastanza denaro, comprɛrɛi un automɔbile = If I had enough money, I should buy a car

(implying that I have not enough money—a condition contrary-to-fact in the present);

Se venisse in tɛmpo, potremmo partire insiɛme = If he came in time, we could leave together

(a condition doubtful in the future).

2. When the if-clause refers to past time, the past perfect subjunctive is used, and the would-clause is in the conditional perfect:

Se avessi avuto abbastanza denaro, avrɛi comprato quell'automɔbile = If I had had enough money, I should have bought that car.

3. Any other condition is expressed by the indicative:

Se Lɛi va in città, mi cɔmpri dell'inchiɔstro, per favore = If you're going to town, buy me some ink, please.

Note that sometimes in Italian, and particularly in the spoken language, the *imperfect indicative* is used in both clauses of a contrary-to-fact condition in the past, instead of the past perfect subjunctive and the conditional perfect:

Se avevo abbastanza denaro, compravo quell'automɔbile = If I had had enough money, I should have bought that car.

The conditional is also used idiomatically to express doubt or uncertainty: *Chi ɛ̀ quello lì? Non saprɛi* = Who is that man there? I don't know.

There remain two more points to consider before we finish the last lesson of this little book. First the translation of "should have" when it means "ought to have". The literal translation of: "I should have read that book" = *Avrɛi lɛtto quel libro* gives no idea of obligation, so we go to *dovere* and use the conditional perfect followed by the infinitive:

Avrɛi dovuto lɛggere quel libro = I ought to have read that book. It would be useful to list the meanings of the various tenses of this semi-auxiliary verb:

Dɛvo lɛggere quel libro = I must, have to, am to read that book.

Dovevo lɛggere quel libro = I had to, was to read that book.

Dovɛtti lɛggere quel libro = I had to read that book.

Dovrɔ̀ lɛggere quel libro = I shall have to read that book.

Dovrɛi lɛggere quel libro = I should, ought to read that book.

Ho dovuto lɛggere quel libro = I have had to read that book.

Avrɛi dovuto lɛggere quel libro = I ought to have read that book.

The second point is the use of the auxiliary with *dovere* when followed by an infinitive, for it is the *infinitive* which determines which auxiliary should be used. Study these examples:

Avrei dovuto *scrivere* quella lettera = I ought to have written that letter.
Sarebbe dovuto *andare* prima di me = He ought to have gone before me.

Four other verbs, besides *dovere*, when followed by an infinitive may take either auxiliary, according to which the infinitive usually takes: *potere*, *volere*, *cominciare* and *finire*:

Non è potuto venire? = Hasn't he been able to come?
Non ha potuto vederla = He hasn't been able to see her.
Ha cominciato a scrivere il libro = He has begun to write the book.
È cominciato a invecchiare = He has begun to get old.

(Verbs conjugated with *essere* are indicated in the Appendix and in the Vocabulary.)

Study these verbs: *condurre*, *distinguere*, *proteggere* and *trarre*.

Translation XV

La mattina dopo partii per Como in compagnia di alcuni americani che proseguivano per Parigi. Como è soltanto un'ora da Milano col direttissimo, e ci arrivai prima delle dieci. Dopo aver fatto un giro per la città mi decisi a salire colla funicolare a Brunate, piccolo borgo sopra una collina a est, da dove c'è una bella veduta del lago. Seduto su una panca a contemplare il panorama, tirai fuori la carta topografica a cercai di orientarmi. In basso si stendeva la città di Como colla sua baia, e con le sue colline oltre le quali si apre la pianura lombarda; in faccia e a destra, il lago, coi suoi monti alti e ripidi, e lontano lontano * all'orizzonte le maestose cime bianche delle Alpi, che brillavano al sole. —Sono ora nel paese di Don Abbondio e di Lucia,— pensai, ricordandomi del famoso romanzo, —e al di là di quelle montagne all'est ci dev'essere Lecco sull'altro ramo del lago—. Consultai di nuovo la carta, pensando, —Invece di rimanere a Como, preferirei un posto più solitario sul lago, un po' fuori di mano. Vediamo un po'.—Seguii col dito l'itinerario del piroscafo: —Como, Cernobbio, Cadenabbia, Bellagio. . . .

* Adverbs and adjectives may be repeated to give emphasis.

Ecco un luogo ridente, su un promontorio, all'incontro dei tre rami del lago; sí, questo va bene. Ci sono cinque o sei alberghi non molto grandi. Tanto meglio.— Scesi di nuovo a Como, e, ritirata la valigia dal deposito m'imbarcai sul piroscafo per Bellagio.

—Buona sera,— dissi al proprietario che stava oziando sulla soglia del suo albergo, —Ha una camera libera?—

—Si accomodi, Signore,— e data la valigia a un portiere che si fece avanti, mi precedette nel vestibolo.

L'albergo era piccolo, ma bianco e pulito; sul davanti aveva un bel giardinetto con balcone e pergola che si stendeva fino alla riva del lago.

—Si fermerà molto?— mi chiese il proprietario.

—No, soltanto tre o quattro giorni.—

—Allora Le posso offrire una bella camera con terrazza e veduta sul lago, lire 2,000 al giorno, tutto compreso; in piú la tassa di soggiorno e per il servizio il dieci per cento. Ce ne sarebbe un'altra piú piccola e senza terrazza con veduta sulle montagne per 1,800. Tutte e due sono belle e ariose, con acqua corrente. Le vuol vedere, Signore?—

—Sí, grazie,— E benché fosse un po' piú caro di quel che avrei voluto pagare, finii per lasciarmi tentare dalla bella vista e scelsi quella con la terrazza.

Ma ogni cosa ha la sua fine. Venne il mio ultimo giorno di vacanza; mi bagnai per l'ultima volta in quelle acque fresche e feci l'ultima gita in barca col vecchio barcaiuolo Antonio. La mattina della partenza mi alzai prestissimo, e, fatta la valigia mi feci portare il caffè sul terrazzino. Mentre mangiavo guardavo passar le barche da pesca con le vele rossicce. Poi a un tratto vidi il mio vecchio amico Antonio, il quale, lasciati i remi, si alzò in piedi, e agitando in aria il beretto, mi gridò:—

—Arrivederci, Signore, buon viaggio; si ricordi di Antonio e torni presto.—

—Certamente—, pensai salendo a bordo del piroscafo per Como, la mia prima tappa del viaggio di ritorno, —certamente, mio caro Antonio, mi ricorderò di te; e, in quanto al tornare presto; sí, anche questo te lo posso promettere: tornerò nel tuo bel paese il piú presto possibile.—

Vocabulary

barca a remi = rowing-boat	prezzo = price
conoscenza = acquaintance	rabbia = anger, rage
molo = jetty	Che rabbia! = How annoying!
motoscafo = motor-boat	importare = to matter

Exercise 30

1. They said they would come at three, but it is half-past and they have not arrived yet.
2. If you go to the theatre, don't come back as late as you did the other time.
3. If I had that book, I should study.
4. If I had had that book I should have studied.
5. If I have that book I shall study.
6. If he had asked *me* where the church was, I should have told him straight away. (Translate in two ways.)
7. He ought to have come earlier if he had wanted to see me.
8. If I had not arrived at Como too late to take the steamer for Bellagio I should not have got to know Antonio (Should not have known . . .). That old boatman with his blue eyes and white beard and with that queer red cap was lounging about on the jetty when I arrived at a run (running), my suitcase in my hand, just in time to see the steamer leave. . . . "How annoying! Who knows how long I'll have to wait!" I thought. "I'm sorry you've missed the steamer. Would you like a boat, sir?" asked the old man, coming up to me. "Thank you," I replied, "it's a bit far to go in a rowing-boat." "Oh, but I have a motor-boat, sir." "No, thank you; I'm afraid that would cost too much." "But, sir, you want to go to Bellagio, and I want to go there too; my home is there (say: *there* is my house . . .), and my wife and children are expecting (waiting for) me for supper. Let's go together; if you wish to pay me, pay me the price of the steamer ticket; if you don't want to pay me, it doesn't make any difference; I shall be going all the same." And so I ended by going with Antonio and in getting to know one of the nicest men I have ever met.

CONCLUSION

LESSON XXX brings us to the end of this little book, and the student who has worked through it conscientiously should now be able to go forward on his own account. His first aim should be to read as much Italian as possible. A beginning could be made with the readers, short stories and plays in Harrap's modern language series, which are provided with notes and vocabularies. The easiest to start with would be: *Andiamo in Italia. Venti scenette italiane*, by Christabel Fowler and Teresa Della Torre; or: E. Goggio, *A New Italian Reader for Beginners*, which contains anecdotes, short stories and a few poems; and three small books of Italian conversation, based on topics of everyday interest, by C. E. Kany and C. Speroni: *Elementary, Intermediate* and *Advanced Italian Conversation*. Two books in the bilingual series might then be tried: *Introduction to Italian*, by Ena Makin; and L. Pirandello, *Quattro novelle*, translated by V. M. Jeffrey; but keep the English side covered up as long as possible! Other editions in the annotated series are, in ascending order of difficulty: (1) C. Collodi, *Avventure di Pinocchio* (the Italian child's classic), ed. E. Goggio, (2) *Modern Italian Short Stories*, ed. T. G. Bergin, a collection of contemporary authors, mostly of the generation that came to fame between the two world wars, as C. Alvaro, M. Bontempelli, G. A. Borgese, G. Lipparini, G. Papini; (3) Massimo T. D'Azeglio, *I miei ricordi*, edited with notes by V. Cioffari and J. van Horne; and (4) A. Manzoni, *I promessi sposi* (the first eight chapters of this famous novel which contain a story in themselves), ed. Geddes and Wilkins.

For those who are interested in plays the Harrap series includes: *Six Easy Italian Plays* (very farcical and of no literary merit, but useful for learning colloquial idiom), ed. E. Goggio; *Modern Italian One-Act Plays* (three in number: G. Verga, *Cavalleria rusticana*, G. Giacosa, *Diritti dell'anima*, and R. Bracco, *Pietro Caruso*), ed. C. A. Swanson; and a play by Pirandello: *Così è, (se vi pare)*. In addition to notes and vocabularies, many of these books have an introduction telling briefly about the author and his work and an appendix containing exercises and drill in idiomatic phrases.

By this time, however, the enthusiastic student will be looking for a dictionary of his own. There is not a large choice; but it is varied, ranging from the very small pocket ones, such as the Collins Gem edition and the similar one in the E.F.G. series, Eyre & Spottiswoode, to the large ones, *e.g.*, G. Orlandi, *Dizionario italiano–inglese, inglese–italiano*, Signorelli, Milan, 1950; or N. Spinelli, *Dizionario scolastico italiano–inglese, inglese–italiano*, S.E.I., Turin, 1951; while those who require a dictionary including commercial and technical terms have a choice of the following: *Modern Italian–English, English–Italian Dictionary*, with commercial supplement, by Lysle-Severino, Allen & Unwin; N. Spinelli, *Dizionario commerciale italiano–inglese, inglese–italiano*, S.E.I., Turin, 1951; and G. Marolli, *Dizionario tecnico inglese–italiano, italiano–inglese*, Le Monnier, Florence, 1950. Between the very small and these larger dictionaries come three medium-sized ones; N. Spinelli, *Dizionario tascabile italiano–inglese, inglese–italiano*, S.E.I., Turin, revised ed. 1952, 2 vols.; J. Purves, *Dictionary of Modern Italian*, Routledge, 1953 and *Cassell's Italian–English, English–Italian Dictionary*, 1958. If an all-Italian dictionary is required a really sound investment would be: G. Cappuccini and B. Migliorini, *Vocabolario della lingua italiana*, Paravia, Turin, revised ed. 1958.

With the knowledge he now has and with the help of a dictionary the student will be surprised at the rapid progress he will make in reading contemporary novels and short stories. One of the main characteristics of the neo-realist writers of post-war Italy (*i.e.*, of post world war II) is the natural spontaneity and unselfconscious freshness of their stories, which are told in a correspondingly simple and straightforward style. Most of the following, therefore, will be found fairly easy to read: L. Bartolini, *Ladri di biciclette* (which made a famous film); E. Vittorini, *Conversazione in Sicilia*, and *Il garofano rosso*; G. Berto, *Il cielo è rosso*, and *Il brigante*; C. Pavese, *La luna e i falò*, and *Prima che il gallo canti*; and, with an interesting present-day Florentine background: V. Pratolini, *Il quartiere, Un eroe del nostro tempo*, and *Cronache di poveri amanti*; while G. Marotta's *L'oro di Napoli* and *San Gennaro non dice mai no* have contemporary Naples for their scene. Two more might be mentioned, rather more difficult than those just listed, and in such complete contrast to one another as to seem to come from two different worlds, yet both giving, in their different ways, a true-to-life picture of Italy today: the tragic and impressive: *Cristo si è fermato a Eboli* by C. Levi; and the delightfully satirical and witty: *Don Camillo, Piccolo Mondo*, by G. Guareschi, while many of the outstanding Italian novels which have appeared recently, Carlo Cassola's *La ragazza di Bube*, Einaudi, Turin, 1958 may be recommended, with Giuseppe Tomasi di Lampedusa's *Il Gattopardo*, Feltrinelli, Milan, 1959, as two of the finest, the latter became internationally famous almost as soon as published.

While reading Italian, grammatical studies should not be neglected if the student wishes to learn to write Italian correctly. He would be well advised to attend some class, or arrange for a teacher or an educated Italian to correct his efforts. The following will be useful, with or without a teacher: V. Cioffari, *Italian Review Grammar*, Harrap, intended for those who have studied Italian for at least a year, and offering many exercises in conversation and drill in colloquial and idiomatic Italian; W. Shewring, *Italian Prose Usage*, a supplement to Italian grammars, Cambridge University Press; and if he would like to study the grammar and read about the language in Italian, the student will find the following of interest and not too difficult: B. Migliorini and F. Chiapelli, *Lingua e stile*, 1952, Le Monnier, Florence; B. Migliorini, *La lingua nazionale*, 1947, the same publisher; G. Devoto and D. Massaro, *Grammatica italiana*, La Nuova Italia, Florence, 1953. Also the following: E. Bianchi, *La lingua italiana*, Salani, Florence, 1943, illustrated, an elementary book on the history of the Italian language, on its structure and position in the Romance family, containing long passages from the classics, both prose and verse in a section devoted to the art of writing; and B. Migliorini, *Conversazioni sulla lingua*, a series of short talks given on the wireless on various aspects of language study, such as: meanings, metaphors, the disappearance of words, the influence of biblical language on Italian, Spanish words in Italian, etc., Le Monnier, Florence, 1949; while a more difficult, but entertaining and at the same time very useful and well-informed book about foreign words which have passed into Italian as a result of the last war and which gives, to the observant reader, an interesting glimpse of contemporary Italy, is: A. Menarini, *Profili di vita italiana nelle parole nuove*, Le Monnier, Florence, 1951.

To the student of the history of Italian literature the following manuals may be recommended: V. Rossi, *Storia della letteratura italiana*, new edition brought up to date by U. Bosco, 1943, 3 vols., Vallardi, Milan, and rather more detailed: N. Sapegno, *Compendio di storia della letteratura italiana*, 1948, 3 vols., La Nuova Italia, Florence; and shorter than either of these: A. Momigliano, *Storia della letteratura italiana*, in one volume, G. Principato, Milan, new ed. 1947, all of which contain full and up-to-date bibliographies. There are many anthologies of Italian literature, a useful one would be *Antologia di letteratura italiana per stranieri*, ed. O. Prosciutti and U. Pittola, Perugia University, 1952; and two inexpensive ones of contemporary works are: *Poeti del novecento*, compiled by G. Spagnoletti, Edizioni scolastiche Mondadori, Milan, 1958; and *Narratori del novecento*, by L. Fiorentino, and the same publisher, 1960; while the *Oxford Book of Italian Verse*, revised and augmented by C. Dionisotti, 1952, is a treasure coveted by many English students of Italian.

For the student who aspires to read Dante in the original there is J. D. Sinclair's edition of the *Divina Commedia* in 3 vols., John Lane, the Bodley Head, revised ed. 1948. This contains brief but adequate notes, an admirable commentary and a very readable English version in prose printed opposite the Italian text. An introduction to Dante studies should include Dean Church's *Essay on Dante* (in *Dante and St. Anselm*, Routledge); E. G. Gardner, *Dante*, Dent; P. H. Wicksteed, *From Vita Nuova to Paradiso* (Manchester University Press); D. G. Rossetti's version of the *Vita nuova* (or in the original in the Temple Classics); and in Italian: M. Barbi, *Dante, Vita, opere e fortuna*, Sansoni, Florence, 1933, and U. Cosmo, *Guida a Dante* (this last has an English translation: *A Handbook to Dante Studies*, trans. by D. Moore, Oxford, Blackwell, 1949). Useful Dante bibliography will, of course, also be found after the relative chapters in each of the manuals of History of Literature mentioned above.

And so, in the hope that this short bibliography will prove useful and will also be an urge to further endeavour, we take our leave of the patient reader, and while advising him to "read, read more, read much more", we would wish him, most cordially, "Buono studio e . . . buon divertimento!"

PART II

KEY TO EXERCISES AND TRANSLATIONS

Preliminary Exercise

1. Virtú, portò, perché, mercoledí, credé, onestà, caffè, città, sincerità.
2. arena (ah-ráy-nah), cupola (kóo-poh-lah), incognito (een-cón-yee-toh), pianoforte (peeah-noh-fáwr-tay), vermicelli (vair-mee-chéll-ee), terra cotta (tay-rrah-cáw-tah), ulti-matum (ool-tee-máh-toom), Galli-Curci (Gah-lee Cóor-chee), Marco Polo (Mahr-coh Páw-loh), Medici (Máy-dee-chee).

Exercise 1 (a)

1. Maria è una donna e Piero è un uomo.
2. Maria e Piero hanno una casa.
3. Piero e Maria hanno un figlio e una figlia.
4. Chi ha un fratello? Maria ha un fratello e anche una sorella.
5. Ha Piero uno zio? Sí, Piero ha uno zio e anche una zia.
6. Dov'è una porta e dov'è una finestra?
7. Chi ha un libro? Piero ha un libro? Che cosa ha Maria? Maria ha uno specchio.
8. Dov'è uno sbaglio? Ecco uno sbaglio in un libro.

Exercise 1 (b)

1. Mary is a woman and Peter is a man.
2. Mary and Peter have a house.
3. Peter and Mary have a son and daughter. (Note that in Italian the article must be repeated before each noun.)
4. Who has a brother? Mary has a brother and also a sister.
5. Has Peter an uncle? Yes, Peter has an uncle and also an aunt.
6. Where is a door and where is a window?
7. Who has a book? Has Peter a book? What has Mary? Mary has a mirror.
8. Where is a mistake? Here is a mistake in a book.

Exercise 1 (c)

1. Maria ha una casa e Piero ha una casa.
2. Piero ha un figlio e una figlia.
3. Ha Maria una zia? Sí, Maria ha una zia e anche uno zio.
4. Dov'è uno sbaglio? Ecco uno sbaglio.
5. Chi ha un libro? Maria ha un libro. Maria dà un libro a Piero.
6. Maria ha un fratello e una sorella.
7. Che cosa ha Piero in una mano? Piero ha un libro in una mano.
8. Maria ha uno specchio? Sí, Maria ha uno specchio.

Exercise 2 (a)

1. Vendo una vacca e compro un gatto.

vendi	compri
vende	compra
vendiamo	compriamo
vendete	comprate
vendono	comprano

2. Mentre scrivo, uso una penna, inchiostro e un foglio.

scrivi, usi
scrive, usa
scriviamo, usiamo
scrivete, usate
scrivono, usano

3. Quando leggo, guardo un libro.

leggi, guardi
legge, guarda
leggiamo, guardiamo
leggete, guardate
leggono, guardano

(Note that the g of *leggere* has the hard sound before the -*o* in the first person singular and third person plural; otherwise it is soft as the *j* in *July* in the other persons, as in the infinitive.)

Exercise 2 (b)

1. Io parlo con Piero.

tu parli
egli, ella, lui, lei, esso, essa parla
noi parliamo
voi parlate
loro, essi, esse parlano

Exercise 2 (c)

1. Who finds a book? I find a book.
2. Are Mary and Peter speaking? Yes, they are speaking.
3. Is Mary writing a letter to Peter?
4. Yes, and while she is writing I am looking at a book.
5. What is Peter buying today?
6. Today Peter is buying a book.

Exercise 2 (d)

1. Dov'è una tavola?
2. Vende una vacca e compra un gatto.
3. Scrivono una lettera a Maria.
4. Mentre lei legge io scrivo.
5. Che cosa vedi? Io vedo una donna e un uomo, un ragazzo e una ragazza.
6. Lei compra uno specchio e io compro un libro.
7. Parlano italiano Maria e Piero? Sí parlano italiano.
8. Lui guarda Maria mentre lei scrive una lettera.

Exercise 3 (a)

1. Dov'è la donna? La donna è a casa.
2. I fratelli e le sorelle di Maria sono in città. Comprano i cappelli e le cravatte.
3. Lo zio di Piero è alto, ma la zia è molto piccola.
4. Ecco la casa nuova. Dov'è l'entrata?
5. Il tetto è rosso e i muri sono gialli.
6. Questo muro è alto ma l'altro è basso.
7. Il giardino è bellino, l'erba è bella e ci sono molti alberi.
8. Piero guarda lo zio: perché ha un cappello giallo, una cravatta azzurra e i calzini sono rossi.
9. Maria non è in casa, è in città e compra gli specchi.

Exercise 3 (b)

1. Where is the woman? The woman is at home.
2. Mary's brothers and sisters are in town; they are buying the hats and ties.
3. Peter's uncle is tall, but his aunt is very small. (The article is often used instead of the possessive "his", "her", etc., when the context makes it quite plain whose "aunt", etc., is meant.)
4. Here is the new house. Where is the door?
5. The roof is red, but the walls are yellow.
6. This wall is high, but the other is low.

7. The garden is pretty; the grass is lovely and there are many trees.
8. Peter is looking at uncle, because he has a yellow hat, a blue tie and his (the) socks are red.
9. Mary is not at home; she is in town, and she is buying the mirrors.

Exercise 3 (c)

1. Gli alberi sono molto alti.
2. La casa nuova ha un tetto rosso e muri gialli. È in un giardino molto bellino.
3. Le finestre sono molto alte, ma la porta è bassa.
4. Lo zio è a casa ma la zia è in città. Lei compra un cappello.
5. Lui è molto alto ma la zia è piccola.
6. Questo ragazzo compra una penna, ma l'altro ragazzo compra calzini e una cravatta.
7. La casa ha cinque porte e diciassette finestre.
8. Loro non scrivono le lettere; guardano il cappello giallo e i calzini rossi di Piero.

Exercise 4 (a)

1. The mother opens the window while the child is sleeping.
2. I do not understand why the lady is going today and not tomorrow.
3. We understand this word, but not the other.
4. This house has twelve rooms.
5. The dining-room has a terrace, and the two large rooms have balconies.
6. The dining-room and the terrace are lovely, but the kitchen is too small.
7. We open the window and we see the garden.
8. We have a very fine garden.
9. Where is Peter's sister? She is in the kitchen.
10. They open the door and they see the terrace.
11. The drawing-room is not small and the chairs are comfortable.
12. The drawing-room is on the ground floor, but the study is on the upper floor.
13. Where do you sleep, Mary and Lucy? We sleep in a room on the upper floor.
14. Do you find Italian easy, madam? (or miss?).
15. Yes, I find Italian easy. Spanish is easy too; but I prefer Italian.

Exercise 4 (b)

1. Questa sedia è molto comoda, ma preferisco l'altra.
2. Non capisco questa parola.
3. Capisce Lei questo libro?
4. Dove sono le signorine? Partono oggi?
5. Sí, partono oggi. Sono in cucina con Piero.
6. Piero dorme al pianterreno.
7. La camera di Maria è al piano superiore.
8. È in casa Piero? No, è in città.
9. Sono in città Maria e Piero? Sí, comprano mele.
10. Perché partono oggi? Non capisco perché.
11. La cucina è piccola, ma la sala da pranzo è grande.
12. Comprano una casa nuova (or: una nuova casa) con un giardino.
13. Preferiamo una casa in città.
14. Ecco lo studio. Piero apre la porta e vediamo lo zio. Lo zio dorme.
15. Mentre lo zio dorme, la zia è in città. È in città con Maria. Comprano cravatte, calzini, cappelli e un soprabito per lo zio.

Exercise 5 (a)

1. Mary is in the garden and Aunt is in the dining-room.
2. John gives some apples to the guests and then leaves for the town in Uncle's car.
3. Uncle is with the children in the drawing-room.
4. What have you got in your pocket, Peter? I have two handkerchiefs and a tie of Uncle's.
5. Where is Peter? He is in the study with the girl.
6. The dining-room chairs are on the balcony.
7. They are looking in the mirror. What do they see?
8. They see Aunt's hat and gloves. They are on the table.
9. Where is Uncle's yellow hat? Uncle's yellow hat is in the river.
10. Poor Uncle! John and Peter buy a new hat for Uncle.
11. Haven't we any bread? Yes, it is on the table in the kitchen.
12. What is there in the river? I do not see anything.
13. Have you any yellow ties, please?
14. No, sir, but I have some white and blue ties.
15. John is very lazy! He never writes to anybody.

Exercise 5 (b)

1. Maria è nello studio con lo zio. Scrivono lettere.
2. Piero compra calzini, fazzoletti e cravatte da un ragazzo nella strada.
3. Giovanni compra un cappello e guanti dallo stesso ragazzo.
4. È un ragazzo molto povero; non ha scarpe.
5. Che cosa ha nella tasca? Ho tre fazzoletti e una cravatta.
6. Che cosa vedi tu nel fiume, Giovanni? Non vedo niente.
7. Guardo nello specchio: vedo i tre bambini col gatto.
8. Maria cerca il gatto nel giardino.
9. Dov'è il pane? Non abbiamo pane.
10. L'uomo nel salotto è il fratello di Giovanni.
11. Dov'è la cravatta di Giovanni? È sulla tavola nella sala da pranzo con i guanti della zia.
12. Non vedo né la cravatta né i guanti.
13. Non ha dell'inchiostro? Sí, è sulla tavola nello studio.
14. Questa sedia è per l'ospite. Ma non è molto comoda.
15. Il libro che Lei cerca è nello studio.

Exercise 6 (a)

1. He sold the two fine horses last week.
2. Three weeks ago I lost a lovely ring in the garden.
3. Two days ago I received a registered letter and a parcel, and I signed a receipt.
4. The cook offered the postman some tea.
5. Last week the postman brought the cook a lovely red rose.
6. The postman has a good salary? but he is of a poor family.
7. Where did Cook go yesterday? She went to the post office and met the postman. She is a good friend of the postman.
8. I went to the post office too, and at the entrance I met the doctor.
9. The doctor is a good friend of the lawyer.
10. Then we met the lawyer too in the writing-room.
11. I bought twelve postcards and twenty stamps; I finished a letter and then we went to a café.
12. Yesterday the postman brought two postcards from the aunt in America.
13. He is a handsome man, the postman, and the cook is not ugly.

Exercise 6 (b)

1. Vendei un bell'anello ieri e comprai questi libri.
2. Perdé un bell'anello tre settimane fa.
3. Dove perdette l'anello? Nel giardino.
4. La zia ricevé un pacco raccomandato ieri e firmò una ricevuta.
5. Maria fu alla posta con la cuoca. Comprarono francobolli e cartoline.
6. Il fratello di Maria è un uomo molto bello.
7. Ricevei una lunga lettera dallo zio ieri e anche due cartoline e un gran pacco.
8. Non ricevé niente ieri Lei, Signor Pazzi?
9. No, ieri non ricevei niente.
10. I teatri in questa città sono molto belli.
11. Sí, fummo al teatro la settimana scorsa.
12. L'avvocato ricevette una cartolina dal dottore ieri.
13. L'anno scorso comprò una macchina, due cavalli, una vacca e una casa con un gran giardino: ora è molto povero.

Exercise 7 (a)

1. When he was in Florence he went to the library every day.
2. Where did you go? We used to go to a café in Tornabuoni Street.
3. Tornabuoni street was one of the smart streets in that town.
4. I met the lawyer in town yesterday. He was in Tornabuoni Street, looking at the new books in the bookshop.
5. He was looking for that book on the history of Italy which we saw in Rome last week.
6. Do you see that old woman without shoes? Once she was very rich; now she is very poor.
7. This morning I was looking for Cook. Where was she? Wasn't she in the kitchen?
8. No, she was in town. She was buying meat and vegetables at the market.
9. Yesterday I met Mary's brother and the postman in town; they were talking to that girl from the bookshop.
10. What a lovely study Mr. Pazzi used to have! It was a large room with a balcony and two windows.
11. The desk was in front of the balcony, and on the round table near the door there was a lovely lamp.
12. It had a beautiful green carpet too, and a large bookcase with many books.

F

Exercise 7 (b)

1. Andava in chiesa tutti i giorni quando era a Firenze?
2. Sí, andava colla zia tutte le mattine.
3. Scriveva a Giovanni tutte le settimane.
4. Cercavo il fratello di Maria. Dove era? (or Dov'era?)
5. Era nella libreria e parlava coll'avvocato.
6. Il dottore entrò mentre loro parlavano.
7. L'avvocato finiva una lettera quando loro entrarono nello studio.
8. Guardava l'avvocato che era vicino alla scrivania.
9. Cercavano quel giornale che quelle donne leggevano.
10. La cuoca era al mercato stamattina, Signora Pazzi?
11. Sí, comprava carne e legumi, pane e vino.
12. Hanno vini buoni al mercato? No, non sono molto buoni.

Exercise 8 (a)

1. Who is that gentleman? He is one of my friends (or a friend of mine).
2. I am writing to a girl friend of mine in Rome?
3. For whom is that registered parcel? It is for my father.
4. How much bread is there in the kitchen, Mary?
5. There isn't any bread; that boy ate all our bread yesterday.
6. Why do you not buy a bookcase for your books?
7. What good wine! Do you drink wine every day?
8. That cook of theirs is very good.
9. What a good fire that is! Yes, Cook always has a good fire.
10. How much wine does that man drink every day? He usually drinks five or six bottles every day.
11. That wardrobe (cupboard) is for my clothes, and this is for yours.
12. Which trunk is yours, miss? This is mine, that is my mother's and that one over there is that gentleman's with the beard.

Exercise 8 (b)

1. Chi è quel signore dalla barba? È un amico di mio padre.
2. Mio padre e mia madre furono in città ieri. Incontrarono quel tuo amico nella libreria (or: quel suo amico).
3. Di chi è questo baule? È di mia madre.
4. Quanti libri ci sono in quello scaffale?
5. Abbiamo diversi (molti) vini buoni, Signore; quale preferisce, rosso o bianco?

6. Un mio amico comprò quella macchina ieri. Quale? Quella macchina lí nell'autorimessa.
7. Che cosa vende quella vecchia? Vende fazzoletti e calzini.
8. Dove compra Lei i Suoi cappelli? Quel Suo cappello nuovo (or: quel Suo nuovo cappello) è molto elegante.
9. Quale vestito preferisce? Preferisco quello azzurro.
10. Quel suo cappello verde è molto vecchio. Non comprò uno * nuovo la settimana scorsa?
11. Molti miei libri sono nel mio baule.
12. Quanti bauli ha Lei, Signore? Ho due bauli. Questo è il mio e quello là è anche il mio.

Exercise 9 (a)

1. When I sell the house I shall buy a car.
2. What time will the train arrive?
3. It will arrive at half-past five. We shall have time to take tea before going to the station.
4. We usually have tea at five.
5. What time will your son arrive, madam? He will arrive by the twenty-to-eight train.
6. When will they leave? John leaves tonight at midnight, but his brothers will leave tomorrow morning for Florence.
7. We generally have dinner at one (eat at one), but tomorrow we shall dine at half-past twelve and take the two-o'clock train.
8. It is eleven o'clock and Cook is still at the market.
9. What will she be buying at the market? She will be buying lots of things at the market, and she will be talking to her friends.
10. According to my father, Cook is a clever woman, but she doesn't look it.
11. I am sure that my son would not sign this letter.
12. Journeys by train are not always comfortable.

Exercise 9 (b)

1. Che ore sono? Sono le tre e mezzo.
2. A che ora arriva il treno? Alle otto meno un quarto.
3. Quanti cappelli ha quella donna? Ne avrà nove, credo.
4. Quando venderemo i cavalli, compreremo una macchina.
5. Sono sicuro che mia madre non comprerebbe quel cappello.

* *uno*, pronoun, does not have the shortened forms like the definite article.

6. Prendiamo il tè alle quattro e mezzo generalmente, ma domani prenderemo il tè alle quattro prima di andare alla stazione.
7. L'avvocato manderà la lettera al giudice domani.
8. Quando arriverà a casa? Non prima di mezzanotte.
9. Stasera i suoi quattro figli saranno a casa.
10. Comprò ieri un cappello grigio e domani comprerà una sciarpa e dei guanti grigi.
11. Sono le quattro meno un quarto e la cuoca è ancora al mercato.
12. Secondo la signora Pazzi la nostra cuoca sarebbe pigra.

Exercise 10 (a)

1. Today we have guests to dinner.
2. Cook has gone to the market to buy meat and vegetables, and the maid has washed the plates, the cups and glasses.
3. Mary will help the maid to lay the table and clean the forks, spoons and knives.
4. When she has helped the maid she will go to the station to meet the guests.
5. The woman had washed all the plates, but she had not cleaned the knives.
6. When you see the doctor he will already have sold his car.
7. As soon as she had broken a cup she let a bottle fall too.
8. Has she broken all the things on the tray? Yes, all.
9. They had been at the doctor's house when they met the lawyer.
10. Will they already have arrived when Charles returns home? Yes, they will already be in the house.
11. She may be intelligent, that maid, but she doesn't look it. She has already broken twelve plates and two glasses. She also let three bottles fall, and we have lost some good wine.
12. What time did Cook return from the market today? She arrived home very late, I think. She must have met the postman on the way.

Exercise 10 (b)

1. Abbiamo invitato il signore e la signora Pazzi (i signori Pazzi) a pranzo oggi.
2. La cameriera (la donna) ha già apparecchiato per dodici.
3. Aveva già pulito i coltelli e le forchette quando la cuoca tornò dal mercato.

4. La cuoca era stata al mercato molto tempo perché aveva perduto la borsa.
5. Appena ebbe perduto la borsa, parlò col poliziotto.
6. Incontrò anche il postino stamane.
7. C'erano molte cose sul vassoio; piatti, bicchieri, tazze e piattini.
8. Ha rotto molte cose? Sí, due tazze, tre piattini e cinque piatti
9. Appena ebbe apparecchiato, gli ospiti arrivarono.
10. Avrà veduto Maria, crede?
11. Ha perduto la borsa nel treno stamane.
12. Tutti i miei libri erano in quel baule che ho mandato a Napoli.

Exercise 11 (a)

1. I've lost my trunk. Have you seen it?
2. No, I've lost my suitcase; I've looked for it everywhere, but I haven't found it yet.
3. Hasn't the porter taken it to the train?
4. No; he may have left it at the hotel.
5. Isn't it already in the carriage? No, I've looked in the carriage; perhaps I've left it in the waiting-room.
6. Have you bought the tickets, madam? No, I have not bought them yet.
7. Has Cook brought the bread and butter and fruit? Yes, she has brought them; she has brought some sausage and a bit of ham too.
8. Where is that porter? Haven't you found him, John? But the train is going and we shall be going without trunks.
9. Here comes the porter. Here he is! Let's go and meet him. But he's got some red roses in his hand!
10. Good Lord! Red roses! But the trunks! Where are they? Where are the trunks? Oh, here they are; here they are at last!
11. Now we are ready. But where is Mary? Run, run, Mary; the train is going. We're off at last. Good-bye, good-bye.
12. But who were those red roses for? They were for Cook.
13. Poor Cook! We've lost her lovely red roses. Mary has let them fall out of the carriage window.

Exercise 11 (b)

1. Abbiamo perduto le nostre valigie, le ha vedute, facchino?
2. No, Signora, non le ho vedute.
3. Le ho cercate dappertutto nella carrozza.

4. Compra i biglietti, per favore, Giovanni.
5. Giovanni e Maria, andate a comprare i biglietti.
6. Ha della frutta? No, non ne ho.
7. Vado io a comprare della frutta? Sí, vada a comprare
   frutta e un po' di prosciutto (or: va' a . . .).
8. Vende anche salame? Sí, lo vende.
9. Compriamo della frutta, pane e burro e un po' di prosciutto.
10. Ha portato anche le salsicce? Si, eccole.
11. Perché non ha portato il baule? Lo ha lasciato nel ristorante
    (or: L'ha lasciato . . .).
12. Andremo noi a cercarlo?
13. No, bambini, rimanete qui, perderete il treno.

Exercise 12 (a)

1. On going out of the post office I met the dentist.
2. Where is the chemist's, please, madam? There is one at the
   corner, miss; there it is.
3. While he was crossing the square a policeman stopped him
   and asked him for his passport.
4. What lovely red roses! Give me one, please!
5. They are not mine, they are Cook's; but I will give you one
   with pleasure.
6. While speaking of it to him (or to her) he missed the bus
   and went home on foot.
7. There is no bus; let us take a carriage. Look, there is one
   in the square, waiting.
8. While she was opening the box, all were looking at her.
9. Have you been to Florence? Yes, sir, we are coming from
   there now.
10. Have you been to Milan, madam? Yes, I've been there.
11. Wait for me, wait for me. We're not waiting for anyone.
    The train is going. Have you given the tip to the porter?
    Yes, I have given it him.
12. Have they given us the tickets? Yes, they have (given
    them to us). And has the porter got his tip? Yes, he has.

Exercise 12 (b)

1. Uscendo dalla chiesa incontrarono il dentista e il dottore.
2. C'era una grande scatola in quel cassetto. L'ha trovata lei?
3. Sí, gliel'ha data.
4. Perché non me lo dà? L'ha già dato a loro.
5. Camminando per via Tornabuoni la cuoca incontrò il
   postino.

6. Ha perduto il suo passaporto. L'ha veduto Lei?
7. No, ma il facchino l'ha trovato. Glielo darà.
8. Gliene dia (or: *dagliene, dategliene*); ma non ne ho piú.
9. Dov'è quella chiesa famosa? Alla cantonata, non la vede?
10. Il dentista le ha dato una ricevuta? Sí, me l'ha data.
11. Hai comprato i biglietti? Sí, li ho comprati e li ho dati a Maria.
12. Ve li ha dati? (or: *Glieli*, or *te li*). Io glieli ho dati. Perché non li avete dati loro? Perché non ce ne aveva dato lui. E perché non ve ne aveva dato? Perché non ne aveva.

Exercise 13 (a)

1. Do not give it to him; give it to her.
2. I met her in town today, but not him.
3. Have you seen the lake? Yes, we went there today. The water was very calm and there were many boats.
4. These sheets are very old; they are not for the guest; let us look for some new ones.
5. This telegram is for you, not for me.
6. The boats arrived at the port laden with fish. (Note carico *di* = laden *with*.)
7. Are the chemists not open today? Yes, madam, they are open.
8. Has the little girl learnt to write already? Yes, she has written a letter by herself.
9. The duke has a long white beard and his hair is white. He is old, but his wife is older than he.
10. The old woman was sleeping; she still had that book in her hand, and the cat was on her knees, sleeping too.
11. The members of the Turin Alpine Club have arrived today.
12. What a girl she is! Yesterday she lost two pairs of gloves in the train, and today in the kitchen she has dropped six eggs (drop = let to fall).
13. Give me a clean towel, please.

Exercise 13 (b)

1. Lo dia a me, non a lui (or: dallo a . . ., datelo a . . .).
2. Quei due uomini con i buoi arriveranno domani.
3. Incontrai loro in città stamane, ma non ho veduto lei.
4. Quel libro era scritto da lui.
5. Questa lettera è per me non è per lui.
6. Mi porti quelle lenzuola, per favore (or: portami . . . portatemi). Eccole.

7. Quelle barche erano cariche di pesce quando arrivarone al porto.
8. Quante uova ha comprate?
9. Quel vecchio è molto elegante. Ha una camicia pulita tutti i giorni.
10. Quella vecchia ha venti paia di scarpe.
11. Fortunata lei! Aveva lasciato il suo portamonete nel treno, e il facchino lo trovò.
12. Ho perduto due paia di calzini nuovi. Li avevo con me la settimana scorsa quando portavo dalla città tutte quelle uova. Li avrò lasciati nell'autobus.
13. Andava a vederla quando io lo incontrai.

Exercise 14 (a)

1. At dinner we shall eat the fish we caught this morning.
2. The young lady with whom I was speaking yesterday is my sister.—She is a nice-looking girl. What is her name?
3. The study in which I work is very comfortable. It is a large room with three windows, from which I have a lovely view of the lake and the mountains.
4. The man to whom you sold the car has left. What, left! and he hasn't paid me for it yet.
5. What is the name of this square? The square through which we are now passing is the Victor Emanuel Square.
6. The gentleman, whose daughter we saw in town this morning, is a professor at the university.
7. The doctor's daughter, to whom you wrote today, is a friend of mine.
8. What time do you get up in the morning, madam? I get up early, generally at six; but my sister is lazy, and she gets up very late.
9. What a glorious sun! How lovely it is here in the heat!
10. Yes, here on the beach one is always happy.
11. Excuse me, madam, the young lady whose ring was lost on the beach is at the door.
12. Do you remember that lovely day on the beach last year? I should think I do! (lit.: and how!). I remember it very well.

Exercise 14 (b)

1. Quella donna a cui lei parlava è la sorella della cuoca.
2. Quel libro di cui lei parlava non è nella biblioteca.

3. La ragazza, da cui ho ricevuto questa lettera, arriverà la settimana prossima.
4. Quell'uomo che ha comprato la Sua macchina è già partito per l'Italia.
5. Il cuoco, i cui piatti erano così famosi, ha lasciato quel ristorante.
6. A che ora si alza tuo padre? Si alza generalmente alle otto, ma ieri si alzò alle sette e partí col treno delle otto per Roma.
7. Si metteva il soprabito, quando arrivò sua sorella.
8. Quella ragazza non si è lavata. Che mani! e che faccia!
9. Scusi, Signore, come si chiama questa piazza?
10. La strada che cerco è vicino a questa piazza.
11. Si è ricordato di quel libro? Sí, fui a quella libreria dove si parla inglese.
12. Parte già lo zio? Sí, si sta mettendo il cappello. Dove sono quei nuovi guanti che gli ho comprati? Eccoli. Lui non se ne ricorda mai.

Exercise 15 (a)

1. The man of whom we are speaking has been here this morning. Didn't you see him, Uncle?
2. Of course Uncle did not see him, for he was in bed.
3. But what time does your uncle get up? Never before ten.
4. And you, what time did you get up this morning? But I have never even been to bed. I travelled in the train all night and slept very badly.
5. What are you looking for, sir? My spectacles; they've just fallen from my nose this moment. Poor me! I can't see anything.
6. Leave it to me, sir; I'll look for them.
7. Here they are, here they are, I've found them. They were under that chair. Thank you, miss.
8. I bought this suit when I was in Milan last week. Do you like it?
9. Yes, I like it very much; that colour suits you very well.
10. The house had a little garden in front, which separated it from the road, and there every evening that old man with the white beard used to work.
11. Has the lawyer arrived? No, he will arrive by the half-past seven train. We will go and meet him at the station.
12. Immediately he had finished the letter, he called up John on the telephone, but the number was engaged.

Exercise 15 (b)

1. Non mi piace il nuovo vestito di Maria, dove l'ha comprato?
2. Quel colore non le sta bene; preferisco il vestito che aveva l'anno scorso.
3. La zia perde sempre i suoi occhiali. Non si ricorda mai dove li ha lasciati.
4. Lunedí scorso li stava cercando per delle ore, e le stavano sul naso tutt'il tempo.
5. Per favore, siamo vicino a Firenze? Sí, ci saremo in cinque minuti.
6. La signora di cui parla è partita ora. Sí, la incontrai quando entravo.
7. Questo non è un letto molto comodo. Com'è il suo? (or: il tuo, . . . il vostro?).
8. Ha dormito bene Signore? No, ho dormito molto male.
9. Parto per Firenze stasera.
10. Viaggerò in treno tutta la notte e ci arriverò alle sei della mattina.
11. Di chi è quel soprabito? È il tuo o il suo? (È il vostro o il suo . . . or: È di Lei, o di lui?)
12. Appena che il professore ebbe finito la lettera, l'avvocato telefonò (or: chiamò per telefono) la polizia.

Translation I

Literal Version

"Good day, sir. In what thing can I serve you" to me asked the clerk when I entered in the office of the tourism Italian at London.

I did not reply immediately, because although I had studied the Italian, not it I had never spoken, and the words not to me were coming quickly to the lips. But, happy of the opportunity of to practise the language before the my journey in Italy, to him I said in Italian, a little timidly:

"Good day. I should have need of some information. I should like to go in Italy for the holidays this summer, but I have little time and money at my disposal."

"Is it the first time that you go in Italy, sir?"

"Yes, not there am I never been."

"I have understood. But, first of all, to me tell, have you the passport in order?"

"Yes, it is in order. I come just now from the office passports, and the consul Italian to me has said that not is necessary a visa special."

"Very good. Then which cities would you like to visit? You yourself interest of art? Then you will want to see Florence, perhaps also Pisa and Siena or Venice? Or have you the intention of to go to Rome and to visit the antiquities? Or of to make a tour through the lakes? Or perhaps you prefer to stop yourself in some station bathing? Or in some place of resort in mountain? To the English please much the beauties natural, it I know; and in Italy there are so many beautiful places . . . Which are your plans, sir?"

"You me should advise. Of art not myself of it I understand much, I must confess it, and very little of antiquities Roman. I was wanting above all to visit Florence, where was born my mother, and perhaps other cities of Tuscany, and to me it would please very much to see Venice if there is time and if the journey not costs too much. Rome is a little too far; it will be for another time."

Free Version

"Good morning, sir. What can I do for you?" the clerk asked as I entered the Italian tourist office in London.

I did not reply at once because although I had studied Italian I had never spoken it and the words did not come very readily. But pleased to have the opportunity of practising the language before my journey to Italy, I said to him rather timidly:

"Good morning. I'm needing some information. I want to go to Italy for my holidays this summer, but I've only a little time and not much money at my disposal."

"Is it the first time you're going to Italy, sir?"

"Yes, I've not been before."

"I see. Then first of all, is your passport in order?"

"Yes, quite. I've just come from the passport office and the Italian consul told me that a special visa isn't required."

"Very good. Now which towns do you want to visit? Are you interested in art? If so, you'll want to see Florence, perhaps Pisa too, or Siena or Venice? Or are you thinking of going to Rome to see the antiquities? Or perhaps of making a tour through the lakes? Or would you rather stay at some seaside resort? Or at some resort up in the mountains? I know the English are very fond of the beauties of nature, and in Italy there are so many lovely places. . . . What are your plans, sir?"

"You must advise me, please. I'm not well up in art, I must confess, and I know precious little about Roman antiquities.

I wanted particularly to go to Florence, where my mother was born, and perhaps to other places in Tuscany; and I'd very much like to see Venice, if there's time and if it doesn't cost too much. Rome is a bit far off; that will have to wait for another time."

Notes

Buon giorno.—Similarly: *buona sera* = good afternoon, good evening; *buona notte* = good night. *mattina* = morning and *pomeriggio* = afternoon, are not used in salutations.

a Londra.—Before names of towns "in" is translated by *a* in Italian, though *in* may be used if the meaning is "within".

sebbene = "although" and *benché* (same meaning) are followed by the subjunctive, see page 143. Conjunctions ending in *-ché* have the acute accent on the final *-é*.

mi venivano . . . alle labbra.—Note the use of the conjunctive pronoun *mi* instead of the possessive adjective, with a part of the body.

contento di.—Some adjectives which in English are followed by "with" or "to" in Italian take *di*: *carico di* = laden with; *soddisfatto di* = satisfied with.

Avrei bisogno.—*Aver bisogno* = to have need. The conditional here rather than the present infers uncertainty in the speaker's mind: *if* I could go to Italy, I should need . . . Note other phrases formed with the verb *avere* and a *noun* as object, which we render in English by the verb "to be" and an *adjective*:

aver fame, lit.:	to have hunger =	to be hungry
aver sete	to have thirst	to be thirsty
aver sonno	to have sleep	to be sleepy
aver ragione	to have reason	to be right
aver torto	to have wrong	to be wrong

in Italia.—"to" before the name of a country is usually *in*; before the name of a town *a*.

a mia disposizione.—The definite article is omitted after certain prepositions (*con, senza, per, di, a* and *da*) when the preposition and the following noun form an adverbial expression, as: *con piacere* = with pleasure; *senza denaro* = without money; *di giorno* = by day.

ufficio passaporti.—Similarly *ufficio viaggi* = tourist office, without any intervening preposition.

benissimo.—From *bene* = well. The ending *-issimo* stands for "very", see page 121.

s'interessa di arte.—Interessarsi = to interest oneself in, here followed by the preposition *di*, may also be followed by *a*, as: *s'interessa alla condizione dei profughi* = he interests himself in the state of the refugees.

l'intenzione di andare.—The infinitive is used after a preposition where in English we have the present participle in "-ing"; see page 125.

stazione balneare.—Bathing resort. *Stazione* here has the original meaning of "station"—that is, stopping-place, place to stay.

villeggiatura.—Comes from the word *villa*, which originally was a large country house, equivalent to country seat. From *villa* we have *villeggiare* = to go and stay in a villa, and the noun, *villeggiatura* = the act of going to stay in the country, also the place where one stays. "Resort" is the best translation in this instance.

Agl'Inglesi piacciono . . ., and in the last paragraph, *mi piacerebbe.* Note the use of the impersonal verb *piacere* = "to please", to translate our verb "to like".

mi dovrebbe consigliare . . . debbo confessarlo.—When the infinitive following *dovere, potere* and *volere* has a pronoun object or objects, these conjunctive pronouns may come either before both verbs, as in the first case here quoted, or they may come after both verbs, as in the second case. They must NEVER come *between* the verbs. Ex.: I can send it to him = *Posso mandarglielo* or *Glielo posso mandare.*

non me ne intendo molto = I don't understand much about it, I am not well up in it. *Intendersi di una cosa* has the meaning of "to be expert in", "to be a good judge of"; *intendersi* also means "to agree", and *intendere* (not reflexive) has three meanings: "to understand", "to intend" and "to hear".

un po' (short for *un poco*) = a little. *troppo* = too, too much; but "too", meaning "also", is *anche*.

Exercise 16

1. Dove va lui per le vacanze quest'estate?
2. Andrà in Italia, se il viaggio non costerà troppo (or: va . . . costa).
3. Parla italiano? Sí, lo parla molto bene (or: benissimo), era nato a Roma.
4. Vuol andare a teatro oggi o domani?
5. Domani, per favore. Non posso andare oggi perché lo zio arriverà stasera e dovrò andare a incontrarlo.
6. Buon giorno, Signora, in che cosa posso servirla?

7. Vorrei vedere delle sciarpe, per favore.
8. Con piacere (or: molto volentieri), Signora. Che colore le piacerebbe? (or: che colore vorrebbe?).
9. Lui va molto spesso al concerto, ma non s'intende di musica.
10. Quando avrà finito con quel libro? Ne avrò bisogno per la settimana prossima.
11. Noi andiamo al mare quest'anno per le vacanze: e non ci andate voi?
12. No, quest'anno andremo in villeggiatura in montagna.
13. Ho bisogno di una gruccia. Me ne può dare uno?
14. Ho molta sete. Mi dia un bicchiere d'acqua, per favore.

Translation II

Literal Version

"Well, sir, you decide then for Florence," continued the clerk, while he was opening a drawer and was taking out various papers and books and an enormous map.

"And would it be possible to go to Florence," I asked, "passing through Genoa and Pisa, and then to return by another road?"

"Very possible."

"What would you say if I went from Florence to Venice, then from Venice to Milan, and in the journey of return I made a tour through the lakes? I know that the ticket of going and return is more cheap; but with that tour, should I have to spend much of more?"

"No, no. Here, here is the thing that does for you; a ticket circular tourist, valid for 45 days; and to you it is convenient, because to you it gives a reduction of the fifty per cent, provided you stop yourself in Italy for a period of at least twelve days."

"It goes just well for me, for myself I shall stop at least two weeks, perhaps even three."

"Let us see a little the map for to fix more exactly the your route. Therefore, leaving from London the morning early, you arrive at Paris the evening towards the six. There you will have the time of to eat before of to leave again with the express Paris–Rome; just your route: Modane–Turin–Genoa–Pisa. It is a very best train. It arrives at the frontier Italian at dawn, and at Pisa in the afternoon. And with the ticket circular you can stop yourself when and where you wish, and you can travel with any train: therefore leave Pisa when you wish and stop yourself at Florence how much to you it seems, naturally always in the limit of the 45 days."

"I understand."

"After Florence the your route is this: Bologna, Venice, Milan, and then Como and Lugano, where you will take the express for Paris. Thus you enter in Italy through the Pass of the Mont Cenis and you exit through the St. Gotthard. Goes it well thus?"

"Thanks, it goes very well indeed. Would you prepare me the ticket? I shall leave Friday next, and I shall travel in second."

"Here, done. This is the ticket; and here there is also a book which perhaps to you will be useful: 'Annual Hotels of Italy', and a magazine tourist with other indications interesting."

"Very kind, thousand thanks."

"Nothing, sir, I pray. Good journey and good enjoyment."

Free Version

"Very good, sir; you decide on Florence then," said the clerk, opening a drawer and taking out various papers and books and a large map.

"And would it be possible to go to Florence," I asked, "via Genoa and Pisa and then come back by another route?"

"Why, yes, of course."

"Supposing I went from Florence to Venice, then from Venice to Milan, and on the return journey go for a tour through the lakes? I know the return ticket is cheaper; but if I go round like that, would I have to pay very much more?"

"Not at all. Here's just what you want; a circular tourist ticket valid for 45 days; and it pays you to get it, for there's a reduction of 50 per cent, provided you stay in Italy for a period of at least twelve days."

"That'll just do for me, for I'll be there at least two weeks, perhaps three."

"Let's look at the map a moment and fix your route. Now, if you leave London early in the morning you arrive at Paris in the evening towards six o'clock. There you'll have time to dine before leaving again by the Paris–Rome express, which goes just the way you want: Modane–Turin–Genoa–Pisa. It's a very good train. It arrives at the Italian frontier at dawn and at Pisa in the afternoon. And with the circular ticket you can stop when and where you want and travel by any train you like; so you can leave Pisa when you wish and stay in Florence as long as it suits you—always of course within the period of the 45 days."

"Of course."

"After Florence here's your route: Bologna, Venice, Milan and then Como and Lugano, where you'll take the express for Paris. So you enter Italy by the Mont Cenis Pass and leave by the St. Gotthard. Will that do?"

"Thank you, that'll do excellently. Will you get me my ticket? I want to go next Friday, and I shall travel second class."

"Here you are. This is your ticket, and here is a book which might be useful: 'Annual Italian Hotel Guide', and a tourist review with other information of interest."

"You are very kind indeed. Thank you very much."

"Don't mention it, sir. A good journey, and I hope you enjoy yourself."

Notes

A buon mercato.—mercato "market", also "bargain"; therefore "at a good bargain", that is "cheap".

Le conviene.—convenire "to agree", "to suit", used impersonally may mean: "to be necessary", or "to be of advantage to": *non ci conviene farlo* = it isn't to our advantage to do it.

purché is followed by the subjunctive. See page 142.

proprio as an adverb means: "just", "exactly"; as an adjective: "own", "proper", "appropriate": *la mia propria casa* = my very own house.

Partendo . . . la mattina presto . . . arriva la sera.—No preposition *in* is required in the adverbial phrases "in the morning", "in the evening"; but with the word *pomeriggio* "in" is used: *nel pomeriggio*. Note the following expressions: *di giorno* = by day; *di notte* = by night; *Vi andrò lunedì* = I shall go there on Monday (no "on" in Italian); *Ci vado il martedì e il venerdì* = I go there *every* Tuesday and Friday; *Il piroscafo fa servizio solamente la domenica* = The steamer goes only on Sundays.

Direttissimo = express train. The names of the trains in Italian, in descending order of speed (!), are: *rapido* = express; *direttissimo* = express through train, stopping more frequently; *diretto* = through train; *accelerato* = stopping train; *treno omnibus* = slow stopper; *treno merci* = goods train.

Prego (from *pregare* = to beg, pray) is commonly used where we might say: "please don't mention it". "excuse me".

Buon viaggio e buon divertimento.—*Buono* is often used in expressions containing a greeting or wish. Just before a meal you say to the others who are going to partake of it: *Buon appetito!* When going to a theatre or concert you may hear: *Buon divertimento*, or *buon concerto*, and if you're going to work, someone might even wish you: *Buon lavoro* or *buono studio*—according to the kind of work.

Exercise 17

1. Parlando (or: mentre parlava) aprí un cassetto e tirò fuori un'enorme carta geografica.
2. Non potrebbe venire con noi al cinema? Dicono che c'è un film molto buono (or: si dice che c'è . . .).
3. Un biglietto di andata e ritorno per Londra, per favore, seconda classe. Devo comprare un biglietto anche per il cane? Sí, Signora, il cane deve avere un biglietto.
4. Non voleva venire a parlarLe ieri; oggi è contento di farlo.
5. Hai messo (or: posto) i colletti dello zio in questo cassetto? (or: mettesti, or if you use porre, ponesti). No, lui stesso ce li ha messi (posti), (or: ce li mise, pose). (Or, to make the pronouns more emphatic: Did *you* . . . no, *he himself*: Hai messo *tu* i colletti . . . No, ce li mise *lui stesso*.)
6. È mai stata a Londra, Signora? Sí, ci sono stata molte volte (*diverse volte, parecchie volte*).
7. Non è arrivato ancora? No, Maria andò a incontrarlo, ma è tornata sola (or: *tornò sola*).
8. Forse è andato per un'altra strada? Sí, è possibile.
9. Ieri si alzò alle sette, ma rimase nella sua camera a leggere il giornale, e scese soltanto alle dieci per prendere il caffè.
10. Mi dia la carta geografica un momento, per favore; voglio cercare Siena.
11. Buon giorno. Ho bisogno di (or: *voglio*) una cravatta per portare con questo vestito.—Ho proprio la cosa che fa per Lei, Signore. Questo blu marino con strisce gialle andrà molto bene con il verde scuro del Suo abito.
12. Dovrebbe comprare un biglietto circolare. È il piú a buon mercato; e può fermarsi dove e quando vuole e quanto le pare. (Using the other modes of address: *Dovresti . . . puoi fermarti . . . quando vuoi e quanto ti pare*; *Dovreste . . . potete fermarvi . . . quando volete e quanto vi pare*.)

Translation III
Literal Version

Of usual I do not sleep well in train: but perhaps this time
I was tired, or I had eaten too well at the restaurant of the
station of Paris (there one eats divinely, but one pays too, very
generously), or perhaps because I was all alone in the compartment and myself I was able to stretch out on the cushions as in
a bed; fact stands that, taken off the shoes, the tie and the
jacket, as soon as I placed the head on the pillow—hired for
100 francs at the station—myself I fell asleep profoundly, and
I continued to sleep like a dormouse all the night.

Myself I awakened that it was already day; the train was
going slowing down and at last itself it stopped. Looking out
of the little window I saw on the platform of a station wayside
a small group of employees of the railway, porters and soldiers,
with two policemen and various other guards, who were laughing and joking among of themselves, with the air of not to take
no notice of us and of our train. But a whistle sharp sent out
by the express Paris–Rome loosened that group. One of them,
the station-master (him one recognized by the cap red), went
to speak with the engine-driver, while all the others, always
talking and laughing, ascended on to the train. The clock of the
station marked the five. Only the five of the morning, and
already it was making hot and there was a lovely sun, a sky
blue and clear, and the air was so mild and fragrant (sweet). I
drew out the watch to regulate it, but in that moment, someone
opened brusquely the door of my compartment, and shouted
with a voice hoarse but strong: "Gentlemen, the customs
Italian, prepare the luggage." Three men in uniform to me
were standing in front on the doorway.

Free Version

I do not usually sleep well in a train; but perhaps this time
I was tired, or I had eaten too much at the station restaurant
in Paris (the food there is marvellous . . . but so are the bills!)
or perhaps it was because I was all alone in the compartment
and was able to stretch out on the seat as if I were in bed;
the fact is, having taken off my shoes, my tie and jacket, no
sooner had I put my head on the pillow (hired for 100 francs
at the station) than I fell fast asleep, and I went on sleeping
like a log the whole night.

It was already light when I awoke; the train was gradually
slowing down, and at last it stopped altogether. On looking out
of the carriage window I saw, on the platform of a wayside

station, a small group of railway officials, porters and soldiers, with two policemen, and various other guards, laughing and joking together, as if they weren't going to take any notice of us and our train. But a shrill whistle from the Paris–Rome express broke up the group. One of them, the station-master—you could see that from his red cap—went to talk to the engine-driver, while all the rest, still laughing and talking, got into the train. It was five o'clock by the station clock. Only five in the morning, and it was already warm, and there was a lovely sun, a clear blue sky, and the air was so mild and fragrant! I took out my watch to put it right, but at that moment somebody suddenly opened the door of my compartment and a loud hoarse voice bawled: "Italian Customs! Get luggage ready, please," and three men in uniform stood before me in the door-way.

Notes

fatto sta che (or: *il fatto è che*) . . . .—The verb *stare* is used in many expressions in place of *essere*. In speaking of the condition of health of a person in greetings, such as: Good morning, how are you? = *Buon giorno, come sta?* Very well, thank you, and how are you? = *Molto bene, grazie, e Lei?* He is ill = *Sta male*. It should be noted, however, that *stare* implies a temporary condition, and *essere* a permanent state: He is lame = *Lui è zoppo*.

tolte le scarpe.—A past participle is often used alone in Italian where we would use a perfect past participle or a dependent clause. When the verb is transitive, the participle agrees with its object; when intransitive, with its subject: *Finita la lettera, uscì* = Having finished the letter (or: When he had finished) he went out; *La ragazza, rimasta sola, cominciò a piangere* = The girl, having remained alone (or: When the girl was left alone), she began to cry.

posi il capo.—We are quite sure whose head it is, so no possessive adjective is necessary.

continuai a dormire.—Some verbs require a preposition after them before a following infinitive. *Continuare* and *cominciare* (see previous note) both take *a*. See also page 126.

andava rallentando.—The use of *andare* to form a progressive tense is not very common; it implies particular attention focussed on the action of the present participle, an action which is progressively increasing. In this sentence it gives the idea that the train is slowing down "more and more" ("more and more", by the way, is in Italian—*sempre più*).

due carabinieri.—There are different kinds of police in Italy (one organization looking after the roads, another after the railways, another after public safety, etc.), but the ones the foreigner notices most are the *carabinieri* (public safety), for they wear a picturesque uniform of the last century, a coat with tails (navy blue), trousers with red stripes, Napoleonic-shaped hat, gold buttons and white gloves, and they always go about in twos.

salirono.—To get into a tram, train, bus, etc., use *salire*; and to get out of such vehicles: *scendere*. *Dove scende lei?* = Where are you getting out?

faceva caldo.—Lit.: it was making hot. Similar idioms with *fare* are: *fare freddo* = to be cold, *fare bel tempo* = to be fine, *fare vento* = to be windy. See, too, page 108.

Exercise 18

1. Buon giorno, Signore, e come sta Lei oggi? Grazie, oggi non sto molto bene. Sono molto stanco.
2. Ha dormito bene nel treno ieri? Sí, grazie, ho dormito benissimo, ho viaggiato in una carrozza-letti.
3. Si mangia bene a quel ristorante dove è stato Lei ieri? Sí, si mangia molto bene, ma è un po' caro.
4. Andate già alla stazione? Ma il treno arriva soltanto alle dieci.
5. Abbiamo fatto un buonissimo viaggio. Non c'era nessuno nel nostro scompartimento, e abbiamo dormito molto bene.
6. Che bel tempo fa! Andiamo a fare una passeggiata sulla spiaggia? (or: faremo una passeggiata).
7. Chiuse la porta e le finestre dello scompartimento, si tolse la cravatta, la giacchetta e le scarpe, pose il denaro, il passaporto e l'orologio da tasca sotto il guanciale, e, sdraiatosi sui cuscini, in un momento s'addormentò.
8. Dove scende Lei, Signora? Io scendo a Firenze, sono salita a Parigi.
9. Lei è piú alto di me; ma Giovanni è piú alto di Lei.
10. Chi è il piú intelligente di quella famiglia? La cuoca; è piú intelligente di quel che Lei pensi (or: . . . *che Lei non pensi*).
11. Quello è l'uomo piú ricco della città. E un suo amico? Mi vuol presentare a lui?
12. Non ho tanto denaro quanto lui; ma ne ho piú di Lei.
13. Non voglio fare una passeggiata; mi fa male il piede.

Translation IV

Literal Version

"You," to me asked the most near of the three, "have you forwarded the luggage?"

"No, it I have all here," I replied quickly, drawing down from the rack the my only suitcase. As I was come in Italy for little time, not I had need of trunks.

"He has only luggage at hand, this gentleman," then two of the Customs officers themselves of it they went, without doubt to look for other victims, while the third, remained alone with me, went on:

"Have you anything to declare, sir?"

"No, nothing."

"Absolutely nothing? No tobacco, cigarettes, cigars, chocolate . . ." a pause . . . "articles of silk? . . . perfumes?"

I outlined a smile.

"But good heavens; what thing myself of it should do I, of perfumes?"

"Oh, sir, one never knows, one never knows! A little present for some girl friend Italian, perhaps?" he suggested; then, with a large piece of chalk white, he drew some his line mysterious on the my case.

"No, sir, leave to stand," he said, when I made for to open it. "It doesn't matter."

"Thousand thanks," replied I, happy of not to have to open the case and put all in disorder.

"You come to pass the holidays in Italy, not is it true? Well. Excellent! Yourself enjoy! Good day." And himself of it he went finally also he.

But, hardly outside in the corridor, he made a step backwards, and, all smiling, himself he faced once again at the door, saying:

"And good luck . . . to that perfume."

Listening to that joker of a Customs officer not myself was I aware that the train was again in motion, and with surprise, looking out of the little window, I saw that already one was passing quickly between high mountains. Myself I accommodated in the my place of corner to contemplate the scenery. The railway, flanked on one side and on the other by precipices rocky was following the course of a torrent, one of those many courses of water which, rising from the Alps, themselves turn upside down in little cascades down for the steep slopes of the long valleys narrow for to empty in those more large, tributaries of the Po. This was a torrent impetuous; every so often one was hearing the swish of its waters above of the noise of the train; and to us it was flowing at the side, as if it wished to say: "There I shall arrive before you."

Free Version

"Have you forwarded your luggage, sir?" the nearest of the three asked.

"No, all I have is here," I quickly replied, and I got down my one and only suitcase from the rack. As I had come to Italy for so short a time I had not needed any trunks.

"This gentleman only has hand luggage," at which two of the Customs officers went off, doubtless to look for other victims, while the third stayed with me and went on:

"Have you anything to declare?"

"No, nothing."

"Absolutely nothing? No tobacco, cigarettes, cigars, chocolate" . . . a pause . . . "silk goods . . . scent?"

I began to smile.

"Good heavens! Whatever should I be doing with scent?"

"Oh, one never knows, sir, one never knows! A little present for an Italian girl, perhaps?" he suggested; then with a large piece of white chalk he drew some mysterious lines on my case.

"No, sir, leave it as it is," he said, when I made as if to open it. "It doesn't matter."

"Oh, thank you," I replied, very pleased at not having to open the case and turn everything upside down.

"You're coming to Italy for your holidays, aren't you? Very good. Excellent. Have a good time. Good morning." And at last he went off too.

But no sooner was he in the corridor than he took a step backwards, and once again his face, wreathed in smiles, peeped round my door as he said:

"Good luck to that scent of yours, sir!"

While listening to that joking Customs officer I hadn't realized that the train was moving again, and it was with surprise therefore, when looking out of the carriage window, that I saw we were travelling rapidly between high mountains. I settled myself down in my corner seat to watch the scenery. The railway, flanked on either side by rocky precipices, followed the course of a mountain stream—one of the many streams which rise in the Alps and hurl themselves in little waterfalls down the steep slopes of long narrow valleys to empty into those larger rivers, the tributaries of the Po. This was a raging torrent; every now and then you could hear the roar of its waters above the rumble of the train; and it flowed there alongside us as if to say: "I'll get there before you."

Notes

spedito.—From *spedire* = to forward, to send. Luggage registered through to Italy from London normally awaits its owner at the Customs house at the frontier station, or it contrives to be in the luggage van of his train. To register luggage is: *fare registrare il bagaglio* (lit.: to make to register). Note this special construction with *fare*. Followed by the infinitive, *fare* expresses the idea of making someone else do something: *Fatelo venire qua* (lit.: make him to come here), *i.e.*, "Have him come here". *Fece chiamare il dottore* = He had the doctor called. Similarly: Please have my luggage brought up = *Per favore faccia salire il mio bagaglio*; Have it taken down, please = *Lo faccia scendere per piacere.*

se ne andarono.—*andarsene* = to go away; a reflexive verb with *ne* added. Here *ne*, "of it", is used in the sense of "thence" *i.e.*, "away". In all the tenses and with the various parts of the verb, *ne* must have its correct position with regard to the reflexive pronoun: *Io me ne vado* = I go away; *Te ne vai?* = Are you going?; *andandosene* = going away; *andatevene* = go away (*voi*); *vattene* = go away (*tu*); *se ne vada* = go away (*Lei*).

Ha qualchecosa da dichiarare.—The preposition *da* implies obligation or necessity. *Avere da* has the same meaning as *dovere*; I must write a letter: *Ho da scrivere una lettera*, or *Devo scrivere* . . . Turn also to page 126.

lasci stare.—Lit.: "let be", "let stand". *Lasciami stare* (*tu*) or *Mi lasci stare* (*Lei*) = Leave me alone, don't bother me.

importa.—*importare* = to matter. *Fare* is also used to mean the same thing: *Ciò non fa niente* = That doesn't matter, that makes no difference; *Ciò fa molto* = That matters a great deal.

tutto sorridente.—*sorridente* is an adjective from the verb *sorridere* to smile. A similar kind of adjective is formed from any verb. Those of the first conjugation form this verbal adjective by adding *-ante* to the stem, and the other two conjugations add *-ente*: *parlare*, *parlante*; *seguire* (to follow), *seguente*; *la lezione seguente* = the following lesson; *gli animali parlanti* = the talking animals. A relative clause is, however, often preferable to this verbal adjective: a singing bird = *un uccello che canta*. Like other adjectives, this verbal adjective is inflected (changing its final *-e* to *-i* for the plural), and it may be used as a noun. Certain of them have been so continuously used as nouns, that they are now regarded as such: *il* (or *la*) *cantante* = the singer; *l'amante* = the lover; *l'insegnante* = the teacher. Refresh your memory on the present participle (page 64).

mi ero accorto.—*accorgersi* "to notice", when not followed by a dependent clause and *che*, is followed by the preposition *di*: I did not notice that girl = *Non mi accorsi di quella ragazza*. I always notice it = *Me ne accorgo sempre*.

finestrino.— *-ino* is a suffix meaning "small". See page 121.

mi accomodai.—*accomodarsi* = to make oneself comfortable, to seat oneself (*comodo* = comfortable). Pray be seated, madam = *Si accomodi, Signora. Accomodatevi* = sit down.

ogni tanto = every now and then, every so often.

ci scorreva allato.—The same construction as *mi stavano davanti*: instead of a preposition governing the pronoun in the predicate—"it flowed alongside us"—the verb governs the pronoun, and the preposition becomes an adverb of place—"us it flowed alongside".

Exercise 19

1. Ha spedito tre bauli o quattro per quel signore dalla barba?
2. Tre solamente; dovrò spedire l'altro domani (or: *avrò da* . . .).
3. C'era una volta una contadina che aveva cento pecore, ventotto vacche, cinquantacinque porci, diciannove capre, un cane e un gatto ed era molto contenta.
4. Qual'è la data di oggi? È il 4 luglio 1940 (*mille novecento quaranta*).
5. In che anno scoprí Colombo l'America? Nel 1492 (*mille quattrocento novantadue*) non è vero?
6. Quanti anni hai, bambino? Compirò sei anni lunedí prossimo, Signorina.
7. Quando è il tuo compleanno? Il nove maggio.
8. Faccia salire il mio bagaglio in camera subito, per favore.
9. Sei milioni di tonnellate di carbone passano per questo porto ogni settimana (or: *tutte le settimane*).
10. La chiesa piú grande del mondo è la chiesa di San Pietro a Roma: ha una superficie di 15,160 (*quindicimila cento-sessanta*) metri quadrati e la cupola è alta piú di 130 (*centotrenta*) metri.

Translation V

(From this point onwards only one English version of the extracts will be given. Where the translation differs a great deal from the original Italian, a literal version will be added in brackets.)

The valley was now getting broader; bare rocky mountains were giving place to hills covered with pines and firs; then these to the plain with its vineyards, farms (houses of farms) and fields yellow with corn and ripening maize. What surprised me most was the small amount of land kept for pasture; almost all of it was cultivated: a succession of yellow fields, dotted here and there with the dark patches (shadows) of the olives and small maples, with their festoons of vines. I was very interested in the cultivation of the vine. The stalks climbed up the trunks and branches of low trees, such as the maple and elm, and hung in graceful festoons from one tree to another; and beneath them some green plant was growing. I could not see very well what it was. "This land must be very fertile," I thought. "And the people want to make the most of it. But how different this landscape is from ours!" At first the colours and the light seemed too strong; I missed the lovely green of the English meadows. "And where are the cows?" I wondered. "Oh, there they are!" In the distance there were two white ones, and I stood up to see better. But I was very surprised to see that, instead of sitting peacefully chewing their cud, these two animals were working! "But those aren't cows!" They were two enormous oxen yoked to a cart laden with hay. "Then they use the ox as a beast of burden here," I thought: "Oh, and the mule too," for as we passed along by a main road I saw several carts drawn by mules; and very soon cars, buses, tall houses and factories all began to appear (did not delay to appear . . .). We were getting near to some large town (there one was getting near).

"Papers, magazines, *Sunday Post.*" I opened the carriage window and calling the newspaper boy I bought a paper for 35 lire and a review for 150. It was still early, but there were plenty of people on the station. "Perhaps they're already going to work," I thought, remembering that in Italy they go to work earlier than we do, for with the great heat in the summer months they need to rest during the day. So, many shops and offices are open from eight to midday, and then they close, and only open again at three or four, and they stay open in the evening until eight, and in some cases even later. The meal times are therefore somewhat different from ours. One might say that the Italians have two meals a day: dinner at one, and supper at eight. Most of them don't eat anything early in the morning; their breakfast consists of coffee and milk and nothing else; but they have a good meal at dinner, and again at supper. That doesn't stop them going to the cafés very often, both in the morning and the afternoon, as I was to find out later (as I came to know . . .).

Notes

coperti di.—Note that an Italian says "covered *of*".

loppio = a low maple, and *olmo* = elm, are both cultivated specially for the trailing of the vine over them. They are both rather short, stunted trees.

lavorassero.—Subjunctive after the verb *maravigliarsi* = to wonder. See page 137.

carico di fieno.—Note the preposition: "laden *of*".

tardarono ad apparire.—*tardare* = to delay, is followed by *a* before a following infinitive.

da noi.—Note the idiomatic use of the preposition *da* to mean: "at our house", "with us", "in our land", etc. *Vado dal dentista* = I'm going to the dentist's. See also page 131.

i più.—Note the adverb used as a noun to mean "majority".

Prima colazione.—Lit. = first lunch—that is, breakfast. Some Italians talk about their midday meal as *colazione* (= lunch), and their evening meal as *pranzo* (= dinner); but this is not so usual as *pranzo* and *cena*; in any case, the two meals are in quantity about the same, whatever they are called.

Ciò non toglie . . . Lit. = that does not prevent that they may go very often. This idiomatic expression is followed by the subjunctive. See page 136, section 2.

spesso, spessissimo.—The *-issimo* superlative ending is not often added to adverbs of manner; the student is advised to use only those he has met in reading, and not to form them for himself.

tanto di mattino che di sera = both in the morning and the evening. Note this use of *tanto . . . che*, meaning literally: "so much . . . as"; note too *di mattino*, "in the morning"; and *di sera* = "in the evening".

Exercise 20

1. Quel signore ha ricevuto tre bauli, ma non il quarto.
2. Il fiume Po è il fiume più lungo d'Italia; è lungo più di seicento chilometri.
3. Sorge dalle Alpi piemontesi, attraversa una pianura molto fertile, e scorrendo dall'ovest all'est, sbocca nel mare adriatico.

4. Il Petrarca nacque nel 1304 (*mille trecento quattro*) e morí nel 1374 (*mille trecento settantaquattro*); egli aveva soltanto 17 anni nel 1321 (*mille trecento ventuno*) quando morí Dante, il quale era nato nel 1265 (*mille duecento sessanta-cinque*).

5. Sa Lei chi è quella Signora? No, Signore; Lei è la terza persona che mi ha fatto quella domanda.

6. Mi ha comprato due dozzine di uova? No. Non potevo comprarne due dozzine, ne trovai soltanto una ventina.

7. Quanto va avanti il vostro orologio al giorno? Non va avanti, rimane indietro dieci minuti al giorno.

8. Qual'era la data di ieri? Ieri era il 10 giugno 1941 (*il dieci giugno mille novecento quarantuno*).

9. L'anno comincia il primo gennaio, e finisce il 31 (*trentuno*) dicembre.

10. Il re Enrico VIII (*ottavo*) ebbe sei mogli, ma non tutte allo stesso tempo.

11. Che bel vigneto! Sí, produce migliaia e migliaia di bottiglie di vino all'anno.

12. Suonavano le dodici un anno fa stasera, e io stavo per andare a letto quando improvvisamente la porta della mia camera s'aprí, e quell'uomo alto e magro mi stette davanti.

Translation VI

"Take your seats, please; seats, please!" (lit.: "In carriage!") and once more we were off. This time I was no longer alone. Two men, one young, the other about fifty, came and sat down in my compartment. The older man, of a very swarthy complexion, had very dark hair and black eyes; the young man, on the other hand, with his fair hair and blue eyes, could easily have been taken for an Englishman. They were commercial travellers, by the look of them (to how much it was seeming), and they were talking loudly and animatedly, but all the time in Piedmontese, a dialect which is so different from Italian that I could not understand them. I read the paper a bit; there was nothing special in it, and in a little more than two hours we were at Genoa.

"Ices, biscuits, sweets, fresh grapes, luncheon baskets!" I looked out of the window. What a noise! What a crowd! Some people getting in; others getting out; some coming to the station to meet new arrivals and others to say goodbye to those who were going; and in the midst of the throng, porters, with bags on their shoulders, trying to push their way through (making themselves forward by dint of pushes), and the news-vendors, ice-cream sellers and the men selling sweets and drinks were doing the same (*non meno di* = not less than). At last I managed to attract the attention of one of these, and I bought a luncheon-basket. It was really very cheap, for I paid only 500 lire for it (it I paid only 500 . . .), and it had a plate of hot macaroni, two slices of roast veal, ham, cheese, fruit, biscuits, two rolls and even a small flask of red wine. I was ravenous, but it was still a little early to have lunch.

"Hope you enjoy your meal, sir!" said the man sitting opposite, with a smile. By now the train was full and there were no empty seats in my compartment. "Thank you, the same to you," I replied, seeing that he was going to eat as well. My other travelling companions were doing the same, and some of them, guessing that I was a foreigner, pointed out objects of interest for me. "This is the gulf of Spezia where the poet Shelley was drowned," they told me. In the distance we could see the white gleam of the mountains of Carrara with the famous marble quarries. Later, while we were passing through a lovely pine forest, they asked me whether I liked music, and told me that there was the house and the tomb of the composer, Giacomo Puccini.

Notes

un uomo sulla cinquantina = a man nearing fifty.

commesso = clerk or employee; *commesso viaggiatore* = an employee who travels for his firm to buy or sell goods.

niente di speciale.—Note this use of *di* before an adjective after a word like "something", "nothing", "anything": *Ho qualchecosa di buono per te* = I've something (of) good for you.

chi arrivava . . . chi partiva = some . . . others. See page 114.

farsi avanti = to come forward, make one's way.

riuscii a richiamare.—*riuscire* takes *a* before a following infinitive.

maccheroni caldi.—Luncheon baskets, or rather heavy paper bags, supplied on the Italian trains often include a small dish of cooked macaroni (with a cover on to keep it hot), and with it there is a small tin fork!

fettone.—*una fetta* = a slice, *fettona* = large slice. See page 121.

fiaschettino.—*fiasca* = flask. See again page 122.

aver una fame da lupi = to have a hunger like wolves, *i.e.*, to be ravenous. For this use of *da*, see page 131.

fare colazione = to have lunch.

colui che = he who, or simply *chi* = he who, the one who . . .
altrettanto = the same to you; lit. = as many, as much as,
again; the same amount again.

mi chiesero se amassi.—The verb of an indirect question has
its verb in the subjunctive if it depends on a main verb in the
past tense. See page 143.

Exercise 21

1. Non faccia nessun caso di ciò che dice; lei ha sempre parlato
   così.
2. Ieri stava un po' meglio; ma oggi sta peggio. Hanno fatto
   chiamare il medico?
3. Qual'è la via più corta (or: *breve*) per andare alla stazione,
   per favore?
4. Vada sempre diritto Signore, fino alla chiesa, e lì volti a
   destra e troverà la stazione di faccia.
5. Parla piano, non vedi che ci stanno ascoltando (or: *parli . . .
   vede*).
6. A che ora fa prima colazione Lei? Alle otto di solito, ma non
   prendo molto, soltanto caffè latte.
7. A che ora si fa colazione qui? Generalmente all'una,
   Signore. Bene. Mancano soltano dieci minuti; ho una
   fame da lupi.
8. Hai (or: *Ha*) mangiato bene sul treno? Sì, molto bene. Ho
   comprato un cestino e dentro c'erano tante buone cose:
   pollo, prosciutto, biscotti, formaggio e frutta.
9. C'era tanta gente e non un posto libero. Ma un signore lì
   vicino alla porta si alzò dicendo molto cortesemente:—Si
   accomodi, Signorina, si accomodi, per favore.—
10. Un altro viaggiatore venne a sedersi nel mio scomparti-
    mento. Era un uomo sulla sessantina, piccolo e grasso,
    calvo e con la barba bianca.
11. Non sono venuti i ragazzi con Lei al teatro? No, sono
    rimasti a casa; volevano sentire la radio; trasmettevano
    un bel concerto dalla Scala.
12. Che cosa fece Lei ieri? Niente di speciale. Son rimasto in
    casa.

Translation VII

At Pisa it was with difficulty that I got free of that crowd of
hotel porters, guides and cabbies who throng around the station
entrance; but having left my case in the cloakroom, once outside, I set off, plan in hand, towards the cathedral square, and
I was there in less than half an hour.

This square has been called the "meadow of miracles"; and there is something marvellous in the sight of those four gleaming white monuments towering up majestically in the middle of a field and standing out so gracefully against the green of the meadow and the blue of the sky. Built at different times—between the eleventh and thirteenth centuries, when Pisa was a powerful maritime republic—the four buildings, baptistry, church, cemetery and leaning tower, are nevertheless all bound together in wonderful harmony. They are romanesque in style, but have their own peculiar and original character, particularly in their external ornamentation of applied arcading with rows of covered galleries above, which gives the marble masses a delicate grace and elegance. In the baptistry I admired the pulpit by Nicola Pisano and I also enjoyed hearing the famous echo. If you sing a single note, the conical dome sends back the echo in a perfect musical chord; if you sing a whole song, it's just as if there were an organ there going full blast. The interior of the cathedral is impressive, with its enormous monolithic columns, and as the light streams down from the huge windows of the central nave, I was able to examine the many works of art there. They also showed me Galileo's lamp (he was a Pisan), and tradition has it that the scientist discovered the laws of the pendulum while watching it swinging. Afterwards I paid 150 lire to go into the Campo Santo (lit.: field holy = cemetery) to see the frescoes; and you have to pay to go up the leaning tower—100 lire. But it is worth it for the magnificent view and also to have the queer sensation of being on a tower that leans so—it is more than four metres from the vertical. You need a stout heart, however, and a strong pair of legs: there are nearly three hundred stairs!

When I came down the tower, I sat down on the grass for a moment. There were other people there, mostly Pisans who had come to picnic their supper in the shade of their monuments. The sun was setting; the soft, clear air was full of the flight of swallows; the white of the marble was changing to a rosy colour. What peace! what calm! As I wended my way back to the station I remembered that this was my first day in Italy: it seemed impossible; I already felt as if I'd been there for some time.

Notes

oretta.—etto, meaning "small", indicates less than an hour; *mezz'oretta* = a little less than half an hour.

maestosi.—Note the use of an adjective for an adverb in *-mente*.

arcate cieche.—Lit.: blind arcades—that is, arcades of which the central space is filled in. A glance at a photograph (if available) of these buildings will show these arcades on the ground floor, while the upper storeys are rows of pillared galleries, the *ordini di loggiati*.

se ci fosse . . . suonasse.—For the use of the subjunctive after *come se*, see page 142.

scoprisse.—Subjunctive after the verb *volere* in the main clause, the statement being a supposition, not an actual fact. See page 136.

ci vuole.—Note the verb *volere* used impersonally with *ci* meaning "to be required" (see page 107). Note the following: *Ci voleva tutta la mia forza* = It required all my strength; *Ci voleva un uomo come lui* = He was the man for it; *È la parola che ci voleva* = That's the word that was wanted; *Quanto tempo ci vuole per andare alla stazione?* = How long does it take to get to the station?

Exercise 22

1. Proprio quando stava per aprire la porta, quel ladro venne arrestato dal poliziotto.
2. La cattedrale di Pisa fu cominciata nell'anno 1063.
3. La torre pendente è fra le piú strane del mondo.
4. Da quanto tempo è in Italia Lei? (or: *Da quando è in Italia Lei?*).
5. Sono in Italia da tre anni.
6. Vale la pena di visitare la torre? Sí, certamente, c'è un panorama magnifico.
7. Ma non andiamo oggi che fa freddo e tira vento. Bisogna aspettare un giorno che faccia bel tempo, o non si vedrà niente.
8. Quanto tempo ci vuole per andare di qua alla chiesa Signore?
9. Non è sceso ancora per la prima colazione? Che cosa faremo? Il treno non aspetta nessuno. Bisognerà partire domani (or: *dovremo partire . . .*).
10. Quel libro era comprato da me, e non lo voglio dare a nessuno (or: *non voglio darlo . . .*).
11. Mi dispiace molto, ma non potrò venire; deve arrivare oggi un mio amico.
12. Si dice che Galileo fece i suoi famosi esperimenti sulla caduta dei gravi dalla sommità della torre pendente.

Translation VIII

Florence is among the most famous of cities by reason of its history and art, and also because of its lovely situation. My stay there was too short to permit me more than a rapid glance at some of the things of historic and artistic importance, but it was enough to give me an idea of the very many lovely things, both of nature and of art, that are to be found in that city on the banks of the Arno, and to make me feel its fascination so strongly that I decided I would return there as soon as ever I could.

The first morning I wakened up early. My boarding-house was on the top floor of an old palace, and on the ground floor there were shops: on one side a florist's, and on the other a seller of antiques and art treasures. I went down the stairs—there was no lift—through the dark passage, cool and sweet smelling from the flowers and plants on view there, and after a look at the old pictures, furniture and jewellery in the antique dealer's window, I went out into the street. With the plan of the town in my hand, I made my way to the Cathedral Square. At Florence, as at Pisa and in many other Italian towns, the cathedral, baptistry and belfry are three buildings separate from one another, but bound together in close unity by the architectural style. Here at Florence the marble is another tint, a shade warmer, almost a pale pink colour, with lines of green, so dark as to look like black. The cathedral was begun in 1296. The interior is dignified and solemn, clear and sober, for it is almost free from ornamentation. I admired the altar of pure silver, but the two famous choir stalls, one by Donatello and the other by Luca della Robbia, which used to be in the cathedral, are now to be found in the museum at the side. The baptistry is octagonal in plan, and the interior is very ornate with marble and mosaic. When I went in they were christening a child; and as I looked at that little group gathered round the font, I remembered that it was here, in this very same place, that Dante was baptized, almost seven centuries ago. There too I saw the beautiful doors in bronze by Ghiberti; those which Michelangelo said were fit to be the gates of Heaven. They represent scenes from the Old Testament, framed in an alternating design * of little statues of the prophets and of round plaques with sculptured heads. The third monument of this group, Giotto's belfry, is a high, square tower, simple and solid in shape, and yet graceful; here too the low reliefs in the bottom

* Lit.: framed by a frieze in which alternate little statues, etc. . . . .

part should be seen, done by followers of Giotto, from designs by the master.

Notes

colà = there, in that place; more emphatic than *là*.

da decidermi = as to make me decide. See page 132, for the use of *da*.

stavano lì esposti.—Many of the shops on the ground floor of the old buildings and palaces have no windows in which to exhibit their goods; these are therefore arranged round the wide stone doorway, on the pavement on either side of the door, and even hanging on the outside walls of the building (whenever this is possible).

esposti.—Note that an adjective (*esposti*, past participle, has here the force of an adjective) agreeing with more than one noun is in the *masculine plural* if the nouns are of different genders; when both nouns are masculine, it is of course masculine, and feminine when both nouns are feminine.

vetrina = shop window. *Finestra* is never used in this sense.

tondo, as an adjective = round, circular; as a noun: circle, dish. *parlare chiaro e tondo* is an idiom meaning: "to speak out flatly".

bassorilievo = low relief—that is, shallow carving or sculpture on a background, from which the figures are shaped to stand out to give the appearance of perspective.

Exercise 23

1. Ho veduto tutti e due quei quadri; questo mi piace piú di quello.
2. Chi è costei? Grida sempre con quella voce?
3. Maria e Lucia suonano bene tutte e due; questa il violino, quella il pianoforte.
4. Ogni volta che ci vado, quell'uomo mi segue fino alla porta.
5. È un gran peccato vendere quel negozio di fiori; ognuno lo dice.
6. Hai visto qualcuno per la strada? No, non ho visto nessuno.
7. Per quanto sia ricca, ciò non m'importa (or: *mi fa niente*), non la voglio per moglie.
8. Chiunque siate, non vi posso lasciar entrare qui (or: *chiunque sia . . . non la posso . . .*; or: *non ti posso . . .*).
9. Chi andava per vedere i quadri; chi andava per farsi ammirare dagli altri; tutti camminavano verso il museo.
10. Che cosa mai è successo? Altri corre, altri cammina, ma tutti vanno verso la chiesa.

G

11. Non bisogna ripetere le opinioni altrui; bisogna avere alcune
    opinioni proprie.
12. Esce Lei stamane? Sí, esco fra poco; ha bisogno di qualche-
    cosa?

Translation IX

From the religious centre I set out for the historical centre of
the town: the Square of the Signoria. It is very picturesque,
with the majestic Palazzo Vecchio (Old Palace) at one side,
built like a fortress with battlemented walls, and near by, the
Loggia dei Lanzi (Lancers' Loggia), where once the lords of the
town: came to make speeches, and where now people come to
admire some of the world's most celebrated statues. From the
piazza you enter into the long avenue (*piazzale* = open space,
large square) of the Uffizi (Offices), which opens out between
the Palazzo Vecchio and the Loggia. It is surrounded on three
sides by the enormous Uffizi palace, so named because it was
destined to be the seat of government offices: today it is a
museum and contains the most important collection of paint-
ings in Italy. On ordinary days you have to pay L.100 ad-
mission, so I postponed my visit until Sunday. When I went I
was surprised to find a crowd of Italians all dressed in their
Sunday best, walking up and down the long, light corridors, or
sitting on the benches between the monuments, chatting and
watching the visitors. They seemed indifferent to all the beauty
of art around them; but if you were to ask one of them, as I did,
where a certain masterpiece is kept or to which school of
painting a certain master belongs, they can almost always give
you a correct answer right away. With them the Sunday walk
in the Uffizi is a habit; those pictures have become part of their
lives.

If you go under the loggia at the end of the avenue you come
out on the Lungarno, one of the streets which run along the
river; and if you turn to the right, a little afterwards you come
to Ponte Vecchio (Old Bridge). This bridge, the oldest in the
town, is very picturesque, with little goldsmiths' shops clinging
on to its sides, which are supported on the outside of the bridge
by wooden brackets. So small are these shops that you would
think that not more than five or six people could get in at once;
but they do, and in large numbers, particularly ladies and
tourists: for, for those who like beautiful necklaces, ear-rings,
brooches, cameos and rings, it is very difficult indeed to resist
the temptation of those windows, or rather show-cases, which

line the very narrow road over the bridge, and which are arranged so tastefully, just at the eye-level of the passer-by.

Having crossed the river, I walked first through dark, narrow back streets between ancient palaces; then, climbing up through avenues and country roads, up over the slopes of a hill I reached the Piazzale Michelangelo. From there you can see the whole of Florence encircled by its hills; hills gently sloping and bathed in sunlight (lit.: laughing in the sun), covered with vineyards and olive groves, dotted here and there with villas and houses, among which every now and then rears up a taller and darker tree, the tree so characteristic of the Tuscan landscape: the cypress. Sometimes one all by itself; at other times there is a lovely row marking the line of some avenue or the contour of some low hill. I could see in the distance the hill of Fiesole with the monastery at the top that I wanted to visit. It was some distance away, but the clear, pure air made it seem quite near. The clock struck twelve noon. How the sun was beating down! Everything you touched was burning hot. I looked around me at the square. Not a soul to be seen, and no noise except the ceaseless chirping of myriads of crickets.

Notes

Signoria = lordship; also: "power", "authority". Name given to the council of chief magistrates, chosen from the merchant class, who ruled Florence at the end of the 13th and during the 14th centuries.

Lanzi.—From *Lanzichenecchi* (landsknecht = German mercenary soldiers who were placed on guard in this loggia).

abiti festivi = holiday clothes, best clothes.

dove si trovi . . . a quale scuola appartenga.—The subjunctive is used here in the indirect question, although the main verb is in the present and not the past tense (see pages 136 and 143) because that verb expresses a supposition: the idea is "were you to ask", "should you ask", "suppose you asked".

li per li (idiomatic) = straight away.

si direbbe che non si possano.—The subjunctive in an indirect statement. See page 143.

sparse . . . di.—*spargere* = to scatter, sprinkle, is followed by *di.*

parer vicino.—Remember that the final -*e* of the infinitive may be dropped before any word except one beginning with *s impure.*

Exercise 24

1. Il verde è un bel colore.
2. Sta studiando l'italiano, già sa parlare francese.
3. Cristoforo Colombo scoprí l'America.
4. La signora Bianchi è in casa; chi la vuole?
5. È caduto dall'albero e si è rotto una gamba. Quando arriverà il dottor Rossi?
6. È un gran pittore; chi lo nega parla da sciocco.
7. Firenze è una delle piú belle città d'Italia.
8. Grazia Deledda, famosa scrittrice italiana, nacque in Sardegna.
9. Sacrificò la vita alla patria.
10. Mio padre è avvocato e mio zio è medico.
11. Buon giorno, Dottore, vorrebbe salire, per piacere.
12. Collane, orecchini, fermagli, cammei e anelli, tutti si vendono in quelle piccole botteghe sul Ponte Vecchio.

Translation X

"Hello! Am I speaking to the Primavera boarding-house? No? Oh, I'm sorry, I've got the wrong number. Hello, Exchange! Please give me number 25,054. Thank you. Hello! Am I speaking to the Primavera boarding-house? Good! Is the English gentleman there, who arrived a short while ago? His name is . . ." "I'm sorry, madam, he's not in. . . . Oh, wait, he's just coming in now. I'll call him; one moment."

"Excuse me, sir," the porter called just as I was coming in for lunch. "You're wanted on the telephone."

"Good lord! the telephone!" I thought. "Who can it be? However shall I make myself understood in Italian?"

But it turned out to be quite easy. It was an old English lady, married to an Italian, who had known my mother, and who wanted to invite me to go and see her in her villa at Fiesole. And very willingly I accepted.

You can go up to Fiesole by tram and by bus; but I preferred to walk. I started out in the afternoon about five. It was still hot, but not too much so; there was a lovely cool breeze coming down from the mountains. I crossed the Cathedral square and followed a long, narrow street until I came into another large square, harmonious in its effect, and surrounded on three sides by fine porticos, and in the middle of it there was a statue of a man on horseback and two very ornate fountains. Over each column of the porticos I noticed a terra-cotta plaque with that famous child in swaddling clothes on a pale blue ground, the work of one of the Della Robbia; then I knew where I was; this was the Santissima Annunziata Piazza (Holy Annunciation Square), and that building was the Foundling Hospital. I continued through other squares and along more roads until I found myself right in the country. Then, always climbing up, sometimes between high walls of villas with their gardens in bloom, other times through woods of cypresses and olives—which cleared every now and then to give a glimpse of the town below—until at last I arrived in the square at Fiesole.

It was market day, and that square presented a very lively spectacle. In the shade of the trees—there are two very fine rows of chestnuts and limes—and of the grey stone buildings, the sellers had arranged their stalls and benches on the pavement, and having covered them with tents, they stood beneath these, crying out their wares. They were selling mostly things made of straw: hats, baskets, carriers, bags, all very gay in colour and design, things for which the little place is famous; there were also leather goods in gay designs and bright colours, which are manufactured in Florence; then, too, other articles, such as shoes, books, post-cards, stockings, cheap jewellery, cloth, rosaries, crucifixes; and biscuits, sweets, and fruit. I saw large baskets full of grapes, pears and figs standing on the ground. As I had to wait for the English lady and some of her friends, I sat down at one of the tables outside under the trees, to drink an iced vermouth and to watch that cheery and animated crowd.

Notes

Pronto (lit. = ready) is used on the telephone, as we say "Hello".

mi riusci (lit. "it succeeded to me", "it turned out to be to me"). This verb is often used impersonally to mean "to turn out to be" and "to seem". *Ciò mi riesce molto strano* = That strikes me as very strange.

portico, with the stress on the first syllable, follows the rule for words so stressed, and does not retain the hard sound in the plural.

Della Robbia.—Luca della Robbia (1400–1482) and his nephew Andrea (1437–1528 *c.*) revived the use of terra cotta for sculpture, and introduced the fashion of glazing their plaques in brilliant colours, particularly a lovely china blue. These blue plaques, with the charming little babe on each, give the square a particularly gay and cheerful appearance.

per lo più = "for the most part".

vermut = vermouth. Italians usually find it difficult to pronounce a word ending in a consonant, and have a tendency to add a final vowel to foreign words which Italian has adopted, such as: *vermutte, autobusse, tramme*; and "beefsteak" has become *bistecca* in Italian. (The first three examples are not spelt with the final vowel; but the fourth, *bistecca*, is so written as well as pronounced.)

Exercise 25

1. Mangia pochissimo quel ragazzo.
2. Sono ricchi, quei forestieri. Hanno un casone in mezzo a un parco.
3. O avete dei gattini? Che piccini (or: *piccolini*), poverini!
4. Vuoi andare alla porta, Mariuccia? Non hai sentito il campanello? Qualcuno ha suonato.
5. Vuoi aiutarmi a portare dell'acqua dal pozzo? Non ho tempo io; quella contadinotta t'aiuterà (or: *vuole aiutarmi . . . l'aiuterà*).
6. Ma di chi parli? (or: *parla?*). Di quella donnetta che è venuta ieri per aiutare la cuoca?
7. Lasciai tutti quei fogli nel mio baule, che ora sarà chiuso; e ho perso la chiave. Non ha chiesto al facchino? Lui avrà la chiave, forse.
8. Ha risposto a quella signorina che Le regalò quel librone? Sí, risposi il giorno dopo.
9. Che cosa rispose quella donnuccia quando le disse che non bisogna canterellare cosí tutto il tempo? Non disse niente, rise soltanto.
10. Salí le scale (or: *gli scalini*) ed entrò nella cameretta. Non c'era nessuno. Pose il pacchetto e i fiori sul tavolino vicino alla finestra.
11. Che casaccia! Chi ci vive? Qualche poveraccio!
12. Hanno un villino in una di quelle stradette di campagna che vanno su per il colle.

Translation XI

We were sitting on the terrace of the English lady's villa after an excellent supper and enjoying the view of the city by night—all a twinkling of lights down there in the valley—when my hosts decided to take me to Siena to see the Palio. "We go every year," they said. "It is a fine sight and most amusing. You'll like it, you'll see." And they were right; I thoroughly enjoyed myself.

We took the *littorina*. By the way, I would not recommend this motor-train for nervous people, but it is the quickest way. It goes so fast that it seems to fly over the rails without touching them; but when it does touch them, it gives such a bump that the travellers bounce up and down on their seats, and the parcels dancing about on the luggage-rack jump out and land on the heads of the people below (lit.: fall on). And so we arrived at the charming, clean and neat little station at Siena. It is very modern, and would make anyone like the modern style of architecture (lit.: very modern and of such as to make to convert to the 20th-century style), so lovely is it in shape and proportion.

Then, after a carriage drive up a steep road, I found myself within the walls of the mediaeval town, which looks down upon the surrounding country from the height of its three hills. The imposing Gothic palaces of grey stone, some battlemented, and the dark, narrow little streets—down some even a carriage cannot pass—all seemed to me rather cold and forbidding at first. But then came the days of the Palio. What a change! Everything and everybody seemed transported with joy: the inhabitants, even the streets and the palaces. Hanging from those sombre buildings were flags, tapestries and pieces of cloth; every window had something; the streets were all a-flutter with banners; and the Sienese, at all hours of the day and night, went walking up and down, arm in arm, singing and laughing, all very merry. This horse race, run in commemoration of some ancient religious festival, is the strangest in the world. It takes place in the middle of the town, in the Piazza del Campo (lit.: Square of the Field), and those taking part dress up in mediaeval costumes in the brightest of colours, but well harmonized together. As I did not know anything about the religious significance, and as I had not backed a horse, I could not share in the wild enthusiasm for the race; all the same, for me it was the most interesting theatrical show, and the scenes which most impressed me were these:

Act I.—A little church in one of the wards. Characters—a priest, a horse, a jockey (all near to the altar); a crowd of people laughing and chatting all the time. The priest recites a prayer, sprinkling meanwhile the horse's nose with holy water. Shouts and laughter of the crowd: "Well done! hurrah! long live the she-wolf!" They all go out laughing. Curtain.

Act II.—A large square the shape of a shell or a fan, crowded with people. There are people at all the windows and people on all the roofs; the square itself is a jostling crowd except in

the space all around reserved for the racecourse. A deafening
roar from the crowd; a mad rush of ten horses; and for just
one minute and a half the air is rent with the shouting and
whistling of tens of thousands of people, with the beating of
drums, the blowing of trumpets, the firing of guns, and the
ringing of the bells of more than twenty churches. Curtain.

Act III.—The main street in the winning ward, at a late hour
of the night. At a long table several hundred people are having
supper in the open air. The scene is lit up by old-fashioned
flares hanging from the ancient palaces. At the head of the
table is the principal actor: the winning horse, with his own
manger, and in it there is—as well as other things—macaroni!
He is eating! The end. Curtain.

Notes

Eravamo seduti . . . a godere.—Note the preposition *a* after a
verb of rest (*sedere*), before a following infinitive.

condurmi.—The few verbs of the second conjugation whose
infinitive ends in *-rre* drop the final *-re* before adding the
conjunctive pronouns.

Noi si va.—The indefinite *si* construction is often used in
conversation together with the subject pronoun *noi* instead of
the ordinary first person plural. This very idiomatic use should
be remembered for conversation, but it should not appear in
written Italian, except when reporting conversation.

Va tanto veloce.—Note the adjective instead of an adverb in
-mente.

in testa alla gente.—Where we should say "on to the heads
of", Italian has "in head to", for *in testa a* has become a prepositional phrase formed by a noun preceded and followed by a
preposition, in the same way as: *in mezzo a* = in the middle of.
See also the last paragraph of this extract: *in capo a* = at the
head of.

scarrozzare = to drive in a carriage.

scarrozzata = drive, driving in a carriage.

abitanti.—From what verb is this noun formed?

partecipare a.—Note the preposition after this verb.

grida e risa.—Irregular plurals of *grido, riso*. See page 70.

l'aria è in tempesta.—Lit.: "the air is in a storm".

Exercise 26

1. Mi diede quel libro prima di partire per Roma.
2. Perché ha detto ciò? Parla senza pensare.
3. Odo dire ciò mille volte al giorno.

4. Hanno fatto aprire quella porta?
5. Sì, la cuoca l'aperse, ma ora non possiamo chiuderla.
6. Invece di leggere un romanzo, dovrebbe studiare quella lezione.
7. Sì, io gliela farei studiare, e subito.
8. La littorina parte alle undici, credo, mi potrebbe prenotare un posto?
9. Gli dissi di comprare i biglietti ieri.
10. Sì, ha cercato di farlo, ma non poteva, tutto era chiuso.
11. Aveva promesso di andare subito, ma non può, non c'è un treno prima di domani.
12. Ti proibisco di andare in quella casa.

Translation XII

Besides being one of the most romantic and picturesque of cities, Venice is also one of the strangest in the world. It is difficult for anyone who has not seen it to imagine what this city of marble and water looks like. There is no vegetation, or very little; no grass, no plants nor trees, except in a few gardens. There are no wide streets, the roads of Venice are canals and waterways; so there are no cars, no buses, no carriages. The Venetian taxi is the gondola or the motor-boat. In this strange place the eye has to get accustomed to a view quite different from that which it sees every day; it is a view of palaces, water and sky; white palaces, yellow palaces, pink palaces, all glittering in the very strong, clear light, and all have the sea lapping their walls at ground-floor level. The ear notes the absence of the usual sounds; the first impression is of a great silence, broken only by the melancholy call of the gondolier as he comes near a street corner, or by the far-off whistle of the steamer which plies regularly to the neighbouring islands.

These and other thoughts were passing through my mind one evening, as I sat at one of the little tables in St. Mark's Square. Several friends were with me—acquaintances I had made at the Lido, where I used to bathe every day—and they had come to hear the evening concert on the Grand Canal.

"And just think, Charles," one of them was saying to me, "this extraordinary city is built in the middle of a lagoon, on an archipelago of nearly a hundred and twenty islands, and it has one hundred and sixty canals and four hundred bridges!"

"It must have a very interesting history," I said.

"Come on, Lewis, the historian," they all shouted.

"Very well," said Lewis. "It was founded in the 5th century —I think—by refugees fleeing before the invasions of the barbarians, and it went on gaining in power and importance by reason of its trade connections with the east. The Venetians, as you know, were a practical and an enterprising people: they managed to seize every opportunity of enriching themselves and of extending their power. In the Middle Ages they acquired the monopoly of the salt trade, a product which was then very scarce and very dear; during the crusades they carried the Christian troops to the east in their boats, and of course, like the crafty merchants they were, they charged a good bit for those voyages. In the 13th century Venice was already an important power in the Mediterranean, with colonies in the Aegean and in Asia Minor; and in the 14th she came forward as the champion of Christianity against the Turks. It was at this period, if I remember rightly, that her ships reached the ports of far-off England. Later, when she had conquered a large part of northern Italy, this maritime republic became one of the five great Italian states. Her decline dates from the 16th century with the opening of new sea routes to the Indies and with the beginning of long wars with Turkey. Today Venice might seem to be a dead city; but it is a very rich museum and a paradise for tourists . . . and for students on holidays," he added, with a smile.

"Good for you, Lewis! Full marks!"

"Thank you, Lewis," I said as I looked around at the square.

In the distance the cathedral façade was facing us; and at either side were the fine porticos with their shops selling glassware and lace, and where a large crowd was now sauntering leisurely to and fro, for it was the hour for the evening walk. The band was playing a slow, sentimental tune, and flying all around were those impudent inhabitants of the piazza—the pigeons. Every now and then they came down on to the pavement or perched upon the tables looking for crumbs. "Let him who needs a real rest come here to Venice," I thought; "for, lulled by the slow rhythm of the gondola, a sense of calm and content enters one's soul here, as in no other place. Here one can be lazy; here no one hurries, there is time for everything, for time itself seems to be standing still."

Notes

Oltre a essere.—Note the infinitive after the preposition where we in English use a present participle. See page 125.

abbia.—Present subjunctive of *avere*. The subjunctive is required here as *chi* has the force of "whoever". See page 138.

Lido.—This most celebrated of bathing-places is at the edge of the lagoon, a short distance by motor-boat from Venice. The English visitor is often surprised at not being able to get down to the sea here without paying for it; and one pays different prices, according to whether one bathes from an hotel or from the large public *stabilimento* (establishment, bathing place). Each hotel, too, has its portion of sea partitioned off, the price for bathing varying according to the class of hotel.

Serenata.—Lit.: "serenade". Each evening during the season a concert is held on the Grand Canal. The orchestra and singers go out in a large, flat-bottomed boat lit up with Chinese lanterns, and the audience follow in gondolas and tie their boats to that of the concert party. At the end of each item two very agile gondoliers leap and crawl over all the boats with money-boxes to coax and smile a good collection out of the spectators.

pratico.—Besides meaning "practical", also means "acquainted with", as: *Non sono practico di queste parti* = I don't know these parts (or: "I'm a stranger here").

si erano acquistati.—Lit. = they had acquired for themselves.

fecero pagar cari . . .—Note that there is no single verb in Italian for "to charge"; it is rendered by *far pagare* = to make to pay.

Trenta con lode.—Lit. = thirty with praise. The usual expression for "full marks and distinction" in Italian schools and universities, as the maximum is generally thirty in most examinations.

basilica.—The name (taken from the Greek) given to Roman law court buildings and subsequently applied to early Christian churches, which in their oblong shape with nave, colonnade and apse, resembled them.

cristallerie e . . . pizzi.—Glass-blowing and lace-making are two of the chief industries of Venice today.

Venga.—Present subjunctive of *venire*, used as an imperative: "Let him come."

Cullandosi al—lit. = cradling, rocking, lulling oneself by . . . *i.e.* being lulled by. Note the preposition used in Italian.

Exercise 27

1. È un ragazzo sfrontato; mi stava guardando tutt'il tempo.
2. Non ha pagato ancora quel biglietto?

3. Non mi permette di vedere quei libri; ha chiuso a chiave la
   porta della sua camera.
4. Che cosa pensa di quell'uomo? È bugiardo; non crede a ciò
   che dice.
5. La bottiglia di vino è sulla tavola nella sala da pranzo;
   quella nuova cameriera dai capelli rossi l'ha lasciata lí.
6. Venezia era una della piú grandi e una delle piú importanti
   città del medioevo. Costruita sopra un arcipelago di
   centoventi isole in una laguna al nord del mare adriatico,
   era destinata a diventare una potenza marittima. I
   veneziani erano un popolo pratico e intraprendente.
   Acquistarono il monopolio del commercio del sale e fecero
   pagar caro quel prodotto. Ai tempi delle crociate seppero
   approfittare dell'occasione per arricchirsi e per estendere
   il loro potere nel Mediterraneo orientale, e le loro navi
   trasportarono migliaia dei fedeli che facevano guerra ai
   turchi. Nei viaggi di ritorno in patria quelle stesse navi
   venivano cariche di marmi e mosaici ricchissimi, i quali
   quella gente marinara adoperarono per abbellire la loro
   città. I bei monumenti ed edifici (or: *edifizi*) veneziani che
   ammiriamo oggi attestano il forte sentimento patriottico
   che animava i figli di questa famosa repubblica marittima
   del medioevo.

Translation XIII

At Venice the life of the town revolves around St. Mark's
Square, or to be more precise round the little café tables there;
at Milan the vital centre is the Cathedral Square, with the
adjacent Victor Emanuel arcade, which also has its little
tables, full at all hours of the day. The arcade, the traditional
rendezvous of the Milanese, is enormous. You enter from the
Cathedral Square, going through a majestic archway, and
when you have gone the whole length you come out into the
Scala Square, where the famous theatre of that name is to be
found. Throughout its length the arcade is flanked by smart
shops and numerous cafés, and I certainly have passed many
pleasant hours there with friends at one of the little tables,
watching and criticizing the people passing, and eating the ices,
which really are delicious.

One day, after a visit to the convent of the church of Santa
Maria delle Grazie (Saint Mary of the Graces) with two
American tourists to see the famous "Last Supper" by
Leonardo da Vinci, I came back to the arcade to rest awhile.

I sat down at my usual table, ordered my vermouth from the waiter, and settled myself to watch the passers-by. I had only a few days' holiday left, and I was thinking that I ought to go to the theatre, at least once. I called the waiter, who was already quite an old friend, for he had helped and advised me so many times, and I asked him for a newspaper so that I could see what was on at the theatres (lit.: the theatre column).

"With pleasure, sir," he replied. "The newspaper boy will go past any minute with the *Evening Post*, and I'll buy it for you myself. But as for theatres, I'm afraid that there'll be very little just now, as it is out of the season. The majority of the theatres are closed and the actors away on holiday. But there are plenty of cinemas. Wouldn't you like to see some good film?" But I already knew that there was not anything special at the cinemas.

While I was waiting for the newspaper boy I bought writing-paper and stamps from the waiter, and there at my little table I wrote home to England to let them know the date I was going back. I was putting the stamps—worth seventy lire—(*da* here stands for "of the value of") on my letter when the waiter returned with the paper. He had already looked at it, and he handed it to me saying: "There is one thing that perhaps may suit you, sir. Do you like music?" On my replying in the affirmative, he went on: "There's a special performance for charity of the lovely opera by Puccini, 'Madam Butterfly'—you must know it, sir—and there's a very good tenor and a Japanese girl singer with a divine voice. It's really worth hearing. But it's being given in a small theatre, a bit away from the centre of town, near to where I live."

"Very good, then, Beppino," I replied—for that was the good man's name—"if it's near your home, come with me tonight and hear 'Madam Butterfly', will you?"

Notes

ci si entra.—The conjunctive pronouns and adverbs (except *ne*) precede *si* when it is used impersonally as here. *mi si dice* = they tell me; *lo si fa così* = it is done like that; but when the *si* is reflexive meaning "to himself", "to herself", etc., it is an indirect pronoun, and therefore precedes the direct *lo, la, li*, etc. *se lo mise in testa* = she put it on her head (lit. = to herself she put in head).

Teatro della Scala.—One of the most famous opera houses in the world; founded in 1778, it holds nearly 3,000 people. It is the height of ambition of every Italian singer (and singers of other countries too) to be well received by the Scala audience.

pensavo che sarei dovuto andare.—A compound conditional tense where we use the simple conditional. See page 146. For the use of the auxiliary, see page 148.

gran che.—Idiomatic use of *che* as a noun. The phrase means: "a great deal", "anything particular", "anything special".

comprai.—One can often buy writing materials and stamps in the cafés in Italy and write letters at the tables there. Stamps may also be bought—as well as at the post office—at any shop that sells salt and tobacco; for these two commodities are government monopolies, and require a special licence—which also applies to stamps.

ai miei.—The possessive adjective is used in the plural without any noun to mean "people", "parents", "relations".

bravo.—Note the difference in meaning in this adjective when it precedes and when it follows its noun. In the first case it means "good", "worthy"; in the second, "clever", "capable", "efficient".

Exercise 28

1. Mi dia di quella carta da scrivere, per favore, voglio scrivere ai miei a casa.
2. Vuole che voi tutti ve ne andiate subito; non può vedere nessuno.
3. Dubito che vengano ora. È tanto tardi.
4. È contento che Lei lo sappia ora; ma non osava dirglielo lui stesso.
5. Sa Lei se siano partiti o no?
6. È il piú cattivo ragazzo che io conosca.
7. Non c'è nessuno qui che sappia suonare il pianoforte?
8. Milano è una delle piú grandi città d'Italia, con piú di un milione di abitanti. È la città piú importante dell'Italia settentrionale, e il maggior centro industriale, commerciale e bancario di tutta la penisola. Quando sono a Milano vado ogni giorno (or: *tutti i giorni*) alla Galleria Vittorio Emanuele, tradizionale luogo di ritrovo dei milanesi, dove ci sono negozi eleganti e numerosissimi caffè. Mi siedo a uno dei tavolini, chiedo un vermut o un caffè al cameriere, e mentre sto bevendo guardo passare la folla. Alcuni vengono qui per passeggiare su e giú, altri per chiacchierare, altri per incontrare degli amici e altri per discutere gli affari; ma tutti ci vengono nella speranza di avere (or:

trovare) un momento di pace e di tregua dal rumore e dal movimento della grande città industriale moderna.

Translation XIV

"Thank you, sir; you are too kind," continued Beppino. "Today, as it just so happens, I'm free, and if you really would like . . ."

So it ended by Beppino coming to the theatre with me, and not only Beppino, but the whole of his large and charming family: his wife, sister, brother, grandfather and four children. But what good-hearted folk! They simply would not let me pay for the tickets, not even for my own, in spite of all my protests. And what a crowd! Rarely in my life have I seen such enthusiasm. We could not reserve seats, there were so many people; in fact (*anzi* = on the contrary), we had to form a queue. But as soon as the doors were opened there was a surge forward (*pigia* = pushing), and with shouts and laughter everyone scrambled to get in first, and I felt myself being carried up the stairs and to a good seat in the gallery. Beppino lost sight of some of his family, but he did not seem to mind; his wife was a bit worried, however, for she had lost a shoe, but luckily it turned up later.

I shall never forget that Italian audience. They were very critical, even severely so; one singer whom they did not like they hissed unmercifully (*senza complimenti* = lit.: without compliments, without any regard to his feelings, without standing on ceremony), and they would not let him go on. They all knew the opera note for note, and they joined in singing the most well-known airs; which was somewhat irritating for me. But when the singer was really good, or if a piece was very well played, the whole audience sat rapt and quiet, as if they were all holding their breath, right up to the very last note, and then there was a storm of applause and shouts of encore that never seemed to be going to end. One of that good tenor's songs got seven encores. And the poor man, to satisfy them, came back and sang it seven times!

As can well be imagined, it was very late when we came out of the theatre; two of the children were already fast asleep, and we were all very tired, but very happy. I had to hurry on to the hotel to pack my suitcase, for I was leaving the following day. They all came with me to the tram, and after many a handshake and cries of "goodbye" and "come back soon", at last I left those delightful people.

Notes

fini per.—finire per = to finish by; this expression in English is followed by the present participle; the Italian equivalent takes the infinitive.

la moglie, la sorella.—The article is preferred to the possessive adjective, for it is quite clear whose wife, etc., is meant.

fare la coda.—to form a queue. *Coda* = tail.

preoccuparsene = to worry about it; *preoccuparsi* takes *di* before its object.

le arie . . . le cantava.—The repetition emphasizes *arie*.

bis = a second time. The Italians shout *bis* in the theatre where we use the French *encore*.

Exercise 29

1. Ero contento che fossero partiti (or: *che se ne fossero andati*).
2. Credevo che voi tutti foste in Italia.
3. Non l'avesse mai veduta!
4. Benché non fosse stata lei che avesse rotto lo specchio veneziano, continuò a piangere.
5. Tua moglie ti chiese dove fossi stato ieri sera?
6. No, entrai senza che lei mi vedesse.
7. Caro Giovanni, Sai dove sono venuto a passare le vacanze? Mio padre ha sempre voluto che io vedessi l'Italia, e ora finalmente eccomi qua! Ho visitato diverse città famose: Pisa, Firenze, Siena, Venezia e adesso sto a Milano, dove ho incontrato alcuni miei amici italiani. Ieri m'accompagnarono al teatro per sentire l'opera. Tutti cantarono molto bene; ma ciò che m'interessava di piú era il pubblico italiano. Che entusiasmo! Avessi visto! Quante volte "bis"! Un tenore molto bravo dovette tornare a cantare sette volte una sua canzone che piacque molto. Sette volte! D'altra parte che fischi, che grida quando c'era uno che non sapeva cantare bene! Peccato che tu non fossi stato con me! Avremmo riso tanto insieme.

Non rispondere a questa; forse dovrò partire per l'Inghilterra fra poco. E scusami questa lettera tanto breve; avrò mille cose da raccontarti; e almeno non ti puoi lagnare che non ti abbia scritto. I meii saluti ai tuoi. Ciao! Tuo Carlo.

Translation XV

The following morning I left for Como, in the company of some Americans who were going on to Paris. By express Como is only one hour from Milan, and I arrived there before ten. After making a tour of the town, I decided to take the funicular up to Brunate, a little village on a hill to the east from where there is a fine view of the lake. While sitting on a seat to look at the view I got out my map to find my bearings. The town of Como stretched out below me with its bay and its hills, and beyond it opened out the plain of Lombardy. In front of me and to the right was the lake with its high, steep mountains, and far, far away on the horizon the majestic peaks of the Alps were shining in the sun. "Now I'm in the country of Don Abbondio and Lucia," I thought, remembering the famous novel. "Lecco must be beyond those mountains to the east, on the other branch of the lake." I looked at my map again, thinking, "Instead of staying in Como, I should really like a quieter place on the lake, somewhere a bit out of the way. Let's look again." My finger followed the steamer route: "Como, Cernobbio, Cadenabbia, Bellagio . . . there's a lovely sunny place (lit. = smiling) on a promontory where the three branches of the lake meet; yes, that will do. There are five or six hotels, none very large. All the better." I went down again to Como, took my bag out of the cloakroom, and embarked on the steamer for Bellagio.

"Good evening," I said to the hotel proprietor, who was lounging about in his doorway. "Have you a room free?"

"This way, sir," and giving my suitcase to a porter who came forward, I followed him into the hall (lit.: "he preceded me").

The hotel was small, but white and clean; it had a lovely garden at the front, with a balcony and pergola which stretched down to the shores of the lake.

"Are you staying long?" the proprietor asked me.

"No, only three or four days."

"Then I can offer you a very nice room, with a terrace and view of the lake, 2,000 lire a day, inclusive; plus the tourist tax and the 10 per cent service. There is, too, a smaller one, without terrace, and with a view over the mountains for 1,800 lire. They are both fine spacious (airy) rooms, with hot and cold water. Do you wish to see them, sir?"

"Thank you." And although it was a bit dearer than I would have liked, I let myself be tempted by the lovely view, and chose the room with the balcony.

But everything comes to an end. The last day of my holidays arrived. I bathed for the last time in those cool waters, and went for a last trip in a boat with the old boatman, Antonio. The morning of my departure I got up early, and when I had packed my case I ordered my coffee to be brought up to the terrace. While I had breakfast (lit.: "while I was eating") I watched the fishing-boats pass with their tawny red sails. Then suddenly I saw my old friend Antonio, and he left his oars and stood up, waving his cap in the air and calling out to me: "Goodbye, sir; a pleasant journey to you. Remember Antonio, and come back again soon."

"Why, of course," I thought as I went on board the steamer for Como, the first stage of my return journey. "Why of course, dear old Antonio, I will always remember you; and as for coming back again soon, why, yes, I can certainly promise you that: I shall come back again to your lovely country at the first possible opportunity."

Notes

col direttissimo.—To travel by train is: *viaggiare col treno*; by car = *coll'automobile, colla macchina* (also *nell'automobile, nella macchina*); also *coll'autobus, con la bicicletta.*

Don Abbondio . . . Lucia.—Two of the principal characters in the historical novel *I promessi sposi* (The Betrothed) by Alessandro Manzoni (1785–1873), one of the greatest figures in Italian literature. The scene of this novel is the country around the lake of Como, particularly near Lecco, a small town at the end of the arm of the lake pointing due south. The extract on page 40 is from this novel (very slightly modified).

i tre rami.—The shape of the lake should be seen on the map. It has three distinct arms meeting at one point. Como, at the end of the arm pointing south-west is a small industrial town, chiefly important for the manufacture of silk; and Bellagio is on the promontory where the three arms meet.

Si accomodi.—We have already used *accomodarsi* for "to seat oneself"; and it is also used in the imperative—*si accomodi*—for many other expressions, such as "This way, please"; "Make yourself at home"; and "Do just as you wish".

imbarcarsi = to embark. *Sbarcare* = to disembark. *S impure* at the beginning of a word is sometimes a shortened form of *dis-*, and therefore negatives the meaning of the word: *coprire* = to cover; *scoprire* = to uncover, discover; *comodo* = comfortable; *scomodo* = uncomfortable.

tassa di soggiorno = a tax levied by the Italian Government on all tourists and visitors. Italians on holiday at hotels and boarding-houses are also required to pay this tax, which varies according to the locality and to the class of hotel.

ArrivederLa—lit.: "to the seeing you again", "au revoir". Note the change of pronoun with the different forms of address: *arrivederti, arrivedervi*; also *arrivederci* is often used.

Exercise 30

1. Dissero che sarebbero venuti alle tre, ma sono le tre e mezzo e non sono ancora arrivati.
2. Se andate al teatro, non tornate tanto tardi come l'altra volta (or: *se va . . . non torni*; or: *se vai . . . non torna*).
3. Se avessi quel libro, studierei.
4. Se avessi avuto quel libro, avrei studiato.
5. Se avrò quel libro, studierò.
6. Se avesse domandato a me dov'era quella chiesa, gli avrei detto subito (or: *Se mi domandava a me dove era . . . gli dicevo . . .*).
7. Sarebbe dovuto venire più presto se avesse voluto vedermi.
8. Se non fossi arrivato a Como troppo tardi per prendere il piroscafo per Bellagio, non avrei conosciuto Antonio. Quel vecchio barcaiuolo dagli occhi azzurri e dalla barba bianca, con quello strano berretto rosso, stava oziando sul molo quando io ci arrivai correndo, con la valigia in mano, proprio in tempo per veder partire il piroscafo. —Che rabbia! Chi sa quanto tempo dovrò aspettare?— pensai. —Mi dispiace che abbia perduto il piroscafo, Signore, vorrebbe andare in barca?— mi chiese quel vecchio, avvicinandosi a me. —Grazie— risposi, —ma è un po' troppo lontano per andarci con una barca a remi.— —Ma, ho un motoscafo, Signore.— —No, grazie, temo che quello mi costi troppo.— —Ma, Signore, Lei vuol andare a Bellagio, e ci voglio andare anch'io; lì c'è la mia casa, e la moglie e i bambini mi aspettano per la cena. Andiamo insieme; se mi vuol pagare, mi paghi il prezzo del biglietto del piroscafo; se non mi vuol pagare, non importa (*non fa niente*); ci vado lo stesso.— E così finii per andare con Antonio e per fare la conoscenza di uno degli uomini più simpatici che abbia mai incontrato.

APPENDIX

ADDITIONAL NOTES ON PRONUNCIATION, ACCENTS AND SYLLABICATION

Pronunciation

The Vowels e and o.—As dictionaries do not always indicate whether *e* and *o* in stressed syllables have the open or close sound, the following notes will be of use:

e is *open* in the following cases:

1. In the diphthong *iɛ*: piɛde, ciɛlo.
2. When followed by another vowel: idɛa.
3. In words of more than two syllables that end in *-ɛro*: sevɛro.
4. When the stressed *e* is in the third from the last syllable: mɛdico, sɛcolo.
5. In the endings: *-ɛndo* and *-ɛnte*, and when *e* is followed by two or more consonants, *except* in the following endings, which are all *close*: -egno, -emmo, -enna, -esco, -etto, -evole, -ezza, and -mente.

Final *e* when stressed is *close*, except in: caffɛ̀, tɛ̀, ahimɛ̀ ("alas"), cioɛ̀ ("that is") and ɛ̀ ("is").

o is *open*:

1. In the diphthong *uɔ*: uɔmo, buɔno.
2. When followed by another vowel: pɔi (except noi and voi).
3. When it is in the third syllable from the end: pɔvero, mɔnaco.
4. When it is followed by a double consonant: dɔnna, fɔlla.
5. When it is a final vowel: comprɔ̀.
6. When it is followed by one or more consonants and the diphthongs *-ia* or *-io*: prɔprio.

The Consonants s and z.—Again, the *voiced* and *unvoiced* sounds are not distinguished in all dictionaries: the following will be helpful:

s is *unvoiced* (like the *s* in *taste*):

1. When followed by *c, f, p, q, t* (all voiceless consonants): aspettare.
2. When at the beginning of a word and followed by a vowel: sạbato.
3. When it is double: tassa.

s is *voiced* (like the *s* in *rose*):

1. When followed by the voiced consonants: *b, d, g, l, m, n, r, v*: ṣbaglio, ṣmemorato.
2. When it comes between vowels: rọṣa, viṣo. There are, however, many exceptions to this rule; we may quote those which have appeared in this book: casa, cọsa, cosí, mese, risa, Pisa, inglese—in all these words the *s* is *unvoiced*, although it comes between two vowels.

z is *unvoiced* (pronounced like *ts*) when it is followed by *-ia, -ie,* or *-io*; grazie, azione.

z is *voiced* (pronounced like *dz*):

1. In verbs ending in *-izzare* which have more than four syllables in the infinitive: analiẓẓare (= to analyse).
2. In words derived from Greek, Hebrew or Arabic: aẓẓurro.
3. In words which begin with *z*: ẓelo (= zeal). But there are some exceptions to this rule; among them we may note: zio, zia, zoppo (all of which we have used in this book), and we may add two other useful words: zucchero (= sugar) and zuppa (= soup). In all these words, the *z* is *unvoiced*, although it is the initial letter.

Accents

In addition to the rules for the written accent, given on pp. 17–18, we must also note that there are some words which take an accent occasionally, when it is necessary to avoid confusion between words of more than one syllable, which are spelt alike, but have different meanings. These are either words which are exactly alike in form, but have a different syllable stressed, as: ancóra = again, àncora = anchor; or they are alike in form, but one has a *close e* or *o*, and the other an *open* vowel: légge = law, lègge = he reads; cólto = cultivated, còlto = gathered. It must be emphasized that such words have the accent *only* when their meaning is not clear from the context; which is not very often.

Some writers put an acute accent on the *i* of words ending in *-io* and *-ia*, when the *i* is stressed, as: signoría, scintillío, gridío, to ensure the correct pronunciation of the word; also in reading you will find that parts of verbs taking the conjunctive pronouns after them often have an accent, as: dàtegliene, dàglielo, fàllo (= do it).

Syllabication

The method of dividing words into syllables differs from that used in English:

1. Every syllable, as far as possible, begins with a consonant: lu-ne-dí; ge-ne-ra-le.
2. Two vowels together forming a diphthong are one syllable, a hiatus forms two syllables: buɔ-no, piɛ-de, vi-a, pa-u-ra.
3. Double consonants are separated: vac-ca, gat-to.
4. Two consonants, of which the first is *l*, *m*, *n*, or *r*, are separated: ac-cɛn-to, per-ché.
5. Any other two consonants are counted in the following syllable: fi-glia, giu-gno.
6. When three consonants come together, provided the first one is not *s*, the first is counted in the preceding syllable, and the other two in the following one: com-pra-re, com-plɛ-to.
7. If *s* is the first of the three consonants, all three belong to the following syllable: co-strin-ge-re, e-stre-mi-tà.

LIST OF COMMON IRREGULAR VERBS

Forms not listed below are regular. When an infinitive is contracted, the original form is given in brackets, to indicate the stem to which the endings are added for the regular parts (present participle, imperfect indicative and imperfect subjunctive—see page 86).

Abbreviations: *fut.*: = future; *impve.* = imperative; *past def.* = past definite; *past part.* = past participle; *pres. ind.* = present indicative; *pres. sub.* = present subjunctive; *imp. sub.* = imperfect subjunctive.

Verbs conjugated with *essere* are marked *; verbs which sometimes take *essere* and sometimes *avere* are preceded by a †.

All the irregular verbs which appear in this book are included. For easy consultation the two auxiliary verbs, *avere* and *essere*, are given together at the end of this list, on p. 220.

*accorgersi = to notice; *past. def.* accorsi, accorgesti, etc.; *past part.* accorto.

aggiungere = to add; see giungere.

*andare = to go; *pres. ind.* vado, vai, va, andiamo, andate, vanno; *fut.* andrò; *pres. sub.* vada, andiamo, andiate, vadano; *impve.* va', andiamo, andate.

*apparire = to appear; *pres. ind.* appaio or apparisco, appari or apparisci, appare or apparisce, appariamo, apparite, appaiono or appariscono; *past def.* apparsi or apparvi or apparii, apparisti, etc.; *past part.* apparso or apparito; *pres. sub.* appaia or apparisca, etc.; *impve.* appari or apparisci, appariamo, apparite.

appartenere = to belong; see tenere.

aprire = to open; *past def.* apersi or aprii, apristi, etc.; *past part.* aperto.

aspergere = to sprinkle; see spargere.

bere (bevere) = to drink; *pres. ind.* bevo; *past def.* bevvi, or bevei or bevetti, bevesti, etc.; *past part.* bevuto; *fut.* berrò or beverò; *pres. sub.* beva; *impve.* bevi, beviamo, bevete.

*cadere = to fall; *past def.* caddi, cadesti, etc.; *fut.* cadrò.

chiedere = to ask; *pres. ind.* chiedo or chieggo, chiedi, chiede, chiediamo, chiedete, chiedono or chieggono; *past def.* chiesi, chiedesti, etc.; *past part.* chiesto; *pres. sub.* chieda or chiegga; *impve.* chiedi, chiediamo, chiedete.

chiudere = to close; *past def.* chiusi, chiudesti, etc.; *past part.* chiuso.

cingere = to gird, embrace, surround; *past def.* cinsi, cingesti, etc.; *past part.* cinto.

cogliere = to gather; *pres. ind.* colgo, cogli, coglie, cogliamo, cogliete, colgono; *past def.* colsi, cogliesti, etc.; *past part.* colto; *pres. sub.* colga; *impve.* cogli, cogliamo, cogliete.

comprendere = to understand; see prendere.

condurre (conducere) = to lead; *pres. ind.* conduco, etc.; *past def.* condussi, conducesti, etc.; *past part.* condotto; *fut.* condurrò; *pres. sub.* conduca, conduciamo, conduciate, conducano; *impve.* conduci, conduciamo, conducete.

conoscere = to know; *past def.* conobbi, conoscesti, etc.

contenere = to contain; see tenere.

*convenire = to suit, agree; see venire.

coprire = to cover; see aprire.

†correre = to run; *past def.* corsi, corresti, etc.; *past part.* corso.

costringere = to compel; see stringere.

costruire = to construct; *past def.* costrussi, costruisti, etc.;
past part. costrutto or costruito.

†crescere = to grow; *past def.* crebbi, crescesti, etc.

dare = to give; *pres. ind.* do, dai, dà, diamo, date, danno; *past
def.* diɛdi or dɛtti, desti, etc.; *past part.* dato; *fut.* darɔ̀; *pres.
sub.* dia, diamo, diate, diano or diɛno; *impve.* da', diamo,
date; *imp. sub.* dessi, etc.

decidere = to decide; *past def.* decisi, decidesti, etc.; *past part.*
deciso.

*dipɛndere = to depend; see spɛndere.

dire (dicere) = to say; *pres. ind.* dico, dici, dice, diciamo, dite,
dicono; *past def.* dissi, dicesti, etc.; *past part.* detto; *fut.*
dirɔ̀; *pres. sub.* dica, diciamo, diciate, dicano; *impve.* di',
diciamo, dite.

*dirigersi = to direct oneself; *past def.* dirɛssi, dirigesti, etc.;
past part. dirɛtto.

discutere = to discuss; *past def.* discussi, discutesti, etc.; *past
part.* discusso.

dispiacere = to displease; see piacere.

disporre = to dispose; see porre.

distinguere = to distinguish; *past def.* distinsi, distinguesti,
etc.; *past part.* distinto.

*divenire = to become; see venire.

dovere = to owe, to have to, to be obliged to; *pres. ind.*
dɛvo or dɛbbo, dɛvi, dɛve, dobbiamo, dovete, dɛvono or
dɛbbono; *fut.* dovrɔ̀; *pres. sub.* dɛva or dɛbba, dobbiamo,
dobbiate, dɛvano or dɛbbano.

emettere = to emit; see mettere.

esporre = to expose; see porre.

estɛndere = to extend; see spɛndere.

fare (facere) = to do, to make; *pres. ind.* faccio or fɔ, fai, fa,
facciamo, fate, fanno; *past def.* feci, facesti, etc.; *past part.*
fatto; *fut.* farɔ̀; *pres. sub.* faccia, facciamo, facciate, facciano;
impve. fa', facciamo, fate.

†giungere = to arrive, to join; *past def.* giunsi, giungesti, etc.;
past part. giunto.

intɛndere = to intend, understand; see spɛndere.

invadere = to invade; *past def.* invasi, invadesti, etc.; *past
part.* invaso.

lɛggere = to read; *past def.* lɛssi, leggesti, etc.; *past part.* lɛtto.

mettere = to put; *past def.* misi or messi, mettesti, etc.; *past
part.* messo.

*morire = to die; *pres. ind.* muɔio, muɔri, muɔre, moriamo,
morite, muɔiono; *past part.* mɔrto; *fut.* morirɔ̀ or morrɔ̀;

pres. sub. muoia, moriamo, moriate, muoiano; *impve.* muori, moriamo, morite.

muovere = to move; *pres. ind.* muovo or movo, muovi or movi, muove or move, moviamo, movete, muovono or movono; *past def.* mossi, movesti, etc.; *past part.* mosso; *pres. sub.* muova or mova, moviamo, moviate, muovano or movano; *impve.* muovi or movi, moviamo, movete.

*nascere = to be born; *past def.* nacqui, nascesti, etc.; *past part.* nato.

offrire = to offer; see aprire.

*parere = to seem; *pres. ind.* paio, pari, pare, paiamo, parete, paiono; *past def.* parvi or parsi, paresti, etc.; *past part.* parso; *fut.* parrò; *pres. sub.* paia, paiamo, pariate, paiano.

perdere = to lose; *past def.* persi or perdei or perdetti, perdesti, etc.; *past part.* perso or perduto.

permettere = to permit; see mettere.

piacere = to please; *pres. ind.* piaccio, piaci, piace, piacciamo, piacete, piacciono; *past def.* piacqui, piacesti, etc.; *pres. sub.* piaccia, piacciamo, piacciate, piacciano; *impve.* piaci, piacciamo, piacete.

piangere = to cry; *past def.* piansi, piangesti, etc.; *past part.* pianto.

†piovere = to rain (impersonal); *past def.* piovve.

porgere = to present, offer; *past def.* porsi, porgesti, etc.; *past part.* porto.

porre (ponere) = to put; *pres. ind.* pongo, poni, pone, poniamo, ponete, pongono; *past def.* posi, ponesti, etc.; *past part.* posto; *fut.* porrò; *pres. sub.* ponga, poniamo, poniate, pongano; *impve.* poni, poniamo, ponete.

†potere = to be able; *pres. ind.* posso, puoi, può, possiamo, potete, possono; *fut.* potrò; *pres. sub.* possa, possiamo, possiate, possano.

prendere = to take; *past def.* presi, predesti, etc.; *past part.* preso.

promettere = to promise; see mettere.

proteggere = to protect; *past def.* protessi, proteggesti, etc.; *past part.* protetto.

†raggiungere = to reach, overtake; see giungere.

riaprire = to open again; see aprire.

riconoscere = to recognize; see conoscere.

ridere = to laugh; *past def.* risi, ridesti, etc.; *past part.* riso.

*rimanere = to remain; *pres. ind.* rimango, rimani, rimane, rimaniamo, rimanete, rimangono; *past def.* rimasi, rimanesti, etc.; *past part.* rimasto; *fut.* rimarrò; *pres. sub.* rimanga,

rimaniamo rimaniate, rimangano; *impve.* rimani, rimaniamo, rimanete.

riprendere = to retake, to continue; see prendere.

rispondere = to reply; *past def.* risposi, rispondesti, etc.; *past
part.* risposto.

*riuscire = to succeed; see uscire.

rompere = to break; *past def.* ruppi, rompesti, etc.; *past part.*
rotto.

†salire = to ascend; *pres. ind.* salgo, sali, sale, saliamo, salite,
salgono; *pres. sub.* salga, saliamo, saliate, salgano; *impve.*
sali, saliamo, salite.

sapere = to know; *pres. ind.* so, sai, sa, sappiamo, sapete,
sanno; *past def.* seppi, sapesti, etc.; *fut.* saprò; *pres. sub.*
sappia, sappiamo, sappiate, sappiano; *impve.* sappi, sappiamo, sappiate.

scegliere = to choose; *pres. ind.* scelgo, scegli, sceglie,
scegliamo, scegliete, scelgono; *past def.* scelsi, scegliesti,
etc.; *past part.* scelto; *pres. sub.* scelga, scegliamo, scegliate,
scelgano; *impve.* scegli, scegliamo, scegliete.

*scendere = to descend; *past def.* scesi, scendesti, etc.; *past
part.* sceso.

sciogliere = to untie, loosen; *pres. ind.* sciolgo, sciogli, scioglie,
sciogliamo, sciogliete, sciolgono; *past def.* sciolsi, sciogliesti,
etc.; *past part.* sciolto; *pres. sub.* sciolga, sciogliamo,
sciogliate, sciolgano; *impve.* sciogli, sciogliamo, sciogliete.

scoprire = to discover; see aprire.

†scorrere = to flow; see correre.

scrivere = to write; *past def.* scrissi, scrivesti, etc.; *past part.*
scritto.

sedere = to sit; *pres. ind.* siedo or seggo, siedi, siede, sediamo,
sedete, siedono or seggono; *pres. sub.* sieda or segga, sediamo,
sediate, siedano or seggano; *impve.* siedi, sediamo, sedete.

soggiungere = to add; see giungere.

*sorgere = to arise; *past def.* sorsi, sorgesti, etc.; *past part.*
sorto.

sorprendere = to surprise; see prendere.

spargere = to scatter, shed; *past def.* sparsi, spargesti, etc.;
past part. sparso.

spendere = to spend; *past def.* spesi, spendesti, etc.; *past part.*
speso.

spingere = to push; *past def.* spinsi, spingesti; *past part.*
spinto.

*stare = to stand, to be; *pres. ind.* sto, stai, sta, stiamo, state,
stanno; *past def.* stetti, stesti, etc.; *pres. sub.* stia, stiamo,

stiate, stiano; *fut.* starò; *impve.* sta', stiamo, state; *imp. sub.* stessi, etc.

*stendersi = to stretch oneself; *past def.* stesi, stendesti, etc.; *past part.* steso.

stringere = to bind fast, hold; *past def.* strinsi, stringesti, etc.; *past part.* stretto.

*succedere = to happen; *past def.* successi or succedei or succedetti, succedesti, etc.; *past part.* successo or succeduto.

svolgere = to unfold; see volgere.

tacere = to be silent; *pres. ind.* taccio, taci, tace, taciamo, tacete, tacciono; *past def.* tacqui, tacesti, etc.; *pres. sub.* taccia, taciamo, taciate, tacciano; *impve.* taci, taciamo, tacete.

tenere = to hold; *pres. ind.* tengo, tieni, tiene, teniamo, tenete, tengono; *past def.* tenni, tenesti, etc.; *fut.* terrò; *pres. sub.* tenga, teniamo, teniate, tengano; *impve.* tieni, teniamo, tenete.

togliere = to take off, from; see sciogliere.

tradurre = to translate; see condurre.

trarre (traere) = to draw, pull; *pres. ind.* traggo, trai, trae, traiamo, traete, traggono; *past def.* trassi, traesti, etc.; *past part.* tratto; *fut.* trarrò; *pres. sub.* tragga, traiamo, traiate, traggano; *impve.* trai, traiamo, traete.

trasmettere = to transmit; see mettere.

trattenere = to hold back; see tenere.

udire = to hear; *pres. ind.* odo, odi, ode, udiamo, udite, odono; *pres. sub.* oda, udiamo, udiate, odano; *impve.* odi, udiamo, udite.

*uscire = to go out; *pres. ind.* esco, esci, esce, usciamo, uscite, escono; *pres. sub.* esca, usciamo, usciate, escano; *impve.* esci, usciamo, uscite.

*valere = to be worth; *pres. ind.* valgo, vali, vale, valiamo, valete, valgono; *past def.* valsi, valesti, etc.; *past part.* valso; *fut.* varrò; *pres. sub.* valga, valiamo, valiate, valgano.

vedere = to see; *past def.* vidi, vedesti, etc.; *past part.* visto or veduto; *fut.* vedrò.

*venire = to come; *pres. ind.* vengo, vieni, viene, veniamo, venite, vengono; *past def.* venni, venisti, etc.; *past part.* venuto; *fut.* verrò; *pres. sub.* venga, veniamo, veniate, vengano; *impve.* vieni, veniamo, venite.

vincere = to win; *past def.* vinsi, vincesti, etc.; *past part.* vinto.

*vivere = to live; *past def.* vissi, vivesti, etc.; *past part.* vissuto.

†volere = to wish; *pres. ind.* vɔglio, vuɔi, vuɔle, vogliamo, volete, vɔgliono; *past def.* vɔlli, volesti, etc.; *fut.* vorrɔ̀; *pres. sub.* vɔglia, vogliamo, vogliate, vɔgliano; *impve.* vɔgli, vogliamo, vogliate.

vɔlgere = to turn; *past def.* vɔlsi, volgesti, etc.; *past part.* vɔlto.

Auxiliary Verbs

avere = to have; *pres. ind.* hɔ, hai, ha, abbiamo, avete, hanno; *past def.* ɛbbi, avesti, ɛbbe, avemmo, aveste, ɛbbero; *fut.* avrɔ̀; *pres. sub.* abbia, abbiamo, abbiate, abbiano; *impve.* abbi, abbiamo, abbiate.

ɛssere = to be; *pres. ind.* sono, sɛi, ɛ̀, siamo, siete, sono; *past def.* fui, fosti, fu, fummo, foste, furono; *imp. ind.* ɛro, ɛri, ɛra, eravamo, eravate, ɛrano; *fut.* sarɔ̀; *pres. sub.* sia, siamo, siate, siano; *imp. sub.* fossi, fossi, fosse, fossimo, foste, fossero; *impve.* sii, siamo, siate; *past part.* stato.

VOCABULARY

Numbers, days, months, seasons (pages 16–17, 95, and 98–99); articles (pages 19–20, 24–25), and personal pronouns (pages 22–23, 58, and 67), are not included in this vocabulary; nor are proper nouns, nor nouns which are the same in spelling and meaning in both languages.

Nouns ending in -*o* are masculine, with the one exception of *la mano*; those ending in -*a* are feminine unless otherwise stated; the gender of other nouns is indicated. Verbs are regular unless otherwise indicated, and where there might be uncertainty as to the stress in the present indicative, or as to the pronunciation of an *e* or an *o*, the first person is appended in brackets. Verbs conjugated with *essere* are marked *, and those which may take either auxiliary are marked †. The preposition most commonly used after a verb or adjective is shown in brackets after the word.

A

abbastanza, *enough*

abbondante (di), *abundant in*

abbozzare (abbozzo), *to outline, sketch*

abete (m.), *fir*

abitante (m.), *inhabitant*

abitare (abito), *to inhabit*

abito, *coat, suit*

abituarsi (abituo), *to accustom oneself to*

abitudine (f.), *habit*

accanto, *at the side of, next to*

accelerato, *stopping train, slow train*

accento, *accent*

*accomodarsi (accomodo), *to seat oneself, to make oneself comfortable*

accompagnare, *to accompany*

accontentare, *to satisfy*

accordo, *accord, chord*

*accorgersi (di) (irreg.), *to notice*

acqua, *water*

acquistare, *to acquire*

acre, *sour, harsh*

acuto, *acute, shrill*

adatto (a), *fit for*

addio!, *goodbye!*

*addormentarsi (addormento), *to fall asleep*

adesso, *now*

adoperare (adopero), *to use*

adornare (di), *to decorate with*

*affacciarsi (affaccio), *to show one's face at (window, door)*

affittare, *to hire*

aggiogare (aggiogo), *to yoke*

aggiungere (irreg.), *to add*

*aggrapparsi, *to cling*

agitare (agito), *to wave*

ahimè!, *alas!*

221

aiutare, *to help*
alba, *dawn*
albergo, *hotel*
albero, *tree*
alcuno, *some, any*
*allargarsi, *to widen*
allato, a lato, *at the side*
allegro, *merry*
allora, *then*
almeno, *at least*
alquanto, *somewhat*
altare (m.), *altar*
altezza, *height*
alto, *high, tall*
altrettanto, *equally, the same to you*
altro, *other*
altrui, *other, others*
*alzarsi, *to get up*
amante (m. and f.), *lover*
amare, *to love, like*
ameno, *pleasing, delightful*
amica, *friend* (f.)
amico, *friend* (m.)
amministrativo, *administrative*
ammirare, *to admire*
analizzare, *to analyse*
anche, *also, even*
ancora, *again*
àncora, *anchor*
*andare (irreg.), *to go*
    andar bene, *to suit, to be all right*
    andar a genio, *to please, to suit one's taste*
andata, *going*, see biglietto
anello, *ring*
angolo, *angle, corner*
anima, *soul, spirit*
animato, *animated*
anno, *year*
annoiare (annoio), *to annoy, bore*

annunciare (annuncio), *to announce*
ansioso, *worried*
antichità, *antiquity, antiquities*
antico, *ancient*
antiquario, *antiquarian, antique dealer*
anzi, *on the contrary*
apparecchiare (apparecchio), *to prepare, lay (table)*
*apparire (irreg.) (either 1st or 2nd group), *to appear*
appartenere (irreg.), *to belong*
appena, *hardly*
appena che, *as soon as*
appetito, *appetite*
applauso, *applause*
appoggiare (appoggio), *to support*
approfittare (di), *to profit by, take advantage of*
appunto, per l'appunto, *precisely*
aprire (irreg.) (2nd group), *to open*
arancia, *orange*
arazzo, *tapestry*
arcata, *arcade*
argento, *silver*
aria, *air*
arioso, *airy*
armadio, *cupboard, wardrobe*
armonia, *harmony*
armonioso, *harmonious*
armonizzare, *harmonize*
arrestare, *to arrest*
*arrestarsi, *to stop*
*arricchirsi (1st group), *to enrich*
*arrivare, *to arrive*
arrivederci!, *goodbye!*
arrosto, *roast*
arte (f.), *art*
articolo, *article*

artista (m. and f.), *artist*
artistico, *artistic*
ascensore (m.), *lift*
asciugamano (m.), *towel*
ascoltare (ascolto), *to listen*
aspergere (irreg.), *to sprinkle*
aspettare (aspetto), *to wait for, expect*
assai, *very*
assalto, *assault*
assenza, *absence*
attenzione (f.), *attention*
attore (m.), *actor*
†attraversare (attraverso), *to cross*

austero, *austere*
autobus (m.), *bus*
automobile (m.), *motor car*
autorimessa (f.), *garage*
autostrada (f.), *motor road, main road*
avanti, *in front*
avanti che, *before*
avere (irreg.), *to have*
*avviarsi, *to start out*
*avvicinarsi, *to draw near*
avvocato, *lawyer*
azione (f.), *action*
azzurro, *blue*

B

bacheca, *show case*
bagaglio, *luggage*
*bagnarsi, *to bath, bathe*
bagno, *bath*
baia, *bay*
balcone (m.), *balcony*
ballare, *to dance*
balneare, *of baths, bathing*
balzare, *to jump*
bambino, -a, *baby*
banca, *bank*
bancario, *banking*
banco, *bench*
bandiera, *banner*
baracca, *hut, tent, stall*
barba, *beard*
barbarico, *barbarian*
barbaro, *barbarian*
barca, *boat*
    barca a remi, *rowing boat*
    barca a vela, *sailing boat*
barcaiuolo, *boatman*
basso, *low, short (of stature)*
    bassorilievo, *low relief*
*bastare, *to suffice*
battere, *to beat*

battesimo, *baptism*
battezzare, *to baptize*
battistero, *baptistry*
baule (m.), *trunk*
beato, *perfectly happy*
bellezza, *beauty*
bellino, *pretty*
bello, *beautiful, fine*
beltà, *beauty*
benché, *although*
bene, *well*
    benissimo, *very well*
beneficenza, *charity*
bere (irreg.), *to drink*
berretto, *cap*
bestia, *beast*
biancheggiare (biancheggio), *to whiten*
bianco, *white*
bibita, *drink*
biblioteca, *library*
bicchiere (m.), *glass, tumbler*
biglietto, *ticket*
    biglietto di andata e ritorno, *return ticket*
bimbo, -a, *child*

binario, *railway track*
biondo, *blonde*
bis!, *encore!*
biscotto, *biscuit*
*bisognare, *to need*
bisogno, *need*
bollo, *stamp, seal*
bontà, *goodness*
bordo, *board*
  a bordo, *on board*
borgo, *suburb, village*
borsa, *purse*
bottega, *shop*
bottiglia, *bottle*
braccetto, *arm*
  a braccetto, *arm in arm*

bravo!, *well done!*
bravo, *good, capable*
breve, *short*
briciola, *crumb*
brillare, *to shine*
bronzo, *bronze*
bruscamente, *brusquely, suddenly*
brutto, *ugly*
bue (m.), *ox*
bugia, *untruth*
bugiardo, *liar*
buono, *good*
burlone, *one who jokes*
burro, *butter*

C

*cadere (irreg.), *to fall*
caffè (m.), *café, coffee*
calca, *crowd*
caldo, *warm, hot*
calma, *calm* (noun)
calmo, *calm* (adj.)
calvo, *bald*
calza, *stocking*
calzino, *sock*
camera, *bedroom*
cameriere, -a, *servant maid (waiter, waitress)*
camicia, *shirt*
†camminare, *to walk*
cammino, *way*
campagna, *country*
campana, *bell*
campanello, *little bell, door bell*
campanile (m.), *belfry*
campo, *field*
canale (m.), *canal*
candido, *pure white, shining*
cane (m.), *dog*
cantante (m. and f.), *singer*
cantare, *to sing*

cantarellare (cantarello), *to hum*
cantonata, *corner*
cantoría, *choir stall*
capelli (m. pl.), *hair*
capire (1st group), *to understand*
capitale (f.), *capital*
capitano, *captain*
capitolo, *chapter*
capo, *head*
capolavoro, *masterpiece*
capostazione (m.), *station master*
cappello, *hat*
cappotto, *cloak, overcoat*
carabiniere, *carabineer, policeman*
caramella, *sweet*
carattere (m.), *character*
carbone (m.), *coal*
caricare (carico), *to load*
carico, *load*
carne (f.), *meat*
caro, *dear*

carro, *cart*

carrozza, *carriage*

carrozza-letti, *sleeping car*

carta, *paper*

  carta da scrivere, *writing paper*

  carta geografica, *map*

cartolina, *post card*

casa, *house, home*

*cascare, *to fall*

cascatella, *little waterfall*

casella, *pigeon hole*

caso, *case, chance*

cassetto, *drawer*

castagno, *chestnut tree*

cattivo, *bad*

causa, *cause*

cava, *quarry*

cavalla, *mare*

cavalletta, *locust*

cavallo, *horse*

celebrare (celebro), *to celebrate*

celebre, *famous*

celeste, *pale blue*

cena, *supper*

cenare, *to have supper*

centesimo, *centime*

centrale, *central*

centro, *centre*

cercare, *to look for*

cerchia, *circle*

certamente, *certainly*

certo, *sure, certain*

cesta, *basket*

cestino, *little basket*

ché, *because*

che, *who, which, that*

  gran che, *of special interest*

che!, *what!, what a!*

che? che cosa?, *what?*

che . . . non, *than*

checché, *whatever*

chi, *who, whom, he who, he whom*

H

chi?, *who?, whom?*

chiacchierare (chiacchiero), *to chatter, gossip*

chiamare, *to call*

chiaro, *clear, light*

chiave (f.), *key*

chicchessia, *whoever, whosoever*

chiedere (irreg.), *to ask*

chiesa, *church*

chilometro, *kilometre*

chiudere (irreg.), *to close*

chiunque, *whoever*

ci (adv.), *here, there*

ciao!, *goodbye, so long*

ciascuno, *each*

cicala, *cricket*

cicerone (m.), *guide*

cieco, *blind*

cielo, *shy*

ciglio, *eyelash*

cima, *top, summit*

cimitero, *cemetery*

cingere (irreg.), *to surround*

cintura, *belt*

ciò, *that, this*

  cioè, *that is*

cioccolata, *chocolate*

cipresso, *cypress*

circolare, *circular*

circondare, *to surround*

circostante, *surrounding*

città, *town*

cittadina, *small town*

coda, *tail*

cogliere (irreg.), *to gather*

colà, *there*

colazione (f.), *lunch*

  prima colazione, *breakfast*

collana, *necklace*

colle (m.), *hill*

colletto, *collar*

collezione (f.), *collection*

collina, *hill*

colonia, *colony*

colonico, *farming, of the farmer*
casa colonica, *farm house*

colonna, *column*

colore (m.), *colour*

colorito, *complexion*

colpevole, *guilty*

colpire (1st group), *to strike*

colpo, *blow*

coltello, *knife*

coltivare (coltivo), *to cultivate*

coltivazione (f.), *cultivation*

colto, *cultivated, educated*

colui, colui che, *he, he who*

comandare, *to command*

comare (f.), *god-mother, neighbour*

come, *as, like, how*

come!, *what!*

come?, *how?*

†cominciare (comincio) (a), *to
begin*

commercio, *trade*

commesso viaggiatore, *commercial traveller*

commissionario, *representative*

comodo, *comfortable*

compagnia, *company*

compagno, -a, *companion*

compiere (compio), *to complete, fulfil*

compleanno, *birthday*

completo, *full*

complimento, *compliment*

compositore (m.), *composer*

comprare (compro), *to buy*

comprendere (irreg.), *to understand*

con, *with*

concerto, *concert*

conchiglia, *shell*

concorso, *competition*

condurre (irreg.), *to lead*

confessare, *to confess*

conico, *conical*

conoscenza, *acquaintance*

conoscere (irreg.), *to know, be
acquainted with*

conquistare, *to conquer*

consigliare (consiglio), *to advise*

consistere (di, in), *to consist*

console (m.), *consul*

consultare, *to consult*

contadino, -a, *peasant*

contemplare (contemplo), *to
contemplate, look at*

contenere (irreg.), *to contain*

contento (di), *contented with,
pleased to*

contiguo, *adjacent*

continuare (a), *to continue*

continuo, *continual*

conto, *account, bill*

contorno, *outline, garnish (of
dish for the table)*

contrada, *regione, quarter,
ward*

contributo, *contribution*

contro, *against*

*convenire (irreg.), *to suit, to
be profitable*

convento, *convent*

convertire, *to convert*

coprire (irreg.) (2nd group), *to
cover*

coraggio, *courage*

coraggioso, *courageous*

corpo, *body*

†correre (irreg.), *to run*

correttamente, *correctly*

corridoio, *corridor*

corsa, *race*

corso, *course*

corteo, *procession*

cortile (m.), *yard, court*

corto, *short*

cosa, *thing*

cosí, *thus, so*

cosí . . . come, *as . . . as, so . . . as*

costà, *there*

costare, *to cost*

costeggiare (costeggio), *to coast*

costí, *there*

costringere (irreg.), *to compel*

costruire (irreg.) (1st group), *to construct*

costui, *that man*

costume (m.), *habit*

cravatta, *tie*

credere, *to believe, think*

†crescere (irreg.), *to grow*

crisi (f.), *crisis*

cristalleria, *glass ware*

Cristianesimo, *Christianity*

Cristiano, *Christian*

criticare (critico), *to criticize*

critico, *critical*

crocefisso, *crucifix*

crociata, *crusade*

cucchiaio, *spoon*

cucina, *kitchen*

cui, *whom, which*

il cui, *whose*

cullare, *to rock*

cuoco, -a, *cook*

cuoio, *leather*

cuore (m.), *heart*

cuscino, *cushion, pl. seats in carriage, car or train*

D

da, *by, with, from*

dappertutto, *everywhere*

dapprima, *at first*

dare (irreg.), *to give*

   dare luogo a, *to give place to*

   dare retta a, *to pay attention to*

data, *date*

datare, *to date*

davanti a, *in front of*

davvero, *indeed*

decadenza, *decline*

decidere (di) (irreg.), *to decide*

*decidersi (a, di) (irreg.), *to decide*

declivio, *slope*

decorazione (f.), *decoration*

degno, *worthy*

denaro, *money*

dentista (m.), *dentist*

dentro, *in, within*

deposito, *deposit, cloakroom*

desiderare (desidero), *to desire*

destinare (destino), *to destine*

destra, *right hand*

deviazione (f.), *deviation*

di, *of*

dí, *day (poetical)*

dialetto, *dialect*

diamine!, *heavens !*

dichiarare (dichiaro), *to declare*

dietro, *behind*

difficile, *difficult*

difficoltà, *difficulty*

dimenticare (dimentico), *to forget*

dio mio!, *Good Lord !*

*dipendere (da) (irreg.), *to depend on*

dire (irreg.), *to say*

diretto, *direct*

*dirigersi (irreg.), *to direct oneself*

diritto (noun and adj.), *right (noun); straight (adj.)*

discepolo, *follower*

discutere (irreg.), *to discuss*

disegno, *design*

disoccupato, *unemployed*
disonore (m.), *dishonour*
disordine (m.), *disorder*
*dispiacere (irreg.), *to displease*
disporre (irreg.), *to dispose, arrange*
disposizione (f.), *disposal*
distanza, *distance*
distinguere (irreg.), *to distinguish*
dito, *finger*
*divenire (irreg.), *to become*
diventare (divento), *to become*
diverso, *different*
divertente, *amusing*
divertimento, *enjoyment*
*divertirsi (2nd group), *to enjoy oneself*
divinamente, *divinely*
divino, *divine*
dogana, *Customs office*
doganiere (m.), *Customs officer*

dolce, *sweet* (adj. and noun)
domanda, *question*
domandare, *to ask*
domani, *tomorrow*
domenicale, *of Sunday*
dominare (domino), *to dominate*
donna, *woman*
dopo, *afterwards, after*
dopo che, *after*
dormire (2nd group), *to sleep*
dottore (m.), *doctor*
dove, *where*
†dovere (irreg.), *to owe, to have to*
dovunque, *everywhere*
dozzina, *dozen*
dubbio, *doubt*
dubitare (dubito), *to doubt*
duca (m.), *duke*
dunque, *then, therefore*
duomo, *dome, cathedral*

E

e, ed, *and*
eccellente, *excellent*
eccetto, *except*
ecco, *here is* (are), *there is* (are)
eco (m. or f.), *echo*
edifizio, *building*
effetto, *effect*
elegante, *elegant*
eleganza, *elegance*
elemento, *element*
emettere (irreg.), *emit*
enorme, *enormous*
*entrare (in), *to enter*
entrata, *entrance*
entro, *within*
entusiasmo, *enthusiasm*

epoca, *epoch*
equestre, *equestrian*
erba, *grass*
esecuzione (f.), *execution*
esercitarsi (esercito), *to practise, exercise*
esitare (esito), *to hesitate*
esperimento, *experiment*
esporre (irreg.), *to expose, exhibit*
*essere (irreg.), *to be*
est (m.), *east*
estate (f.), *summer*
estendere (irreg.), *to extend*
esterno, *exterior*
estivo, *of summer*
estremità, *extremity, end*

F

fa, *ago*
fabbrica, *building*
fabbricare, *to build*
facchino, *porter*
faccia, *face*
   di faccia, *opposite*
facciata. *façade, front*
facile, *easy*
fame (f.), *hunger*
famiglia, *family*
famoso, *famous*
fanciulletta, *little girl*
fantastico, *fantastic*
fantino, *jockey*
fare (irreg.), *to make, to do*
   fare caldo, freddo, bel tempo, *to be hot, cold, fine weather*
   fare caso di, *to take notice of*
farmacia, *chemist's shop*
farsi avanti, *to come forward*
fascino, *fascination*
favore, *favour*
   per favore, *please*
fazzoletto, *handkerchief*
felice, *happy*
feriale, giorno feriale, *ordinary day, week day*
fermaglio, *brooch*
fermare, **fermarsi, to stop*
ferrato, *of iron*
   strada ferrata, *railway lines*
ferrovia, *railway*
festa, *holiday, festival*
festivo, *festive*
festone (m.), *festoon*
fetta, *slice*
   fettona, *large slice*
fiaccheraio, *cab driver*
fiancheggiare (fiancheggio), *to flank*
fiaschettino, *little bottle*

fiasco, *bottle, flask*
fico, *fig*
fidarsi (di), *to trust in*
fieno, *hay*
figlia, *daughter*
figlio, *son*
figurarsi (figuro), *to imagine*
fila, *line, file*
finalmente, *finally*
finché, *until*
fine (f.), *end*
finestra, *window*
   finestrino, *little window*
   finestrone, *large window*
†finire (1st group), *to finish*
fino a, *until, up to*
fioraio, *florist*
fiore (m.), *flower*
fiorentino, *Florentine*
fiorito, *in flower*
firma, *signature*
firmare, *to sign*
fischiare (fischio), *to whistle*
fischio, *whistle*
fissare, *to fix*
fisso, *fixed, fixedly*
fiume (m.), *river*
foglio, *sheet of paper*
folla, *crowd*
fondare, *to found*
fondo, *bottom*
   in fondo a, *at the bottom of*
fontana, *fountain*
fonte (m. and f.), *font* (m.); *fount* (f.)
forchetta, *fork*
forestiere, *foreigner*
forma, *shape*
formaggio, *cheese*
fornaio, *baker*
fornire (di) (1st group), *to furnish, supply with*

forse, *perhaps*
forte, *strong*
fortezza, *fortress*
fortunato, *lucky*
forza, *strength*
  a forza di, *by dint of*
fra, *among, within*
francese, *French*
franco, *franc*
francobollo, *stamp*
fratello, *brother*
freddo, *cold*
fregio (m.), *frieze*
frenetico, *frenzied*
fresco, *cool*

fretta, *haste*
frontiera, *frontier*
fronte (f.), *forehead, front*
  di fronte, *opposite*
frutta, *dessert*
frutto, *fruit*
fumo, *smoke*
funicolare (f.), *funicular railway*
fuoco, *fire*
fuorché, *except*
fuori, *outside, outside of*
  fuori di mano, *out of the way, off the track*
furbo, *cunning*

G

galleria, *arcade, gallery*
gamba, *leg*
gatto, *cat*
gelare (gelo), *to freeze*
gelatiere, *ice cream seller*
gelato, *ice cream*
generale, *general*
generalmente, *generally*
genio, *genius, character, taste* (see andare)
gente (f.), *people*
gentile, *kind*
gesso, *chalk*
ghiaccio, *ice*
ghiro, *dormouse*
già, *already*
giacca, *coat, jacket*
giacchetta, *jacket*
giallo, *yellow*
giapponese, *Japanese*
giardino, *garden*
gigante (m.), *giant*
ginocchio, *knee*
gioia, *joy*
gioiello, *jewel*
giornalaio, *newspaper seller*

giornale, *newspaper*
giorno, *day*
giovane, *young, youth*
giovanotto, *youth, young man*
giro, *tour*
gita, *excursion*
giú, *down*
giudice (m.), *judge*
†giungere (irreg.), *to arrive, to join*
giusto, *right, just*
godere, *to enjoy*
golfo, *gulf*
gondola, *gondola*
gondoliere (m.), *gondolier*
gonna, *skirt*
gotico, *gothic*
gradevole, *pleasant*
grande, *large, great*
*grandinare (grandina) (impers.), *to hail*
grandioso, *grandiose*
grano, *corn, grain*
granturco, *maize*
grasso, *fat*
grave (m.), *weight*

grazie, *thanks*
greco, *Greek*
gridare, *to shout*
gridío, *shouting*
grido, *shout*
grigio, *grey*
grosso, *large*
gruccia (f.), *clothes-hanger, crutch*

gruppo, *group*
guancia, *cheek*
guanciale (m.), *pillow*
guardare, *to look at*
guardia (f.), *guard*
guerra, *war*
guida (f.), *guide, guide book*
gusto, *taste*

H

ha, *he has*

hanno, *they have*

I

ieri, *yesterday*
illuminare (illumino), *to illumine*
*imbarcarsi, *to embark*
*immaginarsi (immagino), *to imagine to oneself*
immensamente, *immensely*
imparare, *to learn*
impetuoso, *impetuous*
impiegato, *clerk*
importanza, *importance*
importare (importo), *to matter*
impressionante, *impressive*
in, *in, to*
*incamminarsi, *to start on the way*
inchiostro, *ink*
incontrare (incontro), *to meet*
indicare (indico), *to indicate*
indicazione (f.), *indication*
indietro, *behind*
indifferente, *indifferent*
indirizzo, *address*
indovinare, *to guess*
industriale, *industrial*
infatidire (1st group), *to annoy, irritate*
inferiore, *inferior, lower*

informazione (f.), *information*
inglese, *English*
ingombrare (ingombro), *to crowd around, to get in the way*
iniziare (inizio), *to begin*
*innalzarsi, *to tower up, rise up*
innocenti, *foundlings* (lit.: *innocent ones*)
*inoltrare, *to go on, forward*
inondare, *to inundate, to pervade, to fill*
insegnare, *to teach*
insetto, *insect*
insieme, *together*
integro, *honest, upright*
intelligente, *intelligent*
intendere (irreg.), *to understand, to intend, to hear*
*intendersi (di), *to be expert, practised in*
intenzione (f.), *intention*
interessante, *interesting*
*interessarsi (a, di), *to be interested in*
intermedio, *intermediate*
interminabile, *unceasing*
interno, *interior*

intimo, *intimate*

intorno, *around*

   intorno a, *round* (prep.)

intraprendente, *enterprising*

invadere (irreg.), *to invade*

invasione (f.), *invasion*

*invecchiare (invecchio), *to become old*

invece, *on the other hand, instead*

   invece di, *instead of*

invitare, *to invite*

isola, *island*

isolato, *isolated*

italiano, *Italian*

itinerario, *route*

L

là, *there*

   al di là di, *beyond* (prep.)

labbro, *lip*

laggiú, *down there*

*lagnarsi (di), *to complain*

lago, *lake*

laguna, *lagoon*

lambire (either 1st or 2nd group), *to lap, lick*

lampada, *lamp*

lampeggiare (lampeggio), *to lighten*

larghezza, *width, generosity*

largo, *wide*

lasciare, *to let, leave*

lato, *side*

latte (m.), *milk*

*lavarsi, *to wash oneself*

lavorare (lavoro), *to work*

lavoro, *work*

legare (lego), *to bind*

legge (f.), *law*

leggere (irreg.), *to read*

leggiadria, *beauty, grace, elegance*

legno, *wood*

lento, *slow*

lenzuolo, *sheet*

lettera, *letter*

letto, *bed*

*levarsi, *to get up, to rise up*

lezione (f.), *lesson*

liberare (libero), *to free*

libero, *free*

libro, *book*

limpido, *clear, limpid*

linea, *line*

lingua, *tongue, language*

livello, *level*

lode (f.), *praise*

loggiata, *series of loggias*

lombardo, *of Lombardy*

lontananza, *distance*

lontano, *far*

loppio, *small maple*

luce (f.), *light*

luminoso, *bright, light*

luna, *moon*

lunghezza, *length*

lungo, *long*

luogo, *place*

lupa, *she-wolf*

lupo, *wolf*

M

ma, *but*

macchina, *machine, engine, car*

macchinista (m.), *engine driver*

madre (f.), *mother*

maestà, *majesty*

maestoso, *majestic*

maestro or maestro, *master*

maggiore, *older, larger, greater*

magnifico, *magnificent*

magro, *thin*

mai, *ever, never*

male, *bad, badly*

malgrado, *in spite of*

mancanza, *lack*

mancare, *to lack*

mancia, *tip (money)*

mandare, *to send*

mangiare (mangio), *to eat*

mangiatoia, *manger*

maniera, *manner, way*

mano (f.), *hand*

*maravigliarsi (di) or meravi-
gliarsi, *to be surprised at*

marciapiede (m.), *pavement*

mare (m.), *sea*

marinaro, *seafaring*

marino, *of the navy, of the sea*

marittimo, *maritime*

marmo, *marble*

marmoreo, *marble* (adj.)

mattina, mattino, *morning*

maturo, *mature*

medico, *doctor*

medioevale, *mediaeval*

medioevo, *middle ages*

meglio, *better*

mela, *apple*

melanconico, *melancholy*

membro (pl. membri), *member*

membro (pl. membra), *limb*

meno, *less*

a meno che . . . non, *unless*

mensola, *bracket*

mente (f.), *mind*

mentre, *while*

meraviglioso (maraviglioso),
wonderful

mercante (m.), *merchant*

mercato, *market*

merce (f.), *merchandise*

merenda, *lunch, picnic*

meridionale, *southern*

merlato, *battlemented*

merlo, *battlement*

mese (m.), *month*

metà, *half* (noun)

metro, *metre*

mettere (irreg.), *to put*

mezzanotte (f.), *midnight*

mezzo, *half* (adj.)

in mezzo a, di, *in the middle
of*

mezzogiorno, *midday*

miglio, *mile*

minore, *less, smaller, younger*

minuto, *minute*

mio, *my*

mirabile, *wonderful*

miracolo, *miracle*

miriade (f.), *myriad*

misero, *wretched*

misterioso, *mysterious*

misto, *mixed*

mite, *gentle, soft*

mobile (m.), *piece of furniture*

moderno, *modern*

modo, *way*

di modo che, *in such a way
that*

moglie (f.), *wife*

mole (f.), *mass*

molo, *jetty*

molto, *much, very*

momento, *moment*

a momenti, *any moment*

monaco, *monk*

monastero, *monastery*

mondo, *world*

monolitico, *monolithic*

monopolio, *monopoly*

montagna, *mountain*

monte (m.), *mountain*

monumento, *monumento*

*morire (irreg.), *to die*

mormorio, *murmur*
mortaretto, *small gun, mortar*
morte (f.), *death*
mosaico, *mosaic*
mostrare, *to show*
moto, *movement*
motoscafo, *motor boat*
movimento, *movement*

mulo, *mule*
muovere (irreg.), *to move*
muretto, *little wall*
muro, *wall*
museo, *museum*
musica, *music*
musicale, *musical*
*mutarsi, *to change oneself*

N

narrare, *to relate*
*nascere, *to be born*
naso, *nose*
natalizio, *of one's birth*
naturale, *natural*
naturalmente, *naturally*
navata, *nave*
nave (f.), *ship*
ne, *of it, some, any*
né . . . né, *neither, nor*
nebbia, *mist, fog*
necessario, *necessary*
negare, *to deny*
negozio, *shop*
nemica, *enemy*
neppure, *not even*
nero, *black*
nervoso, *nervous*
nessuno, *none, no one, nobody*
nevicare (impers.) (nevica), *to snow*

niente, *nothing*
noleggiare (noleggio), *to hire*
nome (m.), *name*
non, *not*
  non . . . che, *only*
  non ostante che, *in spite of the fact that*
nondimeno, *nevertheless*
nonno, *grandfather*
nord, *north*
nostro, *our*
nota, *note*
notare (noto), *to note*
notte (f.), *night*
novella, *short story*
nudo, *bare*
nulla, *nothing*
numero, *number*
numeroso, *numerous*
nuovo, *new*
  di nuovo, *again*

O

o, *or*
occasione (f.), *opportunity*
occhiali (m. pl.), *spectacles*
occhiata, *glance*
occhio, *eye*
*occuparsi (di) (occupo), *to occupy oneself with, to be busy with*

occupato, *busy, engaged*
offrire (irreg.) (2nd group), *to offer*
oggetto, *object*
oggi, *today*
ogni, *every, each*
  ogni tanto, *every now and then*

ognuno, *each one, every one*

olmo, *elm*

oltre, *beyond, besides*

ombra, *shade*

onestà, *honesty*

opinione (f.), *opinione*

opera, *work, opera*

opposto, *opposite*

oppure, *or*

ora, *hour, now*
　or ora, *just now*

oramai, *now, now finally*

orchestra, *orchestra*

ordine (m.), *order*

orecchini (m. pl.), *ear-rings*

orecchio, *ear*

orefice (m.), *goldsmith*

oretta, *short hour, about an hour*

organo, *organ*

orientarsi, *to find one's direction*

oriente (m.), *east*

originale, *original*

orizzonte (m.), *horizon*

ornato, *ornate*
　ornatissimo, *very ornate*

orologio, *clock*

osare, *to dare*

oscillazione (f.), *swing*

oscuro, *dark*

ospedale (m.), *hospital*

ospite (m. and f.), *host, guest*

osservare (osservo), *to observe*

osso, *bone*

ottagonale, *octagonal*

ottimo, *very good, best*

ovest (m.), *west*

oziare (ozio), *to idle, lounge about*

P

pacco, *parcel*

pace (f.), *peace*

padre (m.), *father*

paesaggio, *scenery, landscape*

paese (m.), *country, region*

pagare, *to pay*

paglia, *straw*

paio, *pair*

paladino (noun and adj.), *champion*

palazzo, *palace*

panca, *bench*

pane (m.), *bread*

panino, *roll of bread*

panno, *cloth*

panorama (m.), *view*

paradiso, *paradise*

parco, *park*

parecchio, *much*, pl. *several*

parentesi, *parenthesis*
　fra parentesi, *by the way*

*parere (irreg.), *to seem*

parlare, *to speak*

parola, *word*

parte (f.), *part*

partecipare (partecipo), *to take part in*

partenza, *departure*

*partire (2nd group), *to depart*

pascolo, *pasture*

passante (m. and f.), *passer-by*

passaporto, *passport*

passare, *to pass*

passeggiare (passeggio), *to walk*

passeggiata, *walk*

passo, *step, pace*

pasto, *meal*

patria, *fatherland*

paüra, *fear*

pausa, *pause*

pazzo, *mad*

peccato, *pity*
  che peccato!, *what a pity!*
pecora, *sheep*
peggio, *very bad, worse*
pellicola, *film*
pena, *trouble*
pendere, *to hang*
pendice (f.), *slope*
pendolo, *pendulum*
penisola, *peninsula*
penna, *pen*
pensare (penso), *to think*
pensiero, *thought*
pensione (f.), *pension, boarding house*
per, *for, through*
  per favore, *please*
  per quanto, *however*
pera, *pear*
perché, *why?, because*
percorso, *route*
perdere (irreg.), *to lose*
perdonare (perdono), *to pardon*
perfetto, *perfect*
perfino, *even*
periodo, *period*
permettere (di) (irreg.), *to allow*
però, *however*
persin, persino, *even*
persona, *person*
personaggio, *character, figure*
pesca, *fishing*
pesce (m.), *fish*
pessimo, *very bad, worst*
pezzo, *piece*
piacere (m.), *pleasure*
  per piacere, *please*
†piacere (irreg.), *to please*
piangere (irreg.), *to weep*
pianista (m. and f.), *pianist*
piano (adj.), *quiet, soft, flat, level*

piano (n.), *floor, storey*
  piano superiore, *upper floor*
  pianterreno, *ground floor*
pianoforte (m.), *piano*
pianta, *plant, plan*
pianura, *plain* (noun)
piattino, *saucer*
piatto, *plate*
piazza, *square*
piazzale, *large square, open space*
piccione (m.), *pigeon*
piccolo, *small*
piede (m.), *foot*
  a piedi, *on foot*
piemontese, *Piedmontese*
pieno, *full*
pietra, *stone*
pigia pigia (m.) (pigiare = *to press*), *crowd, mob*
pigliare, *to catch*
pigro, *lazy*
pineta, *pine wood*
pino, *pine*
pio, *pious*
pioggia, *rain*
†piovere (irreg.), *to rain*
piroscafo, *steamer*
pisano, *Pisan*
pittore (m.), *painter*
pittoresco, *picturesque*
pittura, *painting*
piú, *more*
piuttosto, *rather*
pizzo, *lace*
poco, *a little, few*
  un po' di, *a little*
poesia, *poetry, short poem*
poeta, *poet*
poggiare (poggio), *to lean*
poggio, *small hill, mound*
poi, *then, afterward*
polizia, *police*
poliziotto, *policeman*

pollo, *chicken*
pomeriggio, *afternoon*
ponte (m.), *bridge*
porco, *pig*
porgere (irreg.), *to hand, give*
porre (irreg.), *to put*
porta, *door*
portacenere (m.), *ash tray*
portamonete (m.), *purse*
portare (porto), *to bring, carry, wear*
portiere, *door keeper*
porto, *port*
posare (poso), *to alight, to settle*
posizione (f.), *position*
possibile, *possible*
 possibilissimo, *quite possible*
posta, *post office*
postino, *postman*
posto, *place, seat*
potente, *powerful*
potenza, *power*
potere (irreg.), *to be able*
potere (n., m.), *power*
povero, *poor*
pozzo, *well*
pranzare, *to dine*
pranzo, *dinner*
praticare (pratico), *to practise, to frequent*
pratico, *practical, practised, acquainted with*
prato, *meadow*
precedere, *to precede*
*precipitarsi (precipito), *to hurl oneself, to rush*
precipizio, *precipice*
precisamente, *exactly*
predominare (predomino), *to prevail, to dominate*
preferire (1st group), *to prefer*
pregare, *to pray*
preghiera, *prayer*

premere, *to press*
premio, *prize*
prendere (irreg.), *to take*
prenotare (prenoto), *to reserve*
*preoccuparsi (preoccupo), *to trouble oneself*
preparare, *to prepare*
presentare (presento), *to present, introduce*
presto, *early, soon*
prete (m.), *priest*
prezzo, *price*
prima che (conj.), *before*
prima di (prep.), *before*
principale, *principal*
principio, *beginning, principle*
privo, *deprived*
prodotto, *product*
professore (m.), *professor*
profeta (m.), *prophet*
profondamente, *deeply*
profondità, *depth*
profondo, *deep*
profugo, *refugee*
profumatamente, *very generously* (lit.: *with perfumes*)
profumo, *perfume*
progetto, *plan*
proibire (1st group), *to forbid*
promettere (irreg.), *to promise*
promontorio, *promontory*
prontamente, *promptly*
pronto, *ready*
proporzione (f.), *proportion*
proprietario, *proprietor*
proprio, *own, just*
prosciutto, *ham*
proseguire (2nd group), *to carry on, continue*
prossimo, *next*
proteggere (irreg.), *to protect*
protesta, *protest*
provare (provo), *to try*

provincia, *province*
pubblico (adj. and n.), *public,
audience*
pulire (1st group), *to polish,
clean*

pulpito, *pulpit*
purché, *provided that*
pure, *also, yet*
puro, *pure*
putto, *child, baby*

Q

qua, *here*
quadrato, *squared, square*
quadro, *picture*
qualche, *some, any*
qualchecosa, *something, anything*
qualcuno, *someone, anyone*
quale, *which?*
il quale, *which* (rel. pro.)
qualsiasi, *whatever*
qualunque, *whatever*
quando, *when*

quanto, *how much*
in quanto a, *with regard to*
quarto, *quarter*
quasi, *almost*
quegli, *that man*
quello, *that*
quel che, quello che, *that
which, what*
questi, *this man*
questo, *this*
qui, *here*
quindi, *then, therefore*

R

rabbia, *anger, rage*
raccomandare (raccomando),
to recommend, register
raccomandato, *registered*
raccontare (racconto), *to relate*
radio (f.), *wireless*
ragazza, *girl*
ragazzo, *boy*
raggiungere (irreg.), *to reach*
ragione (f.), *reason*
rallentare (rallento), *to slow
down*
ramo, *branch*
rapido (adj.), *rapid*
rapido (noun), *express train*
rapimento, *rapture*
rappresentare (rappresento),
to represent
rauco, *hoarse*
re (m.), *king*

recita, *recitation, performance*
regalare (regalo), *to give a
present*
regalino, *small present*
registrare (registro), *to register*
regola, *rule, order*
regolare (regolo), *to regulate*
regolarmente, *regularly*
relazione (f.), *connection*
religioso, *religious*
remo, *oar*
repubblica, *republic*
resistere, *to resist*
respiro, *breath*
ressa, *crowd*
*restare, *to stay, remain*
rete (f.), *net, luggage rack*
reticella, *little net, luggage rack*
retta, *attention* (see dare)
riaprire (2nd group) (irreg.), *to
open again*

ricevere, *to receive*
ricevuta, *receipt*
richiamare (richiamo), *to call*
riconoscere (irreg.), *to recognize*
*ricordarsi (di) (ricordo), *to remember*
ridere (irreg.), *to laugh*
riduzione (f.), *reduction*
rientrare (in), *to enter again*
rifiutare (di) (rifiuto), *to refuse*
rimandare, *to postpone*
*rimanere (irreg.), *to remain*
rio, *stream, river*
ripartire (2nd group), *to depart again*
ripetere, *to repeat*
ripido, *steep*
riportare (riporto), *to bring back, report*
*riposarsi (riposo), *to rest*
riprendere (irreg.), *to continue, take up again*
risaltare (risalto), *to stand out in relief*
riservare (riservo), *to reserve*
riso, *laugh*
rispettare (rispetto), *respect*

rispondere (irreg.), *to reply*
risposta, *reply*
ristorante (m.), *restaurant*
ritirare (ritiro), *to draw back*
ritmo, *rhythm*
ritrovo, *meeting place*
*riuscire (irreg.), *to succeed*
riva, *bank, shore*
rivista, *review, magazine*
roccioso, *rocky*
romanico, *romanesque*
romano, *Roman*
romantico, *romantic*
romanzo, *novel*
rompere (irreg.), *to break*
rondine (f.), *swallow*
rosa, *rose*
rosario, *rosary*
rosso, *red*
rossiccio, *ruddy, tawny*
rotondo, *round*
*rovesciarsi (rovescio), *to turn upside down, inside out*
rubrica, *section, column of newspaper*
rullio, *rolling, beating (drums)*
ruminare (rumino), *to chew the cud*
rumore (m.), *noise*

S

sabbia, *sand*
sacrificare (sacrifico), *to sacrifice*
sala, *room*
  sala da pranzo, *dining room*
  sala d'aspetto, *waiting room*
  sala di scrittura, *writing room*
salame (m.), *sausage meat*
saldo, *solid*
sale (m.), *salt*
*salire (irreg.), *to go up*

salotto, *drawing room*
salsiccia, *sausage*
saltare, *to jump*
salterellare (salterello), *to keep on giving little jumps*
salubre, *healthy, health-giving*
salutare (saluto), *to greet*
santo, *holy*
  campo santo, *cemetery*
sapere (irreg.), *to know*
sasso, *stone, rock*
sbagliare, *to mistake*

şbaglio, *mistake*

şboccare (şbocco), *to have its mouth in, to empty into, open into*

scaffale (m.), *bookcase*

scala, *stair, stairway*

scaletta, *ladder*

scalino, *stair*

scarpa, *shoe*

scarrozzare (scarrozzo), *to drive*

scarrozzata (f.), *drive, driving in a carriage*

scarso, *scarce*

scatola, *box*

scegliere (irreg.), *to choose*

scena, *scene*

*scendere (irreg.), *to go down*

scherzare (scherzo), *to joke*

sciarpa, *scarf*

scienziato, *scientist*

scintillare (scintillo), *to glitter*

scintillio, *glittering, twinkling*

sciocco, *fool*

sciogliere (irreg.), *to loosen*

scommessa, *bet*

scomodo, *uncomfortable*

scompartimento, *compartment (of railway carriage)*

scoppiare (scoppio), *to burst, explode*

scoprire (2nd group) (irreg.), *to discover*

†scorrere (irreg.), *to flow*

scorso, *last, past*

scossa, *bump, jerk*

scottare (scotto), *to be scorching hot, to burn*

scrittrice, *woman writer*

scrivania, *desk*

scrivere (irreg.), *to write*

scroscio, *splash*

scultura, *sculpture*

scuro, *dark coloured*

scusare, *to excuse*

scuola, *school*

*şdraiarsi (şdraio), *to lie down, stretch out*

se, *if*

sé, *himself,* etc.

sebbene, *although*

secolo, *century*

secondo, *second*

sede (f.), *seat*

*sedersi (irreg.), *to seat oneself*

sedia, *chair*

segnare (segno), *to mark*

seguire (2nd group), *to follow*

sella, *saddle*

*sembrare (sembro), *to seem*

semplice, *simple*

sempre, *always*

senese, *Sienese*

sensazione (f.), *sensation, feeling*

senso, *feeling*

sentimentale, *sentimental*

sentire (2nd group) (sento), *to feel, hear*

senza, *without*

separare (separo), *to separate*

sera, *evening*

serale, *of the evening*

sereno, *clear, bright, serene*

serie (f.), *series*

servire (2nd group) (servo), *to serve*

servizio, *service*

seta, *silk*

sete (f.), *thirst*

settentrionale, *northern*

settimana, *week*

sfrontato, *cheeky*

sfruttare, *to exploit*

şguardo, *glance*

si, *himself,* etc.

sí, *yes*

siccome, *as, because*

sicuro, *safe, certain*

sigaretta, *cigarette*

sigaro, *cigar*

significato, *meaning*

signora, *lady, madam, Mrs.*

signore, *gentleman, sir, Mr.*

signoria, *lordship, authority, council of magistrates*

signorina, *young lady, Miss*

silenzio, *silence*

simpatico, *nice, likeable, charming*

sinceramente, *sincerely*

sincerità, *sincerity*

sincero, *sincere*

singolare, *strange*

sipario, *curtain*

smemorato, *forgetful*

soave, *suave, soft, gentle*

sobrio, *sober*

soddisfatto (di), *satisfied with*

soggiorno, *stay*

soglia, *threshold*

solamente, *only*

soldato, *soldier*

sole (m.), *sun*

solenne, *solemn*

solitario, *solitary*

solito, *usual*

  di solito, *usually*

solo, *only, alone*

soltanto, *only*

soma, *burden*

sommità, *summit*

sonno, *sleep*

sopra, *above*

soprabito, *overcoat*

soprattutto, *above all, especially*

sorella, *sister*

*sorgere (irreg.), *to rise*

sorprendere (irreg.), *to surprise*

sorpresa, *surprise*

sorridente, *smiling*

sorriso, *smile*

sotto, *under*

spagnuolo, *Spanish*

spalla, *shoulder*

spargere (irreg.), *to scatter*

spazio, *space*

specchio, *mirror*

speciale, *special*

  specialmente, *specially*

spedire (1st group), *to send, forward*

spendere (irreg.), *to spend*

speranza, *hope*

sperare (spero), *to hope*

spesso, *often, thick*

spessore, *thickness*

spettacolo, *spectacle, sight*

spettro, *ghost*

spiaggia, *shore, beach*

spillo, *pin*

spingere (irreg.), *to push*

spinta, *push*

sposare (sposo), *to marry*

sposo, *bridegroom*

squillo, *ring (bell), blast (trumpet)*

squisito, *exquisite*

staccare, *to detach*

stagione (f.), *season*

stamane, stamani, stamattina, *this morning*

stanco, *tired*

stanotte (f.), *tonight, last night*

stanza, *room*

  stanza da bagno, *bathroom*

*stare (irreg.), *to be, to stand*

  stare per, *to be about to, on the point of*

stasera, *this evening, tonight*

stato, *state*

statua, *statue*

statuetta, *small statue*

stazione (f.), *station*

*stendersi (irreg.), to stretch oneself, extend

stesso, the same, self

stile (m.), style

stipendio, salary

storia, story, history

storico, historian

strada, street

straducola, back street, alley

straordinario, extraordinary

strapiombare (strapiombo), to lean from the vertical, to be out of the plumb line

stretta di mano, handshake

stringere (irreg.), to grasp, press

studente (m.), student

studiare, to study

studio, study

su, on

subito, straight away

*succedere (irreg.), to happen

suggerire (1st group), to suggest

suo, his

suonare (suono), to sound, ring

superiore, upper, superior

svariare, to vary

*svegliarsi (sveglio), to awake

sventolio, fluttering, waving

*svolgersi (irreg.), to turn

T

tabacco, tobacco

tacere (irreg.), to be silent

tamburo, drum

tanto, so much

tanto . . . quanto, as . . . as, so . . . as, as much . . . as, so much . . . as

tappa, stage, stopping place

tappeto, carpet

tardare, to delay

tardi, late

tasca, pocket

tassa, tax, fee

tavola, table

tavolino, small table

tazza, cup

tè, tea

teatrale, theatrical

teatro, theatre

tegola, tile, slate

telefonare (telefono), to telephone

telefono, telephone

telegramma (m.), telegram

temere, to fear

tempesta, storm

tempo, time, weather

tenda, tent

tenere (irreg.), to hold

tenore (m.), tenor

tentare, to try

tentazione (f.), temptation

termine (m.), term, period

terra, land, earth

terrazza, terrace

terreno, ground, earth

testa, head

Testamento, Testament

tetto, roof

tiglio, lime

timidamente, timidly

tipico, typical

tirare, to throw, to draw

toccare, to touch

togliere (irreg.), to take off

tomba, tomb

tondo (adj. and n.), round, plate, plaque

tonnellata, ton

topografico, topographical

torchietto, *flare, torch*
*tornare (torno), *to return*
toro, *bull*
torre (f.), *tower*
torrente (m.), *torrent*
tovaglia, *table cloth*
tovagliolino, *small serviette, bib*
tovagliolo, *serviette*
tra, *between, among*
tradizionale, *traditional*
tradizione (f.), *tradition*
tradurre (irreg.), *translate*
tralcio, *tendril*
tramontare, *to set* (sun)
tranquillamente, *calmly*
tranquillità, *tranquillity*
trarre (irreg.), *to draw, drag*
trasalire (1st group), *to start, shiver*
trasformazione (f.), *transformation*
trasmettere (irreg.), *to transmit*
trasportare (trasporto), *to transport*

trattenere (irreg.), *to hold back*
tratto, *period, interval*
  a un tratto, *suddenly*
  a tratti, *at intervals*
†traversare (traverso), *to cross*
tregua, *respite*
tremendo, *tremendous*
treno, *train*
  treno merci, *goods train*
  treno omnibus, *slow stopping train*
tributario, *tributary*
tromba, *trumpet*
tronco, *trunk*
troppo, *too, too much*
trovare (trovo), *to find*
truppa, *troup*
*tuonare, *to thunder*
turco, *Turk*
turismo, *touring, travelling*
turista, *tourist*
  turistico, *of the tourist*
tuttavia, *nevertheless*
tutto, *all, whole*

U

uccello, *bird*
udire (irreg.), *to hear*
ufficio, uffizio, *office*
uliveto, *olive grove*
ulivo, *olive*
ultimo, *last*
unico, *only, unique*
uniforme (m.), *uniform*

uomo, *man*
uovo, *egg*
urlo, *shout*
usare, *to use*
*uscire (irreg.), *to go out*
uscita, *exit*
utile, *useful*
uva (collective noun), *grapes*

V

vacanza, *holiday*
vacca, *cow*
*valere (irreg.), *to be worth*
valevole, *valid*

valigia, *suitcase*
valle (f.), *valley*
valore (m.), *value*
vapore (m.), *steam*

vaporetto, *steamer*
vaporino, *steamer*
vassoio, *tray*
vecchio (adj. and n.), *old, old man*
vedere (irreg.), *to see*
veduta, *view*
vegetazione (f.), *vegetation*
vela, *sail*
veloce, *quick, quickly*
velocemente, *quickly*
vendere, *to sell*
venditore (m.), *seller*
veneziano, *Venetian*
*venire (irreg.), *to come*
ventaglio, *fan*
venticello, *breeze*
vento, *wind*
verde, *green*
vermut, *vermouth*
vero, *true*
verso, *towards*
verticale, *vertical*
vestibolo, *hall*
vestire (2nd group) (di) (vesto), *to dress*
vestito, *dress, suit*
vetrina, *shop window*
vetro, *glass*
vi (adv.), *here, there*
via, *road, way*
viaggiare (viaggio), *to travel*
viaggiatore (m.), *traveller*
viaggio, *journey*
viale (m.), *avenue*
vicino, *near, neighbour*
vicolo, *alley*
vigna, *vineyard*
vigneto, *vineyard*
villaggio, *village*

villeggiare (villeggio), *to holiday in the country*
villeggiatura, *stay in the country, country-seat*
villino, *small villa, cottage*
vincere (irreg.), *to conquer*
vincitore (m.), *conqueror, winner*
vincitrice (f.), *conqueror, winner*
vino, *wine*
violino, *violin*
virtú, *virtue*
visione (f.), *sight*
visita, *visit*
visitare (visito), *to visit*
visitatore (m.), *visitor*
viso, *face*
visto, *visa*
vitale, *vital*
vite (f.), *vine*
vitello, *veal*
vittima, *victim*
viva!, *long live!*
vivace, *vivacious*
vivere (irreg.), *to live*
vivo, *lively, bright*
voce (f.), *voice*
volare, *to fly*
volentieri, *willingly*
†volere (irreg.), *to wish, want*
volgere (irreg.), *to turn*
volo, *flight*
volta, *turn*
  qualchevolta, *sometimes*
*voltarsi (volto), *to turn round*
volto, *face*
voluntario, *volunteer*
votare, *to vote*

Z

ẓɛlo, *zeal*
ẓɛro, *zero, nought, nothing*
zia, *aunt*
zio, *uncle*

zɔppo, *lame*
zucchero, *sugar*
zuppa, *soup*

INDEX

The numbers refer to pages